# FINAL JUDGMENT

## The Missing Link in the JFK Assassination Conspiracy

By

## MICHAEL COLLINS PIPER

The Wolfe Press
Washington, D.C.

Third Edition Copyright 1995 by Michael Collins Piper

Published by: The Wolfe Press
Washington, D.C.

Third Edition (This volume is a substantially enlarged, updated, revised edition of FINAL JUDGMENT, first published in January, 1994.)

Printed in the United States of America

Library of Congress Catalog Card Number: 95-60001

ISBN: 0-935036-49-0

# Extra copies of this book ($20 per copy) may be ordered from the authorized American distributor:

Liberty Lobby
300 Independence Ave., SE
Washington, D.C. 20003

Or: call 1-800-522-6292 and use Visa or MasterCard

The author may be contacted in care of Liberty Lobby.

Responsible comment and criticism is invited.

About the Cover . . .

This may be the most unusual cover of any book—and there have been many—published about the assassination of John F. Kennedy. But then, again, *Final Judgment*—like its cover—is extraordinary.

The figures in the background of the cover illustration are taken from age-old folk art illustrating scenes from the Book of Esther in the Old Testament of the Bible.

The Book of Esther (sometimes called "The Megillah," meaning "The Scroll") tells the story of a beautiful Jewish woman, Esther, who became the wife of the King of Persia, alternately described as Ahasueros, Xerxes I or as Artaxerxes II, depending upon which historical source one relies.

Within the King's court, according to the legend, was an evil schemer known as Haman—the king's prime minister—who plotted the destruction of the entire Jewish population of the Persian Empire.

Although Haman's machinations nearly succeeded, Esther brilliantly foiled Haman's plot and, in the end, Haman himself was executed for his treachery. To this day the routing of Haman is celebrated on the holy day known as Purim.

## Dedication

To my late friend, Lois Petersen.

Without Lois, this book simply would not
have been possible.

Thanks, Lois, for everything.

*Mike*

## MOTIVES . . .

"It is interesting—but not surprising—to note that in all the words written and uttered about the Kennedy assassination, Israel's intelligence agency, the Mossad, has never been mentioned. And yet a Mossad motive is obvious.

"On this question, as on almost all others, American reporters and commentators cannot bring themselves to cast Israel in an unfavorable light—despite the obvious fact that Mossad complicity is as plausible as any of the other theories."

Former Rep. Paul Findley (R-Ill.), writing in *The Washington Report on Middle East Affairs*, March 1992.

## ORIGINS . . .

". . . The Israeli origin should be totally covered while attention should be shifted to any other possible factor . . ."

Col. Benjamin Givli, head of Israeli military intelligence, in a cable to his subordinates outlining a campaign of terror in 1954 against British targets in the Middle East to be blamed upon Moslem extremists. Documented in the *Acts of the Olshan-Dori Inquiry Commission* investigating Israel's "Lavon Affair."

## RESEARCHERS . . .

"While the [JFK assassination] researchers have involved themselves in consuming preoccupation with the microanalytic searching for facts of *how* the assassination was accomplished, there has been almost no systematic thinking on *why* President Kennedy was killed."

Longtime JFK assassination researcher Vincent Salandria quoted by Daniel Brandt of *NameBase NewsLine* letter, January-March 1994.

## ILLUSIONS . . .

"There is a type of optical illusion known, in its more pretentious manifestations, as 'camouflage art.' These are paintings, generally of wilderness landscapes, that, viewed up close, look like simple picturesque scenes—a mountain lake with a snow-covered slope reflected on its surface, a field of wildflowers, a forest of birch trees.

"Take a few steps back, however, and the picture changes. The mirrored rock assumes the shape of an eagle in flight, the flowers form themselves into a rearing stallion, the boles of the birch trees become the profile of an Apache warrior. The myriad details resolve themselves into a single, unmistakable image, previously hidden from sight—but only when they are seen from a distance."

From Harold Schecter's *Deranged*, a study of serial killer Albert Fish.

## MIRRORS . . .

"The overwhelming evidence is that a conspiracy—a big conspiracy containing numerous levels of intrigue—led to the Kennedy assassination.

"Everywhere you look, there is another hall of mirrors. Over the years . . . it has become virtually impossible to see what the truth is. Where is the wizard, the wicked witch? All of the above, or none of the above . . .

"What ultimately faces us is a hydra-headed beast, but it is possible to come to grips at least with its claws. Always remembering that the intrinsic nature of this beast is fog and smoke, nevertheless this is not a wholly ambiguous and unknowable world . . ."

From Dick Russell's *The Man Who Knew Too Much*.

## MAGICIANS . . .

"President Kennedy's assassination was the work of magicians. It was a stage trick, complete with accessories and false mirrors, and when the curtain fell the actors, and even the scenery, disappeared. But the magicians were not illusionists but professionals, artists in their way."

From *Farewell America*, by veteran French intelligence officer Herve Lamarr, writing as "James Hepburn."

# Publisher's Preface
## to the Third Edition

Few people know it, but it takes as few as 40,000 copies to be sold for a book to reach the *New York Times* best-seller list. What far fewer people know—but book dealers can attest to it—is that there have actually even been books listed by the *Times* as "best sellers" even though the books have not yet actually been printed! Advance orders from book dealers—presumably—make this unusual phenomenon possible.

Whatever the case, there's much more to the story behind the story of "best-sellers" than meets the eye. And it's a story that most of the major names in the publishing industry probably would prefer left untold.

Nonetheless, a number of books dealing with the JFK assassination have reached the *Times'* list. Interestingly enough, however, Mark Lane's ground-breaking international best-seller, *Rush to Judgment*—which did reach the *Times* list—was never reviewed by the *Times*, which tell us that it is the source of "all the news that's fit to print," until long after the book had become an international *cause celebre*.

In more recent years, particularly in the wake of the release of Oliver Stone's Hollywood blockbuster, *JFK*, several more volumes did reach the *Times'* best-seller list. *Final Judgment* was not one of those volumes. This despite the fact that more than 7,000 copies of *Final Judgment* were sold within two weeks of the book's release in January of 1994—this as a response to a single advertisement in a relatively small-circulation national weekly newspaper.

No more than 200 copies of the book were purchased in bulk by book dealers. All other sales were to individual buyers. In one instance, however, an enthusiastic reader purchased 100 additional copies after his favorable reception of the first two copies that he ordered. Now, as a result of additional direct mail promotions, many thousands more copies of *Final Judgment* are being sold across the country.

Yet, it is a sure bet that not only will *Final Judgment* never appear on the best-seller lists, but that it will never be mentioned in either the *New York Times* or the *Washington Post* (whose editors received copies of the book) or in any of the major media newsmagazines.

That *Final Judgment* has already sold so exceedingly well is quite remarkable, considering the lack of publicity that the book has received. One much-touted JFK assassination work, *The Plot to Kill the President,* by former House Assassinations Committee director G. Robert Blakey, received widespread national promotion when it was released by a *New York Times* book publishing affiliate in 1981. Yet, Blakey's book, according to Blakey himself, sold only some 20,000 copies.

It is important to note, additionally, that since the release of *Final Judgment*, only one minor error of fact that appeared in the first two editions was brought to the author's attention. The error in question had nothing whatsoever to do with the thesis of the book or with even the JFK assassination itself. Needless to say, the error has been corrected in this edition. Otherwise the allegations made and the conclusions reached remain unchanged, although this new third edition contains some 40 additional pages and fully 69 additional footnotes.

Although one particularly harsh review of *Final Judgment* did appear in the pages of a Jewish community newspaper published in Washington, D.C. (referenced in the afterword of this edition), that review never once contradicted any of the factual statements put forth in this volume.

So it is that *Final Judgment*, as of this date, stands unchallenged for its veracity. The only criticism of the volume has been *ad homenim* in nature. Yet, name calling does not a challenge make. If anything, such hysterical and malicious defamation—especially considering the source—lends credence, in its own way, to the thesis of the book.

There is indeed much more to be learned about the assassination of John F. Kennedy. More facts may ultimately emerge that will bring the scenario described in these pages full circle. *Final Judgment* points the direction for those who wish to pursue the matter further. *Final Judgment* is—at least for the time being—precisely what its title suggests.

—G. A. Wolfe

# Author's Preface
# to the Third Edition

Writing a book on so controversial a topic an the JFK assassination—coupling that subject with a highly sensational thesis—has proved quite an adventure and one rather rewarding.

Since the first edition of *Final Judgment* was released, I have been delighted to receive so many wonderful letters from readers containing words of congratulation, encouragement and advice. I have been particularly thrilled by the comments of many people I respect who have said, as one person put it, "I think you've pinned the tail on the donkey."

I have never styled myself as an "authority" on the JFK assassination, by any means, nor would I consider myself an assassination "buff." There are those who have spent much more time and energy, not to mention money, I suppose, in the arena of researching the JFK assassination. The murder of President Kennedy, while a subject of long-standing interest to me, has never been a particular preoccupation of mine.

Be that as it may, I must point out that many of those who have spent years looking into the JFK assassination have been hesitant to acknowledge that there is even any basis for my findings. There are even those who don't wish to even acknowledge the very existence of the book itself.

In this third edition of *Final Judgment* I have pulled no punches in naming their names or in pointing out why I believe—based on the evidence—that some of these "researchers" have been either disingenuous or dishonest or both. Or, to put it bluntly, compromised.

And when I say "compromised" I mean that they have literally been bought off by the very forces responsible for the assassination of President Kennedy. These are difficult words to write but I do not believe that I am overstating the case, as you shall see.

There have been some people who have suggested that *Final Judgment* is somehow "Arab propaganda." For those who may think that, I hasten to add that this is not the case in any way, shape or form. No Arab government—or even any Arab-American source for that matter—had any hand in the preparation or publication or distribution of this book. For the record, one Arab embassy purchased three additional copies of the book after I sent a complimentary copy to its office in New York.

This work—for better or worse—is mine alone. I followed the many leads that fell before me and I reached my conclusions with virtually no outside input prior to finishing the first draft whatsoever.

Some of my critics have pointed out that I am a veteran employee of Liberty Lobby, the populist institution that publishes the national weekly newspaper, *The Spotlight*. These critics note that Liberty Lobby has been critical of U.S. policy toward the state of Israel. This is true. For this I make no apologies nor, for that matter, are any apologies due.

Anyone with even a minuscule amount of knowledge of the history of Israel and its international relations knows full well that the tiny—yet powerful—Middle East state is controversial, to say the very least.

It was precisely because of my association with Liberty Lobby that I was able to gain special insights—particularly *vis-a-vis* U.S. policy toward Israel—which assisted me tremendously in the preparation of this book. Other JFK researchers have not had that unusual advantage.

What's more, as you will see in Chapter 9 and in Chapter 16, Liberty Lobby's weekly newspaper became embroiled in a potentially devastating libel trial after ex-CIA figure E. Howard Hunt brought suit against *The Spotlight* for publishing an article which stated that the CIA intended to frame Hunt for involvement in the JFK assassination.

Successfully handling *The Spotlight's* defense—ironically yet appropriately enough—was none other than Mark Lane, the dean of the Warren Commission critics. Although *The Spotlight* had a certain "right wing" reputation, Lane put aside his ideological differences with Liberty Lobby and skillfully used the Hunt case as a forum to explore the JFK assassination in a legal forum—the first such forum since Jim Garrison's ill-fated prosecution of Clay Shaw.

Thus, having followed the Hunt case from the "inside" from beginning to end—and later having had the opportunity to study Lane's account of the case in his best-seller, *Plausible Denial*—gave me the opportunity to approach the topic of the JFK assassination from a unique vantage point that many other JFK researchers have not had. I thank Mark Lane and Willis Carto, the founder of Liberty Lobby, for that opportunity.

Even to this day, nearly thirty years after Mark first became involved in the JFK assassination controversy, he is still under fire from the powers-that-be for having challenged the "official" government-sanctioned version of what really happened in Dallas. If Mark Lane had not written one word after the publication of *Rush to Judgment*—the book that proved the Warren Commission Report a fraud—the world would still be indebted to him for that singular effort.

Although many other books came on the heels of *Rush to Judgment*—indeed, several books on the JFK assassination actually appeared prior to Mark's book—it was Mark, perhaps through sheer force of personality and true grit and determination, who made the world realize that there was much more to the story than Earl Warren and Company would have us believe.

Aside from having encountered Mark Lane through my long-standing association with *The Spotlight,* I have had the opportunity, likewise, to meet and work with a number of other intriguing and colorful individuals who have, in their own way, been linked to that strange world of intelligence that forever seems tied to the wide-ranging circumstances surrounding the assassination of John F. Kennedy.

Among these people is Col. L. Fletcher Prouty, model for "Colonel X" in Oliver Stone's *JFK.* In the pages of *Final Judgment,* as you shall see, I do not spare my criticism of Oliver Stone. But Stone himself actually came under fire for his association with Colonel Prouty—precisely because

Prouty had been associated with *The Spotlight* which Prouty rightly respects as a source of alternative news and information unavailable in the Establishment press. To Stone's credit, however, he stood behind Prouty who is a gentleman in every sense of the word and a real American patriot who hasn't been afraid to call a spade a spade and hit the CIA for the menace it's become.

In Chapter 16 (and in the Postscript) you will meet an amazing individual whom I am proud to call a new-found friend: he is a former French intelligence officer who provided me with a stunning piece of "inside" information that literally forced me to rewrite the first draft of *Final Judgment*, thereby bringing my thesis and my conclusions full circle. I am not at liberty to reveal his name—at least for now—but suffice it to say that had it not been for his input, this book would not be complete. I am very fortunate to have made his remarkable acquaintance.

Although, in retrospect, I still believe that the first draft of the book presented a compelling case proving Mossad complicity in the JFK assassination that few could dispute, the Frenchman pointed me in a new direction in my research that convinced me—and ultimately many of my readers—that *Final Judgment* was right on the mark.

I also want to say a special "thanks" to my friend and colleague at *The Spotlight*, Tom Valentine who hosts *The Spotlight*'s popular nightly call-in talk forum, *Radio Free America*—the one true independent voice on talk radio in America today. It was Tom who first gave me the opportunity to discuss this book on his program and who has continually given me much encouragement since the book was published.

I am especially gratified because Tom—for many years—was active as a reporter in reporting on research in the field of the JFK assassination. His endorsement of the book has been much appreciated, more than I can say.

I would be remiss not to mention a certain Chicago businessman—we'll call him Larry—who is a long-time reader of *The Spotlight*. As a college student in Washington, D.C. Larry was studying some subject or another and one of his professors suggested that Larry come to *The Spotlight* for further information.

Larry, who is Jewish, was initially horrified. He had heard the Anti-Defamation League-orchestrated lie that *The Spotlight* was "anti-Semitic" (because of its stance critical of Israel, of course). But Larry ventured a trip to Capitol Hill and upon arriving at *The Spotlight*'s editorial offices he was relieved to see that only the American flag hung on the wall—no Nazi uniforms, no swastika banners—only a bunch of newspapermen interested in getting at the truth, no matter how much the truth hurt.

It was Larry who brought to my attention the one factual error that appeared in the first and second editions of *Final Judgment*—my statement (that appeared in Chapter 2) that no Jews had died in the Mossad-orchestrated bombing of Goldenberg's Deli in Paris. Larry had good reason to know why this statement was in error. His aunt was visiting Paris at the time of that tragedy and narrowly escaped death. A traveling companion had urged his aunt to join her to the deli. His aunt opted to visit elsewhere, but her friend went to the deli and was among the victims of the bombing.

Larry remains a tried-and-true fan of *The Spotlight* and after *Final Judgment* was published I was delighted by his favorable response to the book. Some of his friends and family chided him for finding a book such as *Final Judgment* credible—they could not abide the allegation that Israel had a hand in the JFK affair—but I am proud to count Larry among my fans.

There's one more chap worth mentioning. He's a Washington businessman and *Spotlight* reader who—as a consequence of his work—has happened to have been associated with several figures mentioned (sometimes rather prominently) in the pages of *Final Judgment*.

After the first edition of the book came out, I sent him an inscribed copy and I received an acknowledgement saying "Thanks muchly for your final judgment of me and others." In a fashion, I guess, he may have been saying in his own way that my conclusions might not be far off the mark.

I have indeed been fortunate to have had the opportunity to be associated with these people—and many, many others—in the writing of *Final Judgment* and in the wake of its release.

I leave it up to the reader to determine if I have "pinned the tail on the donkey" (as one person put it) and if I am on target. I do believe that I am.

MICHAEL COLLINS PIPER
March 1, 1995

# Acknowledgments

I owe a great deal to so many people who provided me much advice, counsel and assistance in a wide variety of ways. This not to mention the pioneering researchers and investigators whose own work laid the groundwork for this book. They are, of course, too numerous to mention. But their yeoman efforts and dedication deserve full credit.

It is important, however, to single out several authors to whom particular credit is very much due. I have cited their work extensively in these pages. I must hasten to say that although I have relied on their work, **none of these authors either read this manuscript prior to publication nor is my reliance upon their research meant to imply that they share the conclusions reached in the pages of this book.** The conclusions are mine alone.

Stephen Green, Andrew and Leslie Cockburn, and Seymour Hersh, in their own studies of U.S. Middle East policy (*Taking Sides, Dangerous Liaison,* and *The Samson Option,* respectively), provided the basis upon which much of my own research was conducted.

Without their work, the assembly of the evidence provided in the pages of *Final Judgment* would not have been possible. Careful study of their volumes is a must for anyone who wishes to understand the reality of the "special relationship" between the United States and Israel.

The work of Professor Alfred McCoy of the University of Wisconsin at Madison also deserves special note here. McCoy's book, *The Politics of Heroin: CIA Complicity in the Global Drug Trade,* contains a wealth of material included in this volume that brings full circle the nature of the conspiracy that resulted in the JFK assassination.

*Cold Warrior,* Tom Mangold's biography of CIA spymaster James Jesus Angleton, also provided a wealth of information about the mysterious world of the Mossad's favorite CIA man. I have cited his work extensively in these pages. Likewise with *All-American Mafioso,* the highly readable biography of Johnny Rosselli by Charles Rappleye and Ed Becker. *Double Cross,* the Giancana family's biography of Chicago Mafia boss, Sam Giancana, was also most illuminating as was Dick Russell's more recent study, *The Man Who Knew Too Much.*

A special thanks to Gary Wean whose little-noticed, but very important self-published work, *There's a Fish in the Courthouse,* pointed me in several important directions, enriching the pages of my own work considerably. Gary and his associate, Mike Thomas, are fearless Americans who are working to make this country better.

Mark Lane's insights and criticisms have been most valuable, this from the one man who single-handedly proved to the world that the Warren Commission Report was a fraud. His three volumes on the JFK assassination—*Rush to Judgment, A Citizen's Dissent,* and *Plausible Denial*—remain the standard for all serious JFK research.

Victor Marchetti's counsel was likewise appreciated. As publisher of the newsletter, *New American View* (published in Herndon, Virginia), Victor and his right hand, Donna McGrath, have kept a close watch on the U.S.-Israeli relationship and, in particular, on the power of the Israeli lobby in official Washington.

Vince Ryan, John Tiffany, Travis McCoy and Jim Yarbrough, among others, provided helpful suggestions during the writing of *Final Judgment*. Each, in his own way, contributed to this volume.

Willis A. Carto's encouragement and enthusiasm were most important above all. The title was his suggestion—and right on the mark.

A former U.S. Congressman, who must remain nameless, acknowledged to me his own long-time suspicion that the theory presented in *Final Judgment* was correct and encouraged me to follow through with the research and writing. He said it was a book that he himself would have liked to have written. I thank that gentleman for the words of advice.

I also wish to thank another former U.S. Congressman and a retired French intelligence officer (both of whom also must remain nameless) for reading the manuscript and conveying their impressions. The French official provided an interesting "insider's" piece of information that explains a little known (and little understood) facet of the assassination conspiracy.

Special thanks to historian Dr. Alfred Lilienthal, the pioneer American critic of America's disastrous Middle East policy. Lilienthal dared to speak out when few others did. Had John F. Kennedy been permitted to live to pursue the policies that he advised Lilienthal that he wished to pursue, the Middle East might be at peace today.

Thanks also to several others who provided much moral support during the months of research and writing: Robert Wolfe, Larry Showell, Greg Garnett, Donald Malloy, David Lewis, Daniel Hinton, James Jakes, Anne Cronin, Julia Foster, Trisha Katson, Mike, Nick, Jim, Judy, Ruby Lee, and George. My mother, who is my worst critic, actually read the volume and became convinced, her initial doubts notwithstanding.

There are so many others who are due much thanks, many of whom must remain nameless. Research into such a controversial arena is not a pleasant task and I will not burden those good folks with having their names linked to this endeavor. That, I suppose, is a sad commentary on the state of affairs in the world today. Hopefully the publication of *Final Judgment* will have a positive impact upon our future.

MCP

# Table of Contents

# PREFACE

## The Unspoken Truth:
## Israel's Central Role in the JFK Assassination

**Where in the world could anyone come up with the idea that Israel's Mossad had a hand in the assassination of John F. Kennedy? Well, there's more to the story than meets the eye. All of the information which, taken together, proves this contention has already been committed to print. This book, *Final Judgment*, brings all of these facts together for the first time in a frightening scenario that makes sense.**

Considering all of the theories about the assassination of John F. Kennedy that have been circulating for years, how could anyone ever suggest that Israel's Mossad was involved ?

This was the reaction of more than a few people when apprised of the thesis presented in the pages of this book. Yet, I believe, that when you read this volume you will reach the same conclusion: that Israel and its spy agency, the Mossad, did indeed play a critical role in the JFK assassination conspiracy and its cover-up. The evidence, you shall see, is there.

It was several years ago that I first stumbled upon a hint that this was indeed the case. I came across a strange reference in the pages of a controversial work about the JFK assassination which alleged that rogue CIA operatives had been behind the president's murder, A. J. Weberman and Michael Canfield's *Coup d'Etat in America,* first published in 1975. The reference, simple as it was, appearing on page 41, read as follows:

**"After the assassination, an informer for the Secret Service and the FBI who had infiltrated a Cuban exile group and was in the process of selling them machine guns, reported that on November 21, 1963 he was told, 'We now have plenty of money—our new backers are the Jews—as soon as they take care of JFK.' This man had furnished reliable information in the past."**

I barely noticed the reference, but it did intrigue me. Who did this source mean when he referred to "the Jews"? This was the question I needed to answer. My immediate conclusion was this: the source meant Jewish gangsters—such as Meyer Lansky—who had a stake in reviving their Cuban gambling interests that they lost when Fidel Castro came to power. This was the logical answer.

Frankly, I laid the reference aside. It was just one lone remark out of perhaps millions of words written about the JFK assassination. It was nearly a year that went by before I came across the quotation again—while re-reading the same book. I pondered the quote for a moment, thinking, "This is interesting."

However, I once again cast those thoughts aside. I had already reached my own conclusions about the JFK assassination long before: The CIA was primarily responsible, working hand-in-hand with certain elements in "the Mafia" and also in the anti-Castro Cuban movement.

However, in the subsequent year that followed, I began to stumble across some interesting information.

In David Scheim's book, *Contract on America*, which contends that "the Mafia" was solely responsible for the JFK assassination, I saw a variation of the same quote referenced in the Weberman and Canfield book.

However, Scheim's rendition of the quote had deleted the reference to the alleged Jewish backers of the Cuban plotters. I began to think that there might be something more to the story after all, whatever the accuracy of the story allegedly told to the federal authorities.

## THE LANSKY CONNECTION

It was around this time that I learned that a new biography of organized crime figure Meyer Lansky had been released. It was entitled *Little Man: Meyer Lansky and the Gangster Life*. The book—prepared in cooperation with Lansky's family—was little more than a puff piece for the deceased thug. Gossipy, full of inside information, and even entertaining at times, the book still somehow seemed to be missing a lot.

It was then that I returned to my library and pulled a book off the shelf that I hadn't re-read in perhaps fifteen years. It was Hank Messick's biography of Lansky. Re-reading this important book I began to see that Meyer Lansky was not just another gangster. He was "the chairman of the board" of organized crime.

All of the Mafia figures that had been repeatedly implicated in the JFK assassination were, in fact, Lansky's front-men—his subordinates, his underlings. In short, if "the Mafia" had a hand in the killing of JFK, then Lansky had to have been one of the key players.

Yet, as I quickly began to see in reviewing many of the works which allege that "The Mafia Killed JFK," Lansky's preeminent role was being ignored or otherwise under-played.

I was aware of Lansky's close ties to Israel. After all, Lansky fled to Israel when the heat was on in the United States. But how deeply did the Lansky-Israeli connection go?

My research into that question began to turn up some interesting facts relating to an Israeli connection to the assassination of John F. Kennedy. (All of this and more appears in the pages of this book.)

## THE ISRAELI CONNECTION

Why would Israel have an interest in participating in the JFK assassination conspiracy? That was the burning question.

It was just about the time that I had begun to take a second look at the Lansky connection to the Kennedy assassination that several new works about the covert relationship between the United States and Israel were released providing never-before revealed information.

These books, cited extensively in *Final Judgment*, made it all too clear that John F. Kennedy—before his death—was in a pitched battle with Israel. In fact, Kennedy was at war.

This was something that long-time JFK assassination researchers had no reason to know about. Much of the material had long been classified. It was a secret—a deep, dark secret.

Some of JFK's communications with then-Israeli Prime Minister David Ben-Gurion are still classified. Not even top-level intelligence officials with special security clearance have been allowed access to these potentially explosive documents.

This discovery made me realize that there was a lot more to the Kennedy relationship with Israel and a lot more about the JFK assassination than we had ever been told.

## ISRAEL, LANSKY & THE CIA

The long and close relationship between Israel and JFK's foes at the CIA is something which is becoming more and more known to the general public. JFK's own war with the CIA is common knowledge.

At the time of the president's assassination, however, the depth and breadth of the CIA's relationship with Israel's Mossad, however, was not so commonly known.

What's more, as I began to discover, Israel's allies in the Lansky Syndicate had much deeper relations with the CIA than most researchers have realized.

And while the stories of CIA-Organized Crime assassination plots against Castro have been told time and again, the evidence I began to discover told an even bigger story.

The pieces of the puzzle were all there. They simply needed to be put together. As the research continued, I repeatedly found myself stumbling upon new facts and information that continued to verify what was initially in my mind just a theory, but which I now believe to be the truth.

## THE PERMINDEX CONNECTION

It is the little-discussed Permindex connection to the JFK assassination which is the tie that binds—the final proof that Israel's Mossad was at the center of the assassination conspiracy.

In the Permindex connection we find all of the critical elements which tie Israel's Mossad, the CIA and organized crime together in close-knit intrigue linked directly to the murder of President Kennedy.

Although researchers, over the years, have devoted much time and energy to pursuing a wide variety of questions relating to the JFK assassination controversy (focusing on controversies that will never be resolved) they have steered clear of the Permindex connection.

Those who have made any reference to Permindex have described it as some sort of "neo-Nazi" entity—even a remnant of Hitler's SS—but, as we shall see, nothing could be further from the truth.

To understand the forces behind the Permindex connection, which we examine in detail in this volume, is to understand the answer to the biggest mystery of this century: the question of who killed John F. Kennedy.

## INSIDERS AGREE . . .

Just before I began the book I mentioned my theory to a rather well-known former United States congressman. He surprised me when he said, "I think you are on to something. I've believed for years that the Mossad was involved in the Kennedy assassination, but I never really took the time to look into it. I'm glad you're doing it, though. It will be an important book. It's a book I would have liked to have written myself."

Then, just after I finished the book, I sent a copy of the manuscript to another former U.S. congressman, thinking that he might have some interest in the subject. His response was perhaps a bit astonishing.

After the former congressman received the manuscript he wrote me a surprising letter in which he said, "I will tell you this. A retired Western European diplomat and intelligence officer with whom I've been in correspondence (and who has had disastrous experiences with Israel and the Mossad) has been urging me for the last four years to write the book that you have written."

He passed the manuscript on to the Frenchman who in turn wrote me a fascinating letter providing further information confirming my thesis.

## ONE COMPLETE PICTURE

The fruits of my labor appear in this book. I owe so much to all of those JFK assassination researchers who made this book possible. Their pioneering efforts laid the foundation for the construction of a framework which I firmly believe proves Mossad complicity in the assassination of John F. Kennedy.

All of those who sought the truth—and sometimes risked their reputations (and even perhaps their lives) doing it—cleared the way for a final judgment:

Israel was the driving force behind the conspiracy that resulted in the assassination of John F. Kennedy. It is the Israeli connection that pulls all of the pieces of the puzzle together into one complete picture. The role of Israel in the JFK assassination is, indeed, the until-now "missing link."

This is a controversial suggestion, but for the sake of history, it is a story that needs to be told.

MICHAEL COLLINS PIPER
Washington, D.C.

# A Who's Who
# of the JFK Assassination
# Conspiracy and Cover-Up

While the following selection of names in this special "who's who" is by no means complete, it does provide the reader of *Final Judgment* with a brief overview of the facts relating to the involvement of the individuals in question with the circumstances surrounding not only the JFK assassination itself, but also the efforts to not only uncover the truth about the assassination—and also to bury it.

Following each name and description are references to the particular chapters in *Final Judgment* where details about that individual appear in pertinent part. The inclusion of any name in particular is by no means intended to suggest that the individual—unless specifically stated—had foreknowledge that the murder of President Kennedy was being planned.

As we note in these pages, there were many people who were brought into the JFK assassination conspiracy and the subsequent cover-up who had no idea of the actual role that they were playing.

The following "who's who"—if read in this context—provides the reader a quick glance at the key individuals who ultimately prove central to a complete understanding of the entirety of the conspiracy that resulted in the assassination of President Kennedy.

# At Permindex

**Clay Shaw** - If New Orleans District Attorney Jim Garrison had been permitted to carry out an unimpeded investigation and prosecution of Shaw, a CIA contract operative and a former director of the International Trade Mart in New Orleans implicated in involvement with Lee Harvey Oswald, David Ferrie, Guy Banister and other figures central to the JFK assassination conspiracy, Garrison would have divined Shaw's connections—through a shadowy corporation known as Permindex—to not only the Israeli Mossad, but also the international crime syndicate of Israeli loyalist Meyer Lansky. (See Chapter 15)

**Louis M. Bloomfield** - Based in Montreal, Bloomfield was a long-time intelligence operative and a front man for the powerful Bronfman family interests. The Bronfmans were not only key international backers of Israel but also long-time figures in the Lansky crime syndicate. Bloomfield, one of the foremost figures in the Israeli lobby in Canada and one of Israel's leading international operatives, not only served as the chief shareholder in the Permindex Corporation on whose board of directors Clay Shaw served, but also had intimate ties to American intelligence. (See Chapter 15)

**Tibor Rosenbaum** - One of the "godfathers" of the state of Israel and the first director for finance and supply for Israel's intelligence agency, the Mossad, Rosenbaum was a prime financial angel behind the Permindex corporation. His Swiss banking concern, the Banque De Credit International, also served as the chief European money laundry for the global crime syndicate of Miami-based crime chief Meyer Lansky. (See Chapter 15).

**John King** - A close business associate of Tibor Rosenbaum's protege and sometime front man, Bernard Cornfeld, King showed up in New Orleans in the early stages of Jim Garrison's investigation—before Clay Shaw's name had come up—and sought to persuade Garrison (through a bribery attempt) to give up the inquiry. Fortunately he failed in his scheme. (See Chapter 15)

# The Mossad Connection

**David Ben-Gurion** - Prime Minister of Israel; resigned his post in disgust with JFK's stance toward Israel in April of 1963; Said JFK's position threatened Israel's very survival. (See Chapter 4 and Chapter 5)

**Yitzhak Shamir** - A long-time Mossad officer (based largely at the Mossad's chief European office in Paris), Shamir headed the Mossad's assassination squad at the time of the JFK assassination. A former French intelligence officer has charged that Shamir himself arranged the hiring of JFK's actual assassins through a close ally in French intelligence. (See Chapter 5 and Chapter 16)

**Menachem Begin** - In 1963, Begin (later prime minister of Israel) was a roving Israeli diplomat; prior to JFK's assassination he was overheard conspiring with Meyer Lansky's California henchman, Mickey Cohen, in a conversation that suggested hostile intentions by Israel against the American president. (See Chapter 13)

**Luis Kutner** - Although known largely as a "mob lawyer," (who was long and closely associated with Jack Ruby, a sometime-client) Kutner also doubled as an international intelligence operative and functioned as an advisor to an ad hoc pro-Israel lobby group in the United States. (See Chapter 14)

**A. L. Botnick** - Head of the New Orleans office of the Anti-Defamation League (ADL) of B'nai B'rith, an intelligence and propaganda arm for Israel's Mossad; a close associate of New Orleans-based CIA contract operative Guy Banister who helped create Lee Harvey Oswald's pre-assassination profile as a "pro-Castro" agitator. Evidence suggests that Banister's manipulation of Oswald may have been carried out under the guise of an ADL "fact-finding" operation. (See Chapter 15)

**Arnon Milchan** - Israel's biggest arms dealer, Milchan was "executive producer" (i.e. chief financial angel) of Oliver Stone's Hollywood fantasy about the JFK assassination—a fact which may explain Stone's aversion to exploring the Israeli connection to the affair. (See Chapter 17)

**Maurice Tempelsman** - The international diamond merchant and Mossad operative who became the lover of Jacqueline Kennedy Onassis and used his connections to double—perhaps triple—her substantial fortune, thereby coopting the Kennedy family forever. (See the Afterword)

# The CIA Connection

**Rudolph Hecht** - An owner of the CIA-linked Standard Fruit concern, Hecht was a prominent figure in the New Orleans Jewish community and as chairman of the board of directors of the International Trade Mart was Permindex board member Clay Shaw's primary sponsor. (See Chapter 15)

**James Jesus Angleton** - Angleton, the CIA's long-time chief of counterintelligence, was the CIA's primary high-level conspirator in the murder of President Kennedy and the subsequent cover-up. Angleton, who had been coopted by and was totally loyal to the Israeli Mossad, played a major role in the effort to frame Lee Harvey Oswald. *Final Judgment* is the first JFK assassination study to delve into Angleton's role in the conspiracy. (See Chapter 8, Chapter 9, and Chapter 16)

**David Atlee Phillips** - A long-time high-level CIA official, Phillips was the CIA station chief in Mexico City at the time a strange effort was underway to implicate Lee Harvey Oswald as a Soviet KGB collaborator. If anyone in the CIA knew the truth about Oswald, it was Phillips. He confessed publicly that the story about Oswald being in Mexico City was not precisely what the CIA had long claimed. (See Chapter 16)

**E. Howard Hunt** - Long-time CIA officer and liaison to the anti-Castro Cuban exiles. Testimony by ex-CIA contract operative Marita Lorenz placed Hunt in Dallas, Texas the day before the president's assassination. The full truth about Hunt's actual involvement in the affair may never be known, but there is no question that Hunt was deeply involved in the intrigue surrounding the president's murder. Evidence does indeed indicate that there was a conscious effort to frame Hunt for involvement in the crime. (See Chapter 9 and Chapter 16)

**Guy Banister** -The former FBI agent-turned-CIA contract operative whose New Orleans office was a central point for international intrigue involving the CIA, the anti-Castro Cuban exiles and the anti-DeGaulle forces in the French Secret Army Organization (OAS). Under Banister's direction, Lee Harvey Oswald established a public profile for himself as a "pro-Castro" agitator in the streets of New Orleans.

**David Ferrie** - An enigmatic adventurer and CIA contract operative, Ferrie was closely involved with Lee Harvey Oswald during Oswald's stay in New Orleans in the summer of 1963, working alongside Oswald out of Banister's headquarters. The investigation of Ferrie by New Orleans District Attorney Jim Garrison ultimately led to Garrison's discovery of Permindex board member Clay Shaw's ties to both Ferrie and Oswald.

**Marita Lorenz** - A former CIA contract operative, she testified under oath that one day prior to the assassination of President Kennedy she arrived in Dallas in an armed caravan of CIA-backed Cuban exiles who were met by not only Jack Ruby, who later killed Lee Harvey Oswald, but also CIA official E. Howard Hunt. (See Chapter 9 and Chapter 16)

**Guillermo & Ignacio Novo** - Two brothers, veterans of the CIA-backed Cuban exile wars against Fidel Castro. According to Marita Lorenz, the Novo brothers were part of the armed caravan that arrived in Dallas one day before the assassination of President Kennedy. Many years after Dallas, the Novos were later convicted of participating in the murder of a Chilean dissident in collaboration with international adventurer Michael Townley who himself had ties to high-level figures implicated in the JFK conspiracy. (See Chapter 9 and Chapter 16)

**John Tower** - In 1963 Tower was a newly-elected Republican U.S. Senator from Texas with close ties to the CIA. Shortly after the assassination he told associates of his own inside knowledge of the bizarre story of what really happened in Dealey Plaza. The story told by Tower suggests strongly that there were many unseen forces at work, manipulating many of the key players in the JFK assassination conspiracy. It was not until the release of *Final Judgment* that Tower's name was ever connected to the mystery surrounding the JFK assassination. (See Chapter 16)

**Victor Marchetti** - A high-ranking CIA official who left the agency in disgust, Marchetti later made a career writing about the CIA. In a 1978 article he charged that the CIA was about to frame its long-time operative, E. Howard Hunt, with involvement in the JFK assassination. A libel suit resulting as a consequence of Marchetti's article resulted in a climactic finding by a jury that the CIA had been involved in the assassination of the president. (See Chapter 16)

**Robin Moore** - A journalist with long-standing close ties to the CIA, Moore co-authored former CIA man Hugh McDonald's book, *LBJ and the JFK Conspiracy* which promoted James Jesus Angleton's false claim that the KGB was behind the president's murder—another of the disinformation stories that emerged following the assassination. (See Chapter 17)

# The Lansky Syndicate

**Meyer Lansky** - Chief executive officer and de facto "treasurer" of the international crime syndicate; active in gun-running on behalf of the Israeli underground; collaborated closely with American intelligence on a number of fronts; later settled in Israel. Researchers who have claimed that "the Mafia Killed JFK" have pointedly refused to acknowledge Lansky's preeminent positioning in the underworld. (See Chapter 7)

**Carlos Marcello** - The head of the Mafia in New Orleans, Marcello owed his status to Meyer Lansky who was his chief sponsor in the crime syndicate. Marcello could not have orchestrated the JFK assassination—as some suggest—without Lansky's explicit approval. (See Chapter 10)

**Seymour Weiss** - Meyer Lansky's chief bagman and liaison with the political establishment in Louisiana, he later served as a director of the CIA-linked Standard Fruit company and may actually have been a high-ranking CIA contract operative in New Orleans at the time of the JFK assassination.

**Santo Trafficante, Jr.** - Although best known as the head of the Mafia in Tampa, Trafficante actually functioned as Meyer Lansky's chief lieutenant in the crime syndicate and as Lansky's liaison with the CIA in the Castro assassination plots. (See Chapter 12)

**Sam Giancana** - The Mafia boss of Chicago, Giancana was a player in the CIA-Mafia plots against Castro; later murdered, probably at the behest of Santo Trafficante, Jr. His family says that Giancana admitted having been involved in the planning of the JFK assassination. (See Chapter 11)

**Johnny Rosselli** - A roving "ambassador" for the Mafia, Rosselli was the primary conduit between the CIA and the mob in the plots against Fidel Castro; may have arranged the murder of Sam Giancana for Trafficante and was later murdered himself. (See Chapter 11)

**Mickey Cohen** - Meyer Lansky's West Coast henchman; Jack Ruby's role model and a gun-runner for the Israeli underground, Cohen collaborated closely with Israeli diplomat Menachem Begin prior to the JFK assassination; Cohen arranged for John F. Kennedy to meet actress Marilyn Monroe who was assigned the task of finding out JFK's private views and intentions toward Israel. (See Chapter 13)

**Jack Ruby** - A long-time functionary for the Lansky syndicate, Ruby was the Lansky connection man in Dallas and also engaged in CIA-linked gun-running to the anti-Castro Cuban exiles. Evidence suggests there is more to Ruby's sudden "death" than meets the eye. (See Chapter 14)

**Jim Braden** - A veteran personal courier for Meyer Lansky, Braden was almost assuredly in contact in Dallas with Jack Ruby prior to the JFK assassination. He was briefly detained in Dealey Plaza minutes after the president's murder, but those JFK assassination researchers who have mentioned Braden prefer to cast him as a "Mafia" figure rather than as Lansky's man on the scene in Dallas. (See Chapter 14)

**Al Gruber** - A henchman of Meyer Lansky's West Coast operative, Mickey Cohen, Gruber and Ruby spoke by telephone just shortly before Ruby killed Lee Harvey Oswald. It is believed that Gruber gave Ruby the contract on Oswald on behalf of his superiors. (See Chapter 13)

# The French Connection

**Charles DeGaulle** - Repeatedly targeted for assassination by Israeli-allied forces in French intelligence and in the Secret Army Organization (OAS) who were angry that DeGaulle had granted independence to Arab Algeria. The Mossad-sponsored Permindex operation that also had a hand in the murder of JFK, laundered money used in the assassination attempts on DeGaulle. (See Chapter 9, Chapter 15 and Chapter 16)

**Georges deLannurien** - High ranking official in the SDECE, the French intelligence agency; pinpointed by a former French intelligence officer as the individual who (at the behest of Mossad assassinations chief Yitzhak Shamir) contracted the hit team who killed JFK in Dallas. (See Chapter 16)

**Michael Mertz** - A former French SDECE officer and the Paris connection for the Lansky-Trafficante heroin syndicate; alleged to have been one of the actual gunmen in Dallas on November 22, 1963. Said by some to be the legendary CIA contract killer, QJ/WIN. (See Chapter 16)

**Jean Soutre** - A liaison for the French OAS with the CIA's E. Howard Hunt, Soutre maintained contact with Guy Banister's CIA- and mob-linked gun-running headquarters in New Orleans. Soutre may have been in Dallas at the time of the JFK assassination. There is evidence linking Soutre to James Jesus Angleton's intrigue inside the CIA that affected French intelligence in a dramatic way. (See Chapter 15 and Chapter 16)

**Thomas Eli Davis III** - A world-traveling mercenary with apparent links to both Jack Ruby and Lee Harvey Oswald, Davis was taken into custody by the Algerian government for his subversive activities alongside Israeli agents in supplying weapons to the French OAS just prior to the JFK assassination. It is said that CIA operative QJ/WIN (possibly Michael Mertz, one of the reputed assassins of President Kennedy) helped secure Davis's release from prison. (See Chapter 16)

**Geoffrey Bocca** - A former propagandist for the OAS, Bocca later co-authored former CIA contract agent Hugh McDonald's book, *Appointment in Dallas*, which pointed the blame for the JFK assassination away from those who were actually responsible—the first of two suspect books put out by McDonald. (See Chapter 17)

**Christian David** - A French Corsican criminal associated with reputed JFK assassin Michael Mertz, David has claimed knowledge of a French hit team involved in the JFK assassination. David himself was the chief suspect in the murder of a Moroccan dissident, Mehdi Ben-Barka, whose killing was orchestrated by the Israeli Mossad through anti-DeGaulle forces in French intelligence. (See Chapter 16)

# Truth Seekers

**Mark Lane** - Retained by Lee Harvey Oswald's mother to represent her son's interests before the Warren Commission, Lane's book *Rush to Judgment* was the first major critique of the Warren Commission Report. In a libel suit filed against *The Spotlight* newspaper by former CIA operative E. Howard Hunt, Lane proved to the satisfaction of a jury that the CIA had indeed been involved in the JFK assassination. His best-selling book *Plausible Denial* outlined the circumstances of that libel suit and its ultimate conclusion. (See Chapter 9 and Chapter 16)

**Gary Wean** - A former detective on the Hollywood beat of the Los Angeles Police Department, Wean discovered how Meyer Lansky's West Coast henchman, Mickey Cohen, was conspiring against John F. Kennedy on behalf of the Israelis. In a meeting with the former sheriff of Dallas County, Bill Decker, Wean learned a portion of the truth about what really happened in Dallas. (See Chapter 13 and Chapter 16)

# News Twisters

**Edgar & Edith Stern** - Close friends of Clay Shaw, major financial backers of the pro-Israel Anti-Defamation League (ADL) of B'nai B'rith, and owners of the WDSU media empire in New Orleans that not only played a major role in giving vast publicity to Lee Harvey Oswald's pre-assassination profile as a "pro-Castro agitator" but later sought to undermine Jim Garrison's investigation of Clay Shaw. (See Chapter 17)

**Johann Rush** - As a young WDSU cameraman, Rush was on the scene to record Oswald's "pro-Castro" activities. He emerged—many years later—as the brains behind a "computer-enhanced" version of the famous Zapruder film of the JFK assassination that author Gerald Posner cited as "proof" that Oswald acted alone in the president's murder. (See Chapter 17)

**Drew Pearson** - Accused by his own mother-in-law of being a "mouthpiece" for the pro-Israel ADL, Pearson had close ties to not only the Israeli lobby, but also the CIA and to President Lyndon Johnson and his cronies. It was Pearson who floated an unlikely story that Fidel Castro was behind the JFK assassination and who also played a major influence in shaping Earl Warren's perceptions of the tragedy. (See Chapter 17)

**Jack Anderson** - As protege of Drew Pearson, Jack Anderson likewise had strange connections that might have biased his own reportage on the JFK affair. Since 1963 Anderson has promoted a number of conflicting versions about "who really killed JFK" ranging from "the Mafia" to Fidel Castro or a combination of both. (See Chapter 17)

**Jack Newfield** - A liberal columnist and some-time JFK assassination buff, Newfield has been a likewise long-standing devotee of Israel. He made a big splash with a highly fantastic story that missing Teamster boss Jimmy Hoffa had "ordered" two Mafia figures to arrange the killing of President Kennedy. Not surprisingly, Newfield's ridiculous story was given wide play in the Establishment media. (See Chapter 17)

# Theorists and/or Propagandists?

**Oliver Stone** - His Hollywood extravaganza, *JFK*, gave the public a full-blown, full-color, gory-in-every-detail conspiracy theory on the JFK assassination. Yet, Stone's presentation of the conspiracy was far from complete and failed to reach any firm conclusions. He deliberately suppressed the "French connection" which, in turn, was the long-hidden Israeli connection. Not only was Stone's chief financial backer Israel's leading arms dealer but also his film distribution company had its origins in the Lansky crime syndicate. What's more, one of the chief shareholders in the film company was none other than Bernard Cornfeld, long-time associate of Permidex figure Tibor Rosenbaum (See Chapter 17).

**Frank Mankiewicz** - This former publicist for the Israeli Mossad-linked Anti-Defamation League had a peculiar part in the events that took place prior to the murder of Robert F. Kennedy. Then when Oliver Stone began promoting his film *JFK*, Mankiewicz popped up as his key public relations man. (See Chapter 17 and Chapter 18)

**Anthony Summers** - Author of one book hinting that the Kennedy family were responsible for the death—maybe the murder—of actress Marilyn Monroe, Summers wrote another book on the JFK conspiracy. In neither book did Summers reveal explosive information (of which he was aware) that could have helped point in the direction of those same forces which played a part in both crimes. (See Chapter 13)

**Robert Morrow** - A former CIA contract operative who played a major role in activities on the periphery of the JFK assassination conspiracy, Morrow's book on his experiences is rife with detail, yet suspect in the eyes of many who had looked into his claims. Morrow's book absolves the key CIA conspirator, James J. Angleton, of involvement in the JFK conspiracy and portrays him as being "out of the loop" when, in fact, precisely the opposite was true. Is it a coincidence that Morrow's book publisher is an American affiliate of an Israeli publishing company? (See the Afterword)

**G. Robert Blakey** - An unlikely choice to serve as director of the House Select Committee on Assassinations, Blakey had, just two years previously, served as a character witness for a long-time close associate of crime boss Meyer Lansky. When it came time to point the blame in the JFK assassination, Blakey targeted Lansky's protege, New Orleans Mafia boss, Carlos Marcello, but looked no further. Blakey, likewise, found no role by the CIA—or any other intelligence agency—in the JFK assassination. (See Chapter 10)

**David Scheim** - The author of a book that pins the murder of President Kennedy on "the Mafia," Scheim refuses to acknowledge Permindex board member Clay Shaw's intelligence connections and paints Israeli loyalist Meyer Lansky as a low-level syndicate figure with no influence of substance. Scheim's book was published by the American front for an Israeli publishing company. (See Chapter 10)

**Richard Billings** - A journalist with close ties to the CIA, Billings played a major role in the media's campaign to undermine New Orleans District Attorney Jim Garrison's investigation of Clay Shaw. Billings emerged as the prime promoter of the outlandish theory that Garrison was a Mafia front man trying to take the focus off the Mafia and direct the attention toward the intelligence community. (See Chapter 10)

**James DiEugenio** - Although a deep admirer of both John F. Kennedy and New Orleans District Attorney Jim Garrison, DiEugenio has tread lightly when inquiring into the ties between Clay Shaw and the Permindex operation with its multiple links to the Israeli Mossad and the crime syndicate. (See the Afterword)

**Peter Dale Scott** - His years of in-depth research on the JFK assassination have led him directly to the doorstep of the CIA, the Mossad and the Lansky Crime Syndicate, yet he has never been prepared to name names or point in the direction of those very forces, preferring to sidestep the issue. Is he afraid or is he simply ignorant? (See the Afterword.)

*And now, for a final judgment . . .*

# Chapter One

## The Tie That Binds:
### What All of the Most Commonly Accepted JFK Assassination Theories Have in Common— The Never-Mentioned Israeli Connection

**Who killed John F. Kennedy?** That question has plagued the world for a generation. What is it that we do know about the JFK murder that ties all of the differing theories together? What is it that all of the theories have in common?

The blame for the assassination has been placed on numerous power groups, perhaps working independently or together. Most often named have been the CIA (or rogue elements thereof), organized crime and the anti-Castro Cuban network.

Yet, one power in particular—Israel and its spy agency, the Mossad—links all of these forces together. Israel, however, is the central player whose role has been consistently ignored.

"Everybody on earth on November 22, 1963, it sometimes seems, was involved in a plot to assassinate JFK. If all those alleged conspirators—all of whom have denied the allegations—were there, it's lucky anyone got out of Dealey Plaza alive."[1]

These were the words of one journalist, Terry Catchpole, reflecting on the controversy over Oliver Stone's Hollywood all-star extravaganza *JFK* and of widespread interest in the JFK assassination in general.

Catchpole cites groups often alleged to have been involved in some way with the JFK assassination—although this summary by no means is complete (ignoring, in particular, the CIA as an institution):

- Cuban Communists
- Cuban Anti-Communists
- Military-Industrial Complex
- A Renegade CIA Clique
- Organized Crime
- Soviet Communists
- The FBI
- The Mastermind

This final theory, according to Catchpole, is that "the Mafia had actually taken over the Howard Hughes organization from the bedridden recluse, and it was run by a "Mr. X," possibly [organized crime syndicate boss] Meyer Lansky."[2]

Each and every one of these theories, of course, has its own advocates. Each and every one of these theories, additionally, has been intertwined with one or more of the others. And now, the advent of Stone's film, coupled with the subsequent release of several new books on the assassination—most notably Mark Lane's *Plausible Denial,* which proved CIA complicity in the president's murder—has brought new interest in the controversy.

## 'RETIRED CIRCUS CLOWNS'

Perhaps some day there will even be a book which places the blame for the assassination on, as New Orleans District Attorney Jim Garrison used to say, "retired circus clowns." However, it was not retired circus clowns who killed John F. Kennedy, at least so far as we know.

## ISRAEL'S CENTRAL ROLE

This book contends that Israel's Mossad was a prime player alongside the CIA in the complex web of conspiracy that resulted in the assassination of President Kennedy—perhaps even the driving force behind the conspiracy.

It is clearly Israel and its Mossad—as we shall document—which is the one force which ties all of the most frequently mentioned alleged conspirators together: the CIA, the anti-Castro Cuban forces, organized crime and, most specifically—and more significantly than the so-called Mafia—the Meyer Lansky Crime Syndicate.

The connections are far more sinister and go far deeper than most might imagine. In *Final Judgment* we will examine all of this in detail.

## THE EVIDENCE IS THERE

Israel, as we shall see, had a very distinct motive not only to orchestrate Kennedy's removal from office but also to elevate his successor, Lyndon B. Johnson into the White House. As did, of course, many of those other elements in the conspiracy that resulted in Kennedy's murder.

Never once, however—at least in standard assassination research—has the suggestion that Israel had a hand in Kennedy's murder ever been uttered. Yet, the evidence is there—evidence that has lain dormant or has otherwise been ignored or gone unrecognized for its significance.

Indeed, virtually all of the facts brought together in *Final Judgment* have been drawn from recognized volumes in the field of JFK assassination research and in other standard sources.

## ISRAEL'S MOTIVE

One former member of Congress, Rep. Paul Findley (R-Ill.) himself has publicly suggested that Israel indeed may have had a hand in the JFK assassination. In the March 1992 issue of *The Washington Report on Middle East Affairs*, Findley points out:

"It is interesting—but not surprising—to note that in all the words written and uttered about the Kennedy assassination, Israel's intelligence agency, the Mossad, has never been mentioned. And yet a Mossad motive is obvious."[3]

Findley lays out the motive—a motive that we outline in detail in the pages of this book: "Israeli leaders never trusted the Kennedys. They were aware that when President Kennedy's father, Joseph Kennedy, was ambassador to Great Britain, he frequently praised Nazi Germany.

"During John Kennedy's campaign for the presidency, a group of New York Jews had privately offered to meet his campaign expenses if he would let them set his Middle East policy. He did not agree . . . As president, he provided only limited support to Israel.

"On the other hand, Lyndon Johnson had demonstrated his strong support for Israel throughout his political career. The government of Israel, therefore, had every reason to believe that its interests would be better advanced with Johnson as president. And indeed they were. After Kennedy's death, the United States, for the first time, began large-scale shipments of arms to Israel . . .

"Certainly, the Mossad possessed the resources to carry out an assassination almost any place on earth."

Findley concludes: "Am I accusing the Mossad of complicity? Absolutely not. I have no evidence of such. My point is simply this: on this question, as on almost all others, American reporters and commentators cannot bring themselves to cast Israel in an unfavorable light—despite the obvious fact that Mossad complicity is as plausible as any of the other theories."[4]

In these pages we will provide Congressman Findley and the readers with the evidence. We will let the readers make the final judgment.

### 'SOME SUBTERRANEAN ASSOCIATION'

One leading assassination investigator, Carl Oglesby, recently summarized his own decades of personal research. "It was an inside job," he said, "something on the order of the enterprise which we discovered in the Iran/Contra scandal.

"At the same time," he added as a caveat, "I cannot bring myself to believe that an institution such as the CIA [for example] could in any formal and regular sense decide to kill the president.

"So what I am talking about is an off-the-shelf, off-the-books kind of action that must have been put together by some subterranean association cutting through not only the CIA, but to a certain extent the FBI the Dallas police and the military-intelligence agencies themselves." [5]

*Final Judgment* suggests that it was Israel's Mossad that was indeed the very "subterranean association" that did cut through the various entities which found themselves brought into the JFK assassination conspiracy.

In a recent interview another respected JFK assassination researcher, Peter Dale Scott, perhaps lends further credence to the theory we are about to present. Scott believes that there were a variety of forces at work behind the JFK assassination. He specifically fingers "Lyndon Johnson's backers—particularly those who had a stake in the military-industrial complex" and "an intelligence-Mafia connection that included members of the intelligence community who were involved with military-industrial corporate backers of Lyndon Johnson, who in turn were involved with Mafia people. At a minimum," according to Scott, "you have to consider this triad of forces." Note Scott's words: "at a minimum." [6]

This, of course, suggests that other forces were indeed involved. *Final Judgment* not only suggests that it was, in fact, Israel's Mossad, but also clearly pinpoints the Mossad connection.

## 'OTHER INTELLIGENCE NETWORKS'

Scott himself goes one step further, but without naming the Mossad. He says, "In my research, the most suggestive clues have emerged from a relatively restricted circle within what I call the dark quadrant of suppressed relationships or deep politics: a circle within the tripartite world of first, CIA, defense, and other intelligence networks; second, the underworld of organized crime and anti-Castro Cubans; and third, corporate interests with links both to the intelligence and defense communities and also to organized crime."

"The key," says Scott, "is that all those in this dark quadrant would have resisted its exposure whether or not they were key plotters." [7] *Final Judgment* concurs with Scott's judgment. Again, note Scott's words: "CIA, defense, and other intelligence networks."

As we demonstrate—and which is not really so very secret—it is Israel's Mossad—above and beyond any other intelligence network—foreign or domestic—that has been unusually close (almost incestuously so) to the CIA.

## THE MEDIA'S ROLE

What's more, we go one step beyond Scott's conclusions. *Final Judgment* points out the highly significant role of the American media in its role in the cover-up. The cover-up of the JFK assassination conspiracy could never have succeeded without the support of a willing media.

The fact is that Israel and its supporters in the American media have a long and intimate relationship. Until recent years—but even still today—criticism of Israel and its misdeeds have been verboten in the Establishment media, as noted previously in the comments by Congressman Findley.

## 'FALSE FLAGS'

We will illustrate, by several notable examples, how primary friends of Israel in the American media have been key players in floating "false leads" (or "false flags" in intelligence jargon) that have directed attention and suspicion elsewhere. This is a phenomenon never before examined in studying the JFK assassination and which explains, in large part, why the real truth about the assassination conspiracy has remained hidden for so long, all of the research notwithstanding.

(In Chapter 3 we will examine numerous instances wherein Israel's Mossad itself utilized "false flags" to cover up its own role in a wide variety of assassination conspiracies and crimes around the globe.)

## A CHANGE IN MIDDLE EAST POLICY

Professor Scott, like many JFK researchers, has long focused on the change of policy toward Vietnam that took place as a result of John F. Kennedy's assassination. He also points out that there was, additionally, a change of policy toward Latin America.

However, in these pages, we demonstrate beyond question that the most profound—and, in retrospect, probably most lasting and unusual—reversal in the conduct of American foreign policy was in the arena of U.S.-Israeli relations. These facts, unfortunately, have been neglected by even the most serious researchers into the JFK assassination.

## THE THEORIES MESH

The purpose of *Final Judgment*, you see, is not to prove, once and for all, that there was indeed a conspiracy to assassinate President John F. Kennedy and to perpetuate a cover-up of that conspiracy. That has been proven, time and again, in an endless array of books, monographs, magazine articles—even in the pages of several novels.

Instead, *Final Judgment* takes the commonly-accepted theories one step further and binds them all together—all too well—in a frightening scenario that is surely so very close to the truth.

Many desired JFK's removal from the presidency. However, as we note throughout these pages, research over the years has—for a variety of reasons—ignored the bitter conflict between the State of Israel and John F. Kennedy.

Likewise, researchers have—again, for a variety of reasons, innocent and otherwise—ignored the very close connections between Israel and each of the diverse groups all of whom had a reason to want to end John F. Kennedy's presidency: the Meyer Lansky Organized Crime Syndicate, the Mafia, the anti-Castro Cubans, and the CIA.

In *Final Judgment*, we present a theory that, in the free market of ideas, deserves consideration—controversial though it will be.

John F. Kennedy himself put it best: "A nation that is afraid to let its people judge the truth and falsehood in an open market is a nation that is afraid of its people."

What all of the commonly-alleged conspiracies are tied together by is the one strand that has been consistently ignored—and that, of course, is the Israeli connection.

In *Final Judgment* we will consider this (unfortunately) long-ignored hidden aspect of history.

## WHAT THIS BOOK PROVES

What *Final Judgment* proves is not only that Israel had reason to conspire against JFK, but that Israel was in a central position to not only coordinate the assassination scheme (and did) but also the subsequent cover-up—all of this in close collaboration with its co-conspirators in the CIA and organized crime—most specifically those elements intimately linked to syndicate boss Meyer Lansky.

Israel—as much as the Mafia or the CIA, for example—stood to benefit greatly from the death of America's 35th president—and did. JFK's assassination set the stage for Israel to become a major power.

## LOOKING IN ISRAEL'S DIRECTION

Research into the Kennedy assassination is most difficult, if only because the literature is so immense, the web so tangled, and the surfeit of theories and potential conspirators so seemingly unending. What's more, some assassination researchers have latched onto their own unique theories and, as a consequence, have failed to look elsewhere—in the direction of Israel, for example. With all of this in mind, let us proceed on the basis that there are certain areas of agreement.

## GENERALLY ACCEPTED CONCLUSIONS

Our final judgment—outlined in these pages—rests on a foundation composed of the following generally accepted conclusions about the nature of the JFK assassination conspiracy:

• That there was a conspiracy to kill John F. Kennedy;

• That the conspiracy itself involved elements of the U.S. intelligence community, the CIA in particular;

• That Organized Crime figures played a major part in the conspiracy;

• That anti-Castro Cubans were actively participating in the conspiracy, at the urging of and/or manipulation by the CIA and elements of Organized Crime;

• That somehow Lee Harvey Oswald (wittingly or unwittingly) was brought into the conspiracy and that the conspirators planted false evidence to link Oswald with Fidel Castro and the Soviets;

• That Oswald was directly involved in some manner of U.S. intelligence community activities and that he was a knowing participant in those activities;

• That Jack Ruby was either an active participant in the assassination conspiracy itself or was used in some fashion to manipulate Oswald prior to the assassination of JFK;

• That Ruby was actively involved in organized crime activities and that he was, as a consequence of that involvement, also linked with organized crime activities that operated in conjunction (or ran parallel) with U.S. intelligence community activities.

• That the Central Intelligence Agency was cognizant of the activities of both Oswald and Ruby and certainly manipulated both;

• That Oswald was executed by Jack Ruby for the purpose of silencing Oswald forever;

• That a major cover-up of the JFK assassination conspiracy was undertaken following the events in Dallas;

• That the cover-up involved elements of the federal government (including the CIA);

• That the Warren Commission and the House Assassinations Committee were deliberate participants in the cover-up;

• That the cover-up conspiracy was conducted for a wide variety of motivations—both ostensibly "patriotic" and otherwise— including—but not limited to:

a) burying intelligence community connections to the assassination conspiracy;

b) protecting Organized Crime elements involved;

c) preventing hostilities between the United States and foreign nations (whether it be the Soviet Union or Castro's Cuba); and

d) resolving questions about the assassination in the public's mind, both here and abroad.

• That the Controlled Media actively encouraged and/or participated in the cover-up due to its links to the CIA, the intelligence community in general, and Organized Crime.

This is the basis upon which the research for this volume was undertaken. Thus, upon this foundation *Final Judgment* ties together all of the facts and shows how the State of Israel and its spy agency, the Mossad, collaborated with not only the CIA but also key elements in Organized Crime and in the anti-Castro Cuban community in order to orchestrate the assassination of John F. Kennedy and the subsequent cover-up.

## THE EVIDENCE IS THERE

Some of the facts presented—while not necessarily "new"—have been available to researchers for decades.

However, many researchers, regrettably, have not been looking in the right direction. That, of course, is not their fault.

Additional information—particularly in regard to Kennedy's difficult relations with Israel and how U.S.-Israeli relations changed drastically as a result of JFK's murder—has really only recently come into the public forum. In *Final Judgment* we will explore this information in detail.

It is this information—long unavailable to even the most dedicated researchers—that ties all of the previous data together.

The remarkable scenario presented in *Final Judgment* logically incorporates all of the commonly-accepted theories into one broadly encompassing theory that not only makes sense but which brings the diverse elements in the conspiracy together full circle. It is for this reason that *Final Judgment* truly lives up to its name.

The theory presented in the pages of *Final Judgment* may be greeted with the charge of "anti-Semitism"—a standard attack directed upon any utterance even vaguely critical of Israel and its misdeeds.

However, the author leaves it up to the basic honesty and open-mindedness of the readers to determine whether or not the theory presented in this volume makes sense.

## WHAT HAPPENED . . .

Here, in essence, is the basis of the theory presented and documented—sometimes in excruciating detail—in the pages which follow.

•That during his presidency, John F. Kennedy alienated three major international power blocs: the American CIA, Organized Crime, and Israel and its American lobby.

• That in each case, Kennedy's continued tenure in the White House was perceived by each of these power groups as a threat to its very existence.

• That each of these major international power blocs was closely intertwined with the others, often on several levels.

• That when Kennedy's presence in the White House became so intolerable that these forces came together in a wide-ranging conspiracy that resulted in JFK's murder.

• That the power of these forces, together, over the American media played a vital role in the assassination conspiracy cover-up.

*Final Judgment* explores in detail the little-known behind-the-scenes war between John F. Kennedy and Israel and documents how U.S. policy toward the Middle East underwent a drastic reversal upon JFK's assassination.

This book also documents not only the intimate collaboration between the Meyer Lansky Organized Crime Syndicate and Israel, but also the similar incestuous relationship between the Lansky syndicate and Israel's allies in the CIA. Our study will also focus on the singularly important role of Meyer Lansky's positioning in the joint Israeli Mossad-CIA-Organized Crime nexus that came together in the JFK assassination.

Lansky's own role in the JFK assassination conspiracy has been continually ignored or otherwise suppressed—even by those very "authorities" who claim that "The Mafia Killed JFK."

As we shall see, Meyer Lansky was, in fact, the real "overlord" of the international crime syndicate; many of the so-called "Mafia bosses" who allegedly masterminded the JFK assassination were, indeed, Lansky henchmen, front-men, underlings.

The basic facts have virtually all been published in previous works on the JFK assassination and in other studies on the subjects of U.S-Israeli relations, international intelligence intrigue, and organized crime.

It is only now, however, that all of the facts have been finally placed together in a neatly-constructed jigsaw puzzle that presents the whole picture in its rather simple entirety. It is not, as we shall see, as complex as it might at first appear.

However, the bottom line is this: it is clear that not only did Israel have a motive for participating in the JFK assassination, but that it indeed did play a critical part in the conspiracy.

## A THEORY OF POWER POLITICS AT WORK

The conspiracy outlined here was a criminal enterprise involving power politics in its highest—and lowest—forms. This volume:

• Presents international intrigue above and beyond the then-crumbling U.S.-Israel relationship;

• Examines the tragic reality of American involvement in Southeast Asia—which Kennedy sought to prevent—the final result of which guaranteed:

(a) Israel's dominance in Middle East affairs as the United States became bogged down in Asia;

(b) Southeast Asian drug profits for Meyer Lansky's global drug racket (operating in conjunction with the Mossad's ally, the CIA); and

(c) Multi-billion dollar profits in arms production for the backers of Israel's ally—Lyndon Johnson—in the military-industrial complex;

• Explains how the CIA—so closely tied to Israel—was able to continue its subterranean covert activities in Southeast Asia and elsewhere after the elimination of JFK;

• Illustrates how certain special interests (the anti-Castro Cuban movement and Organized Crime) could be manipulated by another special interest—the CIA-Mossad alliance—in pursuit of a mutual goal: ending John F. Kennedy's presidency;

• Points out why the various elements involved in the conspiracy were working in conjunction with one another in covering up the facts about the assassination;

• Details how the Controlled Media—long a primary collaborator with the Lansky-linked pro-Israel lobby in the United States—promoted the Warren Commission's "lone nut" solution of the JFK murder and sought to silence critics of the "official" explanation;

• Reveals how the anger and disgust of one powerful man—in this instance, David Ben-Gurion of Israel—could result in a vendetta carried out by means of a far-reaching conspiracy orchestrated through his own sphere of influence;

• Describes how key American political power brokers—such as J. Edgar Hoover and, most particularly, Lyndon B. Johnson (both connected to the Israeli-linked Lansky Crime Syndicate)—were able to maintain their influence—and expand it correspondingly—upon the death of John F. Kennedy and

• Demonstrates how low-level operatives such as Lee Harvey Oswald and Jack Ruby—both with a diverse array of strange connections—were utilized by conspirators at the top.

All of this taken together makes the conspiracy outlined here one that is not only logical, but one that ties all of the most prominently mentioned conspirators together in a package that is all too uncomfortably neat.

## HOW THIS BOOK IS ORGANIZED: A READER'S GUIDE

In order to outline the conspiracy described in the pages of *Final Judgment*, it is necessary, from the beginning, to consider that conspiracy in its historical context.

A wide array of players were involved and their integral links with one another and with the diverse forces behind the conspiracy make it prudent, at this juncture, to provide the reader with an overview of the material about to be presented.

Here, however, is a summary overview of the chapters which follow and which presents the necessary outline of the approach we take in laying the groundwork upon which we reach our final judgment:

## THE MOSSAD

Chapter 2 explores the accusation that Israel's Mossad did indeed consider assassinating an American president perceived hostile to Israel—in this instance, George Bush—and ponders the likelihood that the Mossad did, in fact, previously collaborate in the assassination of John F. Kennedy.

Chapter 3 reviews the Mossad's historic use of so-called "false flags" in its worldwide acts of terrorism and assassination, leaving others (such as "the Mafia," "right wing extremists," and "Arab terrorists") to take the blame. The point driven home is that the Mossad could have done likewise in the JFK assassination.

## JFK AND ISRAEL

Chapter 4 examines the historic alliance—and then enmity—between John F. Kennedy and his father Ambassador Joseph P. Kennedy not only with the Israeli lobby but also the Israeli-linked Meyer Lansky Organized Crime Syndicate.

Chapter 5 reviews, in depth, the growing conflict between President John F. Kennedy and the state of Israel—facts which have never been seriously examined by students of the JFK assassination.

Chapter 6 outlines how the assassination of John F. Kennedy permitted the Lansky Crime Syndicate- and Israeli-lobby linked Lyndon B. Johnson (a favorite of Israel's allies in the CIA) to assume the presidency and begin an incredible reversal of JFK's Middle East policies, thereby strengthening Israel's global hand.

This important chapter also demonstrates how Israel, the CIA and the Lansky Organized Crime Syndicate stood to benefit from American involvement in the Vietnam War—a little explored aspect of that unfortunate period.

## MEYER LANSKY, ISRAEL AND THE CIA

Chapter 7 is a comprehensive biographical sketch of organized crime figure Meyer Lansky, covering his preeminent role in global criminal enterprises and his links not only to Israel and its Mossad, but also American intelligence.

Chapter 8 explores the close working relationship between Israel's Mossad and the American CIA, and particularly the important role of the Mossad's chief ally in the CIA, James Jesus Angleton, the CIA's chief of counterintelligence

Chapter 9 reviews the conflicts between the administration of John F. Kennedy and the CIA, Israel's primary link in the world of international intelligence. Also considered are the connections of a number of key CIA figures (linked to the JFK assassination) with Israel.

## LANSKY AND THE CUBAN-CIA CONNECTION

Chapter 10 sheds important light upon Meyer Lansky's ties with New Orleans Mafia chieftain Carlos Marcello (often fingered as a key conspirator in the JFK assassination) and upon Lansky's preeminence over the Italian Mafia in organized crime activities.

Chapter 11 continues in this vein, reviewing Lansky's involvement with Mafia figures Johnny Rosselli and Santo Trafficante Jr., and with the anti-Castro Cuban underground and the CIA in assassination plots aimed against Cuba's communist dictator, Fidel Castro.

Chapter 12 is a detailed exploration of Meyer Lansky's predominant role in the international drug racket and how his criminal syndicate worked hand-in-glove with the American CIA in these international ventures.

## LANSKY'S HENCHMEN

Chapter 13 considers a little known angle in the JFK assassination conspiracy: the role of Lansky's West Coast henchman, Mickey Cohen. It was Cohen's close friend and attorney, Melvin Belli, who later emerged as the attorney for Jack Ruby, the Lansky-linked crime figure who murdered JFK's alleged assassin, Lee Harvey Oswald.

This chapter also documents Cohen's close working relationship with the Israeli underground and also connects the murder of JFK's mistress, film actress Marilyn Monroe, with Cohen's pro-Israel activities—an aspect that has been too long ignored.

Chapter 14 is a review of the career of Jack Ruby as an errand boy for both the CIA and the Meyer Lansky Organized Crime Syndicate and his activities connected with the JFK assassination.

## PERMINDEX

Chapter 15, aptly entitled, "The Twain Shall Meet," demonstrates that it was through the little-explored Rome-based intelligence operation known as Permindex that the Israeli Mossad-CIA alliance and the Lansky Crime Syndicate came together and utilized their joint resources to orchestrate the JFK assassination, bringing about the conspiracy documented in previous chapters full circle.

Chapter 16 is, in part, a review of attorney Mark Lane's book, *Plausible Denial*, which documents a little-known libel trial in which a jury concluded that the CIA had a hand in the assassination of John F. Kennedy.

This chapter also examines the critical role that CIA man James Jesus Angleton, Israel's number one contact in American intelligence, played in manipulating the JFK assassination cover-up.

Also examined is the oft-mentioned (but little-understood) so-called "French connection" to the JFK assassination conspiracy which was, in fact, also the Israeli connection.

Chapter 17 is a critical examination of the role that the media played in distorting the public's perception of the JFK assassination conspiracy and how the media pointed the finger of blame elsewhere.

A special analysis exposes how one widely-publicized conspiracy theory (blaming Fidel Castro) was the product of a powerful newspaper columnist with close ties to not only the Israeli lobby in this country but also the Meyer Lansky Organized Crime Syndicate.

## THE CONTINUING COVER-UP

Chapter 18 is a new look at the assassination of Senator Robert F. Kennedy and how RFK's murder ties together not only the CIA, Israel's Mossad, and the Meyer Lansky syndicate, but also the Iranian secret police, SAVAK (itself a creation of the CIA and the Mossad). RFK's assassination was, in fact, an integral part of the JFK assassination cover-up.

The concluding chapter constitutes an overview of the previous chapters and ties together the various aspects considered, outlining the likely nature of the conspiracy that resulted in the assassinations of President Kennedy and his younger brother.

Appendix One considers the covert CIA career of George Herbert Walker Bush and examines his integral links with several of the key players in the JFK assassination conspiracy, examining that critical question, "Where Was George?" Appendix Two reviews Lee Harvey Oswald's little-known link to at least one long-time federal undercover informant who operated in both "right-" and "left-" wing groups.

Our afterword reflects on the nature of the continuing cover-up and of how the truth may never really be told. A special postscript, prepared for the third edition of *Final Judgment* explains the tragic story of how an honest French diplomat may have died as a result of the release of *Final Judgment,* a sad consequence indeed. Another, it seems, of the strange deaths that came in the wake of the assassination in Dallas on November 22, 1963.

What appears in the pages of *Final Judgment,* we believe, is a logically constructed recitation of the facts in the JFK case that lead us to conclude that Israel and its Mossad did indeed have a major hand in the JFK assassination and was, in fact, the prime mover behind the conspiracy.

## REACHING A FINAL JUDGMENT

You be the judge.

You have heard all of the other theories time and again.

**This is the one and only book which ties all of those theories together in a comprehensive summary which makes ultimate sense.**

Read this book and reach your own final judgment.

## Chapter Two

## Off With His Head:
## A Mossad Plot to Kill an American President

**Would Israel's Mossad actually consider assassinating an American president perceived hostile to Israel? A former Mossad agent says "yes." According to ex-Mossad man Victor Ostrovsky, the Israeli spy agency hatched a plan to kill President George Bush.**

Was President John F. Kennedy killed by a conspiracy orchestrated—at least in part—by Israel's spy agency—the Mossad? If so, this would not be the last time that the Mossad planned the assassination of an American president.

According to former Mossad agent, Victor Ostrovsky, elements of the Mossad were plotting an attempt on the life of President George Bush. The reason: according to Ostrovsky, Bush is hated by the Mossad and considered an enemy of Israel.

This amazing revelation was published in the February 1992 edition of the *Washington Report on Middle East Affairs*. The author of the report was former Congressman Paul Findley (R-Ill.), himself a prominent critic of Israel. (Findley's best-selling book, *They Dare to Speak Out: People and Institutions Confront Israel's Lobby*, is a classic exposition of the way Israel's lobby has worked to silence American critics of the foreign nation.)

### BUSH TARGETED BY MOSSAD

Findley reports that Ostrovsky had learned through his sources in the intelligence community that because of President Bush's seeming intransigence toward Israel's demands, the Mossad had begun coordinating plans for the assassination of the American president.

Ostrovsky relayed this information to several members of the Canadian parliament, indicating that the Mossad, and not Israel's elected leadership, is "the real engine of policy in Israel." [8]

One of those attending the meeting with Ostrovsky passed the information on to another former Republican member of the House of Representative, Paul N. (Pete) McCloskey of California. (McCloskey, like Findley, has been a forthright public critic of Israel and is associated with his fellow former lawmaker on the board of the Council for the National Interest, a Washington-based organization that promotes America's interests in Middle East policy-making.)

Upon learning of the potential threat to President Bush, ex-Congressman McCloskey himself flew to Canada where he met with Ostrovsky. According to Findley's account, here is what transpired: "Ostrovsky impressed McCloskey as a patriotic Zionist who believes the Mossad is out of control. Ostrovsky told him the present leadership of the

Mossad wants 'to do everything possible to preserve a state of war between Israel and its neighbors, assassinating President Bush, if necessary."9

"He said a public relations campaign is already underway in both Israel and the United States to 'prepare public acceptance of [vice president] Dan Quayle as president.' After lengthy discussion during which he became convinced that Ostrovsky was 'real' and telling the truth, McCloskey took the next flight to Washington.

"There he relayed the information to the Secret Service and State Department, receiving mixed reactions to Ostrovsky's reliability. An officer of the Navy Department dismissed him simply as a "traitor to Israel."10

## AMERICANS KILLED BY ISRAELI INTRIGUE

Findley points out that in his controversial book, *By Way of Deception*, the aforementioned Ostrovsky documented a Mossad action which was "especially shocking to American readers."11

In that instance, 241 U.S. Marines were murdered by a terrorist truck bomb that plowed into the Marine barracks in Beirut in 1983.

Although Israeli agents learned that the attack was impending, the Mossad headquarters in Tel Aviv ordered its agents to ignore the threat and to not alert the American servicemen to the danger.

"We are not there [in Beirut] to protect Americans," the Mossad leaders explained. "They're a big country. Send only the regular information." According to Ostrovsky, the "regular information" was "like sending a weather report, unlikely to raise any particular alarm."12

"Is it conceivable," asks Findley, "that Israel's Mossad might assassinate George Bush in order to put a more sympathetic man in the White House?

"It is well to remember two earlier occasions when Israeli authorities were willing to sacrifice American lives to serve their own national interests."13

Congressman Findley points out two other occasions where Americans died or otherwise faced extinction at the hands of Israel:

• On June 8, 1967, naval and air forces of Israel deliberately—and without provocation—attacked the American spy ship, the *U.S.S. Liberty*, killing 34 American sailors and wounding 171 others. It was an attempt to destroy the ship and its entire crew.

• During the October 1973 war, Israeli pilots were ordered to shoot down an unarmed U.S. reconnaissance plane that was overflying Israel's secret nuclear bomb development site at Dimona. The plane, however, flew too high for Israel's would-be assassins to reach.

Assessing the potential threat to President George Bush, Congressman Findley concludes, "The U.S. Secret Service will be wise to assume the worst."14

Incredibly enough, at almost the same time Findley's provocative report appeared, several unusual events occurred that seemed to give credence to the allegation that there might indeed be a plot afoot to eliminate George Bush—if not physically, at least politically. Each of these threatening incidents took place during President George Bush's January 1992 trip to the Far East.

The most notable incident, of course, was the President's bizarre public seizure while dining in the company of the Japanese premier. More than a few people speculated—privately—that the president might indeed have been poisoned. This, of course, is speculation, but it is based in reality.

Interestingly, it was while the president was on his Far Eastern junket that *The Washington Post*—the daily newspaper of record in the nation's capitol—inexplicably reversed itself and began publishing a lengthy and glowing seven-part series hailing Vice President Dan Quayle. Obviously this seems to be a confirmation of Victor Ostrovsky's claim that preparations were being made in the United States to make a Dan Quayle presidency palatable.

The *Post*'s unusual flip-flop was made all the more potent when the news arrived that the president had been stricken. Quayle, evidently, already had the Establishment's support if he had been unexpectedly thrust into the presidency. Oddly, prior to the *Post*'s turn-about, the Washington daily had been one of Quayle's most persistent critics. However, something quite alarming also took place during that eventful week.

## A SECURITY BREACH

For two days, during President George Bush's visit in Seoul, South Korea, top-secret information regarding the president's personal arrangements was inexplicably made available to the public.

Incredibly enough, this was during a period when terrorist alert status was already high. Security experts believed that if potential presidential assassins had such action in mind, the security breach would have assisted them tremendously. According to Robert Snow, a spokesman for the Secret Service, "It wouldn't be stretching it" [15]to suggest that the security lapse could have put Bush in danger.

Blame for the lapse in security was laid at the hands of the U.S. Information Service (USIS), a branch of the State Department. For their own part, officials at the State Department were unable to provide an explanation of the bizarre security breach. The White House refused to comment.

The USIS published a list of the names and hotel room numbers of the president's traveling party, which numbered 471 people. (The fact that the president was staying at the U.S. Ambassador's residence was part of the information revealed.) Included on the list were the names and room numbers of 122 Secret Service agents, eight Marine guards, four presidential stewards and six military aides. Also revealed were security control room locations in the hotel where the president was staying as well as the names of the 10 Secret Service agents heading security at the various locations that the president visited while in Korea. The room assignments of top administration officials accompanying the president, as well as those of the thirteen corporate executives along for the trip were also published.[16]

This incredible revelation caused suspicion that perhaps there were those in positions of power who may not necessarily have been concerned for the president's safety. The tentacles of Israel's Mossad do reach far and wide—even into the depths of the U.S. State Department.

Was this breach of security a first step in an assassination attempt—perhaps one to be carried out by some obscure Korean terrorist group acting as a "false flag" for the Mossad?

Retired Air Force Col. L. Fletcher Prouty, himself an acknowledged authority on covert operations—including assassination planning—says that one of the primary necessary measures in any assassination plot is the process of removing or otherwise breaching the intended victim's blanket of security. Prouty, who worked in presidential security with the military, knows whereof he speaks.

According to Prouty, "No one has to direct an assassination—it happens. The active role is played secretly by permitting it to happen . . . This is the greatest single clue . . . Who has the power to call off or reduce the usual security precautions that are always in effect whenever a president travels?"[17]

## IF IN 1991, WHY NOT IN 1963?

The lapse in security during Bush's trip to the Far East may indeed point to something bigger than we might even want to imagine. Congressman Findley's report on the alleged Mossad plot against Bush is thus most provocative. If the Mossad actually considered killing George Bush in 1991, why wouldn't they have considered killing John F. Kennedy in 1963? As we shall see in Chapter 5, JFK's relationship with Israel was strained, to say the very least. Indeed, Israel's then-Prime Minister, David Ben-Gurion, considered JFK a threat to Israel's survival.

## AN INTERESTING FOOTNOTE IN HISTORY . . .

It was only after the second edition of *Final Judgment* went to press that the author learned of yet another Israeli plot to assassinate an American president perceived hostile to Zionist interests.

According to Margaret Truman, daughter of late President Harry Truman, the Jewish underground terrorist movement in Palestine known as the Stern Gang once tried to murder her father.

In a biography of her father Miss Truman discussed the attempt on her father's life by Puerto Rican nationalists. Then, in a little-noticed, but highly significant aside she commented: "I learned in the course of my research for this book that there had been other attempts on Dad's life, which he never mentioned . . . In the summer of 1947, the so-called Stern gang of Palestine terrorists tried to assassinate Dad by mail . . ."[18]

The Jewish terrorists, it seems, had sent the president letters that had been tainted with toxic chemicals. Fortunately, the mail was intercepted and no harm was done. Harry Truman, of course, got the message, though, and rushed to recognize the state of Israel upon its founding in 1948, despite his own reservations and those on the part of his diplomatic advisors.

This clumsy attempt to kill Truman is interesting, to say the very least, and points to a proclivity for political violence on the part of the Israeli leaders in the Stern Gang whom, it should be pointed out, were the very individuals who emerged as the leaders of the Mossad following the establishment of the state of Israel.

## A PATTERN OF EVIDENCE . . .

Very clearly, there is strong evidence—indeed a pattern—to suggest that Israel would indeed consider the assassination of an American president. Harry Truman, we now know, is the first documented target of such a plot. George Bush, it seems, was also a target. And in the pages of *Final Judgment*, we shall see, John F. Kennedy was also a target—and in JFK's case the plot did not fail.

With all of this in mind, let us move forward and examine the hard evidence which will lead us toward a final judgment.

## Chapter Three
## A Bad Habit:
## Israel's Use of "False Flags" in Global Terrorism—
## Pointing the Finger of Guilt Elsewhere

**Researchers in the JFK assassination controversy have repeatedly pointed out the false leads that continue to appear. Most believe that Lee Harvey Oswald, the alleged assassin, was indeed what he claimed to be—the patsy—and that false clues had been laid by the real conspirators to make it appear as though Oswald was an agent of the Soviets or Fidel Castro or both.**

**The use of such "false flags" by Israel's Mossad to cover up its own role in worldwide assassination conspiracies and other criminal activity has been documented time and again. "Arabs," "the Mafia," "right-wing extremists," and others have repeatedly taken the fall for crimes committed by the Mossad or carried out under its coordination.**

The use of "false flag" operations by Israel and its Mossad has been documented repeatedly since the Jewish State first came into being.

This book contends that Israel and its primary collaborator, the CIA, utilized insidious "false flags" in orchestrating the assassination of John F. Kennedy and the subsequent cover-up: "the Mafia," "anti-Castro Cubans," "the Soviets," "Castro agents" and even "right-wing extremists" have all been fingered as those responsible for the JFK assassination. But the real hard evidence points in another direction entirely.

### 'FORGED TRAILS' AND 'FALSE FLAGS'

One major JFK assassination researcher, Professor Peter Dale Scott, has described what he called "the brilliance of the assassination plot."[19]

This was, according to Scott, "that the conspirators had forged trails to induce a cover-up." Scott cites a number of instances: "There were, for example, trails that potentially linked Oswald to Fidel Castro or to the KGB and Khruschev—a trail that might lead to war.

"Moreover, there was false evidence given to the Secret Service that led to a group of anti-Castro Cubans in Chicago whose operations had been authorized indirectly by Bobby Kennedy himself.

"This is just one of several trails that might have led in directions that no one wanted to investigate."[20]

That Israel has had a long and proven record in planting "false flags" is the subject of discussion in this chapter.

In preparation for our consideration of Israel's role in the JFK assassination conspiracy, it is worthwhile to first review some of the more notable instances in which Israel orchestrated criminal ventures—most especially murder—and pinned those atrocities on innocent parties—"false flags."

In Chapter 2 former Congressman Paul Findley was quoted as having cited two cases in which Israel indicated a willingness to sacrifice American lives for its own interests:    (a) the attack on the *U.S.S. Liberty* in June of 1967 and  (b) the intended attack on an American reconnaissance plane that was overflying Israel's secret nuclear bomb development site.   These incidents are particularly intriguing in light of what we will ponder in this volume.

The attack on the *Liberty*—it is generally acknowledged by everyone but Israel and its defenders—was a deliberate attempt to destroy the *Liberty* and its crew and to sink the vessel to the bottom of the Mediterranean. What is most interesting, however, is the reason behind this bizarre and brutal attack.

## THE U.S.S. LIBERTY—BLAMING THE EGYPTIANS

Israel, in fact, hoped to pin the responsibility on a "false flag"— Egypt—and draw the United States into the impending 1967 war on the side of Israel.   It is only because the *Liberty* did not sink and instead was rescued that the history books don't tell us today that "the Arabs" sunk an American spy ship and sparked another "*Lusitania* incident" that forced America to go to war.

## THE NUCLEAR BOMB

The second instance to which Congressman Findley referred is of special interest inasmuch as the intended attack on an American air force reconnaissance plane was designed to protect Israel's secret development of nuclear weaponry.

It was Israel's nuclear offensive that led President John F. Kennedy into the "secret war" with Israel that he was conducting during the three years of his short-lived presidency.   As we shall see in Chapter 5, it was the very issue of Kennedy's intransigence and his opposition to Israel's nuclear development that became a central part of his standoff with Israel and its Mossad.

It was this conflict indeed that played a critical part in setting in final motion the assassination conspiracy that ended John Kennedy's life.

What follows is an overview of some other notable instances in which Israel utilized "false flags" in its international criminal endeavors.

## THE LAVON AFFAIR

Perhaps the best-known instance in which Israel used a "false flag" to cover its own trail was in the infamous Lavon Affair. It was in 1954 that several Israeli-orchestrated acts of terrorism against British targets in Egypt were carried out.   Blame for the attacks was placed on the Muslim Brotherhood, which opposed the regime of Egyptian President Gamul Abdul-Nasser.

However, the truth about the wave of terror can now be found in a once-secret cable from Colonel Benjamin Givli, the head of Israel's military intelligence, who outlined the intended purpose behind the wave of terror:

["Our goal] is to break the West's confidence in the existing [Egyptian] regime . . . . The actions should cause arrests, demonstrations, and expressions of revenge. The Israeli origin should be totally covered while attention should be shifted to any other possible factor. The purpose is to prevent economic and military aid from the West to Egypt." [21]

Ultimately the truth about Israel's involvement in the affair became public and Israel was rocked internally in the wake of the scandal. Competing political elements within Israel used the scandal as a bludgeon against their opponents. But the truth about Israel's use of a "false flag" had come to international attention.

## BLAMING 'RIGHT-WING EXTREMISTS'

A shadowy "right wing" group known as "Direct Action" was accused of the attack on Goldenberg's Deli in Paris on August 9, 1982. Six people died and 22 were injured.

The leader of "Direct Action" was one Jean-Marc Rouillan. It turned out that Rouillan had been operating in the Mediterranean under the cover name of "Sebas" and had been repeatedly linked to the Mossad. All references to Rouillan's Mossad links were deleted from the official reports issued at the time.

However, the Algerian national news service—which has ties to French intelligence—blamed the Mossad for these activities. Angry French intelligence officers were believed to have leaked this information to the Algerians. Several top French security officials quit in protest over this intra-intelligence community scandal.[22]

This is just one of many such Mossad-orchestrated crimes in which others took the blame. There are others.

## FALSE CLUES

On October 3, 1980 a synagogue on Copernicus Street was bombed in Paris. Four bystanders were killed. Nine were injured. The media frenzy which followed the incident was worldwide. Reports held that "right wing extremists" were responsible. Yet, of all of the "right wing extremists" held for questioning, none was arrested. In fact, all were released.

In the upper echelons of French intelligence, however, the finger of suspicion was pointed at the Mossad. According to one report: "On April 6, 1979, the same Mossad terror unit now suspected of the Copernicus carnage blew up the heavily guarded plant of CNIM industries at La Seyne-sur-Mer, near Toulon, in southeast France, where a consortium of French firms was building a nuclear reactor for Iraq.

"The Mossad salted the site of the CNIM bomb blast with 'clues' followed up with anonymous phone calls to police—suggesting that the sabotage was the work of a 'conservative' environmentalist group—'the most pacific and harmless people on earth' as one source put it."[23]

Other Mossad-orchestrated false flag operations also took place on French soil.

## BLAMING THE CORSICAN MAFIA

• On June 28, 1978, Israeli agents exploded a bomb under a small passenger car in the Rue Saint Anne, killing Mohammed Boudia, an organizer for the Palestine Liberation Organization (PLO). Immediately afterward, Paris police received anonymous phone calls accusing Boudia of involvement in narcotics deals and attributing his murder to the Corsican Mafia. A thorough investigation subsequently established that Mossad special-action agents were responsible for the terrorist killing.

## BLAMING THE NEO-NAZIS

• In October, 1976 the same Mossad unit kidnapped two West German students named Brigette Schulz and Thomas Reuter from their Paris hotel. Planted "clues"and anonymous phone calls made it appear that a Bavarian "neo-nazi" formation had executed the abduction.   In fact, French intelligence established that the two German youths had been secretly flown to Israel, drugged, tortured, coerced into a false "confession of complicity" in PLO activities, and then anonymously incarcerated in one of the Israeli government's notorious political prisons.

## BLAMING THE SOUTH KOREANS

• In February 1977 a German-born, naturalized U.S. citizen named William Jahnke arrived in Paris for some secretive business meetings. He soon vanished, leaving no trace. Paris police were anonymously informed that Jahnke had been involved in a high-level South Korean bribery affair and "eliminated" when the deal went sour.

A special team of investigators from SDECE, the leading French intelligence agency, eventually determined that Jahnke had been "terminated" by the Mossad, which suspected him of selling secret information to the Libyans. Along with other details of this sordid case, the SDECE learned that Jahnke had been "fingered" to the Mossad by his own former employer, the CIA.[24]

## BLAMING THE LIBYANS

One of Israel's most outrageous "false flag" operations involved a wild propaganda story aimed at discrediting Libyan leader Muamar Qaddafi— one of Israel's favorite enemies.  In the early months of the administration of President Ronald Reagan, the American media began heavily promoting a story to the effect that a "Libyan hit squad" was in the United States for the express purpose of assassinating Reagan. This inflamed public sentiment against Libya and there were repeated calls for blood.

Suddenly, however, the "hit squad" stories vanished. In fact, it was ultimately discovered that the source of the story was one Manucher Ghorbanifar, a former Iranian SAVAK (secret police) agent with close ties to the Mossad. Even *The Washington Post* acknowledged that the CIA itself believed that Ghorbanifar was a liar who "had made up the hit-squad story in order to cause problems for one of Israel's enemies."[25]

*The Los Angeles Times* itself had already blown the whistle on Israel's scare stories. "Israeli intelligence, not the Reagan administration," reported the *Times*, "was a major source of some of the most dramatic published reports about a Libyan assassination team allegedly sent to kill President Reagan and other top U.S. officials . . . Israel, which informed sources said has 'wanted an excuse to go in and bash Libya for a longtime,' may be trying to build American public support for a strike against [Qaddafi], these sources said."[26]

In other words, Israel had been promoting the former SAVAK agent, Ghorbanifar, to official Washington as a reliable source. In fact, he was a Mossad disinformation operative waving a "false flag" to mislead America.

This was yet another Israeli scheme to blame Libya for its own misdeeds, this time using one "false flag" (Iran's SAVAK) to lay the blame on another "false flag" (Libya). (In Chapter 18 we shall see yet another SAVAK crime carried out on behalf of Israel and its allies in the CIA.)

## BLAMING LIBYA AGAIN

Israel's Mossad was almost certainly responsible for the bombing of the La Belle discotheque in West Berlin on April 5, 1986. However, claims were made that there was "irrefutable" evidence that the Libyans were responsible. A U.S. serviceman was killed. President Ronald Reagan responded with an attack on Libya.

However, intelligence insiders believed that Israel's Mossad had concocted the phony "evidence" to "prove" Libyan responsibility. West Berlin police director Manfred Ganschow, who took charge of the investigation, cleared the Libyans, saying, "This is a highly political case. Some of the evidence cited in Washington may not be evidence at all, merely assumptions supplied for political reasons."[27]

## BLAMING THE SYRIANS

On April 18, 1986 one Nezar Hindawi, a 32 year old Jordanian was arrested in London after security guards found that one of the passengers boarding an Israeli plane bound for Jerusalem, Ann Murphy, 22, was carrying a square, flat sheet of plastic explosive in the double bottom of her carry-on bag. Miss Murphy told security men that the detonator (disguised as a calculator) had been given to her by her finance, Hindawi. He was charged with attempted sabotage and attempted murder.

Word was leaked that Hindawi had confessed and claimed that he had been hired by Gen. Mohammed Al-Khouli, the intelligence director of the Syrian air force. Also implicated were others including the Syrian Ambassador in London. The French authorities warned the British Prime Minister that there was more to the case than met the eye—that is, Israeli involvement. This was later confirmed in repeated reports in the Western press.[28]

## BLAMING THE PLO

In 1970, King Hussein of Jordan was provided with incriminating intelligence that suggested the Palestine Liberation Organization was plotting to murder him and seize power in his nation. Infuriated, Hussein mobilized his forces for what has become known as the 'Black September' purge of the PLO. Thousands of Palestinians living in Jordan were rounded up, some of the leaders were tortured, and in the end, masses of refugees were driven from Jordan to Lebanon.

New data, coming to light after the murder of two leading Mossad operatives in Larnaka, Cyprus suggested that the entire operation had been a Mossad covert action, led by one of its key operatives, Sylvia Roxburgh, who was also known as Sylvia Rafael and is believed to have been born Esther Paltzur.

Miss Roxburgh contrived an affair with King Hussein, known for his weakness for beautiful women, and served as the linchpin for one of the Mossad's major "cover and deception" coups designed to destabilize the Arabs.[29]

In 1982, just when the PLO had abandoned the use of terrorism, the Mossad spread disinformation about "terror attacks" on Israeli settlements along the northern border in order to justify a full-scale military invasion of Lebanon. Years later, even leading Israeli spokesmen, such as former Foreign Minister Abba Eban, admitted that the reports of "PLO terrorism" had been contrived by the Mossad. [30]

## THE ISRAELI DIPLOMAT

It is also worth noting that the attempted assassination—in London—of Israeli Ambassador to England, Shlomo Argov, was initially blamed upon the PLO. The attempted assassination was cited by Israel as one of its excuses for its bloody 1982 incursion into Lebanon.

Yet, ironically, the diplomat in question was considered one of Israel's "doves" and inclined toward a friendly disposition of Israel's longtime conflict with the PLO. He was the least likely target of PLO wrath. What's more, one of the suspects in the crime was found carrying a "hit list" which actually included the name of the head of the PLO office in London.[31]

In fact, it appears that the assassination attempt was carried out by the Mossad—under yet another "false flag"—for two purposes: (a) elimination of a domestic "peacenik" considered friendly toward the Palestinians; and (b) pinning yet another crime on the Palestine Liberation Organization.

## WHO IS POINTING THE FINGER?

These instances cited here are but a handful of Mossad-orchestrated "false flag" operations blamed on a wide variety of alleged "suspects."

The evidence suggests that the assassination of John F. Kennedy was yet another "false flag" conspiracy by Israel's Mossad and its collaborators in the American CIA. In the JFK assassination, the "Mafia" and the "anti-Castro Cubans" were set up as potential fall guys. Even Castro and the Soviets have been implicated. Everybody, it seems, has been fingered but the Mossad.

It was the Mossad and its allies in the CIA and in the controlled American media who have been doing all the fingering. Everybody being blamed by the Mossad and its CIA allies were implicated—one way or the other—and everybody, as a consequence, had a stake in the cover-up.

## JFK AND SECRET DEALS

To achieve the presidency in 1960, John F. Kennedy was forced to cut secret deals—behind the scenes—with a variety of powerful forces intricately linked to Israel. In Chapter 4 we shall examine the history of those deals and how they played a part in the JFK assassination conspiracy.

## Chapter Four

## No Love Lost:
## JFK, Meyer Lansky, the Mafia & the Israeli Lobby

There was a long history of bitter enmity between John F. Kennedy and his powerful father Ambassador Joseph P. Kennedy, and organized crime boss Meyer Lansky, stemming in part from the senior Kennedy's deals with the underworld. This, however, did not stop the Kennedy family from cutting deals with the crime syndicate when it came to winning elections.

The Kennedy family's alleged anti-Semitism didn't do anything to improve JFK's relations with Israel and its American lobby either. Kennedy's intervention in the issue of Algerian independence from France also drew sharp criticism from the Israeli lobby as well. Yet, when John F. Kennedy sought the presidency, he was willing to cut deals with the Israeli lobby—for a price.

By the end of his presidency, however, Kennedy had reneged on his deals, not only with Israel's Godfather, Meyer Lansky, and his henchmen in the Mafia, but also with the Israeli lobby.

John F. Kennedy was very much a product of his father's upbringing—much to the dismay, it might be said, of many of even JFK's most devout disciples. They would, frankly, prefer to forget much of the recorded history of the Kennedy family and present JFK as something just short of being a saint.

That President John F. Kennedy was the son of Ambassador Joseph P. Kennedy, long perceived to be, at the very least, neutral to the ambitions of Nazi Germany—and, at the worst, an anti-Semite and even an admirer of Adolf Hitler—has been a lot for Kennedy's admirers to swallow.

Ambassador Kennedy, of course, fought U.S. entry into World War II. Several accounts of the period suggest that Kennedy himself returned from Britain, where he served as American ambassador, with the intent of launching a major campaign against President Roosevelt's war plans.

However, after a meeting at the White House between the ambassador and the president, Kennedy backed off. What happened during that meeting is ripe for speculation.

### JFK, HITLER AND THE WAR IN EUROPE

What is interesting to note (and definitely little known) is that at the same time Ambassador Kennedy was fighting against American involvement in what became the Second World War, his sons Joe, Jr. and John were also promoting the same agenda.

Joe, Jr., as a student at Harvard, served on the Harvard Committee Against Military Intervention in Europe, described as "a reactionary group that petitioned influential government officials and held rallies opposing American entry in the European war effort."[32]

More significantly, however, it appears that JFK himself was under steady surveillance by J. Edgar Hoover's FBI because of his anti-war activities. JFK was accused by the FBI of voicing "anti-British and defeatest sentiments and blaming Winston Churchill for getting the United States into the war . . . It also appears," charged the FBI, "that Kennedy had prepared for his father at least one of the speeches which his father had made, or was intending to make, in answer to criticism of his alleged appeasement policies . . . In addition Jack Kennedy stated that in his opinion England was through, and his father's greatest mistake was not talking enough, that he stopped talking too soon."[33]

Young Jack Kennedy, as a Harvard student, was more than neutral toward Hitler, it seems. Having visited Mussolini's Italy, Stalin's Russia and Hitler's Germany, JFK recorded in his diary, according to *Time* magazine, that he had come "to the decision that Facism [sic] is the thing for Germany and Italy, Communism for Russia and Democracy for America and England."[34] Youthful musings, but interesting, to say the least.

### KENNEDY AND THE 'FASCIST'

After the war was underway, JFK's father, Ambassador Kennedy, actively considered involvement in a scheme to cut the war short—in opposition to President Roosevelt.

Kennedy's biographer, Richard Whalen, has written of a secret meeting between Kennedy and a prominent critic of the Roosevelt administration, the controversial publicist, Lawrence Dennis. Often described (inaccurately) as "America's leading fascist," Dennis was a former diplomat himself and one of the early leaders in the effort to block American intervention in what evolved into World War II. Consequently, he and Kennedy had much in common.

Kennedy's biographer outlined the circumstances of that secret meeting—a meeting which says much about Kennedy's line of thinking:

"In October 1943, Lawrence Dennis received a telephone call from his friend, Paul Palmer, then a senior editor of *The Reader's Digest*. Before the war, Dennis had contributed to the *Digest*, but the author of *The Coming American Fascism* since had become too controversial for his byline to appear in the nation's largest magazine. Now he received a $500-a-month retainer as an editorial consultant.

"One of his recent efforts had been a memorandum sharply critical of unconditional surrender and the rumored plans to break up Germany. Palmer invited Dennis to lunch in his suite in Manhattan's St. Regis Hotel, saying he would meet someone there who was thinking along similar lines.

"It turned out to be Joe Kennedy. Over lunch, Kennedy said he had been seeing Archbishop Spellman almost daily. He said the Archbishop had returned from Rome with word that Hitler's generals might attempt to overthrow him if they were offered terms less hopeless than unconditional surrender.

"Kennedy grew emotional and castigated Roosevelt. He talked of his two sons in the service, and declared that the war could be ended within two weeks if the German generals were given encouragement.

"Of course, no Church official could speak out against the folly of Roosevelt's policy, but Kennedy could, and this had been Palmer's purpose in arranging the luncheon. The editor asked whether the former Ambasssador would write, or at least sign, an article condemning unconditional surrender. The impact of such an article, given Kennedy's former standing in the administration, could be enormous. But he did not accept the invitiation and the war being fought by his sons and so many other young men raged on."[35]

Ambassador Kennedy no doubt remembered this meeting for the rest of his days. He was very bitter about the war and particularly bitter at Franklin D. Roosevelt. Kennedy once allegedly referred to FDR as "that crippled son of a bitch that killed my son Joe."

(Joe Kennedy, Jr., of course, being the ambassador's eldest son. It was Joe, Jr.'s death that ultimately laid the groundwork for the second son, John, to be groomed for the presidency in his older brother's place.)

## A BUSINESS VENTURE

However, the senior Kennedy's views most definitely did not change as time went by. But as the retired ambassador grew older, he became more pragmatic. This was evidenced in a meeting—in the mid-1950's—between Kennedy and an associate of Lawrence Dennis—a New York-based entertainment executive named DeWest Hooker.

In fact, as we shall see, it may have been efforts by Hooker, as a consequence of his meeting with Joe Kennedy, that no doubt helped John F. Kennedy win his his narrow presidential election victory.

Mr. Hooker hoped to interest Joe Kennedy in a business venture which Hooker believed might be right up the ambassador's alley. Hooker wanted to establish an independent television network, and he felt that Kennedy, himself a veteran movie mogul, might be interested in backing the enterprise. Hooker's memory of that meeting is quite interesting, particularly in the context of the thesis presented in these pages. To appreciate just precisely where Hooker was coming from, however, it is appropriate to review Hooker's remarkable background.

## UNABASHEDLY ANTI-JEWISH

Born to wealth and privilege and a descendent of one of the signers of the Declaration of Independence, Hooker had a varied career. Not only did he act on the Broadway stage, but he also modeled in cigarette advertisements. Hooker also served for a period as a talent agent with the powerful firm MCA and was, at a time during the 1950's one of the highest-paid talent agents in America. Hooker also dabbled in television production and was equally successful.

However, there was an aspect to Hooker's persona that made him, to say the least, *persona non grata* in the entertainment industry: Hooker is unabashedly and frankly anti-Jewish. He will be the first to admit it, no questions asked. A powerfully-built man, Hooker is fearless and not afraid to make his position known.

One of Hooker's proteges was George Lincoln Rockwell, founder of the American Nazi Party. In his memoirs, *This Time the World*, Rockwell credits Hooker as being a major influence on his thinking. In fact, Rockwell dedicated the book to Hooker, along with several others including Sen. Joseph R. McCarthy and General Douglas MacArthur. Hooker, Rockwell declared, was the one "who taught me to know the cunning and evil ways of the enemy."[36] According to Rockwell, Hooker was "the nearest thing to a Nazi since the Bund."[37]

The reason for Hooker's interest in establishing an independent network was highly political: Hooker wanted the new network to be totally divorced from Jewish money and influence. In his judgment, the three existing networks were entirely under the control of Jewish interests. Hooker wanted a network that presented what he called "our way of thinking."

## JOE KENNEDY SPEAKS FRANKLY

It was in 1956 that Hooker had a private meeting in Palm Beach, Florida with Kennedy. After a game of golf, Kennedy and Hooker got down to business. Hooker was there to solicit Kennedy's financial, political and personal backing for his proposed network.

(It was during this period that Sen. John F. Kennedy was then actively seeking the Democratic Party's vice presidential nomination. He lost, but his efforts brought him widespread acclaim within party ranks, and set in place the mechanism for his successful bid for the top spot on the party's national ticket in 1960.)

After Hooker made his presentation to the retired ambassador, Kennedy's response was supportive in spirit, but Old Joe made his final position clear during their four hour conference.

According to Hooker, "Joe admitted that when he was ambassador to England that he had been pro-Hitler. However, in Kennedy's words, 'we' lost the war. By 'we' he didn't mean the United States. When Kennedy said 'we,' he meant the non-Jews. Joe Kennedy believed that it was the Jews who had won World War II.

"Kennedy said, 'I've done everything I can to fight the Jewish power over this country. I tried to stop World War II, but I failed. I've made all the money I need and now I'm passing everything I've learned on to my sons."

"'I don't go with the 'loser'," Kennedy told me. 'I've joined the 'winners.' I'm going to work with the Jews. I'm teaching my boys the whole score and they're going to work with the Jews. I'm going to make

Jack the first Irish Catholic President of the United States and if it means
working with the Jews, so be it. I'm in sympathy with what you're doing,
Hooker'," Kennedy said, 'but I'm not going to do anything that will ruin
Jack's chances to become president.'"[38]

Hooker was, of course, disappointed by Kennedy's response and
ultimately his "fourth" network failed to get off the ground. However,
Hooker at least had the satisfaction of knowing that he and the Kennedy
family were on the same wave length—even if they were willing to
compromise those views for political gain.

## THE NAZIS 'ENDORSE' NIXON

As they parted at the end of their Palm Beach meeting, Hooker asked
Kennedy if there was anything he could do to help the Kennedy family.

"Yes, as a matter of fact, there is something you can do." responded Joe
Kennedy. "I'd like you to use your contacts in the right-wing. Have them
start publishing articles accusing Jack of being controlled by the Jews, of
being a Jewish puppet. This will have the effect of neutralizing Jewish
opposition to Jack (because of me).

"The Jews know my views and naturally they'll assume that Jack is a
chip off the old block. If the right wing starts hitting Jack this will give the
Jews second thoughts—at least the ones who do the voting."[39]

Hooker promised Kennedy he would do what he could. And being a
man of his word, Hooker did influence his right-wing contacts as Kennedy
had asked. Hooker encouraged his friend, Nazi leader Rockwell, and other
"right wingers" to smear John F. Kennedy as JFK's father had suggested.
His efforts succeeded.

As one chronicle of the 1960 campaign noted: "The American Nazi
Party helped too by throwing its support to Richard Nixon—"Nazis for
Nixon, Kikes for Kennedy" was one of its slogans. Another of its placards
read, "FDR and JFK mean JEW deal."[40]

This, of course, was inspired by JFK's father and carried out through
the good offices of DeWest Hooker and his friend George Lincoln
Rockwell, although the historian who penned the description of Rockwell's
sloganeering probably had no idea that it was indirectly the work of Joe
Kennedy.

"Frankly," Hooker says to this day, "As far as I'm concerned, it was my
work that got Johnny Kennedy in the White House."[41] (Hooker's claim is
not completely off the mark, inasmuch as American Jewish leaders claimed
themselves at the time that it was Jewish support for John F. Kennedy that
gave him his narrow victory over Nixon in the 1960 election.)

This interesting—and revealing—episode is not likely to be
memorialized at the John F. Kennedy Library at Harvard or in any friendly
biographies of the Kennedy family. However, there can be little doubt that
Israel and its American lobby had a fairly good idea of what was going on
behind the scenes.

## KENNEDY RILES THE ISRAELI LOBBY

In 1957, while serving in his first Senate term, John Kennedy became involved in a festering international issue that was little noticed among the average American voters, but which was of special interest to Israel and its lobby in America: the question of Algerian independence. The giant Arab colossus, long a French colony, was seeking its freedom and in France itself the nation was engaged in a heated debate over the question. Israel, of course, saw the emergence of another independent Arab republic as a threat to its security and anyone favoring Algerian independence was, thus, advocating a policy deemed threatening to Israel's survival.

Former diplomat Richard Curtiss described Kennedy's surprise entry into the debate over Algeria: "By 1957, as a freshman member of the Senate Foreign Relations Committee, he thought he recognized [the] tragedy of colonial inflexibility unfolding in Algeria. Already one of the congressional library's heaviest borrowers, he now spent additional time in conversation with William J. Porter, an Arabist and the director of the State Department's Office of North African Affairs.

"Porter feared that Washington's uncritical support of its NATO ally, France, in the increasingly brutal French repression of the Algerian natinalists, threatened the whole future of the United States in North Africa. Kennedy also talked to members of the Algerian FLN delegation at the United Nations."[42]

On July 2, 1957, JFK rose before the Senate and gave his maiden foreign policy address on this controversial question. He said, in part: "No amount of mutual politeness, wishful thinking, nostalgia or regret should blind either France or the United States to the fact that, if France and the West at large are to have a continuing influence in North Africa . . . the essential first step is the independence of Algeria."[43]

According to Curtiss: "The speech prompted more mail than any other he delivered as a senator. The foreign policy establishment in New York, a bastion of Atlantic solidarity, expressed righteous indignation."[44] Also, notes Curtiss, "the French were irritated."[45]

Some of Kennedy's critics said that the speech was a political move and that he chose the topic of Algerian independence as the subject of his first major foreign policy address because there was neither a "French" vote nor an "Algerian" vote to contend with in his home state of Massachusetts or in the nation as a whole.

While the latter observation is correct, of course, the fact is that there was one particularly powerful American voting bloc (and source of financial contributions) that did take note of Kennedy's support for Algerian Arab independence: the powerful American lobby for Israel.

As we shall see, in the end, it may have been JFK's initiative on the Algerian question that, in fact, played a major part in shaping the entirety of the conspiracy that ended his life in Dallas, Texas on November 22, 1963.

This gesture by the young senator also angered many French nationalists who wanted to retain French colonial control of Algeria. Many of these nationalists later banded together in the so-called Secret Army Organization—the Israel-backed OAS—and fought against French President Charles DeGaulle who ultimately granted Algerian independence.

In Chapter 12, Chapter 15 and Chapter 16 we will learn more about the so-called "French connection" and how, indeed, it ultimately played a role in the JFK murder, manipulated by Israel's Mossad.

## KENNEDY AND LANSKY

Kennedy had other powerful enemies. An ancient enmity also stood between Joseph P. Kennedy and Meyer Lansky, the foremost Jewish mob boss in America. (In Chapter 7 we shall examine Lansky's history in more detail.) The conflict between JFK and Lansky, however, went back to the days of the president's father's own bootlegging activities.

According to JFK assassination expert, Jim Marrs: "In 1927, a shipment of bootleg whiskey on its way from Ireland to Boston was hijacked in southern New England. Almost the entire guard was killed in the resulting shootout. The hijackers were part of the Luciano-Lansky mob, while it was rumored that Joseph P. Kennedy was involved in the shipment. Kennedy reputedly lost a fortune on the deal and was besieged by widows of the guards seeking financial assistance. Lansky later told biographers he was convinced that Kennedy held a grudge against him personally from that time on and, in fact, had passed the hostility on to his sons."[46]

Long-time Lansky henchman Michael Milan lends support for Marrs' allegation. According to Milan, "Ask Meyer Lansky about Joe Kennedy and you'd see one of the few times that Mr. L. would actually get conniptions. What they said back during Prohibition was that you can't trust Joe Kennedy to keep his word. He stole from his friends so much that he had no friends. And right before World War II, the sonovabitch turned around and said that we should all get on Hitler's side, that the Jews could go to Hell.

"Meyer was ready to bust a blood vessel. His temples were actually throbbing when Sam Koenig told him what Kennedy had said. And then Meyer, almost like he was a born Sicilian, swore a blood revenge on the entire family. 'The sins of the father,' he kept on saying to himself, mumbling like an old *zeydah* vowing revenge. 'The sins of the father.'"[47]

The conflict between Lansky and Joseph P. Kennedy was but one facet of Kennedy's relationship with organized crime. It was a relationship of many parts, and, in the end, clearly had a significant role in helping shape the conspiracy that resulted in the assassination of Ambassador Kennedy's son who had, in fact, finally achieved the presidency.

## A DOUBLE CROSS

Commenting on the theory that organized crime killed JFK (a theory with which Fox concurs), historian Stephen Fox noted that "Gangsters did not normally harm honest lawmen,"[48] such as a president like Kennedy whose admistration had begun cracking down on the national crime syndicate.

However, notes Fox, "For such an extraordinary murder—to kill a president—they must have been extraordinarily provoked. In their terms, it could only have involved a double cross. The Kennedys must have dealt with the underworld in compromising ways. When the Kennedys then turned around and nonetheless went after organized crime, they breached the code and put a contract on the President."[49]

Fox notes that while old Joe Kennedy was an inveterate gambler, with many ties to the underworld, "given his vast wealth, no matter how much he lost the underworld could never have 'owned' him." [50]

Joe Kennedy himself was a regular visitor to Meyer Lansky's Colonial Inn, which Lansky co-owned with New York Mafia boss Frank Costello and an assortment of smaller shareholders including a little-known Dallas nightclub keeper named Jack Ruby. Lansky himself used to brag that among his clients included, "judges, senators, respectable businessmen. Joe Kennedy used to come four or five times a week."[51]

However, as the senior Kennedy's son Jack moved upward in the political arena, his father tried to shut out his past relationship with Frank Costello. According to one of Costello's friends, "The way [Costello] talked about [Joe Kennedy], you had the sense that they were close during Prohibition and then something happened. Frank said that he helped Kennedy become wealthy. What happened between them I don't know." [52]

## KENNEDY AND CRIME

It took the family of Chicago Mafia boss Sam Giancana to fill in the missing pieces of the puzzle. According to Sam Giancana (nephew of the Windy City mobster) and Chuck Giancana (brother of the mobster), JFK—and his father—had indeed double crossed organized crime.

According to the Giancanas, Detroit's "Jewish Mafia," the so-called "Purple Gang" had put out a contract on Joe Kennedy's life for bringing illegal liquor through their territory without their permission during the Prohibition days. However, Kennedy Sr. had gone to Chicago to beg for his life and the Chicago Mafia bosses intervened on his behalf, saving his life. As the Giancana's put it: "Ever after, Kennedy was in Chicago's debt."[53]

The relationship went much deeper, however. According to the Giancanas: "Kennedy's ties to the underworld intersected at a hundred points. Besides making a fortune in bootlegging, Kennedy had made a financial killing in Hollywood in the twenties—with the help of persuasive behind-the-scenes New York and Chicago muscle.

"When Prohibition came to a close, as part of a national agreement between the various bootleggers, Kennedy held on to three of the most lucrative booze distributorships in the country—Gordon's gin, Dewar's, and Haig & Haig—through his company, Somerset Imports."[54]

The Giancanas also say that it was Sam Giancana who smoothed things over with Frank Costello on Joe Kennedy's behalf after Ambassador Kennedy had snubbed the New York mobster. According to the Giancanas, Kennedy was concerned about his son's burgeoning political career and it was at that point that he agreed to cut a deal with organized crime in order to ensure smooth sailing—and in order to get Frank Costello, in Kennedy's words, "off my back."[55]

## A PROMISE TO THE MOB

After Joe Kennedy begged for Giancana's assistance at a meeting in Chicago, Giancana reportedly said, "I've heard nothing today that leads me to think that you can promise me anything in return for my assistance."

Kennedy responded: "I can. And I will. You help me now, Sam, and I'll see to it that Chicago—that you—can sit in the godamned Oval office if you want. That you'll have the President's ear. But I just need time."

Kennedy told Giancana, "He'll be your man. I swear to that. My son— the President of the United States—will owe you his father's life. He won't refuse you, ever. You have my word."[56]

## JFK, THE MAFIA AND MEYER LANSKY

It was during the 1960 Democratic Presidential primary campaign that the Kennedys once again turned to Giancana for critical Mafia support. In fact, according to the Giancanas, the Kennedys—father and son—actually met with Sam Giancana to work out a joint agreement of mutual support, before—and after—the election. As Giancana summarized the agreement: "I help get Jack elected and, in return, he calls off the heat. It'll be business as usual." [57]

Mafia money poured into critical primary states such as West Virginia (where many local political leaders were on the Mafia "pad") and by convention time, JFK was virtually assured the presidential nomination. Although New Orleans Mafia boss Carlos Marcello preferred Texas Senator Lyndon Johnson, an agreement was cut, and a Kennedy-Johnson ticket was set in place. The Democratic ticket was ready for the fall election.[58]

(In Chapter 10 we shall explore the relationship between Carlos Marcello and Meyer Lansky in detail. Marcello, in fact, was a protege of Lansky—his New Orleans front man, pure and simple.)

It turns out, too, that JFK himself was busy with other mob figures other than Sam Giancana, although the history books have discreetly ignored JFK's other crime connections, preferring instead to focus on the Italian-American "Mafia" figures.

According to FBI documents and wiretaps, JFK himself had "direct contact"[59] with Meyer Lansky himself during the 1960 presidential campaign, presumably for the purpose of shoring up mob support for his presidential campaign—a pact that would ultimately prove to have been a proverbial deal with the devil.

## PROBLEMS WITH THE ISRAELI LOBBY

During this same period JFK was also engaged with critical negotations with another important power bloc in American political affairs: the pro-Israel lobby. For obvious reasons, as we have seen, there was indeed no love lost between JFK, his father, Ambassador Kennedy, and the American Jewish community.

Writing in his book, *The Lobby: Jewish Political Power and American Foreign Policy,* Edward Tivnan comments: "Senator Kennedy's record on Israel was vague, certainly not as staunchly supportive as Hubert Humphrey's. And unlike Lyndon Johnson, Kennedy did not rush to Israel's defense during the Suez affair.

"He was also a Catholic. Many Jews associated American Catholics with right-wing, pro-McCarthy, and anti-Semitic causes. Worse, there was the touchy issue of the candidate's father, Joseph P. Kennedy, who, as ambassador to Great Britain in the late 1930's, had been a supporter of Neville Chamberlain's policy of appeasing the Nazis. "[60]

Kennedy's 1957 speech calling for Algerian independence, as we have seen, had not gone over well with Israel's American supporters. Angering the Israeli lobby further, Senator Kennedy had once offered an amendment that would have slashed economic assistance to Africa and the Middle East from $175 to $140 million, this despite the fact that pro-Israel senators said that this was harmful to Israel. [61]

## ABRAHAM FEINBERG

However, John F. Kennedy was ready to deal, and he made moves to appease the pro-Israel lobby. JFK, according to Edward Tivnan, "turned out to be a better diplomat than his father." [62]

Kennedy's contact with the Israeli lobby was New York apparel manufacturer and financier, Abraham Feinberg. Feinberg was president of the Israel Bond Organization and was helping raise private money to finance Israel's secret nuclear development program.

(The financing was done through private, covert means and outside the normal Israeli budget process because the nuclear development program was controversial, in the eyes of not only the Eisenhower administration in Washington but also in the eyes of many Israelis.)

Referring to Kennedy, Feinberg later said, "My path to power was cooperation in terms of what they needed—campaign money."[63] (Feinberg, himself had previously supported JFK's fellow Senator Stuart Symington, a rival for the 1960 Democratic nomination.)

Recognizing the need for not only critical Jewish money, but also Jewish votes, Kennedy arranged to meet with Feinberg and a host of other wealthy Jewish Americans in Feinberg's New York apartment. Following a discussion with Kennedy, Feinberg and his associates agreed to come up with $500,000 on Kennedy's behalf. According to Feinberg: "I called him right away. His voice broke. He got emotional" with gratitude.[64]

## KENNEDY'S 'OUTRAGE'

However, there was much more to the story according to author Seymour Hersh who has investigated Kennedy's relations with Israel and its American lobby:

"Kennedy was anything but grateful the next morning in describing the session to Charles L. Bartlett, a newspaper columnist and close friend. He had driven to Bartlett's home in northwest Washington and dragged his friend on a walk, where he recounted a much different version of the meeting the night before.

"'As an American citizen he was outraged,' Bartlett recalled, "to have a Zionist group come to him and say: 'We know your campaign is in trouble. We're willing to pay your bills if you'll let us have control of your Middle East policy.' Kennedy, as a presidential candidate, also resented the crudity with which he'd been approached. 'They wanted control.' he angrily told Bartlett.

"Bartlett further recalled Kennedy promising to himself that 'if he ever did get to be President, he was going to do something about it.'"[65]—that is, special interest lobbies—particularly foreign pressure groups—dictating American election campaigns and foreign policy through their financial and political clout.

## PARTIALITY 'DANGEROUS'

In a private letter to Jewish American historian Alfred Lilienthal, himself a vocal critic of Israel, Kennedy did, however, reveal his feelings toward the Middle East conflict. The letter, written on September 30, 1960, read in part: "I wholly agree with you that American partiality in the Arab-Israeli conflict is dangerous both to the U.S. and the Free World"[66] In Lilienthal's judgment, Kennedy's comment was "one of the most significant and perspicacious Middle East statements" ever made by any American political figure. [67]

But Kennedy had already cut his deals. Not only organized crime—but the Israeli lobby (of which Meyer Lansky was a critical supporter)—had their claims on John F. Kennedy.

After the election, they expected Kennedy to pay up. In the general election, it was a narrow Kennedy victory over the Republican candidate, Vice President Richard M. Nixon.

The role of the Chicago Democratic political machine (under the thumb of Mafia boss Sam Giancana) in stealing Illinois votes on behalf of the Kennedy-Johnson ticket is now well known and a widely accepted part of American political history.

Sam Giancana and his allies in organized crime—including Meyer Lansky and the Israeli lobby—were confident that they had themselves a president.

## KENNEDY & BEN-GURION—THE FIRST ENCOUNTER

Shortly after his inauguration as president, Kennedy arranged to meet with Israeli Prime Minister David Ben-Gurion. At this meeting, Kennedy said, "I know I was elected because of the votes of American Jews. I owe them my election. Tell me, is there something that I can do for the Jewish people?"

According to Seymour Hersh, "Ben-Gurion was surprised by the frankness and evaded the question by answering, 'You must do what is best for the free world.'" However, Ben-Gurion's real reaction to Kennedy was somewhat different. "What a politician!" is how the Israeli leader described the American leader. [68]

It was the beginning of a bitter and unpleasant relationship between the two men that came to its finish in Dallas, Texas on November 22, 1963. (In Chapter 5 we will examine that unfortunate relationship in detail.)

## KENNEDY TURNS THE TABLES

It was not much longer afterward that Kennedy's organized crime friends began to realize that Kennedy was not proving to be the loyal ally that they had expected he would be. Soon after JFK assumed the presidency, an unexpected war on organized crime began. Robert Kennedy, who had cut his teeth prosecuting mobsters as a counsel for the Senate's "rackets committee," was named attorney general and it was apparent that he was taking his new job seriously.

According to Sam Giancana, "It's a brilliant move on Joe [Kennedy]'s part. He'll have Bobby wipe us out to cover their own dirty tracks and it'll all be done in the name of the Kennedy 'war on organized crime.' Brilliant. Just fuckin' brilliant." [69]

Meyer Lansky's West Coast henchman, Mickey Cohen, reflected in later years upon the Organized Crime-Kennedy alliance and what it meant, particularly after Bobby Kennedy launched his campaign against the underworld.

"I know that certain people in the Chicago organization knew that they had to get John Kennedy in. There was no thought that they were going to get the best of it with John Kennedy. See, there may be different guys running for an office, and none of them may be . . . what's best for a combination.

"The choice becomes the best of what you've got going. John Kennedy was the best of the selection. But nobody in my line of work had an idea that he was going to name Bobby Kennedy attorney general. That was the last thing anyone thought." [70]

(In Chapter 13 and Chapter 14 we shall examine Cohen's own strange and critical role in the JFK assassination conspiracy and its ultimate cover-up—yet another piece of the puzzle brought together in these pages.)

Ultimately, as we shall see, JFK's war against his former allies in the underworld, would lead him to the very doorsteps of the real brains behind the national—and international—crime syndicate, Meyer Lansky.

However, he had already double-crossed his immediate underworld collaborators. That alone was enough to spell JFK's doom.

## JFK MOVES AGAINST THE ISRAELI LOBBY

However, Kennedy was also engaged in some legislative sleight-of-hand that could also prove dangerous to Israel's political leverage in American election politics. Angry at his campaign experiences with the Israeli lobby's fundraisers, Kennedy appointed a bipartisan commission in 1961 to recommend ways to broaden "the financial base of our presidential campaigns."[71]

According to Seymour Hersh, "In a statement that was far more heartfelt than the public or the press could perceive, [Kennedy] criticized the current method of financing campaigns as 'highly undesirable' and 'not healthy' because it made candidates 'dependent on large financial contributions of those with special interests.'"[72]

In 1962 Kennedy submitted five bills to reform campaign financing to Congress and in 1963 two more such bills. But none of those bills survived, having been beaten back by the very special interests that Kennedy sought to counter. [73]

## SECRET WARS

However, Kennedy was more deeply engaged with Israel than on this more subtle level. As we shall see in Chapter 5, Kennedy, in fact, was at war with Israel.

Not only had Kennedy double crossed his allies in organized crime, but he had crossed his pro-Israel financiers. Israel, as we shall see in Chapter 7, was long close to the Meyer Lansky Organized Crime Sindicate.

And Israel, as we shall see in Chapter 8, was particularly close to the American CIA. Kennedy, too, by the middle of his presidency, was also at war with the CIA. This we shall discuss in Chapter 9.

All of these powerful special interests had very special reasons to want to see JFK removed from the presidency and replaced with Lyndon Johnson. There was clearly no love lost between John F. Kennedy and the powerful forces which had helped bring him to the presidency.

A reform-minded President Kennedy also had other long-range plans in the works. The scion of an independent and essentially self-made man who "played the game" to gain power and influence—and to get his son elected president—JFK was indeed very much his father's son. As a consequence, in another important realm, JFK was moving in a direction that could rock the international banking establishment to its core.

There have been widespread rumors, for nearly a generation, that JFK was planning to issue interest-free money—so-called "greenbacks"—independent of the stranglehold of the privately-owned Federal Reserve System. In fact, interest-free United States Notes were issued during JFK's presidency. (Some remain in circulation today.)

## THE MONEY MONOPOLY

There is no question, however, but that JFK—once firmly established in the presidency—fully intended to move against the Federal Reserve money monopoly. In fact, during his private meeting with DeWest Hooker, described earlier in these pages, JFK's father, Ambassador Joseph P. Kennedy, assured Hooker that an ultimate long-term aim of the Kennedy dynasty would be the destruction of what the senior Kennedy described as "the Rothschild-dominated Federal Reserve."

This alone could have assured JFK's removal from the White House. However, there were other more immediate and ultimately dangerous conflicts at work between the forces whose influence JFK sought to dismantle and the hard-driving new Kennedy administration.

## DIVERSE ENTITIES

Let us move forward and examine the strange and intimate connections between all of these Kennedy foes and the dynamics at work between them. However, as we shall see, it is the central thread of Israel and its Mossad that ties all of these diverse entities together.

To begin the process of untangling this hidden web of intrigue, we must first review the long-hidden story of Israel's secret war with John F. Kennedy.

## Chapter Five

## Genesis:
## JFK's Secret War With Israel

The history books have told us of John F. Kennedy's epic struggles with Fidel Castro and the Soviets in the Bay of Pigs debacle and the Cuban Missile Crisis.

Yet, only in recent years have we begun to learn of Kennedy's secret war with Israel. Much of the conflict stemmed from Israel's determination to build a nuclear bomb. This is a hidden history that helps explain in part the dynamic forces at work resulting in Kennedy's assassination.

By mid-1963 Israeli Prime Minister David Ben-Gurion hated Kennedy with a passion. In fact, he considered JFK a threat to the very survival of the Jewish State.

One of John F. Kennedy's first presidential appointments was naming his former campaign aide Myer (Mike) Feldman as his point man for Jewish and Israeli affairs—an important post, especially considering JFK's tenuous relationship with Israel and its American lobby.

According to author Seymour Hersh, "The President viewed Feldman, whose strong support for Israel was widely known, as a necessary evil whose highly visible White House position was a political debt that had to be paid."[74]

However, the administration was determined to make certain, according to Hersh, that nobody—Feldman in particular—would be able to circumvent any administration policy insofar as the Middle East was concerned.

"The President's most senior advisors, most acutely McGeorge Bundy, the national security advisor, desperately sought to cut Feldman out of the flow of Middle East paperwork."[75] Hersh quotes another presidential aide as having said, "It was hard to tell the difference between what Feldman said and what the Israeli ambassador said."[76]

### 'ZIONISTS IN THE CABINET ROOM'

President Kennedy himself had his own suspicions about Feldman, according to the president's close friend, Charles Bartlett (to whom Kennedy in 1960 had previously voiced concerns about Israeli influence as noted in Chapter 4).

Bartlett recalls a visit with the new President at his home in Hyannis Port, Massachusetts one Saturday (the Jewish Sabbath). Talk turned to Feldman's role in the White House bureaucracy. "I imagine Mike's having a meeting of the Zionists in the cabinet room," the president said, according to Bartlett.[77]

The President's brother, Robert Kennedy, himself said that his brother admired Feldman's work, but added, "His major interest was Israel rather than the United States."[78]

However, while Myer Feldman was busy promoting Israel's interests at the White House, the president was sending out a message to the rest of the foreign policy-making establishment in Washington.

Kennedy was making it clear that he was very much interested in finding a path to peace in the Middle East and was, in particular, looking for ways to solve the problem of finding a home for the Palestinian refugees who had been displaced by Israel in 1948.

## KENNEDY'S GOOD INTENTIONS

According to Hersh, "State Department Arabists were pleasantly surprised early in 1961 to get word from the White House, according to [one source], that 'just because 90 percent of the Jewish vote had gone for Kennedy, it didn't mean he was in their pocket.'"[79]

Former high-ranking U.S. diplomat Richard H. Curtiss, writing in *A Changing Image: American Perceptions of the Arab-Israeli Dispute*, elaborated on Kennedy's attitude toward the Middle East controversy. In a chapter appropriately titled: "President Kennedy and Good Intentions Deferred Too Long," Curtiss comments:

"It is surprising to realize, with the benefit of hindsight, that from the time Kennedy entered office as the narrowly-elected candidate of a party heavily dependent upon Jewish support, he was planning to take a whole new look at U.S. Mideast policy.

"He obviously could not turn the clock back and undo the work of President Truman, his Democratic predecessor, in making the establishment of Israel possible. Nor, perhaps, would he have wanted to.

"Kennedy was determined, however, to develop good new personal relationships with individual Arab leaders, including those with whom the previous administration's relations had deteriorated.

"As a result, various leaders of newly independent countries were surprised to find their *pro forma* messages of congratulations upon Kennedy's assumption of office answered with personalized letters from the young American President."[80]

## OLIVE BRANCH TO NASSER

The key Arab leader at the time was Egypt's Gamal Abdel Nasser, the voice of Pan-Arabism. Kennedy was especially intrigued with the possibility of opening up relations with Nasser.

According to Kennedy associate, Theodore Sorensen, "Nasser liked Kennedy's Ambassador, John Badeau, and he liked Kennedy's practice of personal correspondence. Kennedy put off, however, an invitation for a Nasser visit until improved relations could enable him to answer the political attacks such a visit would bring from voters more sympathetic to Israel."[81]

(Unfortunately, however, as noted by Richard Curtiss, "As with most good intentions deferred, the invitation to Nasser for a personal meeting with Kennedy was never issued."[82])

Thus, it was that upon assuming office, Kennedy made positive attempts to contact Arab heads of state asking how the U.S. could help each country in its individual disputes with Israel.

## STANDING BY TRADITION

However, Kennedy wanted one thing in particular understood by all sides in the conflict: the new U.S. president wanted "to make it crystal clear that the U.S. meant what it said in the Tripartite Declaration of 1950—that we will act promptly and decisively against any nation in the Middle East which attacks its neighbor." [83] This policy was directed not only to the Arabs, but Israel as well. Kennedy did indeed mean business.

## ISRAEL'S LOBBY REACTS

Soon after Kennedy assumed office, Israel and its American lobby began to understand the import of Kennedy's positioning in regard to the Arab-Israeli conflict. Israel was not happy—to say the very least—and began putting heat on the White House through the egis of its supporters in Congress, many of whom relied upon support from the Israeli lobby for campaign contributions and political leverage.

According to America's most noted longtime Jewish critic of Israel, Dr. Alfred Lilienthal: "While the President, more often through Vice President Lyndon Johnson, gave much lip service to Israelist aspirations, his administration continued to resist pressures, including a round-robin petition signed by 226 Congressmen of both parties (aided by a large *New York Times* advertisement on May 28, 1962) to initiate direct Arab-Israeli negotiations. Kennedy had decided to shelve his pledge in the Democratic platform to bring Israeli and Arab leaders together around a peace table in order to settle the Palestine question."[84]

## ALGERIA, AGAIN

It was mid-way into Kennedy's presidency that he had the satisfaction of seeing French President Charles DeGaulle grant independence to Algeria—something, of course, as we saw in Chapter 4 that was not looked favorably upon by Israel and its American lobby.

Five years and one day after Kennedy's Senate speech calling for Algerian independence, Algeria became a sovereign state on July 3, 1962. According to former diplomat Richard Curtiss, "Algeria's [revolutionary] leaders had not forgotten the American senator who had championed their cause and they publicly hailed his election."[85]

"Kennedy in turn sent William Porter, the U.S. Foreign Service officer who had explained to him the Algerian cause, as the first U.S. Ambassador to Algeria. [Algerian leader] Ahmad Ben Bella visisted Washington the same year. Afterward, in the words of Ambassador Porter, Ben Bella 'ascribed to Kennedy everything he thought good in the United States.'"[86]

Although pro-Israel propagandists and some American conservatives with close ties to the Israeli lobby said that an independent Algeria would be a "communist" outpost in the Middle East, Algerian Premier Ahmed Ben Bella banned the Communist Party of Algeria on November 29, 1962.[87] In fact, Algeria was very much an Islamic state and it was precisely this which created so much concern for Israel.

## DeGAULLE'S MIDDLE EAST TURN-ABOUT

However, the debate over Algerian independence had sparked a major crisis within France and the French Secret Army Organization (OAS), which fought Algerian freedom, considered John F. Kennedy an enemy only second to Charles DeGaulle.

(In subsequent chapters, in greater detail, we shall see further how JFK's CIA enemies were, in fact, collaborating with DeGaulle's enemies in the OAS, and traitors within his regime—along with the Israeli Mossad.)

Twenty years after Algerian independence, the *Washington Post* commented on the effect that Algerian freedom had upon DeGaulle's Middle East policy and, in turn, upon Israel:

"Diplomatically, France shorn of Algeria, returned under president Charles DeGaulle to its traditional policy of friendship with the Arabs—much to the chagrin of Israel and the 200,000 Algerian Jews who had lived peacefully alongside their Arab neighbors until emigrating to France."[88]

This, we shall see, would later prove to be a major factor in the events which ultimately took place, setting the stage for John F. Kennedy's assassination. In the meantime, however, JFK was shaping a U.S. Middle East policy that would put him directly at loggerheads with Israel.

The new president, cognizant of Israel's political influence in the United States, promptly began making overtures in that direction. Kennedy arranged for a meeting in Palm Beach, Florida in December of 1962 with then-Israeli Foreign Minister (later Prime Minister) Golda Meir.

## 'A TWO-WAY STREET'

It was during that meeting that Kennedy actually went so far as to emphasize American support for Israel, probably the farthest that any American president had gone since Israel was first established.

However, the president tempered that pledge with a hope that Israel recognized that America also had interests in the Middle East. According to President Kennedy, referring to U.S.-Israeli relations, "Our relationship is a two-way street."[89]

## NO 'EXCLUSIVE FRIENDS'

Phillips Talbot, Assistant Secretary of State for Near Eastern Affairs, who was present at the Kennedy-Meir conference prepared a memorandum for the State Department summarizing that meeting. According to the memorandum, summarized by Stephen Green in his monumental study, *Taking Sides: America's Secret Relations With a Militant Israel* :

"The United States, the President said, has a special relationship with Israel in the Middle East really comparable only to that which it has with Britain over a wide range of world affairs. But for us to play properly the role we are called upon to play, we cannot afford the luxury of identifying Israel, or Pakistan, or certain other countries, as our exclusive friends."[90]

According to Green, the thrust of Kennedy's message to Israel was this: "The best way for the United States to effectively serve Israel's national security interests, Kennedy said, was to maintain and develop America's associations with the other nations of the region. [America's]  influence could then be brought to bear as needed in particular disputes to ensure that Israel's essential interests were not compromised."[91]

"'If we pulled out of the Arab Middle East and maintained our ties only with Israel this would not be in Israel's interest,' Kennedy said."[92]

## FOUR PROBLEMS WITH ISRAEL

The American President cited four areas causing a strain in U.S.-Israel relations: 1) Israel's diversion—from the Arab States—of the Jordan River waters; 2) Israel's retaliatory raids against Arab forces in border areas; 3) Israel's pivotal role in the Palestinian refugee problem; and 4) Israel's insistence that the United States sell advanced Hawk missiles to Israel.[93]

The President outlined to Mrs. Meir what has come to be called the Kennedy Doctrine. Kennedy told Meir that U.S. interests and Israel's interests were not always the same. The Talbot memorandum described Kennedy's forthright stance:

"We know," [said Kennedy] "that Israel faces enormous security problems, but we do too. We came almost to a direct confrontation with the Soviet Union last spring and again recently in Cuba . . . Because we have taken on wide security responsibilities we always have the potential of becoming involved in a major crisis not of our own making . . .

## AMERICA'S NEEDS IMPORTANT

"Our security problems are, therefore, just as great as Israel's. We have to concern ourself with the whole Middle East. We would like Israeli recognition that this partnership which we have with it produces strains for the United States in the Middle East . . . when Israel takes such action as it did last spring [when Israel launched a raid into Syria, resulting in a condemnation by the UN Security Council]. Whether right or wrong, those actions involve not just Israel but also the United States."[94]

## AMERICA—NOT ISRAEL—FIRST

Stephen Green believes that Kennedy's position vis-a-vis Israel was an important stand: "It was a remarkable exchange, and the last time for many, many years in which an American president precisely distinguished for the government of Israel the differences between U.S. and Israeli national security interests."[95]

Thus it was that John F. Kennedy informed Israel, in no uncertain terms, that he intended—first and foremost—to place America's interests—not Israel's interests—at the center of U.S. Middle East policy.

## NUCLEAR EXPANSION

This set the groundwork for further tension between the U.S. and Israel over an even more explosive issue: Israel's determination to build a nuclear bomb. Israel had been engaged in nuclear development during the past decade but continued to insist that its nuclear programs were strictly peaceful in nature. However, the facts prove otherwise.

In order to thoroughly examine Kennedy's conflict with Israel over the Zionist State's nuclear intentions, we once again refer to Stephen Green's aforementioned work, *Taking Sides: America's Secret Relations With a Militant Israel*, a treasure trove of little known information relating to U.S.-Israeli relations from the period of 1948 through 1967. Green writes of JFK's discovery that Israel was engaged in nuclear arms development.

When Kennedy was coming into office in the transition period in December 1960 the Eisenhower administration informed Kennedy of Israel's secret nuclear weapons development at a site in the desert known as Dimona. Israel had advanced several cover stories to explain its activities at Dimona.

## A 'HIGHLY DISTRESSING' SITUATION

Israel had kept the nuclear weapons program as secret as possible, but US intelligence had discovered the project. Kennedy termed the situation "highly distressing."[96] Kennedy, upon taking office, determined that he would make efforts to derail Israel's nuclear weapons development. Nuclear proliferation was to be one of Kennedy's primary concerns.

Israel's intended entry into the nuclear arena was, as a consequence, a frightening prospect in JFK's mind, particularly in light of ongoing conflict in the Middle East.

From the very beginning of his presidency, John F. Kennedy found himself at severe odds with the government of Israel. It was a conflict that would never really be resolved until the day JFK died in Dallas. It was not an auspicious start for the New Frontier.

## KENNEDY 'NOT AMUSED' AND DE GAULLE 'ANNOYED'

According to Stephen Green: "The next year—1961—was to be an important one in the process of the nuclearization of the Middle East. In January, [Israeli Prime Minister] David Ben-Gurion informed the Israeli Knesset and the rest of the world that the Dimona reactor was in fact not a textile plant or a pumping station, but 'a scientific institute for research in problems of arid zones and desert flora and fauna.' A new American president, John Kennedy, was not amused."[97]

In Paris, Charles DeGaulle's reaction mirrored that of Kennedy's. His government had been providing nuclear technology assistance to Israel, but with the assurance from Ben-Gurion that the nuclear development was peaceful in nature.

According to Israeli historians Dan Raviv and Yossi Melman: "There was also pressure from President DeGaulle in Paris. The French attitude toward the Middle East began to change just after he took office in 1958 . . . He suspected that the Dimona reactor was destined for military uses and this greatly annoyed the French president."[98] (DeGaulle's later decision to grant Algerian independence, already described, simply exacerbated his own already growing tensions with Israel.)

In Washington, JFK was determined to settle the matter once and for all. Stephen Green described Kennedy's next step: "In May Kennedy and Ben-Gurion met in New York at the Waldorf-Astoria Hotel. Kennedy had already written to Ben-Gurion expressing his extreme concern about the Dimona project, and suggesting regular inspections by the International Atomic Energy Agency. In New York, Ben-Gurion agreed to a compromise—(approximately) annual inspections by U.S. scientists at times and on terms to be determined by the Israeli Defense Ministry.

"Later, Myer Feldman, Kennedy's aide for Middle East matters, would reveal that in return for the periodic U.S. inspections, Ben-Gurion had exacted a promise of provision of advanced Hawk ground-to-air missiles.

"There is no reason to doubt Kennedy's seriousness in wanting to track Israeli nuclear research and forestall weapons development, but whether annual inspections under the terms indicated achieved this result [was, as events unfolded] open to question."[99]

So it was that John F. Kennedy unintentionally found himself already at loggerheads with Israel behind the scenes.

## THE SECRET WAR

Kennedy's friendly overtures to the Arab states were only a public aspect of what ultimately developed into an all-out 'secret war' between Kennedy and Israel.

According to Seymour Hersh: "Israel's bomb, and what to do about it, became a White House fixation, part of the secret presidential agenda that would remain hidden for the next thirty years."[100]

As Hersh notes, quite profoundly we see in retrospect, this secret war with Israel was never once noted by any of Kennedy's biographers.[101]If indeed it had been, as we shall see, the mystery behind the JFK assassination might have been unravelled long, long ago.

## ISRAEL'S NUCLEAR AGENDA

There was an added wrinkle. Although Israel and the American CIA had established a longtime close and ongoing working relationship, the CIA was monitoring Israel's nuclear weapons development.

In March, 1963, Sherman Kent, the Chairman of the Board of National Estimates at the CIA, wrote an extended memorandum to the CIA's Director on the highly controversial subject entitled "Consequences of Israeli Acquisition of Nuclear Capability."

According to Stephen Green, for the purposes of this internal memorandum, Kent defined "acquisition" by Israel as either (a) a detonation of a nuclear device with or without the possession of actual nuclear weapons, or (b) an announcement by Israel that it possessed nuclear weapons, even without testing. Kent's primary conclusion was that an Israeli bomb would cause 'substantial damage to the U.S. and Western position in the Arab world.' [102]

According to Green's accurate assessment, "The memorandum was very strong and decidedly negative in its conclusions" [103]which were as follows:

"Even though Israel already enjoys a clear military superiority over its Arab adversaries, singly or combined, acquisition of a nuclear capability would greatly enhance Israel's sense of security. In this circumstance, some Israelis might be inclined to adopt a moderate and conciliatory posture . . .

"We believe it much more likely, however, that Israel's policy toward its neighbors would become more rather than less tough. [Israel would] seek to exploit the psychological advantages of its nuclear capability to intimidate the Arabs and to prevent them from making trouble on the frontiers."[104]

In dealing with the United States, the CIA analyst estimated, a nuclear Israel would "make the most of the almost inevitable Arab tendency to look to the Soviet Bloc for assistance against the added Israel threat, arguing that in terms of both strength and reliability Israel was clearly the only worthwhile friend of the U.S. in the area.

"Israel," in Kent's analysis, "would use all the means at its command to persuade the U.S. to acquiesce in, and even to support, its possession of nuclear capability."[105]

In short, Israel would use its immense political power—especially through its lobby in Washington—to force the United States to accede to Israel's nuclear intentions.

However, the CIA did not make known its concerns about Israel's determination to produce a nuclear bomb. According to Green, "It is perhaps significant that the memorandum was not drafted as a formal national intelligence estimate (NIE), which would have involved distribution to several other agencies of the government. No formal NIE was issued by CIA on the Israeli nuclear weapons program until 1968."[106]

That the CIA—or at the very least, elements within the CIA—would be interested in protecting Israel's interests is no surprise. As we shall see in Chapter 8, the ties between Israel and the CIA were quite intimate—perhaps too intimate in too many, many ways.

## KENNEDY AND BEN-GURION

In the meantime, President Kennedy was well aware that Israel's nuclear project at Dimona would enable Israel to produce at least one bomb per year—and that was enough to start a world war.

Although Israel's nuclear program was ostensibly "peaceful" in nature, the fact is that the project was entirely controlled by Israel's Ministry of Defense. This alone made the project controversial, even in Israel. It was for this reason that it was critical for Israeli Prime Minister David Ben-Gurion to neutralize JFK's opposition.

There was enough domestic opposition to the program in Israel itself that Kennedy's own steadfast refusal to support Israeli nuclear development could have killed the project altogether.

In the early months of his administration, Kennedy maintained regular contact with Ben-Gurion in an effort to stop the nuclear development. The two leaders had an ongoing private correspondence over the issue.

## A POISONED RELATIONSHIP

According to Seymour Hersh, "Israel's bomb program, and the continuing exchange of letters about it, would complicate, and eventually poison, Kennedy's relationship with David Ben-Gurion."[107]

Ben-Gurion sought to have a private meeting with Kennedy—in the course of an official state visit to Washington—but the president refused to provide a formal invitation.

It was then that, in May 1961, Ben-Gurion pulled his strings at the White House and contrived a meeting with Kennedy through the intervention of New York financier Abe Feinberg.

It was Feinberg, as we have seen in Chapter 4, who had initially smoothed over Kennedy's relations with the American Jewish community during the 1960 presidential campaign and arranged for a massive infusion of Jewish money into JFK's campaign.

(It was this experience, as noted previously, that soured Kennedy's attitude toward Israel and its powerful lobby to a significant extent.)

Feinberg arranged for the American president and the Israeli leader to meet during Ben-Gurion's unofficial visit to the United States where he was scheduled to be honored at a convocation at Brandeis University, a Jewish-oriented center of learning near Boston.

Following the affair at Brandeis, Ben-Gurion journeyed to New York City where he met with Kennedy at the Waldorf Astoria Hotel. According to Hersh, "The meeting with Kennedy was a major disappointment for the Israeli prime minister, and not only because of the nuclear issue."[108]

"'He looked to me like a twenty-five-year-old boy,' Ben-Gurion later told his biographer. 'I asked myself: 'How can a man so young be elected President?' At first I did not take him seriously.'"[109]

## HATRED

Following the meeting, Ben-Gurion complained to Feinberg about his unhappy first meeting with JFK. It was not an auspicious start, and as we shall see, it set a trend. According to Feinberg, "There's no way of describing the relationship between Jack Kennedy and Ben-Gurion because there's no way B.G. was dealing with JFK as an equal, at least as far as B.G. was concerned. He had the typical attitude of an old-fashioned Jew toward the young. He disrespected [Kennedy] as a youth."[110]

What's more, the Israeli Prime Minister had an additional reason to be suspicious of the young American's motives. According to Feinberg, "B.G. could be vicious, and he had such a hatred of the old man."[111] The "old man" in this case was the president's father, former Ambassador Joseph P. Kennedy, long considered not only an "anti-Semite" but a Hitler partisan.

Ben-Gurion's contempt for the younger Kennedy was growing by leaps and bounds—almost pathologically. According to Hersh, "The Israeli prime minister, in subsequent private communications to the White House, began to refer to the President as 'young man.' Kennedy made clear to associates that he found the letters to be offensive."[112]

Kennedy himself told his close friend, Charles Bartlett, that he was getting fed up with the fact that the Israeli "sons of bitches lie to me constantly about their nuclear capability."[113]

Obviously, to say the very least, there was no love lost between the two leaders. The U.S.-Israeli relationship was at an ever-growing and disastrous impasse, although virtually nothing was known about this to the American public at the time.

## 'A MORE SERIOUS DANGER'

President Kennedy's efforts to resolve the problem of the Palestinian refugees also met with fierce and bitter resistance by Ben-Gurion. The Israeli leader refused to agree to a Kennedy proposal that the Palestinians either be permitted to return to their homes in Israel or to be compensated by Israel and resettled in the Arab countries or elsewhere.

Former Undersecretary of State George Ball notes in his book, *The Passionate Attachment*, that "In the fall of 1962, Ben-Gurion conveyed his own views in a letter to the Israeli ambassador in Washington, intended to be circulated among Jewish American leaders, in which he stated: 'Israel will regard this plan as a more serious danger to her existence than all the threats of the Arab dictators and Kings, than all the Arab armies, than all of Nasser's missiles and his Soviet MIGs . . . Israel will fight against this implementation down to the last man."[114]

Clearly, then, by this point, Ben-Gurion perceived the American president's policies to be a very threat to Israel's survival. Ben-Gurion was vowing to fight, as we have seen, "down to the last man."

## KENNEDY'S GESTURE

Despite all of this, the American president remained determined to find a solution to the potential crisis presented by Ben-Gurion's obstinacy.

Kennedy offered to sell Israel Hawk missiles for defensive purposes—as Israel had been demanding—but Kennedy continued to drag his feet on the sale. The president refused to be pushed to the limit by Israel.

Kennedy finally relented and approved the sale, but only after pressure from Israel and its allies in the American Congress. By then, however, it was probably too late. The twig had been bent.

## ISRAEL RELENTLESS

Even the arms sales to Israel did not assuage Israel and its lobby. According to Alfred Lilienthal: "Congress continued to maintain pressures on the White House. The "Israel first" bloc in the Senate attacked the administration for failing to conclude a defense pact to protect Israel and to call an embargo on all arms shipments to the Middle East.

"The legislators reechoed the Ben-Gurion contention that Israel had fallen behind in the arms race. Nasser, they claimed, was ready for a push-button war. Israel [was] easy to pinpoint and destroy and [could not] retaliate against four or five Arab states at once."[115]

By this time—behind the scenes—Kennedy had ordered continuing surveillance of the Israelis and their push for the nuclear bomb. It was a top priority for Kennedy, by all estimations. However, to ensure that Israel's access to intelligence regarding the American spy operation against Israel was limited, the surveillance was being conducted directly out of then-CIA Director John McCone's office.[116]

(This, of course, still did not guarantee that Israel's friends in the CIA [whom we will consider in Chapter 8] did not tip off the Israelis to the hostile operations being conducted.)

Kennedy was still willing, however, to attempt to settle the matter and requested that Israel permit American inspectors the opportunity to come to Israel's nuclear operation at Dimona to verify that—as Israel claimed—the program was peaceful in nature. This was the president's last-ditch effort, apparently, to pacify Israel and, at the same time, find out precisely what was going on at Dimona. But Israel would not permit the inspection.

By this time there was a general understanding at the highest ranks of the Kennedy administration that there was a major problem at hand. The president's inner circle had begun to realize that Israel deemed Kennedy's refusal to knuckle under to Israel's demands as a dire threat to Israel's survival.

According to then-Secretary of Defense Robert McNamara, speaking in retrospect, "I can understand why Israel wanted a nuclear bomb. There is a basic problem there. The existence of Israel has been a question mark in history, and that's the essential issue."[117]

The Israelis—and particularly Ben-Gurion—would no doubt agree. In their view, John F. Kennedy himself was emerging as a threat to Israel's very existence:

JFK would simply not countenance a nuclear Israel and Israel's leaders believed that a nuclear Israel would ensure the continued survival of the Jewish State.

## THREATS AGAINST JFK

The American president continued to demand that Israel permit American inspection of Israel's nuclear development facilities. In response, Israel called on its American lobby to apply pressure on Kennedy behind the scenes.

One of those called into action was Abe Feinberg, the New York businessman who had helped raise critical funds for Kennedy during his presidential campaign. However, even Feinberg was unsuccessful.[118] However, Feinberg did send a message to the president that continued demands for inspection of the plant might "result in less support [from the Israeli lobby] in the 1964 presidential campaign."[119]

According to Hersh, "In the end Feinberg and Ben-Gurion could not overcome the continued presidential pressure for inspection of Dimona. Ben-Gurion's categorical public denial of any weapons intent at Dimona had left the Israeli government few options: refusing access would undercut the government's credibility and also lend credence to the newly emerging anti-nuclear community inside Israel."[120]

## DESERT DECEPTION

So it was that Ben-Gurion finally agreed to allow American nuclear experts to come to Dimona. However, Ben-Gurion had a clever trick up his sleeve. The Israeli Prime Minister hurriedly ordered the construction of what amounted to a phony nuclear plant—one that didn't give evidence of the construction of a nuclear bomb. False control rooms were set in place and dummy operations were displayed.

It was all very carefully orchestrated. Even the Israeli guides who took the Americans through the facility were accompanied by translators who gave the Americans fraudulent translations of the remarks made by the Israeli engineers at the plant.

According to Hersh, "Ben-Gurion took no chances: the American inspectors—most of them experts in nuclear reprocessing—would be provided with a Potemkin Village and never know it."[121]

Ben-Gurion's deception—however successful it may have been—still did not convince JFK that Israel was indeed fully committed to peaceful nuclear development. Kennedy, of course, knew better.

A stand-off between Kennedy and Israel was already in place and it did not bode well for the future.

## THE 'LAST AMERICAN PRESIDENT'

John Hadden, the former CIA station chief in Tel Aviv at the time believes that John F. Kennedy was the last American president to have really tried to stop the advent of the Israeli atomic bomb. "Kennedy really wanted to stop it," said Hadden, "and he offered them conventional weapons [for example, the Hawk missiles] as an inducement.

"But the Israelis were way ahead of us. They saw that if we were going to offer them arms to go easy on the bomb, once they had it, we were going to send them a lot more, for fear that they would use it."[122]

## 'THE TURBULENT YEAR'

By the fateful year of 1963, John F. Kennedy and Israel were decidedly on two different sides, and not only in the realm of the secret—and critical—nuclear controversy.

In fact, it went much deeper than that. Overall Kennedy administration policy toward the Middle East left Israel and its American lobby most dissatisfied. In his memoirs, I. L. Kenan of the pro-Israel American-Israel Public Affairs Committee, a registered lobby for Israel, described 1963 as 'the turbulent year" between John F. Kennedy and Israel. In a chapter in those memoirs, entitled "A Multitude of Promises"—Kennedy presumably the promiser—Kenan scored Kennedy's Middle East policies:

"Kennedy's neutralist strategy, his hope to please both sides in every troubled area, plunged him into a multitude of predicaments in the turbulent year of 1963. His pursuit of former enemies whom he sought to befriend alarmed our allies, whose fears he constantly sought to ally by strong but quiet commitments." [123]

The "enemies" whom Kenan referred to were those Arab leaders—Nasser of Egypt most especially—to whom JFK offered peace. Those "allies"—at least in Kenan's context—really meant just one country—Kenan's foreign principal, Israel.

Kennedy's "strong but quiet commitments," however, were apparently not enough as relations between Israel and the Arab states were strained. War appeared imminent, at least in the eyes of the Israeli leadership.

By the end of April, 1963 Israel's David Ben-Gurion sensed that the Arabs were going to attack the Jewish State, but John F. Kennedy did not share that pessimistic view. Kennedy still hoped for peace in the region and he continued his efforts.[124]

## THE ALGERIAN PROBLEM

Although then-Senator John F. Kennedy's 1957 speech calling for independence for Algeria from France had helped pave the way for that end result, newly-won Algerian freedom came at great cost. Israel was actively seeking to undermine the new regime.

On August 14, 1963 the government of Algerian premier Ben Bella accused Israel of plotting to topple the new Arab regime. The Algerian authorities captured 20 Algerians and 10 foreigners who were engaged in a conspiracy to bring down the government.

"Those foreigners are nearly all Israelites," declared the Algerian information minister. "We are led to believe that we are facing a plot with far-flung ramifications and that behind it is the hand of Israel which is trying to oppose the march of our revolution.

"Ben Bella has made clear the Algerian position on the enclave of imperialism called Israel but which is really Palestine. It is not strange that they are trying to interfere in our internal affairs."[125]

Israel and its allies in the French Secret Army Organization (OAS)—now officially disbanded, but effectively still functioning—were determined to reverse the course of history.

This, however, is not the last time in these pages that we will find the fine hand of Israel and the OAS interfering in the life and work of John F. Kennedy.

## THE LAST PRESS CONFERENCE

Kennedy's efforts to conduct a balanced U.S. Middle East policy were being frustrated at each and every turn. The bitterness was apparent—on both sides. As a result of Israel's manipulation of Congress, both the House of Representatives and the Senate voted in late 1963 to cut off aid to Egypt, a country central to Kennedy's drive for peace.

This, in effect, temporarily—at least—scuttled JFK's peace efforts. His hand of friendship to the Arab world and its leaders, Nasser of Egypt in particular, was being cut off—at the shoulder.

Israel's chief (registered) lobbyist in Washington—I. L. Kenan—described John F. Kennedy's final Washington press conference.

"Kennedy ruefully surveyed the debris of his Nasser policy at a press conference on November 14, 1963. He was sharply critical. The Senate amendment required him "to make a finding which is extremely complicated," and he did not believe that this language would strengthen our hand or our flexibility in dealing with the UAR.

"[Kennedy] went on: 'In fact, it would have an opposite effect. I think it's a very dangerous, untidy world, but we're going to have to live with it; and I think one of the ways to live with it is to permit us to function.'

"If the Administration did not function, the voters would throw it out. Kennedy asked Congress not to make it impossible to function by means of 'legislative restraints and inadequate appropriations.'

"These words," Kenan notes, "were uttered at his last White House press conference."[126]

On many fronts, indeed, JFK's Middle East policy was angering the Israelis, including—perhaps especially—JFK's determination to solve the problem of the Palestinian refugees.

## JFK'S 'GOOD FAITH' IN DOUBT

On November 20, 1963, Kennedy's delegation at the United Nations called for continuing movement toward the implementation of the 1948 UN resolution which called for the right of displaced Palestinian Arabs to return to their homes (in Israel) and for those who chose not to return to their homes to be compensated.

The *London Jewish Chronicle* reported the reaction of the Israelis: "Prime Minister Levi Eshkol summoned the U.S. ambassador . . . and told him that Israel was 'shocked' by the pro-Arab attitude adopted by the U.S. delegation." Golda Meir, the *Chronicle* reported, "expressed Israel's 'astonishment and anger' at the attitude of the U.S." [127]

For its own part, the *Chronicle* noted editorially, "Israel, which has neither been consulted nor informed about the American intention, is not surprisingly questioning the good faith of the United States."[128]

It is not likely that JFK ever got to read the defamatory comments about his Middle East policy published by the *London Jewish Chronicle*. They were printed on November 22, 1963.

So it was that even as John F. Kennedy was preparing to leave Washington for his final journey as president, he was plagued with the problem of Israel and its powerful influence in Washington.

As it turned out, it was during Kennedy's trip to Dallas that one last memorandum was prepared on his behalf relating to the touchy issue of global nuclear arms development.

Although JFK had forcefully opposed French production of nuclear weapons—much as he opposed that of Israel—the American president had, however, begun taking a new look at his stance vis-a-vis the French.

Thus it was that while John F. Kennedy was triumphantly touring downtown Dallas, there was being prepared a "Top Secret, Eyes Only" memorandum from JFK's advisor, McGeorge Bundy, outlining the new, perhaps more lenient, Kennedy policy toward France, which, as we have seen, had itself played a major role in Israel's nuclear development and, unwittingly (much to the disgust of French President DeGaulle) in the drive for atomic weaponry. The memorandum regarding the new policy toward France was also dated November 22, 1963.[129]

By this time, however, John F. Kennedy's fate was sealed. He had pushed Israel and its leaders to the brink.

## BEN-GURION: 'SIGNS OF PARANOIA'

The straw that broke the camel's back, had actually taken place some six months earlier. By spring of 1963, Kennedy and Ben-Gurion were at loggerheads, more seriously than ever before. What's more, Ben-Gurion was suffering a deep personal crisis (part of which, we now see, stemmed from his unhappy relationship with John F. Kennedy).

According to the Israeli prime minister's biographer, Dan Kurzman: "Lonely and depressed, Ben-Gurion felt strangely helpless. Leadership of Israel was slipping from his withered hands . . . Ben-Gurion began to show signs of paranoia. Enemies were closing in on him from all sides. A mere declaration by Egypt, Syria and Iraq in April 1963 that they would unite and demolish the "Zionist threat" threw him into near-panic."[130]

## SECRET CORRESPONDENCE 'INCREASINGLY SOUR'

All of this, of course, contributed immensely to the problems between Kennedy and Ben-Gurion. Seymour Hersh writes: "Kennedy's relationship with Ben-Gurion remained at an impasse over Dimona, and the correspondence between the two became increasingly sour. None of those letters has been made public."[131]

## KENNEDY A 'BULLY'

(Like much of the secret government files on the JFK assassination, the Kennedy exchanges with Ben-Gurion also have not been been released— not even to U.S. government officials with full security clearances who have attempted to write classified histories of the period.)[132]

"It was not a friendly exchange," according to Ben-Gurion's writer, Yuval Neeman. "Kennedy was writing like a bully. It was brutal."[133] Ben-Gurion's response was not passive either.

All of this exacerbated tensions—fierce tensions—between the American President and the Israeli leader. Kennedy's impatience was building. Relations between the United States and Israel were unlike they had ever been before. According to Hersh, "The president made sure that the Israeli prime minister paid for his defiance."[134] When Ben-Gurion once again sought the opportunity for a formal, ballyhooed state visit to Washington, Kennedy rebuffed him.

## ISRAEL'S 'EXISTENCE IS IN DANGER'

It was then that Ben-Gurion made his position all too clear. He was convinced that what he perceived to be Kennedy's intransigence was an all-out threat to the continued survival of the Jewish State. JFK was perceived as an enemy of the Jewish people.

In one of his final communications with Kennedy, Ben-Gurion wrote: "Mr. President, my people have the right to exist . . . **and this existence is in danger.**"[135] (emphasis added) It was at this time that Ben-Gurion demanded that Kennedy sign a security treaty with Israel. Kennedy refused.

On June 16, 1963 Ben-Gurion abruptly resigned as prime minister and defense minister. Thus, the "prophet of fire" ended his fifteen year career as grand old man of Israel. At the time, the Israeli press—and indeed the world press—told the world that Ben-Gurion's sudden resignation was a result of his dissatisfaction with domestic political scandals and turmoil that were rocking Israel.[136]

## A BITTER IMPASSE

However, the primary reason behind Ben-Gurion's departure was the Israeli leader's inability to pressure JFK into accepting Israel's demands. According to Hersh: "There was no way for the Israeli public . . . to suspect that there was yet another factor in Ben-Gurion's demise: his increasingly bitter impasse with Kennedy over a nuclear-armed Israel." [137]Ben-Gurion had failed. The battle had been lost, but the war between the two men was still to be won.

## A MODERN-DAY HAMAN?

What was on Ben-Gurion's mind as he turned over the reins of government to his successor? What was David Ben-Gurion's final act as Prime Minister of the Jewish State? In light of Ben-Gurion's explicit comment to John F. Kennedy that "my people have the right to exist . . . and this existence is in danger," we can certainly make a good presumption.

In Ben-Gurion's eyes, John F. Kennedy was clearly a modern-day Haman—an enemy of the Jewish people. In Jewish folklore, Haman was a descendant of the Amalekites who served as prime minister to King Ahasueros of Persia. It was Haman who sought to convince the king that all of the Jews of his empire should be exterminated forever.

However, according to legend, a beautiful Jewish temptress named Esther used her feminine wiles on Ahasueros and, in the end, it was Haman who was instead put to death. The important Jewish holiday of Purim celebrates the deliverance of the Jews from Haman's intended holocaust.

In the Bible—Deut 25:19, I Sam. 15:8—the ancient Hebrews were urged to "blot out the memory of the Amalekites" from whom Haman descended.

In Israel—in 1963—David Ben-Gurion certainly looked upon John F. Kennedy as a modern-day Haman, a son of the Amalekites. As he pondered the brutal conflict with JFK, Ben-Gurion no doubt remembered the meditation that is read on Purim:

"A wicked man, an arrogant offshoot of the seed of Amalek, rose up against us. Insolent in his riches, he digged himself a pit, and his own greatness laid him a snare. In his mind he thought to entrap, but was himself entrapped; he sought to destroy, but was himself speedily destroyed . . . he made him a gallows, and was himself hanged thereon."

## A FINAL ORDER?

The Israeli leader could not help but ponder further how he might deliver his people from what he perceived to be certain destruction. Ben-Gurion had devoted a lifetime creating a Jewish State and guiding it into the world arena.

And, in Ben-Gurion's eyes, John F. Kennedy was an enemy of the Jewish people and of his beloved state of Israel.

It is the thesis of this volume that Ben-Gurion, in his final days as Prime Minister, ordered Israel's Mossad to orchestrate the assassination of John F. Kennedy. Based upon additional evidence uncovered, we believe that the Mossad took the necessary steps and achieved that goal.

On November 22, 1963, the American president whom Ben-Gurion considered a threat to Israel's very survival came to an unglorious end in Dealey Plaza in Dallas.

That Israel and its leaders believed that drastic measures might be needed to influence the course of history and to ensure the survival of Israel cannot be doubted.

Isser Harrel, who was head of the Mossad until mid-1963, has been quoted as saying that "The government of Israel must act to root out the evil of racism and the monster of anti-Semitism . . ." and that if it could not be done diplomatically, it was to be done in other ways, including, according to Harel, "the secret services, as was the case in my times."[138] In short, by means of murder, if necessary.

Former Undersecretary of State George Ball summarizes the impact of John F. Kennedy's assassination on U.S.-Israeli relations quite succinctly, if somewhat cryptically: "However Kennedy would have succeeded in his relations with Israel must remain one of the many intriguing questions for which his assassination precludes any answer."[139]

## A MOSSAD HIT SQUAD

We know precisely who would have coordinated Mossad participation in the assassination on John F. Kennedy, working in concert with Israeli's allies in the CIA and in Organized Crime (about more of which we shall discuss in these pages.)

Israel's respected *Haaretz* newspaper reported on July 3, 1992 that it was former Jewish underground terrorist-turned-Mossad operative Yitzhak Shamir (later Israeli Prime Minister) who headed a special Mossad hit squad during his service in the Mossad.

The Israeli newspaper reported that Shamir headed the assassination unit from 1955 until 1964—the year after JFK's assassination. "The unit carried out attacks on perceived enemies and suspected Nazi War criminals,"[140] according to an account of the newspaper's report.

"In February 1963 Mr. Shamir dispatched squads on two unsuccessful attempts to assassinate Hans Kleinwachter, a German scientist suspected of helping Egypt develop missiles. Another German scientist working for the Egyptians, Heinz Krug, disappeared mysteriously in September 1962."[141] Shamir's operatives were suspected of having been responsible.

According to the Israeli newspaper, Shamir had recruited members for his Mossad hit squad from former members of the Stern Gang, the underground terrorist group that Shamir led during Israel's fight for independence. The Stern Gang was responsible for the murder, in 1944, of Lord Moyne, Britain's resident Mideast minister, and for the slaying of U.N. mediator Count Folke Bernadotte in 1948.[142]

We have already seen that Kennedy—like Moyne and Bernadotte—was a "perceived enemy" of Israel and its embittered Prime Minister, David Ben-Gurion. And now we know of the existence of the Mossad hit squad that played a major role in the conspiracy that brought about the death of John F. Kennedy. In Chapter 16 we shall learn precisely how this Mossad-orchestrated conspiracy came about.

## THE ENEMIES COME TOGETHER

With Israel's intimate ties to not only the American CIA but also the Meyer Lansky Organized Crime Syndicate—which we will examine in much further detail—the Israeli prime minister and his Mossad operatives had in place a network of allies with whom they could easily collaborate in orchestrating the assassination of John F. Kennedy.

Each of these powerful forces had good reason to take drastic action to put an end to the threat posed by JFK. That they undoubtedly came together in a joint conspiracy we shall document throughout the pages of this volume.

## THE COMING OF THE MESSIAH

With John F. Kennedy lying in a grave in Arlington National Cemetery, Israel was safe—for the time being at least. The modern-day heir of Haman's legacy had been destroyed. That Lyndon Johnson—a man with a steadfast history of loyalty to Israel and its American lobby—was in line to assume the American presidency was a fact not gone unnoticed. Israel's messiah had come.

## Chapter Six

### The Coming of the Messiah:
### Lyndon Johnson Rushes to Israel's Rescue;
### U.S. Middle East Policy Is Reversed

**Within weeks of John F. Kennedy's assassination, Israel was perhaps the most immediate primary beneficiary of Kennedy's death— although this was not something that the controlled media told the American people.**

**The most immediate individual beneficiary of JFK's death was, of course, Lyndon Johnson who was a political favorite of Israel and its allies in Meyer Lansky's Organized Crime Syndicate.**

**It was Johnson who promptly reversed Kennedy's Middle East policy and who, for all intents and purposes, according to one historian, established Israel as America's 51st state.**

There can be no question but that the assassination of John F. Kennedy accomplished several very specific things insofar as the U.S.-Israeli relationship was concerned:

1) It removed from the White House a president—John F. Kennedy— who had—to put it lightly—greatly displeased Israel with his firm neutral stance and his refusal to be bullied by Israel's demands;

2) It placed in the Oval Office a president—Lyndon Johnson—who completely reversed long-standing U.S. Middle East policy and placed the United States firmly in Israel's camp—with a vengeance.

3) It allowed Lyndon Johnson to reverse JFK's Vietnam policy and begin escalating U.S. involvement in Southeast Asia. This permitted Israel to advance its own geo-political stance in the Middle East; and

4) It enabled Israel's allies in the CIA and the Meyer Lansky Organized Crime Syndicate to gain a lock on drug-trafficking in Southeast Asia as a proximate result of U.S. involvement in the region.

*Israel was clearly—and beyond doubt—the primary international beneficiary of Lyndon Johnson's presidency which only became possible through the assassination of John F. Kennedy.*

### ISRAEL'S SURVIVAL

If protection of its national security interests and its very survival can be considered a motive—and surely it can be—then Israel, perhaps above all, obviously had a major interest—and motivation—in helping orchestrate the assassination of President Kennedy. Indeed, the very survival of Israel has been a cornerstone of its foreign policy from that nation's earliest beginnings. Thus, elimination of a perceived enemy to Israel's survival— that is, John F. Kennedy—would only be a logical course of action.

This especially, of course, in light of the fact that the man who succeeded Kennedy—Lyndon Johnson—had long and often proven a history of personal affinity for Israel and its international interests.

## JOHNSON'S LANSKY CONNECTION

Johnson, too, had a long and sordid record of involvement in criminal activities—including murder—that have finally begun to surface. The record is far too complex to examine here—besides which, popular literature on the subject is quite complete.

Nonetheless, it is certainly worth noting that one major Johnson backer was Meyer Lansky's Louisiana henchman, Carlos Marcello. According to John W. Davis, Lansky's man Marcello funnelled at least $50,000 a year in payoffs to then-Texas Senator Lyndon Johnson who, in turn, helped kill in committee all rackets-related legislation that might have been harmful to the Lansky Organized Crime Syndicate.[143]

There are indications, however, that Johnson's ties to Lansky and his associates go even deeper. When Lansky himself was living in Israel, one of his American cronies, Benjamin Sigelbaum, came visiting. [144]

It was Mr. Sigelbaum (not to be confused with Benjamin "Bugsy" Siegel whom Lansky had ordered killed in 1947) who was involved with longtime Johnson intimate Bobby Baker in two major dealings: the purchase of a bank in Tulsa, Oklahoma and in Baker's controversial Serv-U Vending Machine Company.[145]

Another of Baker's business collaborators, was Edward Levinson, who operated the Fremont Casino in Las Vegas as a front man for longtime Lansky friend and business partner, Joseph (Doc) Stacher (who ultimately died in exile in Israel). [146]

What's more, author Robert Morrow, a former CIA contract agent, has revealed that one of Baker's closest associates, with whom he was reportedly "thick as thieves," was a mob courier named Mickey Weiner who was "a complete user of [Baker's] office, of all the [Baker] facilities on [Capitol] Hill." [147] Needless to say, Baker's office and Baker's "facilities" were one and the same with those of Lyndon B. Johnson.

It was this same Mickey Weiner who, as we shall see in Chapter 7, was one of Meyer Lansky's chief couriers between his Miami banking operations and his European money-laundering center at the Banque de Credit International (BCI) in Geneva, Switzerland.

(BCI, as we shall see in detail in Chapter 7, Chapter 12 and Chapter 15, was operated by an Israeli banker, Tibor Rosenbaum, former Director for Finances and Supply for Israel's Mossad.)

Mr. Baker, who served time in federal prison for his criminal activities during his time as Johnson's protege (and as his reputed bagman), would have been the one person who could have sent Lyndon Johnson to prison if he had revealed all.

Indeed, it was Johnson's involvement with Bobby Baker that had led John F. Kennedy to begin laying the groundwork for dropping Johnson from the Democratic ticket in 1964. But even with Kennedy's death, the stench of corruption surrounding the Lansky-linked Baker still threatened Johnson.

## JOHNSON FACES PRISON?

Washington lobbyist Robert N. Winter-Berger recalls a visit by then-President Johnson to the office of House Speaker John McCormack while Winter-Berger was there. Johnson burst in unexpectedly. Unconscious of Winter-Berger's presence, Johnson began shrieking and shouting and condemning his longtime friend and protege, Bobby Baker. "John, that son of a bitch is going to ruin me. If that cocksucker talks, I'm gonna land in jail," Johnson roared. "I practically raised that motherfucker and now he's gonna make me the first President of the United States to spend the last days of his life behind bars." [148]

According to Winter-Berger Johnson suddenly realized that he was present. Speaker McCormack assured the president that Winter-Berger was "all right" and that Winter-Berger was close to one of Baker's other associates, Nat Voloshen.

Johnson asked Winter-Berger to have this message relayed to Baker. "Tell Nat to tell Bobby that I will give him a million dollars if he takes this rap. Bobby must not talk." [149] Baker did not talk. Baker went to jail. Johnson did not.

Obviously, Johnson's Lansky connection is far more complex than we might even be able to determine—but the interplay between Johnson and his intimates and those of the Lansky syndicate is indisputable, to say the least.

## SUDDEN POLICY CHANGES

Needless to say, when Lyndon Johnson became president, the Kennedy war against organized crime came to a sudden halt. There were other important policy reversals as well, including, of course, the change in Vietnam policy (about which we will explore further in this chapter and in Chapter 9.)

What, of course, however, is most significant about Lyndon Johnson's assumption of the Oval Office were the profound—and immediate— changes in U.S. policy toward Israel and the Arab world that came rapidly upon LBJ's sudden succession to the presidency.

## 'GOOD NEWS' FROM DALLAS

The earliest evidence we can find that Israel and its lobby in America were delighted by Lyndon's elevation to the presidency comes in a memo that I. L. Kenan, director of the American-Israel Public Affairs Committee (AIPAC) sent out to top-ranking figures in AIPAC and others in the Israel lobby.

Hailing Johnson's "front-rank pro-Israel position"[150] during his Senate career, the memo was dated November 26, 1963, just one day after John F. Kennedy was buried in Arlington National Cemetery. The memo, incidentally, was formally noted "Not for Publication or Circulation."[151]

Clearly, those in the Israeli camp didn't want their seeming delight in Kennedy's passing—and Johnson's sudden good luck—to be in the public record.

What is additionally interesting are Kenan's memoirs of his service as one of the Israeli lobby's top men in Washington. The memoirs contain, as we have seen, a chapter about John F. Kennedy cryptically—perhaps critically—entitled—"A Multitude of Promises" along with the intriguing—and accurate—reference to 1963 as "The Turbulent Year," (for U.S.-Israeli relations).[152]

The very next chapter—about Lyndon Johnson—is warmly entitled "Israel's Texas Friend." Johnson—who was, in Kenan's words, the "New Man in the White House"—proved to be a very loyal friend of Israel.

Seymour Hersh points out that one of Johnson's first symbolic acts as president was to dedicate a synagogue in Austin, Texas—less than six weeks after assuming the presidency. In fact, Hersh notes, Johnson was the first American president in history to dedicate a synagogue. It was, we shall see, a very symbolic act indeed.[153]

Lady Bird Johnson, the new president's wife, later tried to explain why her husband was so fond of Israel and its friends in the American pro-Israel lobby. "Jews have been woven into the warp and woof of all his [Johnson's] years," she said.[154]

### ISRAEL'S INTERESTS FIRST

In Israel, Johnson's presidency was greeted with pleasure. The Israeli newspaper *Yedio Ahoronot* said that in a Johnson presidency the issue of "U.S. interests" would not be as much of a problem in U.S.-Israeli relations as they had been under Kennedy.[155] In other words, Johnson—unlike Kennedy—would be willing to set aside American interests in favor of Israel's. The Israeli journal added, "There is no doubt that, with the accession of Lyndon Johnson, we shall have more opportunity to approach the President directly if we should feel that U.S. policy militates against our vital interests."[156]

### MOURNING IN ISLAM

In the Arab world, however, the response was far different. According to former diplomat Richard Curtiss, who spent much time in the region, "The mourning stretched across the Arab world, where to this day faded photographs on humble walls depict the young hero."[157]

In Algeria, the new Arab republic that had achieved independence with help from John F. Kennedy, Premier Ahmad Ben Bella telephoned the U.S.

ambassador to say, "Believe me, I'd rather it had happened to me than to him."[158] Kennedy's friendly gestures for peace were being remembered.

In Egypt President Nasser realized that the death of John F. Kennedy would have a profound impact upon the Arab world. With Kennedy's departure, Nasser later said that "[French President Charles] DeGaulle is the only Western Head of State on whose friendship the Arabs can depend."[159]

However, according to DeGaulle's biographer, Jean Lacouture, DeGaulle was "a friend neither of the Arabs, nor of Israel, but only of France."[160] One might say that similar words could likewise be applied to John F. Kennedy: "a friend neither of the Arabs, nor of Israel, but only of America." And Israel certainly did not consider JFK a friend.

## MOURNING IN PARIS

In Paris, DeGaulle—who had granted Algerian independence and who had suffered numerous attempts on his own life in retaliation—was thoroughly stunned by the murder of the American president. He interrupted a Cabinet meeting to announce: "John Fitzgerald Kennedy has been assassinated. He was one of the very few leaders of whom it may be said that they are statesmen. He had courage and he loved his country."[161] According to DeGaulle's biographer, "It was a tribute without precedent and one that was never repeated."[162]

In fact, as we shall see, the very same elements that had conspired against the life of DeGaulle were indeed those same elements who had brought about the assassination of John F. Kennedy. And if DeGaulle did not know it then, he ultimately would.

## SUSPICIONS

There was additional fall-out in the Arab world as a consequence of Kennedy's assassination. According to Curtiss, the fact that Kennedy's alleged assassin, Lee Harvey Oswald was promptly murdered by Jack Ruby—in Curtiss's words—"an American Jew with gangster connections,"[163] suspicions about Israel's complicity in the crime were widespread.

According to Curtiss: "The circumstances gave rise to many conspiracy theories, including one believed by virtually all Arabs that the assassination was to prevent an impending U.S. policy change in the Middle East."[164]

Curtiss's next comment, however, has proven wrong in the light of what we are about to explore in the pages of *Final Judgment*: "No Middle East connection of any sort has ever been discovered, however."[165]

Curtiss notes that, "Instead, ironically, the assassination five years later by an Arab-American in California of President Kennedy's younger brother, an outspoken supporter of Israel, made Robert Kennedy the first American victim of the Palestinian-Israeli dispute to be killed on U.S. soil."[166] (However, as we shall see in Chapter 18, there is—as in the assassination of

John F. Kennedy—a lot more about the murder of his younger brother than really meets the eye.)

Nonetheless, as Alfred Lilienthal, the veteran critic of U.S. Middle East policy, has written, "There is little question that Kennedy intended to move decisively in his second term. The assassination of President Kennedy in Dallas on November 22, 1963, shattered the possibility that his second term might see Washington start to free itself from the grave burdens of U.S. partisanship on the Arab-Israeli conflict and of continuous politicking for domestic votes."[167]

## MOVING FAST

Arab hopes for peace had been shattered and a new American president in Washington was—in the meantime—busy ingratiating himself with Israel's representatives in the American capital.

"You have lost a very great friend, but you have found a better one," the new president told one Israeli official. [168] Although Johnson's quote has been oft-repeated, it is not quite certain just who that official was. The quote, indeed, may even be apocryphal—another legend in the Lyndon Johnson legacy.

However, most sources believe that Johnson's comment was probably made to Ephraim Evron, the number two man in Israel's embassy in Washington. It was Evron who ultimately became a very close friend of Lyndon Johnson.

At the time of the Kennedy assassination—interestingly enough— Evron was in Washington in charge of Israeli intelligence operations, working closely with James Jesus Angleton, Israel's man at the CIA. Thus, it seems likely, that whatever Angleton knew about JFK's assassination, Evron likely knew—and vice versa. And perhaps, we might speculate, Johnson also thus knew as well. (In Chapter 8 and in Chapter 16 we will consider Angleton's peculiar part in the JFK assassination conspiracy in full detail.)

According to Johnson aide Harry McPherson, "I think [Evron] felt what I've always felt, that some place in Lyndon Johnson's blood there are a great many Jewish corpuscles." [169]

The aforementioned McPherson, speaking on tape for the LBJ Library Oral History Project, interestingly described himself as the Johnson White House's "staff anti-Semite," [170] McPherson explained that this meant that he had to maintain "a continuing relationship with B'nai B'rith, the Anti-Defamation League, to some extent the Zionist organization, and others who want various things,"[171] presumably a difficult task. As a consequence, McPherson was especially tuned in to Johnson's relationship with Israel and its lobby in Washington.

In fact, as the record shows, Johnson had a long and close relationship with Israel and its partisans. Israel knew that it had a loyal devotee of its interests in the White House now that John F. Kennedy was out of the way.

## A LONG-TIME FAVORITE OF ISRAEL

Israel, of course, had been keeping a close watch on Lyndon Johnson for a long time. About Johnson, Israeli intelligence man Evron said as follows: "Johnson's feeling about Israel came out very early in the [Suez] crisis in 1957 when he was [Senate] majority leader. When at that time President Eisenhower and Secretary of State Dulles wanted to force us to withdraw from Sinai, they threatened us with economic sanctions. Johnson persuaded Senator William Knowland of California, who was then minority leader, to come with him to the White House and tell the President that it just wouldn't do."[172]

The Arab States were also watching Johnson closely, particularly after he assumed the presidency. Particularly concerned was Egyptian President Gamal Abdel Nasser with whom JFK had hoped to build bridges. In fact, as we have seen, it was during his last White House press conference that JFK bemoaned the efforts by Israel and its partisans to sabotage his Middle East peace initiatives, especially in regard to relations with Nasser.

## THE CHANGE IN POLICY BEGINS

According to author Stephen Green, as early as March 5, 1964 Nasser told Assistant U.S. Secretary of State Phillips Talbot that "The U.S. had shifted its policy into more active support of Israel." [173]

This was just little more than three months after John F. Kennedy had been assassinated and Lyndon B. Johnson was catapulted into the presidency.

Nasser's assessment was on target. According to intelligence historian Richard Deacon, Johnson's new policy was keeping in line not only with Israel's demands, but those of Israel's friends at the CIA:

"President Johnson had already swung away from the tentative pro-Arab stance of the Kennedy administration which had always been frowned upon by the CIA."[174]

Deacon reports that Walt Rostow, the president's national security advisor believed that US policy towards Israel would serve as an effective check on Soviet support for Arab countries. "Thus," according to Deacon, "Rostow reflected almost totally the views of the CIA hierarchy."[175]

Johnson, himself, also had long-standing ties to Israel's friends in the CIA from his years of service in the Senate.

As Senate Majority Leader, Johnson worked closely with the CIA on a regular basis and was considered a "CIA friend" in Congress.

Unquestionably, however, Lyndon Johnson did indeed begin a major shift in U.S. Middle East policy—keeping in line with his joint devotion to not only the CIA's interests, but those of Israel's as well.

This, of course, had a momentus impact on the course of American foreign policy and was an immediate and absolute turn-about of the policy that had been pursued by the late President Kennedy.

## THE NUCLEAR BOMB

Interestingly enough, Israel's initial benefit from the death of JFK was, in fact, the removal from the White House of a president who vehemently opposed Israel's nuclear weapons development.

According to Stephen Green:   "Perhaps the most significant development of 1963 for the Israeli nuclear weapons program, however, occurred on November 22 on a plane flying from Dallas to Washington, D.C., Lyndon Baines Johnson was sworn in as the 36th President of the United States, following the assassination of John F. Kennedy.

"In the early years of the Johnson administration the Israeli nuclear weapons program was referred to in Washington as 'the delicate topic.' Lyndon Johnson's White House saw no Dimona, heard no Dimona, and spoke no Dimona when the reactor went critical in early 1964."[176]

Thus it was that the critical point of dispute between John F. Kennedy and the Mossad-dominated government of Israel was no longer an issue. The new American president—so long a partisan of Israel—allowed the nuclear development to continue. This was just the beginning.

## HUBERT HUMPHREY & THE LANSKY SYNDICATE

Johnson was also cementing his long-standing ties to Meyer Lansky's Organized Crime Syndicate. In 1964—seeking his first full term in the White House—Johnson selected Minnesota Senator Hubert H. Humphrey as his vice-presidential running mate.

As the *Washington Observer* newsletter noted: "Humphrey was first catapulted into public office as Mayor of Minneapolis in 1945 via the machinations and campaign slush funds raised by the notorious Kid Cann, king of the Minneapolis underworld.

"Cann, whose real name was Isadore Blumenfeld, along with his brothers (who were known by their aliases, Harry and Yiddy Bloom) were partners with Meyer Lansky in the ownership of many of the plush resorts in Miami, along with Humphrey's chief advisor, Max Kampelman, a top figure in the Israeli lobby in Washington."

"Blumenfeld and Lansky were partners in the syndicate that owned the Sands and Fremont Hotels—gambling operations in Las Vegas—until they sold their interest in the Sands to Howard Hughes.  When Humphrey and his top aides are in Miami," the *Observer* reported, "they enjoy[ed] free accommodations at the syndicate's plush hotels."[177]

(Alan H. Ryskind, writing  in his critical biography of Humphrey, demonstrated how then-Minneapolis Mayor Humphrey managed to look the other way when Blumenfeld got himself into a widely-publicized set of difficulties[178]—just one of HHH's favors for the Meyer Lansky Organized Crime Syndicate.)

Thus, in the 1964 presidential election—which was Johnson's to lose—Lansky and his partners in Israel were assured a dream ticket come November. Both Johnson and his vice president were bought and paid for.

Lansky and Israel made sure there wouldn't be any problems with any independent upstart second-generation multi-millionaire Irishmen like John F. Kennedy who was not only the son of a notorious anti-Semite but a bull-headed proponent of America's interests to boot.

Thus, having become ensconced in the presidency, Lyndon Johnson was in a position to do many favors for Israel.

## THE FOREIGN AID PORK BARREL

Perhaps his most drastic efforts in service to Israel involved massive increases in U.S. taxpayer-financed foreign aid giveaways. Although John F. Kennedy himself had been generous to Israel in that regard, Johnson made Kennedy look like a piker.

Former Undersecretary of State George Ball comments that in the foreign aid realm: "The Israelis were proved right in their assumption that Johnson would be more friendly than Kennedy."[179]

According to author Stephen Green, citing U.S. Agency for International Development data: "Over the next few years—the first three years of the Johnson administration—[the level of foreign aid] support [to Israel] would change both qualitatively and quantitatively. U.S. government assistance to Israel in FY 1964, the last budget year of the Kennedy administration, stood at $40 million. This was substantially reduced from the levels of assistance in previous years. In FY 1965, this figure rose to $71 million, and in FY 1966, to $130 million."[180]

## ARMING ISRAEL'S WAR MACHINE

Green notes further that under Lyndon Johnson, United States military aid to Israel also saw a drastic increase:

"More significant, however, was the change in the composition of that assistance. In [JFK's] FY 1964, virtually none of the official U.S. assistance for Israel was military assistance; it was split almost equally between development loans and food assistance under the PL 480 program. In [LBJ's} FY 1965, however, 20 percent of U.S. aid was military in nature, and in FY 1966, fully 71 percent of all official assistance to Israel came in the form of credits for purchase of military equipment.

"Moreover, the nature of the weapons systems we provided had changed. In FY 1963, the Kennedy administration agreed to sell five batteries of Hawk missiles valued at $21.5 million. This however was an air defense system. The Johnson administration, in FY 1965-1966, provided Israel with 250 modern (modified M-48) tanks, 48 A-1 Skyhawk attack aircraft, communications and electronics equipment, artillery, and recoilless rifles. Given the configuration of the [Israel Defense Forces], these were anything but defensive weapons.

"The $92 million in military assistance provided in FY 1966 was greater than the total of all official military aid provided to Israel cumulatively, in all the years going back to the foundation of that nation in

1948."[181] Green summarizes the massive extent of Johnson's giveaways: "Seventy percent of all U.S. official assistance to Israel has been military. America has given Israel over $17 billion in military aid since 1946, virtually all of which—over 99 percent—has been provided since 1965."[182]

## ISRAEL'S INTERESTS FIRST

It was clearly Lyndon B. Johnson who set the precedent for unlimited aid to Israel. All told, however, the death of John F. Kennedy and Lyndon Johnson's assumption of the Oval Office marked a major change in overall U.S. policy. As Stephen Green writes, in all too clarifying detail in *Taking Sides: America's Secret Relations With A Militant Israel*:

"In the years 1948-1963, America was perceived by all of the governments in the Middle East as a major power that acted upon the basis of its own, clearly defined national self-interest. Moreover, U.S. Middle East policy was just that—Middle East policy; it was not an Israeli policy in which Arab countries were subordinate actors.

"In the years 1948-1963, Presidents Truman, Eisenhower, and Kennedy firmly guaranteed Israeli national security and territorial integrity, but just as firmly guaranteed those of Jordan, Lebanon, and the other nations of the region. That was what the Tripartite Declaration of 1950 was all about.

"For successive Israel governments in this period, the boundary line between U.S. and Israeli national security interests was drawn frequently, and usually decisively. Truman's policies on arms exports to the middle East, Eisenhower's stands on regional water development and on territorial integrity during the Suez Crisis, and Kennedy's candor with Mrs. Meir—all of these were markers on this boundary line.

"Nevertheless, during this time U.S. financial support for Israel far exceeded that given any other nation in the world, on a per capita basis. And U.S. diplomatic support for Israel in the UN and elsewhere was no less generous.

"But the limits to U.S. support for Israel were generally understood by all of the countries of the region, and it was precisely these limits that preserved America's ability to mediate the various issues that composed the Arab-Israeli dispute.

"Then, in the early years of the Johnson administration, 1964-1967, U.S. policy on Middle Eastern matters abruptly changed. It would perhaps be more accurate to say that it disintegrated. America had a public policy on the nonproliferation of nuclear weapons, but suddenly had a covert policy of abetting Israel's nuclear weapons program. We had a public policy on arms balance in the region, but secretly agreed, by the end of 1967, to become Israel's major arms supplier.

"Officially, the United States was "firmly committed to the support of the political independence and territorial integrity of all the [Middle Eastern] nations," while consciously, covertly, the Johnson "Middle East team" set about enabling Israel to redraw to her advantage virtually every one of her borders with neighboring Arab states.

"It was, of course, a policy without principle, without integrity. But it was also ineffective, in the sense that Israel steadily continued to act in ways that ignored U.S. national security interests."[183]

## VIETNAM—ISRAEL BENEFITS

These incredible facts about the sudden reversal of traditional U.S. policy have gone too long ignored in the context of considering the question of who stood most to benefit by the assassination of John F. Kennedy. Israel clearly stood most to benefit—and did.

All of this is most ironic when one considers the fact that Israel repeatedly and pointedly refused to support Johnson's Vietnam policy, much to the dismay of "Israel's Texas Friend." "Dammit," Johnson once complained to his "staff anti-Semite" Harry McPherson, "they want me to protect Israel, but they don't want me to do anything in Vietnam." [184]

Clearly, Israel's allies in the CIA now had a free hand to conduct their own private war in Vietnam—one CIA benefit resulting from Kennedy's removal from the presidency. (In Chapter 9 we will examine Kennedy's war with the CIA in further detail.)

Johnson's reversal of JFK's decision to begin withdrawing U.S. forces (and CIA personnel) from Southeast Asia was, in its own sense, a CIA coup. The CIA also expanded its own power during the Vietnam conflict.

Likewise with Johnson's many friends in the defense industry both at home in Texas and elsewhere. The defense contractors reaped untold billions in profits from Johnson's dirty little war in Southeast Asia—a war that probably spelled the end of Johnson's popular chances for a second term.

## VIETNAM—ISRAEL'S DIRTY LITTLE SECRET

However, what has been unfortunately ignored is that Israel, too, had much to gain from U.S. involvement in Vietnam.

As Stephen Green points out, a direct and proximate result of U.S. military adventurism in Southeast Asia was Israel's ability to advance its own military muscle and political influence in the Middle East.

After all, Israel could now argue, with the United States bogged down in Southeast Asia, Uncle Sam needed its close, reliable, democratic ally in the Middle East looking out for America's interests in the region.

According to Green: "In a period in which the Johnson White House was becoming increasingly obsessed with the war in Vietnam, Israel's military leaders offered to impose stability upon the peoples and countries of the Middle East—it was to be a 'Pax Hebraeca.'

"There were, of course, costs involved for America. The United States would have to take the initial steps toward becoming what three previous Presidents had said we never would be—Israel's major arms supplier. We would also at least temporarily forfeit our role as primary mediator of the multifaceted Arab-Israeli dispute.

"The new arrangement would necessitate throwing our long-standing nuclear nonproliferation treaty to the winds, the 1968 treaty to the contrary notwithstanding.

"Perhaps most important, U.S. national security interests in the region would become merged with Israel's to a degree that was, and is to this day, unique in the history of U.S. foreign relations."[185]

Israel—above all—stood to benefit immensely from U.S. involvement in Vietnam, something which would not have occurred had JFK lived.

There is yet an additional irony in the relationship of the United States and Israel vis-a-vis the Vietnam conflict that is very much worth noting,

After the war in Vietnam was underway, dragging Lyndon Johnson deeper and deeper into the muck of public discontent, Israel was beginning to encounter its own difficulties as it flexed its muscle in the Middle East.

Although America's entry in Southeast Asia had given Israel a free hand in its own sphere of geographic influence, the tiny Jewish state found that it now needed the United States—perhaps more so than ever. Israel's aggression against its Arab neighbors had rallied the Arab world against Israel.

With the United States in too deep in Southeast Asia, Israel and its American lobby perceived U.S. energy to be focused in the wrong direction. Thus it was that many of the very voices urging U.S. withdrawal from the arena of Vietnam were those who were most stridently demanding that the U.S. re-insert itself into the Middle East cauldron.

## WHERE SHOULD AMERICA FIGHT?

It was on the eve of the 1967 War—a war that could have been the end for Israel—that the *Washington Star* (in its June 4 lead editorial) pointed out the strange paradox.

"Many of those, both at home and abroad, who most loudly condemn the American presence in Vietnam, were the first to urge total American involvement in the Middle East.

"And having made the leap from isolation to intervention, they have gone on to argue that our commitment in the Middle East is additional justification for disengagement in Asia. The nation, so this line of reasoning goes, cannot afford involvement in both areas.

"A choice must be made. And the Middle East is logical place for the United States to intervene," [186]according to the *Star*'s assessment of the attitude of the pro-Israel advocates of withdrawal from Vietnam who were urging U.S. intervention in the Middle East.

So it was that Israel, which initially reaped benefits from U.S. involvement in Southeast Asia, ultimately began banging the drum for U.S. withdrawal—but it was only well after the damage of the Vietnam War had already been done. Israel was placing its own interests—not America's interests—first.

## LANSKY, THE CIA & VIETNAM

It should be noted, too, that Israel's friends in the Meyer Lansky Organized Crime Syndicate also stood to benefit from the Vietnam conflict. In Chapter 12 we shall examine in detail the little-known collaboration between the Lansky syndicate, its Mossad-linked banking money launderers, and the CIA in the drug pipeline out of Southeast Asia.

The Lansky crime empire began operating major global drug trafficking, largely under CIA cover, throughout Southeast Asia during the Vietnam War, during which time the drug problem began escalating to a major degree in the United States and elsewhere.

Now, many years later, the CIA's role in the global drug market is only now just coming to the surface. The Iran-contra scandal, for example, shed some light on this little known aspect of the underbelly of world affairs. Thus, the joint Israel-Lansky-CIA combine shared a major benefit from American involvement in Vietnam. They had Lyndon Johnson to thank.

## A PASSIONATE ATTACHMENT

Israel and its covert allies did indeed have a messiah in Lyndon Baines Johnson. In his book, *The Passionate Attachment*, former Undersecretary of State George Ball summarized the results of Johnson's Middle East policies: "First, the administration put America in the position of being Israel's principal arms supplier and sole unqualified backer.

"Second, by assuring the Israelis that the United States would always provide them with a military edge over the Arabs, Johnson guaranteed the escalation of an arms race . . . Third, by refusing to follow the advice of his aides that America make its delivery of nuclear-capable F-4 Phantoms conditional on Israel's signing the Nuclear Non-Proliferation Treaty, Johnson gave the Israelis the impression that America had no fundamental objection to Israel's nuclear program.

"Fourth, by permitting a cover-up of Israel's attack on the *Liberty* [see Chapter 2], President Johnson told the Israelis in effect that nothing they did would induce American politicians to refuse their bidding. From that time forth, the Israelis began to act as if they had an inalienable right to American aid and backing."[187]

As Stephen Green concluded in his discussion of the incredible changes in U.S. policy toward Israel that took place during the Johnson era:

"By June of 1967, for a variety of reasons that prominently included 'domestic political considerations,' Lyndon Johnson and his team of foreign-policy advisors had completely revised U.S.-Israeli relations. To all intents and purposes, Israel had become the 51st state."[188]

## Chapter Seven

## Israel's Godfather:
## The Man in the Middle
## Meyer Lansky, the CIA, the FBI & the Israeli Mossad

**If it had not been for international crime boss Meyer Lansky there might not be a state of Israel today. This is something that Israel would rather be forgotten.**

**Israel was established as a state, in major part, through the political, financial and moral support of Meyer Lansky and his associates and henchmen in Organized Crime. Lansky's interests and Israel's interests were almost incestuous. In fact, Lansky's chief European money laundering bank was an operation run under the auspices of a high-ranking, longtime officer of Israel's Mossad.**

**Lansky's intimate ties with not only American intelligence (including both the CIA and the FBI) made the Russian-born mobster the "untouchable" leader of the global organized crime syndicate.**

During John F. Kennedy's short-lived presidency, he was not only at odds with Israel and its powerful lobby in America. Kennedy, as we saw in Chapter 4, had also double-crossed his secret allies in the criminal underworld who had helped him achieve the presidency. The president's brother, Attorney General Robert F. Kennedy, was waging a relentless war against organized crime.

In the years prior to Kennedy's ascendency to the presidency, a little-known, but immensely powerful underworld figure by the name of Meyer Lansky had schemed and shot his way to the top of the crime syndicate.

That syndicate was not just national—it was international—and the uncrowned king of crime was Meyer Lansky—the so-called "chairman of the board" of that incredible criminal empire which spanned the globe.

It was Meyer Lansky, early in his criminal career, who had emerged as one of the leading sponsors of the state of Israel and whose most intimate associates were among the chief financial patrons of the influential Israeli lobby in America.

What's more, as we shall see, Lansky had also forged close ties with Israel's allies in the American CIA—an agency that, in itself, had entered into a bitter war with John F. Kennedy.

Thus, when JFK came to blows with not only Israel and its allies in the Lansky Organized Crime empire, but also with the CIA, the American president had unwittingly forged a deadly alliance among his fiercest foes.

### THE MAN IN THE MIDDLE

It is the Meyer Lansky connection which explains how Israel's Mossad was able to utilize and manipulate, among other elements, the anti-Castro Cuban community—itself working with not only the CIA but also the

Lansky Organized Crime Syndicate—in the conspiracy to assassinate John F. Kennedy.

To begin our investigation of the shadowy crevices of the underworld where Israel's Mossad, Organized Crime and the CIA came together in the Kennedy murder, it is most appropriate to begin with Lansky.

It is Lansky (individually) and his crime syndicate which tie all of these diverse strands together, pointing the finger toward the until-now undisclosed role of Israel in the JFK assassination.

A spokesman for the Bahamas Commission of Inquiry which was investigating organized crime in the islands, once said, "At one stage, we began to wonder whether the name of Meyer Lansky was not some vast journalistic piece of fiction, so ghostly and mythical a figure did he appear." [189] But exist he did.

Meyer Lansky, in fact, is a pivotal player in the international conspiracy that resulted in the assassination of John F. Kennedy—all of the literature propagating the theory that "The Mafia Killed JFK" notwithstanding.

## WHO WAS MEYER LANSKY?

The most concise summary of the origins and rise to power of Meyer Lansky appeared in a lengthy profile of Lansky that appeared on the front page of *The Wall Street Journal* in 1969. It reads, in pertinent part:

"Born Maier Suchowjansky in Grodno, Russia, Lansky arrived in the U.S. at age nine. His family settled in New York's immigrant slums. By the time he was 27, young Maier had five arrests on his record, on charges ranging from disorderly conduct to suspicion of murder, but he was never convicted. He had begun his painstaking climb up the underworld ladder.

"It was during the 1920's that Lansky became a pal and partner of Bugsy Siegel. The two became a formidable pair, first as hired gunmen for Legs Diamond, soon as leaders of their own gang, called the 'Bugs and Meyer Mob.'

## A MEMBER OF THE BOARD

"Their specialty was protecting liquor in transit from hijackers to East Coast gangs. They were good at it, and when an alliance called the Eastern Syndicate was formed to coordinate rum-running Lansky and Siegel were named to the board. Lansky was put in charge of handling the syndicate's finances.

"By the early 1930's the Eastern syndicate began to form a loose alliance with other regional mobs. Thus was the national syndicate born. Each gang retained its own identity and pursued its own activities, with the federation coming together occasionally to discuss matters of common interest. Final decisions rested with individual gang leaders, with one acting as federation chairman. The first chairman was Lucky Luciano, head of the Mafia in the East.

## TIES TO U.S. INTELLIGENCE

"During World War II, Lansky played a part in an incredible alliance between the underworld and the U.S. Navy . . . Apparently, the Navy decided East Coast piers could be protected from sabotage only with the aid of the Mafia.

"Lucky Luciano was [by then in prison], but he still held power and the loyalty of Mafia members. Luciano's attorney and Meyer Lansky were recruited to persuade Luciano to give the arrangement his blessing. After several months of prison visits, Luciano agreed . . . After the war, Lucky was paroled and sent home to Italy on promise he would never again enter the U.S.

## CHAIRMAN OF THE BOARD

"With Luciano gone, a triumvirate of Lansky, Joe Adonis and Frank Costello took over leadership of the syndicate. By the late 1950's, Costello had been ousted from power by his colleagues and Adonis had been deported. Lansky sat alone at the top."[190]

In the meantime, Lansky had already cemented his ties with the Washington establishment. In fact, those ties were long-standing.

## LANSKY & CUBA

(In Chapter 10, we shall discuss Lansky's critical role in helping win President Franklin Delano Roosevelt the Democratic presidential nomination in 1932.)

Roosevelt himself sent Lansky as a personal emissary to Cuba to meet with Cuban strongman Fulgencio Batista. FDR believed that Batista's authoritarian rule was stirring popular discontent which could be exploited by a growing communist movement in Cuba. Through Lansky FDR hoped to influence Batista to institute reforms that would quell the communist threat. It was during this period that Lansky had begun establishing his lucrative gambling empire in the tropical paradise and a long and profitable personal and business relationship with Batista and other Cuban leaders who made millions in kickbacks from Lansky's casino operations.

(Among those on the receiving end of Lansky's pay-offs was Carlos Prio Soccaras, whom, we shall see in Chapter 14, ultimately became a business partner in gun-running activities with  Dallas nightclub operator and Lansky Syndicate henchman, Jack Ruby.) [191]

(In Chapter 11, we shall examine Lansky's Cuban gambling activities and his Israeli Mossad-linked European money laundering operations. In Chapter 12 we shall examine Lansky's international narcotics trafficking, and his consequent connections with the CIA, in detail.)

Although Batista was in and out of office several times during the next two decades, the Cuban strongman remained the *de facto* leader of the island through successive puppet regimes until the advent of Fidel Castro on New Years Day, 1960.

However, Lansky also had extensive contacts much farther away from American shores. Lansky—as we shall see here—was a key force in establishing the State of Israel.

## ALLIANCE & RIVALRY

To understand Lansky's preeminent leadership position in organized crime, however, we must first look at the strange and complex alliance— and rivalry—between the Italian and Jewish elements in the organized crime world.

*The Wall Street Journal's* account of Lansky's rise to power hints at these contradictions, but doesn't explore them in the fashion needed. Two interesting things left out of the *Journal* summary of Lansky's career should be mentioned.

It is generally known that Lansky launched his criminal career working in conjunction with the famed Mafia figure Charles "Lucky" Luciano. Their alliance is noted in the *Journal* account and a recent Hollywood extravaganza entitled *Mobsters* highlighted the youthful exploits of Lansky, Luciano, Benjamin Siegel and Frank Costello.

## LUCIANO GETS FRAMED

However, it may have been Lansky, through his political contacts, who arranged the criminal indictment and subsequent imprisonment of Luciano. It was Luciano's imprisonment—and ultimate deportation—that smoothed Lansky's further advancement in organized crime.

In his own memoirs Luciano provides a detailed account of how he was, in fact, framed on the white slavery and prostitution charges that resulted in his imprisonment. Luciano does not blame Lansky, by any means, although, as we shall see, he may have had his suspicions.

Luciano doesn't ask the reader to believe that he (Luciano) wasn't engaged in extensive criminal activity. He does present a very cogent case, however, that he was not guilty of the crimes for which he was convicted. Indeed, Luciano was never brought to trial for any of the crimes in which he was engaged with Lansky.

In any case, it is quite possible that Lansky, in fact, did have some role in framing Luciano on the prostitution charges. Tom Dewey's war against Lucky Luciano, the Mafia chieftain's imprisonment, and his subsequent deportation smoothed the way for Lansky's rise to the top.

## BOSS OF ALL BOSSES

It was upon Luciano's deportation, that Luciano actually named Lansky as his official spokesman. According to Luciano, "I worked it all out with Lansky, and that's the point where Meyer became the real treasurer of the outfit. I put him in charge of my money and later on he started to take care of the finances of quite a few guys."[192] .

Lansky was—despite his Jewish origins—the *capo di tuti capi* ("boss of all bosses") in Luciano's absence. Theoretically, Lansky could never be a "member" of the Mafia, but he certainly ranked higher than even "made" members who had been inducted into the so-called "honored society."

## LANSKY, DEWEY & THE CIA

Both Dewey and Lansky did, of course, stand to benefit from Luciano's imprisonment. The case of Dewey and his Lansky connection is most interesting.

As a consequence of his prosecution of Luciano, Dewey won widespread political fame and in 1938 ran, unsuccessfully, for governor of New York. In fact, at that time, Lansky reportedly donated fully $250,000 (in 1938 dollars) to Dewey's campaign.

Dewey did not win that race, but during the remaining period of his service as New York's "racket-busting" prosecutor he did obtain a conviction of one of Lansky's Jewish rivals in organized crime, Louis "Lepke" Buchalter, who eventually died in the electric chair.

Then, in 1942 when Dewey once again—this time, successfully—sought the governorship, Lansky provided additional financial support and political muscle. Dewey, as governor, commuted Luciano's sentence. In return for his freedom, Luciano agreed to go into exile to his homeland of Italy. Thus, Lansky's influence widened in Luciano's absence abroad.

This would not be, however, the end of the Dewey-Lansky relationship. Dewey later became a major stockholder in the Mary Carter Paint Company in the late 1950's.

According to former CIA contract agent Robert Morrow, "Carter Paint was originally an active corporation set up by Thomas Dewey [and CIA director] Allen Dulles to use as a CIA front. In 1958, Dewey and some friends had bought controlling interest in the Crosby Miller Corporation, with two million dollars in CIA money—authorized by Allen Dulles. Then, in 1959, the Crosby Miller Corporation was merged with the CIA-owned paint company. As an example of one of its early activities, it provided laundered CIA money for the Bay of Pigs army. In 1963, Mary Carter Paint spun off its paint division, after a Florida land scandal, and became Resorts International." [193]

Resorts International, Inc. controlled virtually all of the resorts in the Bahamas and throughout the Caribbean where Lansky reorganized his gambling operations after being forced out of Cuba in 1960.

Resorts International ultimately set up a subsidiary known as International Intelligence, Inc. (Intertel) ostensibly designed to curtail organized crime involvement in the casino industry. However, in reality, this was a myth.

There are those who suspect that Intertel—like Resorts International and Mary Carter Paint before it—was not simply a CIA operation, but a joint CIA-Lansky operation—an intelligence network interacting with Israel's Mossad. [194]

Perhaps not surprisingly, Dewey's admiring biographer, Richard Norton Smith, writing in *Thomas E. Dewey and His Times*, never mentions Dewey's Mary Carter Paint Company—or Lansky's support for Dewey's political endeavors. Another Lansky connection gone unmentioned. All of this illustrates the depth of Lansky's political influence and his wide range of connections.

## FRANK COSTELLO 'RETIRES'

There is also the question as to whether Lansky may have had a hand in the unsuccessful assassination attempt against his other boyhood friend, the aforementioned Frank Costello, who was often called "the Prime Minister of the Mafia." Whatever the truth, the attempt on Costello forced the "prime minister" into early retirement and gave Lansky further influence in organized crime.

## LUCIANO REMEMBERS . . .

"Lucky" Luciano, who had initially smoothed Meyer Lansky's way to the top, later rued the day that he had placed so much trust in his early gangland associate. In 1961, well after his influence in the international crime syndicate had begun to dwindle, Luciano reflected upon his relationship with Lansky. "In [Shakespeare's] *Julius Caesar*, you remember a guy by the name of Cassius? He was a pain in the ass. It seems like everybody's got a Cassius in his life."

According to Luciano, his Mafia associate Vito Genovese was his own Cassius. However, upon further thought he added, "Come to think of it, I even had two Cassiuses in my life, the other one bein' a guy by the name of Meyer Lansky. But I didn't get on to him for a longtime." [195]

In his waning days Luciano considered offers from Hollywood producers who wanted to film his life story. However, Luciano—in exile in Italy—got word from home that there were "orders" that he not participate in any such venture. It was then that Luciano saw the whole picture—the whole truth about what "the Mafia" had really become.

## 'THE BOSS OF EVERYTHING'

"When I realized that Meyer Lansky was right in the middle of this, that's when I knew he had us all by a string. Why should Lansky, bein' a Jew, give a shit whether or not some fuckin' movie had a bunch of Italian names in it? Because he was pullin' the wires and everybody was dancin' to his tune on the other end, like a bunch of puppets.

"Lansky held the purse strings, too; he was the treasurer and he was really tryin' to be the boss of everythin'. He was so hungry for power behind the scenes he'd kiss anybody's ass and do anythin' he had to do so that in the end, he—Meyer Lansky, my old partner and a Jew—would wind up the real boss of bosses of all the Italians and the Jews—and without a single fuckin' vote on the [organized crime syndicate] council.

"I never really knew what it meant when we was kids and I used to call him the Genius. But at the age of sixty-four, I finally got wise." [196]

## THE GUIDING HAND

So it was that Meyer Lansky—though not an Italian—did, indeed, become, as he was to be called, "the chairman of the board" of the organized crime syndicate, even more powerful than the "Mafia" itself.

If, as some claim, "The Mafia Killed JFK," it couldn't have been done without the foreknowledge—and guiding hand—of Meyer Lansky.

And as we shall see in this chapter—and further throughout the pages of this work—Lansky's connections with Israel and its Mossad (as well as Israel's allies in the CIA), demonstrates that Israeli loyalist Meyer Lansky is an integral player who bound together the diverse elements which came together in the JFK assassination conspiracy.

## HIDING BEHIND 'THE MAFIA'

In *Little Man*, his recent friendly biography of Meyer Lansky, Robert Lacey dismissed rumors of Lansky's role in the JFK assassination when he wrote that: "Meyer was mentioned most frequently of all in that happiest of hunting rounds for conspiracy theorists, the assassination of President John F. Kennedy." [197]

This is the **only** reference in Lacey's book to even the most tenuous link between Lansky and the JFK murder. However, as we shall see, the connections are very deep indeed. Yet, contrary to what Lacey contends, Lansky's name seldom appears in any significant fashion in most standard accounts which contend that organized crime played a role in the assassination.

The fact is that Lansky's name has been continuously and conveniently buried behind a host of Italian Organized Crime ("Mafia") figures. In Chapter 10 and Chapter 11 we review, extensively, Lansky's connections with the more famous—perhaps infamous—Italian-surnamed underworld figures linked to the Kennedy assassination.

As we shall see, in fact, those individuals in question were, practically to a man, Lansky's underlings. However, Lansky's name is hardly mentioned at all in standard accounts which suggest that organized crime—particularly "the Mafia"—played a part in the president's murder.

## 'THE REAL LEADERS OF CRIME'

Lansky's most authoritative biographer, organized crime writer Hank Messick pinpoints the tendency of the media—and the law enforcement community—to overlook the broad and penetrating reach of the Meyer

Lansky Organized Crime Syndicate, focusing instead on the media's hype of "the Mafia"—the Italian wing of the criminal underworld.

Says Messick: "The real leaders of crime have remained hidden while the nation's law enforcement agencies have chased minor punks. And naive is he who believes this development is accidental. Research reveals that non-Mafia leaders of crime have been hiding behind the vendetta-ridden society [the Italian Mafia] for decades. . . Attempts to frame me have been made, and I've been smeared as anti-Semitic from coast to coast by gangsters who used religion as a cloak."[198]

In his own memoirs, Lansky's crony, Charles "Lucky" Luciano revealed one rather interesting fact. According to Luciano, it was Lansky himself who suggested that the the newly-assembled national crime syndicate dub itself "the Union Siciliano"—a sobriquet which gave the criminal underworld a decidedly "Sicilian" imagery.[199]

### 'KOSHER NOSTRA'

According to veteran JFK assassination researcher Peter Dale Scott, "It is relevant that [then-Senate rackets committee counsel Robert F.] Kennedy did not use the word 'Mafia' when presenting, in his 1960 book *The Enemy Within*, his model of organized crime as an endemic, multi-ethnic, partially institutionalized syndicate."[200]

According to Scott: "What Robert Kennedy had meant by the 'syndicate' was very different from what [Mafia experts meant by the term] La Cosa Nostra."[201] According to Scott, "anyone speaking about organized crime . . . does so under conditions of great political restraint."[202]

To put it bluntly: the term "Mafia" does not account for the substantial—and indeed predominant—role of Meyer Lansky and his Jewish associates in the national crime syndicate.

Because of political constraints and fear of being accused of "anti-Semitism," many have been afraid to point out the important role of Jewish criminals in the world of crime.

One Jewish gangster, Lansky's West Coast henchman, Mickey Cohen, discussed the Italian-Jewish conflict in organized crime in his memoirs. He said, frankly: "See, I don't want to pull any wool over anybody's eyes because I'm writing a true autobiography, right? And I certainly don't want to mince any words, but I really don't consider the Mafia or anything of that type the only strength [in organized crime].[203]

Cohen differentiated between the Italian elements in organized crime, popularly known as "the Mafia" and "La Cosa Nostra" and the Jewish forces sometimes satirically called, "the Kosher Nostra."

"It's an organization. It's more what I would refer to as a syndicate. . . So it was an organization, but it wasn't the Mafia. Being Jews, Benny and me and even Meyer couldn't be a real part and parcel of that [the Mafia]."[204]

(The "Benny" to whom Cohen referred was the aforementioned Benjamin "Bugsy" Siegel, the lifelong friend and crime partner of Lansky's. It was Lansky who ultimately ordered Siegel's assassination.

(We will learn much more about the Lansky-Siegel-Cohen connection in Chapter 13 where we uncover Cohen's own pivotal role in the JFK assassination conspiracy.)

It was not, in fact, until the infamous Mafia conclave at Appalachian, New York, in 1957 when the media began hyping "the Mafia" as a major force in organized crime.

Americans had long been aware of legendary mobsters such as Al Capone and Lucky Luciano, but general awareness that a national crime syndicate did indeed exist was not commonplace.

Following a police raid of the Appalachian conference—attended exclusively by top Italian-surnamed Mafia figures from around the country—public attention began focusing on "the Mafia"—thanks to the media.

## MAFIA IN TURMOIL/LANSKY ON TOP

The official story has always been that a local policeman just happened to stumble upon the Mafia conclave at the home of Mafia figure Joseph Barbara. He called in reinforcements and a major "bust" took place. However, according to Hank Messick, the police had been tipped off by a Lansky associate that the meeting was about to take place. Messick described the consequences of the Appalachian raid :

"The delegates were scattered before any alliance could be reached. And the publicity caused the greatest heat since the 1930's. It focused not only on the men who attended the session but on the entire Mafia. What's more, it continued for well over a year as state and federal officials tried to find some charge to stick against the delegates they had captured or identified.

"Not only were Mafia leaders immobilized by the continuing publicity, but also they were demoralized. Almost instinctively they rallied to Lansky and other non-Mafia syndicate leaders for advice and assistance."[205]

Perhaps not coincidentally, one of the young attorneys who played a key role in the Appalachian raid was one Justin Finger. It was Finger who later went on to become chief of the "civil rights division" of the Anti-Defamation League of B'nai B'rith, the primary intelligence and propaganda arm of Israel's Mossad in the United States. [206] In subsequent chapters, Chapter 17 in particular, we will examine the role of the ADL in the JFK assassination cover-up in more explicit detail.

Obviously, the Appalachian raid was a critical event in Lansky's continuing rise to power. It solidified Lansky's hold over the crime syndicate.

Michael Milan, a low-level Jewish organized crime figure who grew up in Lansky's sphere of influence claims to have, in fact, been ritually inducted into the Mafia—by Lansky himself. It was to Lansky that Milan swore his allegiance. Writing in his memoirs, Milan remembers the event fondly: "'Omerta' whispered Meyer Lansky, only half believing in the ritual itself, but not wanting to show the slightest sign of disrespect to . . . [Mafia] traditions."[207]

In any case, as we have seen, Meyer Lansky's predominant role in the criminal underworld was already well in place.

## THE HOOVER-LANSKY CONNECTION

Lansky's role in the Office of Strategic Services (OSS)-Naval Intelligence operations during World War II and his work on behalf of Franklin Delano Roosevelt in handling Batista may account for the fact that Lansky seldom faced harassment from the federal authorities.

Writing in *Secret File*, Hank Messick comments: "Was Lansky rewarded? No final answer is possible, but he has been strangely immune to prosecution on the Federal level. Twice the IRS Intelligence Division has recommended prosecution, and twice the Justice Department has declined. Lansky remains the only top man in the national crime syndicate to escape untouched. Because of his brains and the troubles of his colleagues, he rules as undisputed chairman of the board."[208]

Lansky himself acknowledged his role in the so-called "Operation Underworld." "Sure, I'm the one who put Lucky and Naval Intelligence together," he told his Israeli friend, Israeli newsman Uri Dan. Lansky's reasons were interesting: "The reason I cooperated was because of strong personal feelings. I wanted the Nazis beaten. I was a Jew and I felt for those Jews in Europe who were suffering. They were my brothers."[209]

Former Lansky associate (and covert FBI operative) Michael Milan also points toward another critical Lansky connection that may have accounted for his immunity from federal harassment.

"I also knew that [J. Edgar Hoover] and Meyer Lansky sometimes broke bread together. Mr. L. was never rousted, was rarely served with federal subpoenas, and was generally left alone to conduct his business. Mr. L., on the other hand, didn't go around shooting anybody like people in some of the other [Mafia] Families, and making life embarrassing for the cops and the feds.

"So in this way everybody got along. Mr. H. could worry about his fifth column [the communists]. Mr. [Costello] could worry about keeping peace among the different Families and looking forward to retirement, and Mr. L. could worry about the cash flow in his Las Vegas casinos."[210]

## THE ANTI-DEFAMATION LEAGUE

J. Edgar Hoover's own connections to the Lansky Crime Syndicate and to the pro-Israel lobby have been the subject of rumors and controversy for many years.

It was the pro-Israel Anti-Defamation League (ADL) of B'nai B'rith that was largely responsible for the establishment of the J. Edgar Hoover

Foundation in 1947. (Top Lansky associates have long been generous financial backers of the ADL.) The Hoover Foundation's first president was Rabbi Paul Richman, Washington director of the ADL.

Hoover's longtime associate, Louis B. Nichols, the FBI's Assistant Director in charge of the Records and Communications Division of the Bureau, was the FBI's key contact with the ADL when the ADL helped orchestrate mass sedition trials against key critics of President Franklin D. Roosevelt's foreign policy.

Nichols went on to serve as president of the J. Edgar Hoover Foundation, but only after he left the FBI. Upon retirement from the bureau he signed on as Executive Vice President of Schenley Industries, a major liquor firm run by ex-bootlegger and Lansky associate Lewis R. Rosenstiel.[211] Rosenstiel himself was a very close friend of the FBI director in spite of, or perhaps precisely because of, his ties to Lansky.

## THE ADL AND ORGANIZED CRIME

The liquor industry, largely controlled by Jewish families such as the Bronfman family, and others, have been major contributors to the ADL, financing a large portion of its budget over the years. [212] These same liquor interests—obviously, as we have seen—had longtime contacts with Lansky from his earliest years in the bootlegging and rum-running rackets.

The origins of Hoover's sponsor—the ADL—is quite interesting. The organization's initial impetus came not so much out of a desire to defend members of the Jewish faith, but, more so, in particular, Jewish mobsters.

In the early part of this century New York City Police Commissioner Thomas Bingham had begun a dedicated investigation of organized crime in his city. By 1908 Bingham was under fire and being accused of being "anti-Semitic" for pointing out the role of certain Jewish gangsters in organized crime.

Ultimately, Bingham was forced out of office and organized crime took hold in New York City. One of the immediate beneficiaries of Bingham's departure was mobster Arnold Rothstein, Lansky's mentor and the undisputed Jewish underworld leader prior to the younger Lansky's rise to power.

The source of the attacks on Bingham was a public relations committee formed by a corporate attorney by the name of Sigmund Livingston. By 1913 Livingston's committee had formally incorporated as the Anti-Defamation League of B'nai B'rith.[213]

So it was that "crime buster" J. Edgar Hoover was himself a beneficiary of ADL largesse (a large portion of which, as we have seen, came from the coffers of Lansky and his criminal syndicate.)

## LOOKING THE OTHER WAY

Critical J. Edgar Hoover biographer Curt Gentry notes that Hoover's FBI was never strongly concerned with Lansky's activities. According to

Gentry, "The Dallas and Miami field offices [of the FBI] had blind spots. As a result, there were no taps or bugs on [Lansky's protege, New Orleans Mafia boss Carlos] Marcello, [Lansky's Tampa Mafia underling Santo] Trafficante, and, except for a brief period, Meyer Lansky."[214]

(In Chapter 10, Chapter 11, and Chapter 12 we will explore Lansky's relationships with Marcello, Trafficante and other "Mafia" figures further.)

Gentry adds: "There was a rumor, often heard in the underworld, that Meyer Lansky had his own man very high up in the FBI. William Sullivan had his own suspect, someone close to both the director and [Hoover's close friend and second in command, Clyde] Tolson, who was reputedly living far above his means. This was one case the FBI never solved."[215]

This same Sullivan happened to be the number three man at the FBI behind Hoover and Tolson. As head of the Bureau's highly-secretive Division Five, Sullivan was in charge of domestic counterintelligence. Also in charge of the FBI's participation in the Warren Commission investigation, Sullivan was not only a close friend of James Angleton, head of the Mossad desk at the CIA, but also—incredibly enough—a CIA conduit within the FBI itself.[216] (We will examine Angleton's role in the JFK assassination in much further detail in Chapter 8 and in Chapter 16).

As head of the FBI's Domestic Intelligence, Sullivan was in charge of the infamous COINTELPRO operations against, among others, Dr. Martin Luther King, Jr. and a bevy of left-wing (and right-wing) political groups.[217] COINTELPRO relied heavily on the Israeli lobby's Anti-Defamation League for continuing and ongoing intelligence reports as it had since at least before World War II.

### A DEAD WITNESS

Clearly a man with much inside knowledge, Sullivan was shot to death in a strange hunting accident on November 9, 1977 just prior to the time that he was to be called to testify before the House Select Committee on Assassinations.

Sullivan, who had resigned from the FBI, having broken with Hoover, had told investigators that he had become disenchanted when Hoover told him personally, "I am most concerned about having something issued so we can convince the public that Lee Harvey Oswald is the real assassin." [218]

Whatever Sullivan did know about Hoover—and perhaps Hoover's relationship with Meyer Lansky—will never be known.

### HOOVER'S DEAL

According to Sam and Chuck Giancana, in their biography of Chicago Mafia boss, Sam Giancana, "Hoover himself had been on the [organized crime] pad for years."[219]

The Giancanas say that Hoover had worked out a deal with Lansky's boyhood friend and criminal associate Frank Costello. The New York mobster would pass horse race betting tips to columnist Walter Winchell, a Hoover intimate. Winchell, in turn, would pass the information on fixed races to Hoover. Hoover would arrange his real bets through his associates while making minimal bets on his own ticket at the horse races. According to the Giancanas, "Hoover won every time." [220]

That Hoover was well versed in Lansky's criminal activities there is no question. His intelligence sources were legendary.

## WHAT HOOVER KNEW

Gentry sums it up well, noting that Hoover, although an inveterate gambler, knew all about what was happening in Lansky's Las Vegas casinos even though he, Hoover, avoided Las Vegas like the plague:

"[Hoover] knew who was skimming from the casino profits—and how much they were taking in. He knew where the money went and how it made its way to the top bosses.

"He also knew that some people, well connected with this place, were very unhappy with the Kennedys, John and Robert, unhappy to the point they were talking about killing them."

"Eventually the FBI discovered that most of the "skim" loot went to Meyer Lansky in Miami. In a typical month in 1963, the skim from one casino amounted to $123,500, of which Lansky kept $71,000, then transmitted the rest to the New Jersey mobster Gerald Catena.

Catena distributed in the north and Lansky in Florida. Each recipient would have a small percentage of his share deducted for casino employees who kept mum about the operation. There were also couriers, $300,000 to a Swiss bank, $100,000 to the Bahamas."[221]

(Later in this chapter and in Chapter 11, Chapter 12 and Chapter 15 we shall discuss Lansky's Swiss bank connections. They are central to the joint Lansky-CIA-Israeli Mossad operation that resulted in the assassination of John F. Kennedy.)

Even in the late 1960's, according to Gentry , "Hoover still had a blind spot so far as [Lansky] was concerned."[222]

## THE ANGLETON CONNECTION

However, in 1993 author Anthony Summers provided what may be a critical missing piece of the puzzle. Summers created a media sensation when he alleged in his new biography of Hoover, *Official and Confidential*, and on the PBS series "Frontline," that Lansky blackmailed Hoover with supposed photos of Hoover engaged in homosexual activity. Although such rumors about Hoover had been commonplace for years, no well-known author had affixed his own name to the charge.

Citing numerous sources—some suspect and virtually all of them unsavory—Summers claimed that not only Lansky, but also several others had access to similar photos (which Summers is apparently unable to produce). Summers reports that former OSS man and later longtime CIA counterintelligence chief James Jesus Angleton also had control of the Hoover photos, as did former OSS chief William Donovan.

The question, though, is whether Angleton, Donovan and company gave the photos to Lansky—or vice-versa—either option being possible in light of Lansky's own longtime association with American intelligence.[223]

That both Lansky and Angleton were in possession of such evidence is quite interesting in light of their joint interest in the welfare of the state of Israel, a subject we will be examining shortly.

Angleton, as we shall see in Chapter 8 and Chapter 12, had been directly involved with the Lansky crime syndicate through the CIA's dealings with Lansky's drug-smuggling allies in the Corsican and Sicilian Mafias. He was also Israel's chief patron at the CIA.

Angleton, who headed the Israeli desk at the CIA, was the one individual at the CIA who was most particularly close to Israel, so much so that he was often accused by critics of being a co-opted agent of Israel.

## THE GODFATHER

Clearly, Meyer Lansky was very much a "godfather" in organized crime, far more influential than even the most powerful Mafia boss in any city in America. All of this, then, accounts for Lansky's preeminent role in the underworld.

It is for this reason, then, that when we refer to the "Meyer Lansky Organized Crime Syndicate" we are referring to not only the "Mafia" but also to the powerful Jewish interests that are inter-connected here.

It was the Meyer Lansky Organized Crime Syndicate that played a pivotal role in the establishment of Israel. Lansky, you see, was Israel's modern-day "Godfather." Lansky was with Israel from the beginning.

## GUN-RUNNING FOR ISRAEL

According to Hank Messick, "Certainly Jewish gangsters have long and openly supported Jewish causes and the State of Israel. On the night Lansky's ex-partner, Bugsy Siegel, was executed, the Flamingo was taken over by Moe Sedway [a Lansky henchman]. When asked how he so conveniently happened to be in Las Vegas, [Sedway] explained that he was there to arrange a United Jewish Appeal fund drive." [224]

Robert Lacey points out in his biography of Lansky that Israeli agents were introduced to Lansky in the summer of 1948, the year that Israel became a state. Lansky permitted the Haganah (Jewish terrorist underground) fund-raiser, Joseph Baum, to hold a $10,000 benefit at (Lansky's gambling house), the Colonial Inn. He gave a donation himself. Lansky told them: "I'm at your service."[225] (As we noted in Chapter 4, one of the smaller shareholders in the Colonial Inn—at least at one point—was a Dallas nightclub keeper named Jack Ruby.)

Lansky also provided other "technical assistance" to the Israeli gun-running operations in the United States.

In one instance, a Pittsburgh arms dealer's shipment of weapons to the Arabs who were fighting the Jews in Palestine was tossed overboard after Lansky talked to his friends at the New York docks. On other occasions, arms intended for the Arabs were, instead, hijacked by Lansky's henchman and shipped to Israel.

Lansky also wasn't above putting the squeeze on rackets buddies—Jewish and non-Jewish alike—to buy Israel bonds. "Hey, these are a great investment," he would say.[226]

In fact, according to journalist Robert Friedman, Lansky was later a major contributor to radical New York-born Rabbi Meir Kahane who founded the militant Jewish Defense League.

Kahane, who was ultimately assassinated, actually served, at one point, in the Israeli parliament. [227] And, as we shall see in Chapter 8, Kahane himself had unusual connections to American intelligence that bring his Lansky connection full circle.

## OPERATION UNDERWORLD

It was Lansky's connection with the OSS-Naval Intelligence enterprise known as "Operation Underworld" that brought him into a strange global network that ultimately paved the way for the establishment of the state of Israel.

Operation Underworld was stationed at Rockefeller Center in New York and supervised by a British intelligence operative named William Stephenson (who was said to be Ian Fleming's inspiration for the fictional character, James Bond.) It was Stephenson who worked closely with the Anti-Defamation League (ADL) of B'nai B'rith as well as the FBI in coordinating anti-Nazi intelligence operations in the United States.[228]

(In later years, following the establishment of Israel, the Lansky Organized Crime Syndicate-financed ADL emerged as an unregistered foreign agent for Israel, handling intelligence and propaganda operations for the Jewish State, in collaboration with the FBI and the CIA. In Chapter 17 we will examine the ADL's role more fully, particularly in regard to its manipulation of the media. )

In any case, as we shall see in Chapter 15, it was Operation Underworld's William Stephenson who became a critical player in the establishment of Israel's Mossad.

Stephenson's top aide was Louis Bloomfield, later an attorney for the Lansky-linked Bronfman bootlegging family and himself a key player in the conspiracy to assassinate John F. Kennedy. (We shall examine Bloomfield in detail in Chapter 15 as well.)

There is little question but that Stephenson and Bloomfield were in close contact with Lansky and his henchmen during this period. Lansky himself, as we have seen, acknowledged his own role in Operation Underworld.[229]

Following World War II, the activities of Operation Underworld and many of the key players shifted to a new front: the establishment of Israel.

## A NEW FRONT

Both Stephenson and Bloomfield were integral to gun-running operations on behalf of the Jewish terrorist underground that later emerged as the government of the new Jewish State in 1948.

It was in 1947 that Rudolph Sonneborn (husband of New York publisher Dorothy Schiff) set up an entity known as the Sonneborn Institute. It was this institute that provided the Jewish Haganah, and later the Irgun, in Palestine with arms and money. The Institute's coordinator for arms smuggling to the Jewish underground was Louis Bloomfield. Working with Bloomfield were liquor baron Samuel Bronfman, one Hank Greenspun (about whom we shall see much more later in Chapter 17) and Lansky himself.[230]

It was during the 1947-1948 period that Teddy Kollek, later mayor of Jerusalem, was in charge of the Haganah station in Lansky's then-base of operations, New York City. He was said to be the formal liaison with American organized crime. [231]

Kollek worked with the Lansky Syndicate and ultimately had contact with yet another key player in our story, one James Jesus Angleton—a controversial figure indeed.[232]

It was Angleton, an OSS man, who later became a top-ranking figure in the American CIA and Israel's chief contact—some would say co-opted agent and loyalist— within CIA ranks.

Angleton worked closely with Jewish underground activities both in London and in Italy and was instrumental in orchestrating U.S. intelligence collaboration with the Corsican Mafia and the Sicialian Mafia in intelligence operations during these same years and thereafter.

(In Chapter 8 and Chapter 16 we shall examine Angleton's CIA activities, working closely with Israel and of his pivotal role in the JFK assassination and cover-up conspiracy in detail.)

Clearly, during the period of the establishment of Israel, Meyer Lansky was directly and intimately involved with all of the major players. Many of these same people would later be involved with Lansky in what some call "the crime of the century."

The Russian-born Jewish immigrant had come a long way from the slums of Brooklyn to a singular and pre-eminent role in global power politics. Indeed, Lansky was emerging as the "godfather" of a newly born nation: Israel.

## BASE OF OPERATIONS

The real key to the Lansky connection with Israel is money. The newly-established State of Israel not only needed money to exist, but the organization of a new government was an ideal opportunity for Lansky and his confederates to establish their own worldwide financial—and criminal—network. In its early years Israel was "untouchable." The emotional memories of the experiences of the Jewish people during World War II—indeed throughout history—were the foundations upon which Israel had been established. Criticism of Israel was verboten. The new Jewish State was an ideal cover under which Lansky and his criminal syndicate could operate unfettered.

## MONEY LAUNDERING

Lansky's status as organized crime's chief financier and grand wizard of money laundering put Lansky in a particularly central position. Organized crime writer Ed Reid's description of Lansky pinpoints Lansky's role precisely: "With his brother Jake, [Lansky] rules the gambling roost of the crime syndicate and may be the direct link between unknown moneyed nabobs who stash away mob dollars in foreign banks and the cash vaults of the U.S. criminal cartel."[233]

It was Lansky's foreign banking connection that draws him into the web of Israel's international intrigue to the utmost.

## RABBI TIBOR ROSENBAUM

Lansky's primary link with Israeli intelligence and financial operations came through the entity of the Banque de Credit International in Geneva Switzerland. This bank emerged as Lansky's primary European money-laundering operation.[234] This bank was the brainchild of one Tibor Rosenbaum.

An Orthodox rabbi, Rosenbaum served for a period as international vice president of the World Jewish Congress (of which Lansky-connected Bronfman family member Edgar Bronfman has served as president). Rosenbaum also was a co-founder of the World Zionist Congress and a director of the Jewish Agency in Geneva, Switzerland.[235]

However, and most importantly, Rosenbaum had served as Director General for Finance and Supply for Israel's secret intelligence agency, the Mossad. Rosenbaum was, very clearly, a key figure in Israel's international intrigue and a critical player in the world of organized crime syndicate boss Meyer Lansky.

Rosenbaum, among other things, also served on the board of the Swiss-Israel Trade Bank, established by Pinchas Sapir, Israel's Finance Minister and a Mossad officer. [236] It was during the time he served on the Swiss-Israel Trade Bank that Rosenbaum created the Banque de Credit International (BCI).

BCI—Meyer Lansky's European money laundering bank—was very much an Israeli government/Mossad operation, critical to the survival of the Jewish State.

Indeed, one of the board members of BCI was Zwi Recheter, director of the Bank Hapoalim, one of Israel's largest banks and a wholly-owned subsidiary of Israel's Histadrut, the national labor confederation. [237]What's more, BCI held the bulk of funds for the World Jewish Congress and the Jewish Agency, no minor deposits by any means.

BCI was to become Meyer Lansky's primary overseas money laundering bank—sharing those money laundering services that the bank provided to Israel's Mossad. In fact, during its heyday, BCI included among its board of directors two longtime Lansky associates, Edward Levinson and John Pullman.[238]

As we noted in Chapter 6, Levinson was one of the operators of the Fremont Casino in Las Vegas, a front man for Lansky's close friend , Joseph "Doc" Stacher, and a frequent business partner of Bobby Baker, reputed "bagman" for Lyndon Johnson. John Pullman, about whom we shall learn more later in this chapter and in Chapter 12 and Chapter 15, was Lansky's key international money handler.

The extent of Lansky's Israeli connection—through Rosenbaum's BCI—first became part of the public record in 1970 during the criminal trial of Alvin Malnik, one of Lansky's lieutenants.

Testimony in the trial revealed that one of the main money laundering channels for the illegal proceeds of the Lansky Crime Syndicate's narcotics, vice and gambling rackets in the United States was Tibor Rosenbaum's BCI. Rosenbaum's bank received its Lansky Crime Syndicate cash flow mainly through the Lansky-dominated Bank of World Commerce in Nassau, Bahamas.

The middleman was a Swiss national, Sylvain Ferdmann, a courier for Lansky. Ferdmann was an official of Rosenbaum's bank, an associate of the Bank of World Commerce (controlled by Lansky's longtime crony, John Pullman) and a legman for Investors Overseas Services (IOS), the fiefdom of financier Bernard Cornfeld.

Cornfeld, in fact, was sponsored by Rosenbaum, and had emerged as a major money launderer for Lansky's global drug-trafficking. Millions in small bills were transferred from Lansky's casinos, often masked as Israeli Bond sales and contributions to Jewish philanthropies.[239] This, of course, an outrageous betrayal of honest supporters of the Zionist cause.

(In Chapter 12 we shall examine in detail how as a result of active U.S. involvement in the region, the Lansky Syndicate used the cover of CIA covert activities in Southeast Asia to carry out multi-billion dollar drug smuggling operations.)

Investigative reporter Jim Hougan focused on the Lansky-Rosenbaum connection and its central link to Israel's international operations—particularly those of the Mossad:

"During the Second World War [Rosenbaum had become] a hero of the resistance through his underground activities on behalf of the Jews.

"After the war he became a delegate to the World Zionist Congress in Basel, where plans were made for the creation of Israel, and worked in various European capitals for the Palestine Liberation office (forerunner of the Jewish Agency). This was at the height of Zionist terrorist attacks in Palestine. A superb clandestine operator, Rosenbaum is said to have been instrumental in providing weapons to the Haganah and Stern Gang. That would tend to explain why the International Credit Bank [i.e. Banque de Credit International or BCI], 'Rosenbaum's Baby," became gambling czar Meyer Lansky's Number One conduit abroad.

"Rosenbaum was more than a friend to the Jews, however. When his bank was rocked with scandal after the collapse of [Bernard Cornfeld's] IOS, the newspaper *Ha'aretz* solemnly declared, 'Tibor Rosenbaum is Israel.' And the paper wasn't far from wrong. While Rosenbaum's bank facilitated the flight-capital schemes worked by IOS, it also served as a source of secret funds for the Mossad, Israel's intelligence service, and as one of the country's primary weapons brokers. At one point 'as much as ninety percent of the Israeli Defense Ministry's external budget flowed . . . through Rosenbaum's bank on the Rue de Conseil General.'

"In economic matters he was equally important, founding the Israel Corporation with the help of Baron Edmond de Rothschild, a French aristocrat committed to the Zionist cause. The raison d'etre of the Israel Corporation was to raise money among the world's Jews, money to be invested in a variety of public and semi-public Israeli enterprises.

"By finding money abroad to fund development projects in "the homeland," Rosenbaum and Rothschild freed Israeli tax monies to be spent on the country's critical military needs. Accordingly, [Rosenbaum] became the "Mr. Fixit" of Israeli finance, cementing friendships with the country's most important military and political leaders.

"The mix of Mob, Mossad, IOS, and Rothschild monies was an intoxicating one in which the common denominator appears to have been a love of Israel. Certainly Rosenbaum and Cornfeld shared that affection with Lansky and the French baron."[240]

## THE ISRAEL CORPORATION

There is yet another interesting Lansky-BCI-Israel link in the aforementioned Israel Corporation. It was Rosenbaum's BCI that held the bulk of funds for the Israel Corporation, a $200 million investment trust. The founders of the Israel Corporation included a host of longtime figures who moved in Lansky's sphere of influence.

Prominent among them was Sam Rothberg of the National Distilleries. Rothberg, in fact, was one of the initial investors in Lansky's first Las Vegas casino, established by Benjamin Siegel, the Flamingo Hotel.

Rothberg was one of the leading lights in the American Jewish community and the U.S. director of the Israeli Bonds drive. It was Rothberg who later came to Lansky's aid and fought against Lansky's forced return to the United States to face criminal charges following Lansky's flight to Israel (more about which later in this chapter.)

Others included two interesting figures in particular:

• Shaul Eisenberg, a former Mossad gun-runner who had been a key figure in Israel's nuclear bomb development programs and

• Philip M. Klutznick, a top-ranking figure in the Anti-Defamation League (ADL) of B'nai B'rith.[241]

The ADL connection here is interesting in that it further backtracks to Lansky's BCI-Rosenbaum linkage.

Klutznick, who had been associated with the Lansky-linked Sonneborn Institute gun-running operations coordinated by Louis M. Bloomfield (mentioned earlier), had become chairman of the board of the American Bank and Trust Company.

This firm was a subsidiary of the Swiss-Israel Trade Bank of which Rosenbaum had been a director. Swiss-Israel Trade Bank, in fact, assumed management of the American Bank and Trust Company on a very memorable day: November 22, 1963.[242]

Installed as one of the new directors of the company was New York businessman Abe Feinberg. It was Feinberg, as we saw in Chapter 4, who was instrumental in arranging highly critical American Jewish financial support for the 1960 presidential campaign of then-Senator John F. Kennedy.

American Bank and Trust had an unhappy ending. The company was looted in 1975-76 by financier David Gravier who subsequently was supposed to have died in an airplane crash in Mexico.

Tibor Rosenbaum's BCI also, incidentally, had a similarly unhappy ending. The bank collapsed in 1974 resulting in a scandal that shook Israel to its core. In his book, *Jews and Money: The Myths and the Reality*, author Gerald Krefetz details the scandal surrounding the collapse of the Lanksy-Mossad banking operation.

## THE ADL-LANSKY BANKS

The Bank of Miami Beach and the City National Bank of Miami were Lansky's chief money laundering banks in the United States and both included several Lansky associates, most notably one Max Orovitz, as directors.

In 1963, in fact Lansky began planning the installation of his gambling casinos in the Bahamas in Orovitz' office. And, finally, when Lansky himself ultimately settled in Israel, he initially took up residence in the Dan Hotel in Tel Aviv. Owner of hotel was Lansky's Miami banker friend, Orovitz.

Lansky's Miami banks were central to Lansky's gambling operations in Cuba and throughout the Caribbean.

According to former CIA contract agent Robert Morrow, the Bank of Miami Beach "was originally set up to service Cuban casinos operated by organized crime and continued to perform laundering services through the 1960s—and was still considered mob-connected. It was considered a sister bank of the Miami National Bank in the 1960s, sharing many of the same directors and performing many of the same services." [243]

These Miami banks, additionally, have close ties to the Anti-Defamation League of B'nai B'rith, Israel's intelligence and propaganda arm in this country. For example, Leonard Abess was chairman and founder of City National Bank of Miami. His bank managed ADL Foundation funds and Abess himself served as ADL national vice chairman. [244]

City National's chairman, beginning in 1982, was Donald Beazley, who was a former director of the mysterious Australian Nugan Hand Bank.[245] The Nugan Hand Bank, the subject of an interesting study by Jonathan Kwitny entitled *The Crimes of Patriots*, has been repeatedly linked to international drug money trafficking out of Southeast Asia conducted through the conduit of CIA operations in the region.

(And as we shall see in Chapter 12, Lansky utilized the CIA's activities in Southeast Asia as a cover for his drug-running operations which were, in fact, carried out hand-in-hand with the CIA.)

In Chapter 12, and in Chapter 15, however, we shall see the Lansky-Rosenbaum connection once again, and in further detail. Their linkage is critical to recognizing the important role that Israel played in the conspiracy that resulted in John F. Kennedy's assassination.

## THE GODFATHER GOES HOME

It was in 1970, finally, that Meyer Lansky pulled up stakes and settled in Israel. Under Israel's unique "Law of Return" any Jew from anywhere in the world could claim Israeli citizenship. That is what Lansky did.

At home in the United States, Lansky was under criminal investigation. Exile in Israel seemed a likely way of escaping the trouble. Israel was an ideal location for Lansky to relocate his operations and he set about plans for setting up the Jewish State as the new, formal headquarters for his global crime syndicate.

As Hank Messick put it: "As chairman of the board of the Syndicate International, [Lansky] could operate just as easily—perhaps more easily—from Tel Aviv as Miami Beach."[246] Lansky's longtime associate Joseph (Doc) Stacher had already gone to Israel to live. So had a wide-ranging assortment of other American Jewish mobsters, including Lansky's good friend Phil "The Stick" Kovolick.

The Mossad-dominated government of Israel seemed to welcome these criminals as new countryman. Israel, according to *Newsweek*, "appeared to be motivated by self-interest. Each year, Lansky and his underworld associates pour vast sums into Israeli bonds and Israeli philanthropies.

## MOB MONEY IN ISRAEL

"As the daily *Ha'aretz* saw it, the government seemed afraid of losing the millions of dollars in illicit money first 'laundered' in mob-controlled institutions and then funnelled into Israeli business and industry."[247]

Lansky's initial entree to Israel was quietly orchestrated. Word leaked out that a wealthy "Miami philanthropist" had taken up residence in the Jewish State. However, circumstances beyond Lansky's control made matters difficult for the grand wizard of the underworld.

During his stay in Israel, two American grand juries (in March of 1971 and in June of 1972) handed down indictments against Lansky and several of his associates. The first indictment charged—correctly, of course—that Lansky had been skimming millions from the Flamingo Hotel and Casino in Las Vegas. The second indictment charged Lansky with income tax evasion.

There were more than a few honest, law-abiding Israelis who objected to the "chairman of the board" staking his future in Israel, and the political pressure was such that there was widespread clamor for his deportation.

It didn't help matters that fearless crime reporter Hank Messick's biography of Lansky appeared during that same period and portions of it appeared in the Israeli press. Many Israelis quickly began to realize that the "Miami philanthropist" was, instead, the kingpin of the international crime syndicate.

Lansky himself made his own loyalties clear, however. In a friendly series of interviews with *Ma'ariv*, an Israeli daily, Lansky said, "I don't care what they wrote and write about me in America. I care what they think of me in Israel."[248]

Between the public outcry in Israel and pressure from American authorities, the Israel government buckled and agreed to expel Lansky.

However, the "boss of all bosses" appealed his expulsion all the way to the Israeli Supreme Court. The emotional issue of a Jew who had made "aliyah" and settled in Israel under the Law of Return—and who was then being expelled to face possible punishment in a criminal court in another country—played heavily in Lansky's favor.

However, despite Lansky's best efforts—including an offer of $10,000,000 if he was permitted to remain—he was forced to return to the United States.

## LANSKY IN DECLINE

By this time, Lansky was in ill health and even underwent open heart surgery. However, as the *Wall Street Journal* noted: "Whenever the heat [was] on—an investigation made public, a grand jury inquiry, a new task force of federal crime fighters on his trail—stories suddenly abound that Meyer Lansky is dying of cancer or some other terminal illness. In the files of the New York State Police, there exists a report made out in the 1920's that says Meyer Lansky is a bad guy, all right, but there's no need to worry because he's a sickly man who won't live out the year."[249]

But Lansky's traditional magical powers over the American criminal justice system were still with him. First of all, a jury in his home base of Miami acquitted him on the income tax evasion charges. Then, in mob-controlled Nevada, the criminal charges against Lansky were thrown out of court on the basis that Lansky was in ill health.

And in Washington, U.S. Solicitor General Robert Bork decided that going after Lansky—the ruling boss of international organized crime—was not in the nation's best interests. Bork decided that the Justice Department just didn't have a case against Lansky. The case was dropped. [250] Lansky had once again prevailed—to nobody's surprise.

(Bork later suffered an ignominious rejection by the Senate when nominated for the Supreme Court. However, it was not Bork's pandering to Lansky that weighed against him—although it probably should have.)

Lansky's remaining years were quiet ones spent with his wife and dog and an assortment of other aging racketeers. He still maintained some oversight over his business operations but increasing health problems continued to plague him. The mastermind behind the global crime syndicate finally died on January 15, 1983.

## A GLAMOROUS FOLK HERO

In his final years—and posthumously—Lansky (with the willing help of Hollywood and the rest of the media) became a folk hero of sorts. Gangsterism was being made fashionable—even as the glory days of John F. Kennedy and Camelot were being trashed by that same media.

Lansky's days with Benjamin Siegel were glamorized in films such as *The Gangster Chronicles, The Neon Empire*, and in *Mobsters*, where a host of teen idols played Lansky, Siegel, Frank Costello, and Lucky Luciano in their early years.

Author Robert Lacey—who had previously written a glowing profile of the British royal family—turned his attention to the royal family of the international crime syndicate and produced—with the help of the Lansky family—a Lansky biography, *Little Man: Meyer Lansky and the Gangster Life*. Lacey's epic tells much—but ignores a lot. He would have us believe that Lansky was, more than anything, a devoted family man, and not the ruthless thug that he truly was.

Even as Lacey's Lansky biography was hitting the bookstores, yet another Hollywood production brought Lansky to the screen. This film, *Bugsy*, starring heart-throb Warren Beatty as Benjamin Siegel, cast the highly-regarded actor Ben Kingsley (who had even played Mahatma Gandhi) as a wise and all-knowing Meyer Lansky.

However, the Hollywood versions of the life and times of Meyer Lansky were far from the truth, no matter how colorful a story they told about the evil genius they portrayed.

Thus, even in death, Meyer Lansky prevailed. Lansky's central role As a virtual middleman between the high-level forces that conspired in the assassination of John F. Kennedy has been cleverly buried by a willing media. "Israel's Godfather" was lionized almost as a misunderstood statesman. Meyer Lansky, however, was not that.

Instead, Lansky was a cynical, cold-blooded killer who had ordered the death of his closest friend—Benjamin Siegel—and who certainly had no qualms about helping orchestrate the murder of an American president who threatened not only his own survival, but that of his beloved State of Israel.

## Chapter Eight

## Thick as Thieves:
## A Dangerous Liaison—
## James Jesus Angleton and the Unholy Alliance
## Between Israel, the CIA
## and the Meyer Lansky Organized Crime Syndicate

By 1963 John F. Kennedy was not only at war with Israel and the Meyer Lansky Organized Crime Syndicate, but he was also at war with their close ally in the international intelligence underworld—the CIA. That was a deadly combination.

The CIA and Israel had forged a close-working strategic alliance in the previous decade. Their joint enterprises around the globe tied the CIA and Israel together inextricably. Israel's interests—and the CIA's interests—were often one and the same, perhaps too often. Likewise with the Meyer Lansky crime network.

What's more, Israel's chief contact at the CIA in Washington, James Jesus Angleton, ultimately played a pivotal role in the JFK assassination conspiracy cover-up. Angleton, too, had close links with the same forces in the Lansky Syndicate.

At the Central Intelligence Agency headquarters at Langley, Virginia there was one man—just one man alone—who knew perhaps better than any other American, Israel's intentions and attitudes toward President John F. Kennedy. This was the enigmatic James Jesus Angleton.

Angleton was so close to the Israelis during his tenure at the CIA that, following his death in 1987, a monument was unveiled in Israel by its government in his honor.

This is evidently one of the few known public monuments to any American CIA official anywhere in the entire world. Clearly quite an honor for Angleton but actually one of several memorials to Angleton in Israel.

According to Andrew and Leslie Cockburn, co-authors of *Dangerous Liaison: The Inside Story of the U.S.-Israeli Covert Relationship*, Angleton was "a man who for nearly a quarter of a century was one of the most powerful and mysterious figures in the CIA."[251]

According to the Cockburns, "Angleton was involved in many strange and secret dealings in the world of intelligence, but the Israelis like to talk of him as having been especially close to them, which is why they paid public homage to his memory."[252]

Recruited into the Office of Strategic Services (OSS) while at Yale University, Angleton was a fast-rising star in the world of clandestine activities, and following the abolition of the OSS after World War II, Angleton entered into service with the Central Intelligence Agency after the CIA was established in 1947.

By 1954 Angleton assumed the highly sensitive post of chief of CIA counterintelligence. What's more, Angleton's influence within the CIA itself was of a greater magnitude than what otherwise might be expected. Angleton was a very powerful—and secretive—man.

## POWERFUL PATRONS

According to Tom Mangold, Angleton's biographer, CIA Director Allen Dulles and his deputy, Richard Helms, who later went on to become CIA director during the administration of Lyndon Johnson, were Angleton's mentors. However, Mangold says, Helms was Angleton's "chief patron."[253]

(Dulles, of course, was later fired as CIA director by John F. Kennedy and then, in a twist of fate—or by design—served on the Warren Commission which ostensibly investigated JFK's murder.

(And it would be Helms, along with Angleton, who would later sign off on a controversial intra-agency memo that would ultimately—and apparently unwittingly—blow the lid off the CIA's involvement in the conspiracy to assassinate President Kennedy. In Chapter 16 we shall examine that memo in detail.)

## A POWER UNTO HIMSELF

According to the CIA spymaster's biographer, "Angleton's long-standing friendships with Dulles and Helms were to become the most important factor in giving him freedom of movement within the CIA. [Angleton] was extended such trust by his superiors that there was often a significant failure of executive control over his activities. The result was that his subsequent actions were performed without bureaucratic interference. The simple fact was that if Angleton wanted something done, it was done. He had the experience, the patronage, and the clout.

"In the sixties the Counterintelligence Staff, for example, had its very own secret slush fund, which Angleton tightly controlled. This fund gave him easy access to a large amount of money that was never audited (as other such funds were). Angleton argued that he would have to be trusted, without outside accountability, because it would have been difficult to allow mere clerks to go through his accounts—if only because sources would have to be revealed. The [directors of central intelligence] (including Helms) agreed to this unusual arrangement, which gave Angleton a unique authority to run his own little operations without undue supervision." [254]

In short, according to Peter Dale Scott, Angleton "managed a 'second CIA' within the CIA"[255] and one, as we shall see, that was collaborating all too comfortably close with Israel's Mossad.

## INTERNATIONAL INTELLIGENCE BOSS

However, Angleton's influence went even further. Angleton, in fact, was the "official CIA liaison for all Allied foreign intelligence agencies"[256]—in particular, and most especially, the Mossad. Through these connections, Angleton was able to manipulate intelligence activities around the globe.

A friend of Angleton recalls: "That's the job that was so sensitive and that's the one that you don't read about. While he was liaising with everyone, he was getting them to do favors for either the CIA—things the CIA didn't want to carry out directly; like they've never killed anyone, right?—or for his own agenda.

"Even on a more mundane level, he could use his contacts with Israeli intelligence, which he kept to himself, as authority for whatever line he was trying to push at the CIA. You know, 'My Israeli sources tell me such and such,' and no one was going to contradict him, since no one else was allowed to talk to Israeli intelligence.

"I always had the impression that he used the Israelis in this way, getting them to say that the Russians had not really broken with the Chinese or whatever. They would be perfectly happy to do him the favor. On top of all that he felt that he was getting the benefit of Israeli networks and connections all over the place, not just in the Communist bloc." [257]

One friend of Angleton's (who didn't necessarily share the counterintelligence chief's infatuation with Israel and the Mossad) commented: "You have to understand that Jim's central dominating obsession was communism, something that for him was the essence of absolute and profound evil.

"For him nothing else really mattered,but he would use anyone and anything to combat it. Sure he liked Israelis . . . but he was not a 'co-opted Israeli agent,' as some people in Washington used to call him."[258]

## BEN-GURION'S MAN IN WASHINGTON

Most important to Angleton, however, was his relationship with the Mossad. In fact, he was the CIA's longtime, self-appointed man at the agency's Israel desk.

Angleton's biographer, Tom Mangold, points out that "The legends alone surrounding his twenty years as head of the Israeli Desk would fill another book, as indeed would the truth."[259]

And although Mangold's account of Angleton's career devoted hardly any attention to Angleton's intimate ties with Israel and its Mossad, Mangold does state flatly: "I would like to place on the record, however, that Angleton's closest professional friends overseas, then and subsequently, came from the Mossad and that he was held in immense esteem by his Israeli colleagues and by the state of Israel, which was to award him profound honors after his death."[260]

Angleton, in fact, had long-standing direct ties with Israeli Prime Minister David Ben-Gurion himself, dealing with the Israeli leader on an intimate basis. If there was anyone in the CIA who knew of Ben-Gurion's distaste for JFK, it was Angleton. As a devoted friend of Israel—and chief liaison with the Mossad—Angleton had to be fully aware of the raging conflict between the Israeli prime minister and the American president who refused to bow to Israel's demands.

And considering President Kennedy's efforts to build bridges with the Soviet Union and his efforts to wind down the Cold War, one knows, beyond question, that Angleton—hard-line, even fanatical anti-communist that he was—viewed Kennedy's overtures with outrage and disgust. All of this not to mention Kennedy's own conflicts with the CIA which we will review in Chapter 9.

## KENNEDY A THREAT

Clearly, John F. Kennedy was not only a threat to Israel and the CIA and their allies in the Meyer Lansky Organized Crime Syndicate, but also to James Jesus Angleton himself. Kennedy's war with the CIA could spell an end to Angleton's career and the world-wide intelligence empire that the strange and calculating counterintelligence boss had assembled.

The ties between Angleton's CIA and the Mossad were such, according to historian Steven Stewart, that they "had the effect of ensuring that virtually every CIA man in the Middle East was also working at second hand for the Israelis . . . as the CIA's policy changed almost overnight, in an extraordinary *volte-face*, from being largely pro-Arab to becoming almost totally pro-Israeli"[261]—a close relationship indeed.

## THE CIA AND ISRAEL: EARLY DAYS

It is the CIA's relationship with Israel that is most significant in terms of that agency's global intrigue—and, of course, in light of the CIA's documented role in the assassination of John F. Kennedy (which we examine in more detail in subsequent chapters). And it was Angleton who was, as we have seen, the prime mover behind the CIA-Israeli Mossad's close working relationship—in fact, from its very beginnings.

The late Wilbur Crane Eveland, a former advisor to the CIA and former member of the policy-planning staffs of the White House and Pentagon, had written extensively on the U.S.-Israeli relationship. In his book, *Ropes of Sand*, Eveland reviewed the beginnings of what Andrew and Leslie Cockburn call the "dangerous liaison"—America's covert relationship with Israel.

This covert relationship was conducted primarily through the egis of Angleton's Israeli desk at the CIA. Eveland writes of its origins:

"CIA operations had started before Allen Dulles became director that had long-range implications from which the United States might find it difficult to disengage.

"Stemming from his wartime OSS liaison with Jewish resistance groups based in London, James Angleton had arranged an operational-intelligence exchange agreement with Israel's Mossad, upon which the CIA relied for much of its intelligence about the Arab states." [262]

as not necessarily initially based on
/olf Blitzer, longtime Washington
*t*, the CIA-Mossad relationship began

militants seized the U.S. Embassy in
sis of 1979-1981), the militants seized
ased.
eli intelligence agencies, mostly in the
re-tapped, and offered bribes to U.S.
in sensitive intelligence and technical

ying on Israel, although this didn't
it was necessary for the CIA and the
James Jesus Angleton who stepped
to have been largely responsible for

y joint ventures over the years, all
e.
ncluded assassination plots. In fact,
d that he hoped that "the Nasser
rring to what he perceived to be an
dent)—CIA Director Allen Dulles
er.
oster Dulles (brother of the CIA
dogs.
actions against Israel's enemies in
rthrow the nationalist government
of communist fanatics such as Angleton considered to be
"leftist"—fell apart when the CIA's paid henchmen, Syrian nationals (who
evidently were patriots), turned themselves in and exposed the CIA's plot to
the Syrian government.

At the time, CIA director Dulles commented, "I guess that leaves
Israel's intelligence service as the only one on which we can count, doesn't
it?" [266]

## ANGELTON'S ZR/RIFLE TEAM

The CIA's now-best known assassination plot, of course, was the
agency's collaboration with organized crime in a scheme to kill Cuban
leader Fidel Castro. (We will examine the Castro assassination plot in much
further detail in Chapter 11.)

It is interesting to note, however, at this juncture, that as part of the plot
against Castro the CIA established its now-infamous ZR/Rifle Team,

incorporating a wide array of foreign assassins and mercenaries—skilled and dangerous men who were trained in murder.

The ZR/Rifle Team, in fact, was one of Angleton's pet in-house CIA projects which he ran in conjunction with his CIA colleague, William Harvey.

This, in the long run, as we shall see in Chapter 16, gave Angleton and his Israeli allies access to the "talent" necessary to achieve a successful operation in Dealey Plaza in Dallas, Texas on November 22, 1963.

## A FIRM ALLIANCE

According to intelligence historian Richard Deacon, Israel's relationship with the CIA (and Angleton, in particular) had been firmly cemented: "On the American side the Israelis had won a certain amount of unofficial support from the CIA even during the Eisenhower era. The CIA had been realistic enough to realize that the Eisenhower appeasement policy towards the Arab world would ultimately be disastrous for every American interest, military or economic.

"For this reason they had maintained a policy of allowing all intelligence operations in Israel to be carried out entirely by the Mossad. In short, what this meant was that the CIA had no office or station chief in Tel Aviv, but that certain officers in the US Embassy there co-operated with the Mossad.

"In theory this entailed an exchange of intelligence between the two sides and in practice this worked rather better than one could have expected normally.

"The key figures in this arrangement were originally [Mossad chief] Isser Harel, Ephraim Evron, who later became deputy Israeli ambassador in Washington, and James Angleton, chief of the CIA Counter-Intelligence." [267] (Evron, as we saw in Chapter 6, also became particularly close to John F. Kennedy's successor, Lyndon Johnson, who reversed U.S. policy toward Israel and the Middle East—and in favor of the CIA's interventionist policies in Southeast Asia—immediately upon assuming office.)

According to intelligence historian Deacon, Angleton exploited the new intimate relationship between the CIA and the Mossad for use internationally:

"Angleton, having seen the folly of U.S. foreign policy during the abortive Suez operation, decided to counteract the State Department's bias towards the Arabs by close cooperation with Israel. It was he who first saw the need for a new policy in the Middle East and safeguards against increasing Russian influence.

## A REVERSAL OF POLICY

"He and Evron worked well together and, as a result, the CIA helped Israel with technical assistance in the nuclear field. Evron was eager to grasp this opportunity for he had been one of the prime instigators of the aggressive challenge to [John F. Kennedy's] policy of friendship for Nasser [and] was instrumental in paving the way to a reversal of the pro-Arab policy which for a while dominated American thinking, not only under Eisenhower, but also the Kennedy administration."[268]

According to Deacon, Evron was Israel's most powerful figure in Washington, more highly regarded than even the Israeli ambassador and was welcomed as a collaborator and Mossad liaison officer to Angleton's Central Intelligence Agency.

## THE NUCLEAR PROBLEM

The evidence also suggests that Angleton was a key player in attempts within the CIA to cover up Israel's secret nuclear weapons development program—the sticking point which led to the break between John F. Kennedy and Israeli Prime Minister David Ben-Gurion, resulting in Ben-Gurion's angry resignation from office. (All of this, of course, we examined in detail in Chapter 5)

What's more, it appears that not only did Angleton help in the cover-up, but he also was evidently instrumental in assisting Israel's nuclear development.

As we noted in Chapter 5, following an American U-2 spy plane photographing Israel's "peaceful" nuclear reactor in the Negev desert in 1960, shock waves reverberated through official Washington at the highest levels.

John Hadden, who was the CIA station chief in Tel Aviv before his retirement in 1960, apparently reported that an Apollo, Pennsylvania company, the Nuclear Materials & Equipment Corporation, was an Israeli front, providing bomb-grade uranium for Israel's nuclear weapons development.

## THEODORE SHACKLEY

However, Hadden faced much opposition from within the CIA. One individual in the CIA, the assistant to the deputy director for covert operations, was constantly attacking and belittling Hadden's claims. This was Theodore Shackley.

It was Shackley, whom we shall see in Chapter 11, was a key CIA player in the CIA-Meyer Lansky Organized Crime Syndicate assassinations plots against Fidel Castro. It was also Shackley, whom we shall see in Chapter 12, was a key player in the CIA in Southeast Asia during the joint CIA-Lansky drug-trafficking operations in the region.

Later, following his retirement from the CIA, Shackley entered into lucrative international arms dealing ventures with Shaul Eisenberg, a key Mossad operative and a major figure in Israel's nuclear development program. Shackley, as we shall see in the appendix, was also a close CIA colleague of later CIA director George Herbert Walker Bush, himself, evidently, a major player in the web of intrigue that we find surrounding the JFK assassination.

Here, however, we see Shackley engaged in covering up Israeli operations in the nuclear development arena—along with Angleton.

According to Hadden, Angleton "had no interest in stopping"[269] the NUMEC operation, and certainly did not. Hadden comments: "Why would someone whose whole life was dedicated to fighting communism have any interest in preventing a fiercely anti-communist nation from getting the means to defend itself?" [270]

What's more, one of Angleton's "closest colleagues" from his days in the OSS in Italy (more about which we will review later in this chapter) was a former leader of the Jewish underground, Meir Deshalit, the older brother of Amos Deshalit, a physicist who was one of the leaders in Israel's drive to build a nuclear bomb.[271]

## SECRET MEMORANDUM

As we noted, in Chapter 5, an internal CIA memorandum issued during the presidency of John F. Kennedy cast negative light on Israel's nuclear development program.

However, according to historian Stephen Green, "It is perhaps significant that the memorandum was not drafted as a formal national intelligence estimate, which would have involved distribution to several other agencies of the government. No formal NIE was issued by CIA on the Israeli nuclear weapons program until 1968." [272]

There is no question, of course, considering Angleton's close ties with Israel and its Mossad, that Angleton (and perhaps the aforementioned Shackley) were instrumental in burying this memorandum.

The CIA-Mossad joint operations relating to Israel's nuclear development continued for a generation.

Interestingly enough, many years later, the CIA and Israel jointly arranged the kidnapping of Mordechai Vanunu, a nuclear technician who blew the whistle on Israel's nuclear weapons development. A woman used to lure Vanunu in the kidnaping conspiracy was a CIA covert action operative who also did occasional work for the Mossad.

## ANGLETON'S POWER INCREASES

With the advent of the Lyndon Johnson administration and the amazing reversal of U.S. policy toward Israel, outlined in detail in Chapter 6, and with the close relationship between Angleton's Mossad liaison, Evron, and Lyndon Johnson, Angleton's influence in Middle East policy-making became even greater.

According to Andrew and Leslie Cockburn: "One long-serving official at the CIA's ancient rival, the code-breaking National Security Agency, states flatly that 'Jim Angleton and the Israelis spent a year cooking up the '67 war. It was a CIA operation, designed to get Nasser [of Egypt].' Such a verdict, from a source inside an agency that had the inclination and the facilities to monitor both the CIA and the Israelis, must carry some weight." [273]

Now all of the aforementioned is particularly relevant when one considers Angleton's preeminent role in the CIA-Mossad alliance. However, much new additional information has come to light which ties Angleton even further into the international web of conspiracy that resulted in the assassination of John F. Kennedy.

## ANGLETON, LANSKY & THE OSS

Angleton, in fact, had intimate ties to Meyer Lansky-linked organized crime operations in Europe stemming back from his service in the OSS in England (working with British intelligence) and in Italy.

It was during his years in the OSS in England that Angleton may have come into contact with another young American, Clay Shaw, an army officer detailed to the OSS in its operations in England.

And it was during this same period that Meyer Lansky himself was engaged in joint covert operations with the OSS, as noted in Chapter 7.

The aforementioned Shaw, as we shall see, in Chapter 15, is the focal point of contact between not only the CIA and low-level elements in the intelligence community—Lee Harvey Oswald among them—but also between Meyer Lansky's European money laundering operation based at Mossad officer Tibor Rosenbaum's Banque de Credit International [first examined in Chapter 7).

## THE JEWISH UNDERGROUND

At the tender age of 27, Angleton—then stationed in Rome—was the youngest counterintelligence branch chief in the entire OSS and the only non-Briton in Italy cleared to share intelligence secrets of the top-secret Ultra program which was cracking Nazi codes.

Italy, indeed, became a central point of contact for Angleton and his international intelligence connections, and particularly for his work on behalf of the state of Israel.

By 1951 Angleton was engaged in "the underground Jewish network that ran down from Eastern Europe through Italy to the ports where shiploads of immigrants were loaded for Palestine." [274]

It was this refugee network, according to Richard Deacon, writing in *The Israeli Secret Service*, a history of the Mossad, that was "paving the way for an ultimate intelligence network for the future state of Israel." [275]

One of Angleton's Israeli contacts in the Jewish underground in Europe was Teddy Kollek (later to become mayor of Jerusalem.). Kollek, in fact, emerged to become "a close personal friend." [276]

Kollek, as we saw in Chapter 7, was the Haganah station chief in New York during the 1947-1948 period, engaged in arms smuggling to Palestine in conjunction with Meyer Lansky and Major Louis M. Bloomfield—whom we shall see in Chapter 15, was associated with not only the aforementioned Clay Shaw, but also with Tibor Rosenbaum's Banque De Credit International.

## TIBOR ROSENBAUM, AGAIN

But there is an even more pivotal contact between Angleton, Major Bloomfield, Shaw and Lansky: the same Tibor Rosenbaum. In Chapter 7 we met Rabbi Tibor Rosenbaum of the Banque De Credit International.

It was Rosenbaum, who went on to serve as Director General for Finance and Supply for the Israeli Mossad, who was one of the prime movers in the refugee-turned-intelligence network with which Angleton worked so closely.

Interestingly enough, it was also during this same period that the terrorist Menachem Begin (who later became prime minister of Israel) was coordinating Israel's Irgun operations in Europe.

(In Chapter 13, we shall find, Begin was also operating in the United States in conjunction with a key figure in the Lansky Organized Crime Syndicate in joint efforts on behalf of Israel—and against John F. Kennedy.)

## THE CORSICAN MAFIA CONNECTION

Angleton's connections with organized crime and the Lansky operations, however, go even deeper.

It was through a secret CIA asset, one Jay Lovestone, that Angleton manipulated what his biographer called "an odd little operation that Angleton had been quietly running all on his own since 1955." [277]

Through an aide, Stephen Millet, who was the counterintelligence officer who handled the Israeli desk for Angleton, the CIA spymaster was maintaining close links with the criminal underworld in Italy and France.

For details on the activities of Angleton and his Lansky-linked organized crime associates we turn to the work of Robert I. Friedman.

In his biography of militant New York-born Rabbi Meyer Kahane (later a member of the Israeli parliament), we learn that it was the aforementioned Lovestone who provided Kahane and his closest associate and fellow rabbi, Dr. Joseph Churba, with financing and support. (Lansky, himself, as we saw in Chapter 7, was a contributor to Kahane's later activities in support of Israel.)

Churba and Kahane functioned as CIA assets in churning up Jewish support—and otherwise—for the war in Vietnam, a venture, we have seen, which proved fruitful for not only the CIA, but its allies in Israel and their allies in the Lansky Syndicate.

## THE CIA'S HIRED GUNS

According to Friedman, "Churba and Kahane also received support from legendary cold warriors Jay Lovestone and Irving Brown, who had been top officials of the American Communist Party in the 1920s before undergoing a 'Damascus Road' conversion and who subsequently ran the AFL-CIO's powerful International Affairs Department under the tutelage of the CIA.

"It was under the CIA's direction that Lovestone and Brown—using Corsican and Italian mafiosos—set up right-wing death squads in Marseilles and other European cities after the Second World War to break the burgeoning left-wing labor movement.

"Thanks to Brown, by 1953 his key contact in the Marseilles underworld, Pierre Ferri-Pisain, had control of the city's port, where he built an international heroin trafficking empire.

"This was not the first time that American intelligence purchased the services of the Mafia. Prior to the Allied invasion of Sicily in the Second World War, the OSS established contacts with the Sicilian Mafia through the same Lucky Luciano who allowed [the Jewish underground] to smuggle weapons from Hoboken to the Irgun in Palestine. The Sicilian Mafia provided intelligence on the Germans, and after the war assassinated hundreds of Italian left-wing political activists."[278]

According to historian Alfred McCoy, "After the CIA withdrew [from active involvement] Marseille's Corsicans won political protection from France's intelligence service, the SDECE, which allowed their heroin laboratories to operate undisturbed for nearly 20 years. In partnership with Italy's Mafia syndicates, the Corsicans smuggled raw opium from Turkey and refined it into no. 4 heroin for export. Their biggest customer was the United States . . ."[279]

In Chapter 7 we examined Lansky's pivotal role in arranging the accommodation between the OSS and the Sicilian Mafia in the famed "Operation Underworld."

## ANGLETON, THE CIA & THE FRENCH CONNECTION

In Chapter 12 we will examine the Lansky-CIA manipulation of the Corsican and Sicilian organized crime elements in the drug trade in particular detail.

In Chapter 12 , Chapter 15 and Chapter 16, we will also examine the role of French Corsican gangsters and French intelligence operatives in the JFK assassination—linking Angleton further to the events in Dallas on November 22, 1963.

Here, now, we see that it was Israeli Mossad ally James J. Angleton who was, in fact, the prime mover behind the CIA operations utilizing the Corsican and Sicilian organized crime elements in Angleton's "anti-communist" ventures.

That all of this was run through the Angleton's Israeli desk at the CIA is quite interesting, to say the least.

This, of course, ties Angleton and the CIA and their collaborators in the Mossad even further into the Lansky network—and into the nexus revolving around the conspiracy that led to the murder of John F. Kennedy.

However, Angleton's French intrigue went beyond his connections with the Corsican crime syndicate. He and the CIA were also dabbling in internal French politics, intefering with the political aims of French leader Charles DeGaulle and his political alliance. The CIA, in fact, was backing the Socialist Party.

Historian Alfred McCoy notes that: "On the surface it may have seemd a bit out of character for the CIA to be backing so far left [a party] as a Socialist Party. However, there were only three major political parties in France—Socialist, Communist and Gaullist—and by a simple process of elimination the CIA wound up allying itself with the Socialists.

"While General DeGaulle was too independent for American tastes, Socialist leaders were rapidly losing political ground to the Communists and thus were willing to collaborate with the CIA."[280]

That Angleton and the CIA would be actively working against DeGaulle is intriguing, particularly in light of further evidence we shall examine in Chapter 12, Chapter 15 and Chapter 16 which ties the CIA and its allies in Israel to joint operations against DeGaulle. It was from this same sphere of intrigue, as we shall see, that the JFK assassination evolved.

## THE NOSENKO AFFAIR: PLACING BLAME

After John F. Kennedy was killed, it was Angleton who emerged as the CIA's "overseer" of the Warren Commission investigation into the assassination of Kennedy. In fact, as we shall see in Chapter 16, Angleton maneuvered himself into this position. JFK assassination researcher Peter Dale Scott has written of what he called "the recurring presence of Angleton in the background of the Warren Commission investigation."[281] Indeed, Angleton, Israel's point man at the CIA, was well-placed to help cover up the Middle East state's central positioning in the conspiracy—and did.

It was Angleton who emerged in the period of the Warren Commission investigation as the leading CIA critic of Russian Soviet defector Yuri Nosenko. It was Nosenko, who defected to the United States in 1964, who claimed to have been the KGB's case officer who handled Lee Harvey Oswald during Oswald's sojourn in Russia (presumably as a defector.)

Nosenko's most provocative claim was that, contrary to some suspicions—and allegations—the Soviet KGB had absolutely nothing to do with the assassination of John F. Kennedy. Thus, those such as Israel's man at the CIA, Angleton, who wanted to hang the blame on the KGB for the president's murder, had what appeared to be a *bona fide* Soviet defector on their hands whose claims ran contrary to the propaganda line they sought to promote.

Angleton was Nosenko's loudest and most vociferous accuser, determined to prove Nosenko a liar. Angleton subjected Nosenko to 1,277 days of torture, questioning and deprivation, but Nosenko stuck to his story.

Angleton was clearly determined to disprove the one man who was clearly well-informed enough about the Soviet KGB to dispute the claim that the Soviets were behind the JFK assassination. Eliminating the Soviets as a suspect would, of course, shift suspicion elsewhere.

Looking elsewhere for those with not only the means and the opportunity—but also the motive—to kill John F. Kennedy would have, of course, pointed in the direction of Angleton's own CIA and its allies in the Israeli Mossad. In Chapter 16 we shall see how Angleton did indeed play a key role in the JFK assassination cover-up.

## A HOUSE OF CARDS

Revelation of either a CIA role or an Israeli role in the murder of JFK would have inevitably destroyed not only America's relationship with Israel, but it would have brought the international house of joint CIA-Mossad-Lansky Crime Syndicate conspiracies tumbling down.

And James Jesus Angleton, as the CIA's intimate liaison with Israel, would have been destroyed in the process. Likewise with his CIA patrons, Allen Dulles and Richard Helms.

(In Chapter 16 we shall review the activities of Angleton and Richard Helms further, particularly as they relate to the cover-up of the truth about the JFK assassination conspiracy..

(In Chapter 18 we shall see how Helms' close relationship with the Iranian secret police, SAVAK—created jointly by the CIA and the Mossad—tie Helms himself even further into the realm of conspiracy in the continuing cover-up of the JFK assassination.)

Angleton's "chief patron" Richard Helms left the CIA in 1973. This was the beginning of the end of the CIA career of James Jesus Angleton. Angleton himself was fired from the CIA on December 20, 1974. Revelations about Angleton's involvement in the CIA's domestic spying and other covert activities on American soil were too much for even the CIA to handle.

In his remaining years, Angleton habitually met with Washington reporters, feeding them tidbits, stroking them with information, convincing them all that they were getting "the inside story"—particularly in regard to the matter of the JFK assassination.

## FANTASY IN BOOK FORM

The ultimate parlay of Angleton's Kennedy assassination disinformation appeared in Edward Jay Epstein's book, *Legend: The Secret World of Lee Harvey Oswald* (published in 1978).

Epstein, a Warren Commission "critic" who has never been held in high regard by more sturdy critics of the commission, first came to prominence as the author of *Inquest*, a book-length study of the commission, originally written as his master's thesis at Yale University, long a recruiting ground for the CIA.

It was not until some years later, however, that Epstein came forth with *Legend*. As pointed out, however, by assassination researcher, Carl

Oglesby, it was Angleton who was "Epstein's chief source for the narrative unfolded" [282] in *Legend*.

Epstein's book presented the thesis that Oswald had been recruited by the Soviet KGB during his Marine service. Later KGB asset Oswald killed JFK, but not necessarily on the Kremlin's orders. Evidently, we are led to assume, Oswald got out of control.

Oswald's KGB connection, according to Epstein, was subsequently covered up by a Soviet mole in the CIA and then the FBI's legendary communist hunter, J. Edgar Hoover, helped in the cover-up, for reasons of his own—a fanciful story indeed. Whatever the case, it was Angleton who was Epstein's most important source of "inside" information in the weaving of this particular "legend." And interestingly enough, it was the controlled media which had otherwise scoffed at JFK conspiracy allegations that responded so favorably to this "new" conspiracy story.

As Carl Oglesby noted at the time *Legend* was published: "*Time* called Epstein 'a careful, academic researcher' and said his evidence that Oswald was a Soviet spy was 'strong.' *The New York Times Review of Books* called it "fascinating, alarming and perhaps enormously significant' and praised its 'explosive qualities.' The normally chaste Wilfred Sheed swallowed the whole Angleton kaboodle and chimed in on his own that 'Cuba itself seems the most likely conspirator' with Oswald. 'This one," he concluded, 'is a beauty.'"[283]

(And as we shall see in Chapter 17, the controlled media's own extensive links with Israel and its lobby in America, particularly the Lansky Syndicate-funded Anti-Defamation League [ADL] of B'nai B'rith, accounts for the media's desire to place the blame for the JFK assassination elsewhere, other than on Angleton's CIA and his allies in Israel.)

## FOOLED BY A FALSE FLAG

Interestingly, many American conservatives (who were certainly no admirers of the Kennedy administration) fell for the Angleton-sponsored fantasy that the KGB was behind the JFK assassination.

They wanted, more than anything perhaps, to believe that a communist had killed JFK. It was wholly in line with their anti-communist worldview and tailor-made for those who wanted to wave the proverbial "red flag." (This red flag, as we shall see in these pages, however, was, in fact, yet another Israeli false flag.)

Noting the conservative outcry that "a communist killed JFK," Peter Dale Scott has written of "the loud and irresponsible campaign of the American Security Council, the largest p.r. lobby for the military-industrial complex, to support the intelligence-fed claim that a KGB assassin 'had been trained at an assassin's school in the USSR for assignment later on the North American continent.'"[284]

Since the publication of the second edition of *Final Judgment*, a former publicist for the American Security Council has acknowledged to this author his own sincere belief that there had been a communist role in the

JFK assassination. He acknowledged that, for political reasons, he had indeed been a part of the effort to pin the assassination on the Soviets.

However, having read *Final Judgment* he has concluded that, as he put it, "I think you have pinned the tail on the donkey." In other words, that he now believed that the Israeli Mossad was indeed the prime mover behind the JFK assassination. "It was an angle that I never even conceived possible—until now," he said.

There is no question but that conservative elements did indeed stress the "communist" angle in the JFK assassination following the president's murder—for very obvious political motivations.

One prominent "right wing" journalist of the time, Revilo P. Oliver— then a key figure in the John Birch Society—was actually called before the Warren Commission to elaborate on his controversial and widely-publicized theory that the Soviets had JFK executed because he [JFK] was not doing enough to advance the international communist conspiracy.

However, shortly before his death in 1994 Oliver told associates that had he not been so ill, he would have relished the opportunity to write a favorable review of *Final Judgment* which had just been released in its first edition earlier in the year. Oliver himself evidently realized that he, too, had been taken in by the Angleton-inspired myth.

Needless to say, however, the myth that the Soviets were somehow involved in the JFK assassination was an ideal cover story and one that James J. Angleton was very much the prime mover behind.

### 'A MANSION HAS MANY ROOMS'

All of this is interesting and illustrates the lengths to which Angleton would go in order to fabricate a story targeting his enemies for the blame— and clearing his friends. However, Angleton's most provocative and widely known statement, often presumed to be in reference to the JFK assassination—came when he was quoted in *The New York Times* —two days after he was fired from the CIA by then-Director William Colby.

Angleton's cryptic remark was as follows: "A mansion has many rooms. I'm not privy to who struck John." [285] Angleton, however, insisted that the reference had nothing to do with the JFK assassination.

Angleton died a broken man on May 11, 1987—driven out of the CIA to which he had devoted his lifetime. Angleton was correct: "A mansion has many rooms." There was yet another secret room—so to speak—a shadowy intelligence operation working closely with Organized Crime and the CIA in a wide variety of ventures both in the United States and around the globe: James Jesus Angleton's beloved allies in Israel's Mossad.

## Chapter Nine
## A Little Unpleasantness:
## JFK's War With Israel's Allies at the CIA

**Just six weeks before John F. Kennedy was shot, a top administration official warned that a CIA-orchestrated coup in America was a fearful possibility. The CIA—like its allies in Israel— had good reason (in its own perception) to want to see JFK removed from the White House and replaced with Lyndon B. Johnson. JFK's battle with the CIA over the Bay of Pigs debacle was just the beginning. JFK was—by the last days of his presidency—not only fighting the CIA's efforts to involve the United States ever more deeply in Southeast Asia, but he was also moving toward dismantling the CIA entirely. The CIA's very existence was in danger.**

In 1972 the *Washington Observer* newsletter published perhaps what was one of the first hints—in print—that the Kennedy family itself suspected that the CIA had a hand in the assassination of John F. Kennedy.

According to the *Observer*, "Back in 1963, shortly after President Kennedy's assassination, Robert F. Kennedy, while he was still Attorney General, conducted his own private investigation, which ran parallel with the official inquiry into the assassination conducted by the Warren Commission. Kennedy's investigation featured trips to this country by an Inspector Hamilton, former Chief Inspector of Scotland Yard. Hamilton, an old friend of Joseph P. Kennedy, had been retained by the attorney general to help unravel the real truth about the murder of JFK.

"After long conferring with the members of the Kennedy family and making a few discreet soundings with his own contacts, Hamilton zeroed on the fact that the assassination of John Kennedy had occurred very shortly after his brother Bobby had made some preliminary moves for direct personal control of the CIA, whose leadership he blamed for the Bay of Pigs fiasco.

"Hamilton, following the *cui bono* ("whom does it benefit?") reasoning, reached the conclusion that Bobby's move to seize control of the CIA had something to do with the murder of his elder brother."[286]

### THE BAY OF PIGS

That the Bay of Pigs debacle was a major bone of contention between the Kennedy brothers and the CIA is now very much a recognized part of history. The bitterness that developed between JFK and the CIA over the failed attempt to invade Castro's Cuba was a serious point of conflict between the president and the intelligence agency. The Bay of Pigs and its aftermath was a sore spot between Kennedy and the CIA, but not the last. It did, however, set in motion events leading to the final showdown between JFK and the CIA, what, in fact, was ultimately the assassination of the American president.

The family biographers of Chicago Mafia boss, Sam Giancana, who participated in the infamous CIA-Organized Crime plots against Fidel Castro (which we will examine in more detail in Chapter 11) report that Giancana was very much aware that the CIA was unhappy with the Kennedys. "Within the CIA, the dismay at having been betrayed by both the President and attorney general, as well as the President's open promise to dismantle the intelligence agency's power, soon turned to hatred, creating a ripple effect that would blacken the moods of the men [Giancana] dealt with in his covert operations. These men expressed their outrage at the Bay of Pigs operation along with their fear that Kennedy now posed a very real threat to the CIA's continued autonomy, perhaps its very existence." [287]

## KENNEDY MOVES AGAINST THE CIA

In his best-selling, *Plausible Denial*, in which he pinpoints the CIA's role in the JFK assassination conspiracy, veteran JFK assassination investigator Mark Lane commented on the CIA's move against the president:

"If the CIA operatives, officers, and former officers believed that the defense of their Agency and their nation required the elimination of President Kennedy because he was about to dismantle their organization, one could comprehend, while neither accepting nor condoning their viewpoint, that their concept of self-defense required them to use deadly force. Most relevant, therefore, is not what Kennedy was or was not about to do vis-a-vis the CIA, but what the leaders of the Agency believed he might do.

"John F. Kennedy made it clear that he planned to destroy the CIA. *The New York Times* reported on April 25, 1966, under a subheadline, 'Kennedy's Bitterness,' that 'as the enormity of the Bay of Pigs disaster came home to him, [Kennedy] said to one of the highest officials of his Administration that he wanted 'to splinter the CIA in a thousand pieces and scatter it to the winds.'

"He clearly was not suggesting a modest legislative proposal or executive order to modify or reform the organization. The total destruction of the Agency was his apparent objective." [288]

## CONTROLLING THE CIA

Lane points out that Kennedy's preliminary actions against the CIA had already been set in motion and that the president was very clearly moving toward ultimate evisceration of the agency.

"[Kennedy] dealt with the CIA through the implementation of a three-point emergency program designed to control the agency. He fired its most culpable and powerful leaders, he appointed a high-level committee, the Cuban study group, to investigate the misdeeds of the organization so that he might determine what additional short-range limitations were required and, in the interim, he dramatically reduced the powers and jurisdiction of the Agency and established strict limits as to its future actions through National Security Action memoranda."

"Kennedy then sought to control the Agency by sharply reducing its ability to act in the future through National Security Action Memoranda 55, 56 and 57. These documents, in theory, eliminated the ability of the CIA to wage war. The CIA would not be permitted to initiate any operation requiring greater firepower than that generated by handguns." [289]

That all of these actions upset the CIA and its allies is undoubted. One man on the scene at the time was Col. L. Fletcher Prouty, who served as liaison between the Defense Department and the CIA during the relevant period.

According to Prouty, "Nothing I had ever been involved in in my entire career had created such an uproar. NSAM 55 stripped the CIA of its cherished covert operations role, except for small actions. It was an explosive document. The military-industrial complex was not pleased." [290]

## THE CIA AND VIETNAM

However, Kennedy's conflict with the CIA went well beyond the issue of Cuba. The burgeoning issue of U.S. involvement in Southeast Asia had positioned the president at odds with the CIA even further.

By late 1963 JFK's conflict with the CIA was in full force and although it was not the subject of heated public discussion, the word was leaking out through official and un-official channels that there was something afoot at the highest levels.

On October 3, 1963, the dean of America's newspaper columnists, Arthur Krock, was writing frankly in the *New York Times* of Kennedy's war with the CIA—a war which was intensifying over the issue of Vietnam. Krock's front page article, in fact, was entitled, "The Intra-Administration War in Vietnam."

## KENNEDY'S TRUSTED CONDUIT

But what is so astounding about the column is that Krock quoted a high-level administration source as having suggested that if there were ever a *coup d'etat* in the United States, one might expect that it would be the CIA which was responsible—this just weeks before JFK was murdered.

The significance of this astounding column is that it was Arthur Krock who affixed his name to this explosive report: Krock was a longtime close friend and confidant of the Kennedy family and had even ghost-written several published works on behalf of the president's father, Ambassador Joseph P. Kennedy.

The columnist was a key Kennedy link in press circles and would have been the first and foremost choice of President Kennedy if JFK had wished to utilize the press to bring his conflict with the CIA into the public arena. As Mark Lane so aptly described the column: "This was John F. Kennedy sending out a message to the American people through his trusted conduit Arthur Krock." [291]

This column remained forgotten in the wake of the president's assassination, but it was in 1992 that Lane surfaced the prophetic warning and began bringing it to the attention of American audiences who now had a renewed interest in the Kennedy assassination.

## OUT OF CONTROL

Lane described the column: "Krock pointed out that John F. Kennedy had gone to war against the CIA. He concluded that Kennedy no longer could control the CIA.

"The columnist stated that President Kennedy sent Henry Cabot Lodge, his Ambassador to Vietnam, with orders to the CIA on two separate occasions and in both cases the CIA ignored those orders, saying that it was different from what the agency thought should be done. In other words, the CIA had decided that it—not the president—would make the decisions as to how American foreign policy should be conducted." [292]

Lane pointed out that a source for Krock's column was a report filed for the Scripps-Howard newspapers by foreign correspondent Richard Starnes who had interviewed a number of high-ranking administration officials and others who expressed their concern about the CIA's intransigence.

## A CIA-SPONSORED COUP D'ETAT?

According to Krock's column: "Among the views attributed to United States officials on the scene, including one described as a "very high American official . . . who has spent much of his life in the service of democracy . . . are the following:

The CIA's growth was "likened to a malignancy" which the "very high official was not sure even the White House could control . . . any longer."

"If the United States ever experiences [an attempt at a *coup* to overthrow the Government] it will come from the CIA and not the Pentagon." The agency "represents a tremendous power and total unaccountability to anyone."

"Whatever else these passages disclose, they most certainly establish that representatives of other Executive branches have expanded their war against the CIA from the inner government councils to the American people via the press.

"And published simultaneously are details of the agency's operations in Vietnam that can come only from the same critical official sources. This is disorderly government. And the longer the President tolerates it—the period already is considerable—the greater the real war against the Vietcong and the impression of a very indecisive Administration in Washington.

"The CIA may be guilty as charged. Since it cannot, or at any rate will not, openly defend its record in Vietnam or defend it by the same confidential press 'briefings' employed by its critics, the public is not in a position to judge. Nor to this department, which sought and failed to get even the outlines of the agency's case in rebuttal.

"But Mr. Kennedy will have to make a judgment if the spectacle of war within the Executive branch is to be ended and the effective functioning of the CIA preserved. And when he makes this judgment, hopefully he also will make it public, as well as the appraisal of fault on which it is based.

"Doubtless recommendations as to what his judgement should be were made to him today by Secretary of Defense McNamara and General Taylor on their return from their fact-finding expedition into the embattled official jungle in Saigon." [293]

It is ironic, indeed, that Krock's column concluded with its reference to the trip by McNamara and Taylor to Southeast Asia.

For, as Col. Fletcher Prouty points out, upon their return they "reported to the President that it looked to them, after their visit to Saigon, as though things could be put under control and that we would be able to withdraw all personnel [from Vietnam] by the end of 1965.

"Now we can see why they chose that date," comments Prouty. "This was the date the President had used in his own discussions with his closest advisers. They all knew that he planned to announce a pullout once he had been re-elected." [294]

It was soon thereafter, however, that John F. Kennedy was indeed gone from the scene and the president's plans for withdrawal from Vietnam, so carefully drawn, were now being reversed by the new President.

## THE CIA PREVAILS

In his book *Plausible Denial,* Mark Lane summarizes the events which occurred:

"Just four days after the death of President Kennedy, Lyndon Johnson signed NSAM 273 that began to reverse the policy of withdrawal from Vietnam and signified the beginning of the escalation of the conflict. The CIA had prevailed. The effort in Southeast Asia was to become a massive land-based war."

"During March, 1964, Johnson signed NSAM 288 that repudiated Kennedy's plan to end the U.S. military participation in the war that year. In the months that followed, Johnson increased the military commitment from under 20,000 troops to approximately a quarter of a million." [295]

" Years later . . . after the deaths of more than 50,000 Americans and more than a million Vietnamese, Laotians, and Cambodians, the war finally ended with the military defeat of the United States. "[296]

However, as we have seen in Chapter 6, the war in Vietnam proved a boon to the CIA's allies in Israel, allowing the Middle East state to flex its muscles in the region.

And in Chapter 12 we shall see that a joint CIA-Meyer Lansky Crime Syndicate venture in the international drug racket out of Southeast Asia proved so very profitable, conducted under military cover in the midst of U.S. involvement in Vietnam.

## THE CIA AND THE JFK ASSASSINATION

It was not until the release of *Plausible Denial* that the extent of the CIA's involvement in the JFK assassination was fully outlined. Suspicion of the CIA's complicity was commonplace over the years, but Lane's book proved the matter once and for all.

And, significantly, his book was a written summation of a libel trial in Miami some years previously in which the jury had concluded that the CIA had indeed been involved in the JFK assassination conspiracy and cover-up.

## E. HOWARD HUNT

The circumstances of how the trial came about are interesting. It was in 1978, that a Washington-based weekly newspaper, *The Spotlight*, published an article by former high-ranking CIA official Victor Marchetti which alleged the CIA intended to frame longtime CIA operative E. Howard Hunt for involvement in the Kennedy assassination.

Hunt, of course, was the CIA's chief political liaison with the anti-Castro Cuban community during the period leading up to the JFK assassination and who had, subsequently, over the years, been mentioned as a suspect in the assassination conspiracy.

(Hunt had organized, on the CIA's behalf, several anti-Castro Cuban groups, including the Revolutionary Democratic Front. Hunt's Cuban point man in the RDF, Antonio de Varona, in fact, personally received funding for the RDF from Meyer Lansky himself.) [297]

Marchetti's article suggested that there was then so much growing suspicion that the CIA had been involved in the JFK assassination that the CIA had decided that it would sacrifice Hunt and say that Hunt was a "renegade" operative involved in the president's assassination.

## HUNT A FREE-LANCE OPERATIVE?

However, according to Marchetti, the CIA intended to say that Hunt and his co-conspirators had been operating independently—that the CIA as an institution had not been part of the conspiracy.

Although the editors of *The Spotlight* felt Marchetti's article served, if anything, as an advance warning to Hunt about what his former employers had in mind, the ex-CIA man decided to sue, even though he ultimately admitted under oath that he believed *The Spotlight*'s story seemed plausible.

When the case finally went to trial in federal court in Miami, the newspaper suffered a devastating loss. The jury found in favor of Hunt and ordered *The Spotlight* to pay $650,000 in damages.

Fortunately—for *The Spotlight*—an error in the trial judge's instructions to the jury gave the populist weekly grounds for an appeal. When the case was successfully appealed and ordered for retrial, Mark Lane—an attorney—stepped in for the defense.

Among the big names deposed during the Hunt case were: former CIA Director Richard Helms; former CIA Director Stansfield Turner; former CIA chief for the Western Hemisphere David Phillips; and former CIA and FBI man (and Watergate celebrity) G. Gordon Liddy.

The most damning evidence against Hunt came, however, when attorney Lane presented the deposition of former CIA operative Marita Lorenz to the court.

## HUNT & RUBY IN DALLAS

Miss Lorenz testified that one day prior to the president's assassination she arrived in Dallas (traveling from a CIA "safe house" in Miami) in a two-car caravan.

Accompanying Miss Lorenz on what she described as a secret mission were several CIA operatives who were armed with telescopic rifles. According to Miss Lorenz she had not been apprised of the purpose of the mission.

Upon arrival in Dallas, according to Miss Lorenz, they met with not only E. Howard Hunt, who was functioning as the CIA operatives' paymaster, but also nightclub operator Jack Ruby who later executed the president's alleged assassin, Lee Harvey Oswald.

When Hunt himself took the stand, attorney Lane, while questioning Hunt, pointed out numerous inconsistencies in Hunt's testimony.

Hunt himself had told several stories, over the years, about where he had been on the day the president was assassinated.

It was Miss Lorenz' testimony, however, that convinced the jury that the CIA had been involved in the Kennedy assassination. The jury found in favor of *The Spotlight* and dismissed Hunt's claim.

## THE JURY'S VERDICT

Leslie Armstrong, a Miami resident who was jury forewoman in the case, issued a statement in conjunction with the release of Lane's written account of the trial:

"Mr. Lane was asking us [the jury] to do something very difficult. He was asking us to believe John Kennedy had been killed by our own government. Yet when we examined the evidence closely, we were compelled to conclude that the CIA had indeed killed President Kennedy."[298]

In *Plausible Denial* Lane recounts this exciting trial and demonstrates other compelling evidence that his own research has uncovered which proves that the CIA did indeed have a hand in the president's assassination and its cover-up.

(In Chapter 16 we shall examine the case of Hunt in further detail, examining evidence which points further toward the involvement of Israel and its CIA allies in the JFK assassination and the subsequent cover-up.)

## THE NOVO BROTHERS

In an interview, Lane described how Miss Lorenz had gone even further in her testimony, naming the names of other CIA operatives who had been in the two-car caravan in which she travelled from Miami to Dallas.

According to Lane, "Before Miss Lorenz testified, I asked her, 'Will you tell me the names of the people who traveled with you in that two-car caravan?'

"She said that she wouldn't name names. 'That could get me killed,' she said. 'Don't ask me that question. I want you to promise me that you won't ask me that question.' However, " according to Lane, "Mr. Hunt's lawyer asked her that question and she answered it, to my surprise. She said that it was the Novo brothers."

According to Lane, "The Novo brothers—Guillermo and Ignacio—are very interesting characters. I've done some research on them.

"I can assure you," said Lane, "that the first time I heard their name connected with the Kennedy assassination was when Miss Lorenz gave their names to Hunt's lawyer. She had not told me anything before that.

"After her testimony to Hunt's lawyer, I asked Miss Lorenz, 'Why did you tell them?' She said—referring to Hunt, the CIA and his lawyers—'If they are so dumb as to ask me that question, then it is not my fault if I give them the answer. It's on their heads," said Miss Lorenz. "If you had asked me, it would have been a different story. However, if the CIA—through Hunt and his lawyers—asked that question, then it's on the record and it's their fault, not mine.'

## THE HUNT-BUCKLEY CONNECTION

"These Novo brothers that Miss Lorenz named have been involved in a series of intelligence related crimes. They were involved in the murder in Washington, D.C. in 1976 of former Chilean government official Orlando Letelier and Ronnie Moffit, a woman who was with him. A man named Michael Townley who was connected with the Chilean secret police was involved in planning the Letelier murder with the Novo brothers. When Townley was indicted, he testified against the Novos.

"Townley was questioned by the FBI who asked Townley to show them where in New York City he had his first meeting with the Novos. Townley pointed out a building at 500 Fifth Avenue and showed the FBI the office on the 41st floor where the first meeting was held."[299]

According to Lane, research indicates that the meeting was held in the office of then-U.S. Sen. James Buckley (C-N.Y.). Now a federal judge on the U.S. District Court of Appeals for the District of Columbia, Buckley is the brother of former CIA operative and conservative fortnightly*National Review* founder William F. Buckley, Jr.

(E. Howard Hunt was William F. Buckley's immediate superior in the CIA during the period that the two served together in the CIA in Mexico for nine months in the period of 1951-52. Hunt himself is also believed to have been operating as the CIA's station chief in Mexico City during the months prior to the JFK assassination—a point which, as we shall see in Chapter 16, is quite significant.)

According to Lane, "The testimony by Townley made reference to a William Sampol who worked in James Buckley's office. Sampol was a cousin of the Novo brothers."[300]

## GEORGE BUSH

Lane points out that the murder of Letelier took place during the time that George Bush was director of the CIA: "There is evidence that Bush was given information that indicated that the Chilean government was responsible for the murder of Letelier. However, Bush gave information to selected friends in the news media the story that Letelier was killed by his own supporters who wanted to make him [Letelier] a martyr.

According to Lane, "It was William F. Buckley, Jr who took that story from Bush and ran with it. The media followed Buckley's lead, but the story turned out not to be true." (In Chapter 20, as we shall see, it was George Bush who, in many ways, had very close connections to a number of the key players in the strange netherworld of international intelligence as it is linked to the JFK assassination.)

As Lane points out: "The Novos were both convicted of the Letelier murder and sentenced to prison. These are the brothers that Marita Lorenz testified were in the two-car caravan of killers traveling from Miami to Dallas for the purpose of assassinating President Kennedy."[301]

## MULTIPLE MOSSAD CONNECTIONS

Evidence now available from former Mossad operative Victor Ostrovsky suggests that Israel's Mossad, in fact, was indirectly connected with the Letelier assassination for which the Novo brothers (implicated in the JFK assassination) were convicted.

(It was Ostrovsky, coincidentally enough, whom we learned in Chapter 2, had exposed a Mossad plot to assassinate the former director of the CIA, George Bush, after Bush, serving as U.S. President, ran afoul of Israel.)

According to Ostrovsky, commenting on the Letelier murder: "Nobody pointed the finger at the Mossad. And while the Mossad had no direct involvement in the hit ordered by Chilean DINA [secret police] Chief Manuel Contreras Sepulveda, it had played a significant indirect role in the execution through a secret deal with Contreras to buy a French-made Exocet surface-to-surface naval missile from Chile.

"The death squad didn't use Mossad personnel in killing Letelier but they certainly used Mossad know-how, taught to them as part of the deal Contreras made to supply the missile."[302]

It was the Novo brothers, however, who took the fall and served time in prison. No Mossad agents, however, were charged with the crime.

It is interesting to note, nonetheless, that Michael Townley himself had an interesting further connections with Israel.

His wife, Ines, although a Chilean Christian, had spent time on an Israeli Kibbutz with her first husband, and maintained a long-standing "devotion to the cause of Israel." [303] Part of Townley's deal with the federal prosecutors, in the case of the Novo brothers, involved a plea bargain in which his wife received immunity from prosecution, although she had been implicated in various terrorist enterprises alongside her husband. [304]

However, Townley's other connection with Israel is far more significant, particularly in the context of our discussion of his connection with the Cuban Americans who have been implicated in the JFK assassination.

During Townley's long career as an international adventurer, he served—apparently during the period from 1961-1966—as a mutual funds salesman for financier Bernard Cornfeld's Investors' Overseas Service (IOS) [305] It was in Chapter 7 that we first came across the IOS, in examining the relationship of Meyer Lansky's Organized Crime Syndicate to the Israeli Mossad-linked Banque De Credit International (BCI).

## TIBOR ROSENBAUM'S PROTEGE

During the criminal trial in 1970 of one of Lansky's Florida lieutenants, Alvin Malnik it was publicly revealed that one of the key money laundering channels for the illegal proceeds of Lansky's narcotics, vice and gambling rackets was BCI, the brainchild of the Israeli Mossad's former Director-General for Finance and Supply, Tibor Rosenbaum.

Rosenbaum's BCI received its Lansky Crime Syndicate cash flow mainly through the Lansky-controlled Bank of World Commerce in Nassau, Bahamas. The middleman was a young Swiss, Sylvain Ferdmann, a courier for Lansky.

Ferdmann was not only an official of Rosenbaum's bank, and an associate of the Bank of World Commerce (controlled by Lansky's longtime crony, John Pullman) but—like Michael Townley himself—also a legman for Investors Overseas Services (IOS).

Townley's employer, Cornfeld, in fact, was initially sponsored by Rosenbaum who had emerged as a major money launderer for Lansky's global drug-trafficking. Millions in small bills were transferred from Lansky's casinos, often masked as Israeli Bond sales and contributions to Jewish philanthropies through BCI and the IOS.

It is thus interesting, to say the least, that Michael Townley, with his Israeli Mossad connections during not only the period of the JFK assassination but also during his participation in the Letelier murder, should be associated with the Novo brothers who have been implicated in both crimes themselves.

That former New York Senator James Buckley's office should have, perhaps by coincidence, served as the meeting place where the Letelier assassination was planned is also interesting.

As we've noted already, E. Howard Hunt (himself implicated in the JFK assassination) and Buckley's brother, publisher (and Hunt's ex-CIA support staffer) William F. Buckley, Jr. were longtime friends stemming from their CIA days.

Hunt's own longtime intrigue with the Cuban American community in anti-Castro activities as the CIA's chief liaison with the Cubans, of course, has long been widely noted.

## THE BUCKLEY-ISRAELI CONNECTION

However, what is not so widely known is that the Buckley family— including brothers James and William—had substantive links to Israel through their various family oil enterprises. In 1971 the *Washington Observer* newsletter shed some interesting light on the Buckley family oil concessions in Israel, established by Buckley's father.

Buckley, Sr. incorporated Pan-Israel Oil Co (headquartered in Jerusalem) with Buckley, Sr. as president. Directors of the company included several Israelis. Simultaneously, Israel-Mediterranean Petroleum, Inc. was incorporated under the laws of Panama. The principal offices of the firm were in Jerusalem at the same address where Pan-Israel Oil Co. was located. James L. Buckley was one of the vice presidents. All of the voting stock for the two companies was held in the voting trust. No members of the Buckley family, however, held votes. The voting trustees had Jewish names.

Pan-Israel and and Israel-Mediterranean jointly owned eight petroleum licenses, all located in Israel. The two companies also owned Mana Oil Distributors and Tri-Continent Drilling Co., a subsidiary of the Pantepec Oil Company (later absorbed by Pantepec International Petroleum, Ltd.).

President of PIP, Ltd. was John W. Buckley who, with his brother James L. Buckley, served on the board of directors. These companies, together conducted global operations with oil properties in Australia, South America, Canada, Libya, Spanish Sahara, the Philippines and Israel.[306]

That the Hunt- and CIA-linked Buckley family should also be so closely tied to the Novo brothers, implicated in both the JFK and Orlando Letelier assassinations is intriguing.

More so, perhaps, because the Novo brothers' associate in the Letelier assassination—at least—was himself intimately tied to the Meyer Lansky Organized Crime Syndicate and an Israeli Mossad-sponsored money laundering operation.

Incredibly enough, however, there is yet another bizarre Buckley family link to a key player in the strange world of JFK's alleged assassin, Lee Harvey Oswald, and the JFK assassination conspiracy.

## THE BUCKLEY-DeMOHRENSCHILDT CONNECTION

This link came in the person of the colorful Russian nobleman, George DeMohrenschildt, who befriended Oswald upon the young American's return from exile (some would say "CIA service") in the Soviet Union.

DeMohrenschildt, who is reputed to have worked for various international intelligence agencies, had a long-standing relationship with the CIA, dating back to the days of the CIA's predecessor, the Office of Strategic Services (OSS), in which, incidentally, E. Howard Hunt himself had served. [307]

The European nobleman, however, travelled around the globe primarily in his capacity as an oil engineer. It was in this guise that he came into contact with the Buckley family. As early as 1945 DeMohrenschildt worked directly under Warren Smith, then the president of the Pantepec Oil Co., the Buckley family's Mexican oil company, established in 1914. DeMohrenschildt and Smith eventually formed the Cuban-Venezuelan Oil Trust Co. The Buckley Family's Pantepec, interestingly enough, had, by that time, already shifted its focus to Venezuela. [308]

Despite all these more tenuous Buckley links, there is, however, firm evidence of a link between the Buckleys and DeMohrenschildt. It turns out that in DeMohrenschildt's address book is listed one "Buckley, W.F."[309] Another interesting connection indeed.

### DeMOHRENSCHILDT AND HUNT

DeMohrenschildt's career also seems to have intersected on a regular basis with that of William F. Buckley, Jr.'s friend and CIA mentor, E. Howard Hunt.

Both Hunt and DeMohrenschildt had worked for the Agency for International Development (AID); Hunt for the Economic Cooperation Administration (ECA), a subsidiary of AID and DeMohrenschildt in the late 1950's for the International Cooperation Administration, the AID subsidiary which was the successor to the ECA.

Hunt and DeMohrenschildt also both popped up in Cuba in 1956 in the stormy period before Fidel Castro pushed the Meyer Lansky Organized Crime Syndicate off the island. While DeMohrenschildt said later that he was there on oil business, Hunt was attending a meeting of CIA station chiefs from the Caribbean and Central American regions.

In 1960 both Hunt and DeMohrenschildt also appeared in Guatemala when troops were being trained there for what was ultimately to be the Bay of Pigs debacle, initially intended for the purpose of toppling Castro. DeMohrenschildt said that he and his wife were on a walking tour of Central America. Hunt, however, was serving as the CIA's liaison with anti-Castro Cuban groups. [310]

By 1963, however, DeMohrenschildt had settled in Dallas and had befriended Lee Harvey Oswald who, of course, by this time, was mixing easily with the anti-Castro Cuban elements that were directly under the thumb of the CIA's chief liaison with those forces—E. Howard Hunt.

The role of DeMohrenschildt in the JFK assassination conspiracy will probably never be fully known.

In the end, the globe-hopping nobleman died (ostensibly by his own hand) on the morning of March 29, 1977 just shortly before he was scheduled to meet with an investigator of the House Select Committee on

Assassinations. DeMohrenschildt's wife, in fact, believed that her husband's suicide had somehow been induced.

## THE ANGLETON-ISRAEL-CIA CONNECTION

Whatever the case, there is yet another bizarre coincidence, DeMohrenschildt had just met—before his death—with author Edward Jay Epstein. In Chapter 8, as we have seen, it was Epstein who was the primary literary promoter of the theory that Lee Harvey Oswald was under Soviet influence when he assassinated John F. Kennedy. The primary source for Epstein's theory was Israel's ally at the CIA, James Jesus Angleton.

## THE CIA AND THE OAS

It was during the same period of JFK's war with the CIA that the CIA was actively engaged in an effort to topple French President Charles DeGaulle, lending aid and support to the Israeli-backed French Secret Army Organization (OAS) that was fighting DeGaulle's decision to grant independence to Algeria.

Although the Church Senate Committee hearings on clandestine CIA activities later concluded that there had been no CIA involvement with the OAS,[311] there is very strong evidence to the contrary.

General Maurice Challe, former commander in chief of French forces in Algeria and leader of the military revolt against DeGaulle in April of 1961, emerged as one of the key figures in the OAS. Although Challe insisted that he "'had no contact personally with any foreign countries' and that in fact he had deliberately avoided all such contacts as as not to incur any possible charge of having been brought in on foreign bayonets.

"Nevertheless," according to historian Alistair Horne, "some of [Challe's] subordinates appear to have made informal, and highly tentative, soundings with representatives of various countries that might be considered sympathetic, among them Portugal, Spain, Israel and South Africa."[312]

"Rumors of clandestine United States involvement ran extremely strong in France. Undeniably, during his time at NATO headquarters the popular Challe did make firm friends of a number of high-ranking United States generals who made no secret of their aversion to what DeGaulle was doing to NATO, going so far—over a plethora of Scotch—as to express enthusiasm for anyone who might rid France of her turbulent president, or, at least, force him to change his tune."[313]

"There were also rumors that the CIA had promised Challe United States recognition if they succeeded—in order to keep the communists out of North Africa. Any hopes, however, that all this may have engendered in the bosom of the conspiracy were to be swiftly dashed when [John F. Kennedy's] Ambassador to Paris, General James M. Gavin, firmly assured DeGaulle that if any rebels attempted to land on French bases where there were American troops, these would at once open fire."[314]

There is further evidence that the CIA was engaged in intrigue with the OAS. According to historian Alexander Harrison, "In early December 1961, a 'Colonel Brown' of the CIA station in France requested a meeting with [OAS leader General Raoul] Salan. Brown offered Salan enough weaponry to equip an army of 50,000 men."[315]

Although some have speculated that the purported CIA operatives were not, in fact, really with the CIA, General Salan himself said, "I was sure they were serious, because they knew all the right people, and their credentials were perfect." In fact, in the end, some arms were indeed delivered.[316]

Interestingly enough, the CIA did have one liaison, at least, to the OAS. He was E. Howard Hunt, the agency's political handler for the anti-Castro Cuban exiles. In Chapter 15 and Chapter 16 we will examine Hunt's OAS connections further, particularly as they relate to the key players involved in the JFK assassination conspiracy.

That Israel and its allies in the CIA would be conspiring against Charles DeGaulle during the same period when they were likewise conspiring against John F. Kennedy, as we shall see, is quite significant indeed.

## THREE POWERFUL FORCES

All of these strange—perhaps not so strange—connections illustrate the never-ending cycle which continually links key players in the international intrigue between not only the CIA and the Israeli Mossad, but also the Meyer Lansky Organized Crime Syndicate—three powerful forces all of which desired the removal of John F. Kennedy from the White House.

Like Israel and the Lansky Syndicate, the CIA was, for all intents and purposes, an aggrandizing international power-unto-itself unwilling to have its influence curtailed by an independent-minded American president with an agenda of his own. Thus it was that the CIA entered into the JFK assassination conspiracy.

With John F. Kennedy now not only at odds with the Lansky Crime Syndicate and Israel, but also their collaborators in the CIA, the American president had arrayed against him a powerful alliance with not only the means and the motive, but also—as we now see—the opportunity to end his presidency.

## Chapter Ten

### Little Man's Little Man:
### Meyer Lansky & Carlos Marcello—
### Did the Mafia Kill JFK?

**Meyer Lansky's Louisiana front-man, Carlos Marcello, has become a favorite target for JFK assassination researchers who like to claim that "The Mafia Killed JFK."**

**The fact is that Marcello's most formidable chief accuser, G. Robert Blakey, staff director of the House Select Committee on Asssassinations, had been on the payroll of a key figure in the Meyer Lansky Organized Crime Syndicate.**

**Marcello was only one cog in the Lansky Syndicate. His key placement in New Orleans—scene of much of the pre-assassination planning—makes him the perfect fall guy. Marcello also had ties to Israel's allies in the CIA. There's a lot more to the Marcello story than meets the eye.**

It was Lee Harvard Oswald's pathetic cry, "I'm just a patsy," that has become immortalized. Ironically, though, one of the most widely alleged JFK assassination masterminds—New Orleans' widely-publicized supposed "crime boss"—might himself be able to make that same claim. We are speaking, of course, of the colorful Carlos Marcello—nicknamed "Little Man"—a sobriquet he happened to share with Meyer Lansky.

### BLAMING MARCELLO

One book, John W. Davis's *Mafia Kingfish: Carlos Marcello and the Asssassination of John F. Kennedy*, names Marcello as the likely mastermind of the JFK murder. Standing alone, with no further evidence such as that we have cited in the pages of *Final Judgment*, in this chapter and elsewhere, Davis' contention seems wholly reasonable. But, as we've said, his conclusions are not based on the totality of all the evidence available.

### DISTORTING THE TRUTH

David Scheim, writing in *Contract on America: The Mafia Murder of President John F. Kennedy*, likewise blames "the Mafia" for the JFK assassination and also points the finger at Carlos Marcello in particular. For whatever reason, however, Scheim is devoted to underplaying (even ignoring) the critical role of Meyer Lansky in the underworld.

In Scheim's view, Lansky was little more than a bit player—this in direct contradiction to even standard histories of organized crime which, by virtue of reality, are forced to recognize Lansky's particular influence.

Scheim, in fact, goes to great lengths to suggest that Lansky was of little consequence in the whole scheme of things. He writes: "The late syndicate financier Meyer Lansky could take no action without the approval of Mafia superiors."[317] This is simply not true in any sense whatsoever. That Scheim even suggests this indicates that he is determined to ignore the entire picture.

Scheim notes, incorrectly, that Lansky's alleged "Mafia superiors" kept him under constant surveillance through one Jimmy "Blue Eyes" Alo whom Scheim describes as a *"caporegime"* in the Genovese Mafia family out of New York.[318] Alo was indeed closely associated with Lansky, but, in fact, was not only a close personal friend, but also a working partner. He was not, contrary to Scheim's bizarre concoction, a Mafia handler of Meyer Lansky.

## CLAY SHAW AND THE CIA

Scheim's own determination to ignore the role of the intelligence community in the JFK assassination conspiracy—particularly that of the CIA—is also interesting. In his book Scheim goes to great lengths to portray New Orleans District Attorney Jim Garrison as a tool of the Mafia and an associate of Carlos Marcello. He also comes down hard on Garrison's investigation of international businessman Clay Shaw.

According to Scheim, "Equally bizarre was Garrison's prosecution of Clay Shaw, who became his prime culprit. A retired director of the New Orleans International Trade Mart, Shaw was a soft-spoken liberal who devoted most of his time to restoring homes in the Old French Quarter."[319] What Scheim fails to note—and what he could not miss inasmuch as he is self-portrayed as a longtime JFK assassination researcher—is that Shaw was, indeed, involved with the CIA.

## IGNORING THE FACTS

This was a fact well known among JFK assassination researchers at the time Scheim's book went to press. There is simply no rational excuse for Scheim's deliberate deletion of this critical fact.

Be that as it may, in Chapter 15 we shall examine Shaw's central positioning in the conspiracy that involved not only the CIA and the Mafia and the Meyer Lansky Organized Crime Syndicate, but also Israel's Mossad.

Obviously, in order to perpetuate the myth that "The Mafia Killed JFK," Scheim is forced to avoid the facts that damage his thesis. And this is precisely what he has done.

Scheim's own book (and the aforementioned work by John W. Davis) both rely heavily on a previously-released work, *The Plot to Kill the President: Organized Crime Assassinated JFK* by G. Robert Blakey and Richard N. Billings.

(Scheim's book, in fact, is hardly more than a re-write of much of the same material and, actually, constitutes little more than a history of the

Mafia, available in many standard sources. Scheim's book, all in all, fails miserably in its attempt to lay the blame anywhere for that matter.

(And in light of the facts that we are uncovering in the pages of *Final Judgment* it is probably worth noting that Scheim's publisher, Shapolsky Publishers, is an affiliate of an Israeli-owned company—a fact that could perhaps have something to do with the decision to promote a book pinning the assassination of JFK on "the Mafia.")

That Scheim and Davis relied upon the Blakey/Billings work is unfortunate, particularly since this book comes from what can only be charitably described as suspect sources.

Blakey, of course, was director of the House Assassinations Committee which concluded that there had probably been a conspiracy behind the president's assassination and that, more than likely, elements of the "Mafia" may have been been involved.

## SABOTAGING GARRISON

Richard Billings, who served alongside Blakey in the House Committee investigation, was no stranger to the JFK assassination conspiracy. In fact, Billings had been the *Life* magazine editor who led a team from his magazine to New Orleans ostensibly to collaborate with then District Attorney Jim Garrison in his investigation into the JFK murder.

Garrison notes, however, that *Life*, instead, did just the opposite. *Life* ran several major articles which linked Garrison to organized crime—to the Mafia—to Carlos Marcello, specifically, thereby discrediting Garrison to many who believed the tales.[320]

As a consequence when Blakey and Billings teamed up to write the book based on their experiences with the House Assassinations Committee, they reserved harsh criticism for Garrison and suggested that he was pointing the finger, wrongly, at the intelligence community and, in effect covering up for Marcello's involvement in the crime.

Billings, it also just happens, was an in-law of C. D. Jackson, the publisher of *Life* magazine whom investigative journalist Carl Bernstein has described as "[*Life* owner] Henry Luce's personal emissary to the CIA."[321] Billings also—perhaps not coincidentally—played a recurring role in *Life's* coverage of CIA-backed Cuban exile raids on Castro's Cuba.

## ORGANIZED CRIME 'EXPERT'

So it was that Blakey and Billings' work put much emphasis on Marcello as having been one of the prime movers in the conspiracy. Yet, Blakey's allegations—in particular—can only be described as suspect, to say the very least.

A professor of law and the director of the Notre Dame University Institute on Organized Crime, Blakey is considered one of the nation's leading authorites on the underworld.

Previously a special prosecutor in the Justice Department under then-Attorney General Robert Kennedy, Blakey is the author of the famous Racketeer Influenced and Corrupt Organizations (RICO) statute that has become a major tool in federal organized crime and white collar prosecutions.

Thus it is that Blakey's conclusions about the role of "the Mafia" (and specifically Carlos Marcello) in the JFK assassination conspiracy have received widespread recognition and credibility.

However, just two years before he was selected to serve as chief counsel and staff director of the House Assassinations Committee, Blakey had a different relationship with organized crime: *he had been on the payroll of a top figure in the Lansky Syndicate.*

## BLAKEY'S LANSKY CONNECTION

After *Penthouse* magazine had published an article alleging that the La Costa Country Club in Carlsbad, California was linked to the underworld, several of La Costa's founders filed a lawsuit against *Penthouse*.

It just so happens that one of the plaintiffs in the La Costa case was Morris "Moe" Dalitz, a former Detroit and Cleveland bootlegger-turned-Las Vegas casino boss, who had long-standing and close personal and business ties with Meyer Lansky.

Brought in as part of Dalitz's legal team was Robert Blakey himself, an unusual position for a self-promoted "crime fighter" such as Blakey. The crime fighter, in fact, provided an affidavit on Dalitz's behalf against *Penthouse*.[322]

Dalitz—the man for whom Blakey was working—was very much an integral part of the Lansky Syndicate.

### 'THE LITTLE JEWISH NAVY'

According to FBI organized crime expert William Roemer, "Moe Dalitz started his criminal career way back in the Prohibition Era. He had been one of the admirals in 'the Little Jewish Navy' in Detroit when, as a rum-runner, he ferried booze across the Detroit River from Canada to quench the thirst of the many Motor City citizens who were eager to taste the whiskey, wine, and beer forbidden by the 'Noble Experiment.'"[323] This was the beginning of a long, lasting, close working relationship between Lansky, "the chairman of the board of organized crime" and Morris Dalitz.

### DALITZ, SIEGEL AND LANSKY

In fact, according to Roemer, it was Dalitz who was the prime mover behind the Syndicate's move against Benjamin "Bugsy" Siegel, Lansky's boyhood friend and fellow racketeer who was shot dead in 1947.

According to Roemer, it was Lansky who sent Dalitz to Las Vegas to inquire into the activities of Ben Siegel. Dalitz, reports Roemer, "was the main contributor to the growing opinion that everything was not on the up and up. His report was the major reason why Lansky, [Frank] Costello, et al, made their report to the [organized crime] assembly in Havana in December 1946 and later in June when it was finally decided to chop Bugsy." [324]

(In Chapter 13 we shall review the Lansky-Siegel connection further and examine the role that Siegel's successor as Lansky's West Coast henchman, Mickey Cohen, played in the JFK assassination conspiracy.)

The removal of Siegel as Lansky's Las Vegas operative opened the way for Morris Dalitz to become, "the godfather of Las Vegas."

It would be nearly thirty years later before Robert Blakey, the chief proponent of the theory that "The Mafia Killed JFK" would end up on Morris Dalitz's team.

Unfortunately for Blakey, Dalitz and La Costa, *Penthouse* prevailed, beating back the libel suit and, in effect, repudiating Blakey's character references on behalf of the Lansky Syndicate.

So it was that the chief proponent of the theory that "the Mafia Killed JFK" had lined up in defense of one of Meyer Lansky's closest associates— Moe Dalitz—a legendary figure in the underworld himself.

It was in Chapter 4, incidentally, that we learned that it was Dalitz's notorious "Purple Gang" in Detroit that had put out a contract on the life of Ambassador Joseph P. Kennedy, father of the future president, during Prohibition for interfering in their "territory." Kennedy, as we saw, made contact with Chicago Mafia chieftain Sam Giancana who intervened on the elder Kennedy's behalf, convincing Dalitz and company to cancel the proposed "hit."

## ISRAEL HONORS DALITZ

Dalitz himself did not suffer as a consequence of the *Penthouse* victory in the libel suit. Instead, in 1983 Dalitz was honored by the pro-Israel Anti-Defamation League (ADL) of B'nai B'rith with its prestigious annual "Torch of Liberty Award."

Evidently the ADL—a favorite charity of top-level figures in the Lansky syndicate—did not see any problem with giving its highest honor to one of the top leaders of organized crime.

Dalitz's service to the cause of Israel was apparently deemed more significant than his activities in the underworld.

Despite this high honor, Dalitz was gunned down several years later on the streets of Las Vegas. When the bullets of his would-be assassins failed to accomplish their goal, another party was called in to finish the job.

Dalitz was poisoned to death in his hospital room where he was recovering from his bullet wounds.[325] This was obviously a major loss to not only organized crime but also to the Israeli lobby in America.

(In Chapter 7, of course, we examined the long-standing ties of the Lansky Syndicate to Israel. In Chapter 13 and Chapter 15 we shall examine that relationship further.

In Chapter 17 we shall examine Israel's ADL and its impact on the American news media and, in one instance, of how a longtime ADL collaborator floated a "new" theory about the JFK assassination—a cover story that seems to have been orchestrated by Israel's friends at the CIA.

Robert Blakey clearly prefers to look at the Italian elements of the underworld, but no further. The differences between "the Mafia" and organized crime as a whole as we saw in Chapter 7 and which we shall discuss in this chapter and in Chapter 11 and Chapter 12 are deep and significant.

## BLAKEY AND THE CIA

Blakey, likewise, has refused to acknowledge the role of American intelligence, specifically the CIA, in the JFK assassination.

No wonder then that prominent JFK assassination researchers such as Mark Lane, writing in *Plausible Denial*, and Jim Marrs, writing in *Crossfire*—among many others—have commented critically on Blakey's close relationship with the CIA during the period of the House Assassinations Committee investigation.

In his own book, *Conspiracy*, Anthony Summers documents—in frightening detail—the CIA's subversion of the House investigation which, it appears, was aided and abetted by Blakey himself

Blakey himself did nothing to allay the suspicions of his critics by first clearing his own book with the CIA. The concluding paragraph of Blakey's book—which another JFK assassination researcher, Carl Oglesby, caustically remarked should have appeared on the opening pages rather than buried at the end of the book—read as follows:

"Pursuant to agreement with the Select Committee on Assassinations, the Central Intelligence Agency and the Federal Bureau of Investigation reviewed this book in manuscript form to determine that the classified information it contained had been properly released for publication and that no informant was identified. Neither the CIA nor the FBI warrants the factual material or endorses the views expressed." [326]

Thus, while Blakey was busy pointing the finger at Carlos Marcello and away from the CIA and its allies in the Israeli Mossad, the facts about the Lansky-Marcello relationship belie Blakey's claim that "the Mafia" was the driving force in the JFK assassination conspiracy.

## LOUISIANA FRONT MAN

The fact remains that whatever role Marcello or any of his underlings played in either the JFK assassination or the cover-up, Marcello was nothing more than a front-man for the "boss of all bosses"—Israel's longtime patron, Meyer Lansky himself. Marcello was indeed, Little Man's Little Man. Lansky was, in fact, much, much bigger—in terms of power and influence—than Carlos Marcello would ever be, Marcello's fame and reputation notwithstanding.

To understand the fatal flaws in the Davis, Scheim, Blakey-Billings theories—and to underscore the thesis of *Final Judgment*—it is vital to remember this all-important fact.

Interestingly, Davis himself makes clear that Marcello was, in fact, a protege of Lansky. The author does not, however, place the significant emphasis on Lansky's superiority over Marcello that must be made in presenting any theory that "The Mafia Killed JFK."

For the full story of the Lansky-Marcello relationship we are indebted to Hank Messick, the fearless investigative reporter who specialized in Organized Crime coverage. In his biography of Meyer Lansky, Messick described how Lansky picked Marcello out of relative obscurity and set up Louisiana's supposed "Mafia boss" in business. Messick told how Lansky (through his partner and longtime associate Frank Costello) first moved into Louisiana.

Under heat from New York reform Mayor Fiorello LaGuardia, Lansky and Costello had decided that New Orleans was an ideal location to relocate their slot machine operations. Costello met in New York with then-Louisiana Governor Huey Long who agreed to open up his state to Organized Crime.

Lansky-Costello associate "Dandy Phil" Kastel was sent in to take charge of the project. However, it was Lansky himself who went to New Orleans to cut the final deal with Long. The two met at the Roosevelt Hotel which was owned by a mutual crony, Seymour Weiss. [327]

(This was not the first meeting between Lansky and Long, however. The two had first met at the 1932 Democratic Convention in Chicago which nominated then-New York Governor Franklin Delano Roosevelt for president. It was during that brokered convention that Lansky bribes, along with Long's support, enabled FDR to win his party's nomination. Lansky's longtime associate and primary link to the Italian underworld, Charles "Lucky" Luciano, described that momentous meeting in his historic posthumously-published memoirs.)[328]

## THE LONG-LANSKY DEAL

It was during their second fateful meeting that Long and Lansky cut a deal which sealed their fates irrevocably and which, in fact, ultimately led to Long's untimely demise at the hands of an assassin. Here was the deal: in return for allowing Lansky's syndicate to operate in Louisiana, Long agreed to take a $20,000 monthly kickback. Lansky's slot machines were installed by a company chartered for "charitable contributions." However, out of the first $800,000 made by Lansky and his cronies in New Orleans, widows and orphans got exactly $600.[329]

This cozy arrangement between Lansky's Organized Crime syndicate and Huey Long's powerful Louisiana political machine made possible the rise of Carlos Marcello. Lansky biographer Messick described the origins and nature of the Lansky-Marcello relationship as follows: "Lansky was smart enough, however, to recognize that even the innovation of slot machines which paid off in mints as well as cash would not suffice forever. [Lansky's] brother Jake was listed as an officer of the Louisiana Mint Company, the new outfit controlling the slots, but something more was needed.

"In the Algiers section of New Orleans, across the Mississippi, he found Carlos Marcello. Born in Tunis, he had come to New Orleans in 1910 and made a living in a variety of ways, none of them successful. Nor had he bothered to become a U.S. citizen.

"Lansky gave Marcello a franchise for the Algiers section, allowing him to keep two-thirds of the slot profit. By 1940 he had 250 machines in operation and proved himself as an effficient businessman. Later he was given a piece of the plush Beverly Club, the biggest rug joint (a posh gambling casino) in the area and at that time second to the Beverly Hills Club outside Newport, Kentucky."[330]

## MARCELLO TOOK THE HEAT

Messick's concluding comments regarding the Lansky-Marcello relationship, however, are probably the most significant: "As a front man, Marcello worked out perfectly. In years to come he was touted as the Mafia boss of Louisiana—despite his birth in Tunis—and resisted all efforts to deport or jail him.

"With all the heat on Marcello, the role of Lansky was almost forgotten—exactly what Meyer wanted. Ultimately, Lansky was able to shift Kastel to Las Vegas and leave Marcello and Weiss to run New Orleans."[331]

"Meyer Lansky once explained why he left New Orleans to Marcello and others to run. 'There was just too frigging much to do elsewhere,'he said."[332]

As Messick elaborated even further, if only to drive home the point: Even Marcello's famous Beverly Club was not, in reality, Marcello's personal fiefdom. According to Messick, "Costello and Kastel were partners, Marcello had a small piece, but Lansky was the real boss." [333]

Aaron Cohn, who was director of the New Orleans Crime Commission, lends credence to Messick's analysis of the relationship. According to Cohn, "The Commission had long been suspicious of the massiveness of Marcello's holdings—which were much too large to be controlled by a single don—even one as powerful as Marcello." [334]Marcello, in short, was indeed fronting for Meyer Lansky.

All of this, of course, taken together, sheds a more accurate light on the truth about the Lansky connection and Carlos Marcello.

## LANSKY, MARCELLO & THE CIA

There is also evidence that Marcello was working directly with the CIA in at least one other sphere of influence that also links Lansky, whose own connections with American intelligence we examined in Chapter 7 and which we will examine further in Chapter 11, Chapter 12 and Chapter 14.

According to Sam and Chuck Giancana, in their biography of Chicago Mafia boss, Sam Giancana, "Marcello was a co-conspirator with the CIA in gunrunning operations and a fervent supporter of the anti-Castro exiles. It was an arrangment [Giancana] said more than once, aimed at returning Cuba to its pre-Castro glory—meaning its lucrative casinos and vice rackets." [335]

But there was another realm in which the Lansky-CIA-Marcello nexus had a close working relationship: the illicit traffic in narcotics. The Senate Committee on Government Operations report to the 88th Congress on "Organized Crime and Illicit Traffic in Narcotics" had pinpointed New Orleans—at that time—as having been the key distribution point for drugs coming into the United States.

Most observers believe that one of Marcello's "legitimate" businesses, a shrimp-boat operation, was, in fact, part of the drug-smuggling—and gun-running—network.

(In Chapter 12 we shall see, in fact, that Lansky was the prime mover behind that drug network working in conjunction with the CIA.)

Needless to say, Marcello's central positioning in New Orleans made it such that it was inevitable that the Mafia chieftain would have an inside track to gaining first-hand knowledge about developments—at least in New Orleans—in the JFK assassination conspiracy.

## MARCELLO, FERRIE, BANISTER & THE CIA

After all, Marcello's personal pilot was CIA contract agent David Ferrie, (now widely known as a result of his portrayal in Oliver Stone's Hollywood extravaganza, *JFK*). Ferrie's still-undetermined part in the JFK assassination conspiracy, and his apparent association with alleged assassin, Lee Harvey Oswald, is but another piece of the whole puzzle.

It was Ferrie's associate, Guy Banister, whose New Orleans private detective agency (a conduit for CIA arms to the anti-Castro Cuban exiles) employed several other Marcello cronies. Banister, who had been with the Office of Naval Intelligence, and was later special-agent-in-charge of the Chicago office of the FBI, had re-located to New Orleans. [336]

According to the Giancanas, Banister had long been close to the Chicago Mafia and that it was their good offices that brought Banister into Marcello's sphere of influence when the former FBI man went to New Orleans, initially working for the city police department.[337]

(During the summer of 1963 the Cuban Revolutionary Council, a creation of the CIA's chief liaison with the anti-Castro Cuban groups, E. Howard Hunt, also maintained offices in the same building as Banister. [338] We first met Hunt, of course, in Chapter 9 where we learned of a libel trial in which both Hunt and the CIA were directly implicated in the JFK assassination.)

Banister, clearly, was the intermediary between the CIA and the Lansky-Marcello operation in New Orleans. And it was through his office that Lee Harvey Oswald, was being set up as the patsy. (In Chapter 11, Chapter 14, Chapter 15 and Chapter 16 we shall examine that aspect of the JFK assassination conspiracy further.)

Without question, New Orleans and the Marcello fiefdom were an integral part of the Lansky Organized Crime Syndicate. But to suggest that Marcello was the driving force behind the JFK assassination conspiracy is to ignore the whole picture.

## LANSKY & THE LONG ASSASSINATION

As a passing historical note, it is probably appropriate to refer to the demise of Huey Long and the role that Lansky and his associates played in that important political event.

By 1935, Long had been elected to the Senate and had risen to national prominence. In fact, Long was generally considered a major threat to Franklin Delano Roosevelt's 1936 re-election chances. Long had made it clear that if he didn't run as a Democrat—or as a third party candidate—in 1936, he certainly intended to play a major part in that election, and not on FDR's side.

This, obviously, was of major concern to FDR. Thus, a Justice Department investigation of Long and his finances was unleashed. Such an inquiry was dredging up Long's tangled financial arrangements and threatened to break the back of the very profitable machine that Long had assembled. There were more than a few Louisiana political figures and Long associates who were frightened of their impending demise alongside Long at the hands of federal prosecutors.

As Messick notes—and this is ironic—it was in a Dallas, Texas hotel room that the federal authorities made the decision to indict Long. The colorful Louisiana Senator was shot that same day by a "lone assassin" who was himself promptly shot to pieces by Long's bodyguards.

To this day there are myriad conspiracy theories relating to Long's murder. Some say that the alleged assassin never fired a shot—instead, that he swung a punch at Long and that the "murder weapon" was planted on the scene afterward by the bodyguards who wanted to cover up the fact that it was one of them who accidentally shot Long when firing at his assailant. There are those, however, who say that Long was, in fact, deliberately shot by one of his bodyguards.

The Giancana family, in their biography of Chicago Mafia boss, say that Sam Giancana later claimed that "Some of our friends in New York had him hit—worked it out with a New Orleans [Mafia] boss. They figured it out so it would look like a loony did it."[339]

The real truth may never be known. Whatever the case, Long died in the hospital some hours after the shooting. What we do know is that Long's death removed from the scene a major threat not only to the Roosevelt administration, but to the Long machine which relied so heavily on the

Lansky Organized Crime Syndicate. With Long out of the picture, the federal authorities gave up their interest in Louisiana and its murky political underworld.

The evidence now indicates that Long's death could have been prevented. Hank Messick told the story: at a meeting in Hot Springs, Arkansas at the Arlington Hotel, shortly after Long's death, Frank Costello filled Lansky in on the truth about Long's departure. "We could have saved him," Costello told Lansky, "but I didn't see much use in it. The doctors had their orders to let him die."[340]

This apparently was Meyer Lansky's first major involvement in the assassination of an American political figure with whom Organized Crime had collaborated. It would not be the last time, however.

That Lansky's lieutentnant, Carlos Marcello had his own reasons for wanting John F. Kennedy out of the way cannot be doubted. The Justice Department under Robert F. Kennedy had targeted Marcello repeatedly.

John Davis's interesting biography of Marcello provides a detailed analysis of the Kennedy campaign against Marcello. No wonder Marcello made his famous oft-told exclamation, "*Livarsi na petra di la scarpa*" (Take the stone from my shoe.") Yet, such an emotional outburst does not an assassination order make.

In fact, there is no evidence anywhere whatsoever that Marcello took any further affirmative action to have his order—if indeed one can call it an order—fulfilled.

## STALKING LANSKY THROUGH MARCELLO

It's worth noting, in this regard, that Robert Kennedy's systematic prosecution and harassment of Marcello would have only been a logical first step in the Justice Department's ultimate prosecution of Meyer Lansky.

This, of course, is a standard procedure in all similar organized crime prosecutions: first the underlings are targeted—then the boss. In this case, of course, it would have been the so-called "chairman of the board," Meyer Lansky.

Seth Kantor, Jack Ruby's acquaintance and biographer, summarizes it well: "As Attorney General, [Robert F. Kennedy] got more indictments on members of America's criminal industry than had any previous prosecutor, pursuing them relentlessly.

"Meyer Lansky, for instance, no longer was safe behind the bolted doors of that industry's executive suite. The Attorney General put together what was known inside the Justice Department as the OCD (Organized Crime Division) and was stalking Lansky's secret operations in the Bahamas and Las Vegas."[341]

The assassination of John F. Kennedy and the demise of Robert Kennedy's campaign against organized crime as a direct consequence prevented this from happening. The end of the Kennedy war on organized crime was a major consequence—a major victory—for the organized crime fiefdom of Meyer Lansky.

Of course, as we have said, even if the JFK murder was strictly a "Mafia" operation—with no tentacles leading elsewhere—it would have been Lansky who ordered it from the start.

Meyer Lansky was Carlos Marcello's immediate superior in the world of organized crime and not vice versa. There is simply no way of getting around Lansky's critical positioning in the center of the vast conspiracy. What we are demonstrating here is that the conspiracy reached above and beyond "the Mafia." And that is central to our thesis.

## LANSKY'S 'KOSHER NOSTRA'

Interestingly, Ruby biographer Seth Kantor differentiated between what he called "Lansky's 'Kosher Nostra'" and what he separately referred to as "the hot-blooded Sicilian Cosa Nostra." [342]Certainly, Carlos Marcello breathed a sigh of satisfaction when John F. Kennedy died in Dallas. However, Meyer Lansky was, of course, the ultimate beneficiary.

Any major operation such as the assassination of a president—even if proposed by Marcello single-handedly—would have first had to have been cleared by Marcello through his boss, Meyer Lansky. Thus, it would have been Lansky himself who most certainly had to have given the go-ahead, even if the Kennedy assassination plot originated with Marcello alone.

The evidence, of course, suggests, however, that Marcello and his associates in New Orleans were simply pawns in a more far-reaching conspiracy that originated elsewhere. Their proximity to Oswald and the New Orleans end of the conspiracy, however, makes them an easy target for those who seek to find a "Mafia" conspiracy behind the murder.

## WEASEL WORDS

As noted previously, those very sources who point to Marcello as the mastermind of the JFK murder choose to ignore Marcello's secondary positioning to Meyer Lansky in the syndicate chain of command. Lansky-linked Robert Blakey's House Assassinations Committee gingerly skirted around the issue, however. In its final report the committee concluded:

"Given the far-reaching possible consequences of an assassination plot by the commission [i.e. the national "commission" of Organized Crime], the committee found that such a conspiracy would have been the subject of serious discussion by members of the commission, and that no matter how guarded such discussions might have been, some trace of them would have emerged from the surveillance coverage [by federal authorities].

"It was possible to conclude, therefore, that it is unlikely that the national crime syndicate as a group, acting under the leadership of the commission, participated in the assassination of President Kennedy.

"While the committee found it unlikely that the national crime syndicate was involved in the assassination, it recognized that a particular organized crime leader or a small combination of leaders, acting unilaterally, might have formulated an assassination conspiracy without the consent of the commission."[343]

These are weasel words, to be sure. However, one could also conclude from the committee's presumption that if indeed Organized Crime did play some significant role in the assassination conspiracy, that it was not a conspiracy that originated with "the Mafia," for example. Perhaps then the conspiracy originated elsewhere. That, of course, is the conclusion presented in *Final Judgment*.

Unwittingly, then, the House Committee has provided us even further basis for the conclusions drawn here.

## LANSKY NOT MENTIONED

The House Committee report had nothing to say about the Lansky-Marcello connection. This is par for the course in standard accounts of the JFK assassination which promote the theory that "The Mafia Killed JFK." What is also particularly interesting is that Robert Lacey's Lansky biography, *Little Man*, never once mentions Lansky's sponsorship of Marcello, or does Marcello's name appear once in the book. The New Orleans connection is barely mentioned at all, and only in passing. Was Marcello—who even the FBI has said headed "the first family" of the Mafia—that unimportant?

Could it be that because Marcello's name has been repeatedly linked to the JFK assassination that for Lacey—a very friendly biographer who worked closely with Lansky's family—to bring up Marcello's much-abused name would obviously draw in the Lansky connection to the JFK assassination?

Is it possible that Marcello and his associates such as David Ferrie were deliberately drawn into the periphery of the assassination plot in order to deliberately plant the possibility that the blame for the assassination could be laid upon Marcello and the Mafia—in the event, perhaps, that the image of Lee Harvey Oswald as a "pro-Castro agitator" failed to work?

This is indeed a possibility and would fit firmly into the long-standing Israeli Mossad policy of using "false flags" in its criminal endeavors.

Clearly, there's a lot more to the relationship between Meyer Lansky and key "suspects" in the JFK assassination than meets the eye. All of which, again, points toward Lansky's central role in the international conspiracy which we document.

## Chapter Eleven

## Cuban Love Song:
## Meyer Lansky, the Mafia, the CIA and
## the Castro Assassination Plots

Two top "Mafia" figures—Johnny Rosselli and Santo Trafficante, Jr.—were key figures in the CIA-Organized Crime assassination plots against Cuba's Fidel Castro and often linked to the JFK assassination, Trafficante in particular.

Although both Rosselli and Trafficante were major players in the criminal underworld, both were, in fact—like Carlos Marcello—subordinates of Meyer Lansky.

Rosselli and Trafficante were Lansky's point men in Lansky's dealings with Israel's allies in the CIA and the anti-Castro Cuban movement in assassination plots against Fidel Castro.

Carlos Marcello is not the only major "Mafia" figure whose connections with Organized Crime syndicate boss Meyer Lansky have been ignored by Lansky's friendly biographer Robert Lacey. The legendary Johnny Rosselli is never mentioned either. Was neither Marcello nor Rosselli worth mentioning? Were they really that insignificant? Not according to standard accounts of Organized Crime history. Both Marcello and Rosselli have particular prominence in the annals of criminal folklore, especially in relation to the Kennedy assassination.

### ROSSELLI A MAJOR PLAYER

It is quite significant that Lacey has chosen to delete Rosselli from his account of Lansky's life:

• Rosselli was a major figure in Organized Crime in Los Angeles, where Lansky's longtime associate Ben Siegel—and Siegel's successor as Lansky's West Coast operative, Mickey Cohen—represented Lansky's interests.

• Rosselli was a major figure in Organized Crime in Las Vegas, where Lansky maintained major gambling operations. He was Chicago Mafia boss Sam Giancana's primary representative there;

• Rosselli was a major figure in Organized Crime in Havana, representing the interests of the Chicago Mafia, where Lansky also dominated gambling operations.

By all standard accounts, Rosselli was very much a key figure in the modern "Mafia" as we know it.

In short, while Marcello's activities were based almost entirely in his Gulf Coast fiefdom (and extending into Texas), Rosselli operated as almost a roving ambassador for the Italian wing of Organized Crime (popularly called "the Mafia."), primarily the Chicago branch.

Yet, Rosselli's ties to Lansky have been ignored by Lansky's biographer Robert Lacey. Why? Lacey's biography (which is otherwise quite detailed) would suggest—by virtue of ignoring both Marcello and Rosselli—that Lansky had no connections with them at all, or that any connections he did have were so insignificant that they weren't even worth mentioning.

Rosselli's name—like that of Marcello—has also been prominently linked to the Kennedy murder.

One can only wonder why Lansky's biographer failed to bring in these clearly important connections. Even Tiger (described in the index as "(Lansky's dog)" is mentioned—not once, but twice. (Carlos Marcello is not mentioned at all.)

### WHERE WAS TRAFFICANTE?

Rosselli was also particularly close to Lansky's Florida and Havana lieutenant, Santo Trafficante, Jr, who is also practically a "non-person" in Lacey's account of Lansky's ventures. And, as we shall see, it may well have been Trafficante who arranged Rosselli's own ultimate assassination on behalf of the CIA.

Like Rosselli, Trafficante was also a major figure in the annals of crime and much more so than even Rosselli, was an intimate working partner of Lansky. In fact, as we shall see in much more detail in Chapter 12, Trafficante—although a "Mafia" leader—was Lansky's immediate underling in the gambling and narcotics rackets.

In Lacey's biography of Lansky, Trafficante is also given short shrift. In fact, he is hardly mentioned at all, except in minor passing—just eight times. In fact there are fewer references to Trafficante than there are to yet another Lansky dog, Bruzzer, who rates 13 references, including a detailed review of the dog's sad final days.

In Kennedy assassination folklore this is also particularly relevant, inasmuch as we have been told repeatedly that Trafficante once told one Jose Aleman, Jr., a wealthy Cuban exile, that JFK was scheduled to be hit. However, interestingly enough, the rest of the story goes untold. According to J. Edgar Hoover biographer Curt Gentry, it was, in fact, Aleman's impression that although Trafficante may have been aware of an assassination plot against Kennedy that Trafficante himself "wasn't its principal architect." [344] Who, then, was?

### THE LANSKY-CIA ALLIANCE

All of this is interesting about Rosselli and Trafficante, particularly in the context of their central involvement in CIA-Organized Crime assassination plots aimed at Fidel Castro who had seized control of Lansky's gambling operations in Havana.

There is much, much more to the Rosselli-Trafficante link with Meyer Lansky that needs to be explored, for this connection opens up another area:

Lansky's long-standing and intimate ties with Israel's allies in the CIA. Indeed, as we shall see in Chapter 12, Lansky's CIA linkage goes far beyond Cuba and the Caribbean. It even extended into Southeast Asia.

As we saw in Chapter 7 (and which has been repeatedly documented by perhaps hundreds of writers over and over again), organized crime—Meyer Lansky in particular—had much to lose when communist revolutionary Fidel Castro came to power in Cuba.

Prior to the advent of Castro, Cuba had been a primary gambling money-making base of operations for the Meyer Lansky Organized Crime Syndicate and its Mafia lieutenants. Anthony Summers summarizes the situation well:

"Castro's predecessor, the dictator Batista, had long been a puppet on strings pulled by American intelligence and the mob. In 1944, when the United States feared trouble from the Cuban left, Lansky reportedly persuaded Batista to step down for a while. When he came back in 1952, it was after the current President, Carlos Prio Socarras, was persuaded to resign, a departure reportedly eased by a bribe of a quarter of a million dollars and a major stake in the casino business.

"It was now that the gambling operation already established in Cuba became a Mafia bonanza . . .When the Batista regime began to crumble before a revolution of popular outrage, the mob hedged its political bets by courting Fidel Castro.

"Many of the guns which helped him to power in 1959 had been provided courtesy of Mafia gunrunners, a policy which did not pay off. Lansky saw the writing on the wall and flew out of Havana the day Castro marched in."[345]

## CASTRO vs. LANSKY

Investigative reporter Jim Hougan described the relationship between the Meyer Lansky Organized Crime Syndicate and the Cubans—both Castro and his enemies.

"In 1960 [Johnny] Rosselli was one of a handful of operators . . . responsible for managing the Mob's investments in Cuba. According to the FBI, these operations were owned by Santo Trafficante and Meyer Lansky, with New Orleans' Carlos Marcello and Chicago's Sam 'Momo' Giancana having smaller pieces of the action.

"The Mob's relationship to the *arrivista* Castro regime was a stormy one. On the one hand, some of its members had been active in the revolution, ferrying guns to Castro's guerrillas. On the other hand, the new Cuban premier seemed determined to eradicate those social evils that the Mob found most profitable: drugs, prostitution, and gambling. Castro had, moreover, jailed both Trafficante and Meyer Lansky's brother Jake in the wake of his triumphal march upon Havana."[346]

In Chapter 14 we shall see that one of the key mob gun-runners on Castro's behalf was Lansky errand boy, Jack Ruby, working in conjunction with other Lansky associates.

However, the initial mob support for Castro went sour when Castro proved to be a danger to the Lansky syndicate's lucrative operations in Cuba. It was at this point, then, that Ruby—like his mob associates—did a complete turn-around and began working against Castro.

Although many syndicate figures still hoped that they could resume operations in Cuba after Castro was removed from office, Lansky was more realistic and practical. He began looking to the Bahamas as his next Caribbean gambling base of operations.

Still, Lansky maintained his ties with the anti-Castro Cubans. It was during this period, after all, that the CIA was preparing to move against Castro. Lansky would play a major role in that effort.

## ETHNIC TIES

For an even more obscure reason—one which has often gone un-noticed—perhaps unmentioned—Lansky had another reason to be disenchanted with Fidel Castro and supportive of anti-Castro Cuban elements.

The fact is that many of the anti-Castro Cubans who had settled in Miami and elsewhere following Castro's rise to power were Cuban Jews.

American CIA-financed anti-Castro propagandist Paul D. Bethel, writing in the December 15, 1965 issue of the *Latin America Report* (subtitled the "*Free Cuba News*") gives us some interesting facts about the status of Jews in Cuba before and after the advent of Castro. Bethel noted that of a total of 11,000 Jews in Cuba at the time of Castro's takeover, only 1,900 remained at that time. The rest had already joined the anti-Castro Cuban colonies which had largely migrated to the Miami and New Orleans areas. Of those remaining, an additional 1,300 were leaving at the time of Bethel's report .[347]

The affluent Cuban Jewish community was, in fact, an important faction within the overall anti-Castro Cuban community. Their ethnic ties with Lansky can't have gone un-noticed by Lansky. Castro's well-documented war against religion in Cuba would certainly have stirred Lansky just as much as Hitler's war against the Jews in Germany had done previously. This, coupled with Lansky's financial loss in Cuba, made him all the more inclined to strike against Castro in cooperation with the CIA.

## LANSKY FUNDS CIA FRONT GROUPS

Although Anthony Summers' previously-cited book on the JFK conspiracy, aptly titled *Conspiracy,* devotes very little attention to Meyer Lansky's pivotal role in Organized Crime, he does make reference to a CIA anti-Castro operation funded by Lansky.

CIA operative E. Howard Hunt put together the Revolutionary Democratic Front, a coalition of anti-Castro Cubans, headed by Manuel Antonio de Varona, a former president of the Cuban Senate. In fact, as Summers tells us, de Varona met with Lansky for financial support and also received funds through the Washington, D.C. firm of Edward K. Moss and Associates, which represented the interests of Lansky operatives Dino and Eddie Cellini.[348]

(In Chapter 9 we first met the aforementioned CIA operative, E. Howard Hunt, and learned how he was implicated, in a little-publicized libel trial, in the JFK assassination conspiracy. In Chapter 16 we shall learn much, much more about the circumstances which led up to that trial.)

## THE ASSASSINATION PLOTS

Now although the famous CIA-Mafia assassination plots against Castro have been reported time and again, the key organized crime players in the tale are always the aforementioned Santo Trafficante, Jr., Johnny Rosselli and Sam Giancana of Chicago.

Rosselli's biographers note that it was CIA contract agent Robert Maheu, a longtime acquaintance of Rosselli, who  initiated the CIA's dealings with organized crime in the anti-Castro plots. [349]

(It was this same Maheu, a former FBI agent as well, who had worked directly under the former special-agent-in-charge of the Chicago FBI office, Guy Banister. [350] It was Banister, as we saw in Chapter 10, who was the direct link between the Lansky-Marcello-CIA gun-running  operations on behalf of the anti-Castro Cuban network.)

Maheu, who had become friendly with Rosselli during business trips to Las Vegas, had been approached by the CIA to open up negotiations with the Mafia for this special, mutually-beneficial, operation. Thus, the initial plot was set in place. However, there were subsequent developments:

"Once the basic groundwork was laid, Rosselli decided to introduce two new players into the picture.  One was Rosselli's Chicago boss, Sam Giancana, and the other was Santo Trafficante, Meyer Lansky's colleague in the Havana casinos. Trafficante's connections could prove helpful in moving the plots along, and besides, Mafia tradition required that as the local don, he be informed of any activity taking place in his domain."[351]

So it was that the CIA and Organized Crime entered into a complex— and controversial—liaison for a mutual aim: the elimination of Cuban dictator Fidel Castro.

There is no question that Trafficante, Rosselli and Giancana did indeed help coordinate assassination plots against Castro with representatives of the CIA. (This, as we have said, has been thoroughly documented time and again. To discuss this here would belabor the point.)

However, as one author succinctly put it: "Lansky was the top man in the CIA-Mafia plot against Castro, but the only journalist who had guts enough to point this out was [columnist] Victor Riesel." [352] JFK assassination researcher Peter Dale Scott acknowledges that Lansky was indeed involved in the CIA plots against Castro,[353] but, Lansky's role has been obscured, ignored, or otherwise gone unmentioned.

In fact, as we shall see in Chapter 12 when we examine the Lansky-Trafficante relationship further, Trafficante was Lansky's subordinate. All of Trafficante's anti-Castro operations in league with the CIA were being conducted with Lansky's approval and under Lansky's watchful eye.

## LANSDALE, SHACKLEY & CLINES

The latter phase of the CIA's anti-Castro operations were known as Operation Mongoose. General Edward Lansdale was in charge of the operation. Working under Lansdale was CIA operative Theodore Shackley. Shackley's deputy was Thomas Clines. Headquarters of the operation—known as JM/Wave—were in Lansky's own city of Miami and based on the campus of the University of Miami.

Part of the CIA's campaign against Castro included its so-called ZR/Rifle Team project. Skilled assassins, recruited from around the globe (and often from the ranks of professional mercenaries and from within organized crime) were on retainer for use in the CIA's own private "hit team" or terrorist army, as the case may be. One of the prime in-house supervisors of the ZR/Rifle Team project was the CIA's counterintelligence chief, Israel's loyal ally, James J. Angleton.

The Operation Mongoose days were only a part of a long and friendly relationship between the Meyer Lansky Organized Crime Syndicate and American intelligence—a relationship, as we have seen, which began at least as early as World War II.

In Chapter 12 we shall once again see the CIA, Lansdale, Shackley, and Clines operating in tandem with Lansky and his underlings—this time in another part of the world: Southeast Asia.

This secret relationship laid the groundwork for the ultimate collaboration between the Lansky syndicate and the CIA with their allies in the Israeli Mossad in the conspiracy that resulted in the assassination of John F. Kennedy.

## ROSSELLI & THE JFK ASSASSINATION

That Rosselli, for example, was entwined in some aspect of the JFK assassination conspiracy seems certain. Evidence suggests that Rosselli was definitely engaged in activities during the summer and fall of 1963 that tied him directly to several of the key figures in the assassination conspiracy.

Rosselli's biographers themselves have suggested that Rosselli was indeed involved in the assassination itself. According to Rappleye and Becker: "The strongest indication that John Rosselli had a hand in the pre-assassination planning is a report of a direct contact between Rosselli and Jack Ruby in early October 1963. There were two meetings, both taking place in small motels near Miami, and both observed by the FBI. One of the federal investigators probing Rosselli's murder thirteen years later came across an FBI report on the meetings and relayed its contents, on a confidential basis, to Washington, D.C. reporter William Scott Malone.

"An accomplished investigator himself, Malone said in an interview he was confident of the integrity of his source, and said the FBI had determined the actual site of the Miami meetings."[354]

## ROSSELLI, BANISTER & THE CIA

According to Rappleye and Becker, Rosselli visited Guy Banister's office at 544 Camp Street in New Orleans. It was in the same controversial building that the Cuban Revolutionary Council (CRC) had an office. The CRC, as we saw in Chapter 9, was the brainchild of the CIA's chief liaison with the anti-Castro Cuban exiles, E. Howard Hunt, himself implicated in sworn testimony in the JFK assassination.)

Rosselli's biographers even go further, asking : "Was Rosselli, in fact, in Dallas? FBI surveillance loses his trail on the West Coast between November 19 and November 27."[355]

## COLLABORATION IN A KILLING

According to the Giancanas, the president was deliberately lured to Dallas where the operation could be carried off to the specifications of the plan. "The politicians and the CIA made it real simple," Sam Giancana explained. "We'd each provide men for the hit. I'd oversee the Outfit [Mafia] side of things and throw in Jack Ruby and some extra backup and the CIA would put their own guys on to take care of the rest." [356]

So it was that Johnny Rosselli and Sam Giancana—along with Santo Trafficante, Jr.—were brought into the JFK assassination conspiracy.

(In Chapter 17 we shall see how Rosselli became the central figure in a spurious—but widely publicized—newspaper story which suggested that Fidel Castro was behind the JFK assassination. The story was concocted by two journalists with close ties to not only the CIA and the Lansky Crime Syndicate, but also the Israeli lobby.)

The full story of Sam Giancana's role in much of these matters—the JFK assassination in particular—never became known until his own nephew and brother went public in 1992 with their book *Double Cross*.

## GIANCANA EXECUTED

Giancana never had the chance to talk even if he had wanted. He was murdered execution style in his own home in Chicago on June 19, 1975. The Establishment media hyped it as yet another "Mafia killing." The Giancana family doesn't think that's what it was. They say it was a CIA double cross, just like John F. Kennedy himself had double-crossed Sam Giancana. (In Chapter 4 we saw how Kennedy had not only cut a secret deal with organized crime, but also with Israel's American lobby.)

As it just so happens, Giancana was killed the very day that congressional investigators were on their way to Chicago to interview the Mafia leader about reported CIA-organized crime plots against Castro.

Sam and Chuck Giancana frankly assert in their own book that it may have been Johnny Rosselli who helped arrange Giancana's murder. According to the Giancanas they believe that the CIA contracted out the Giancana murder and that the CIA had arranged it through Trafficante.

The Giancanas believe that Trafficante, in turn, saw to it that Rosselli arranged the Chicago hit on Sam Giancana. As they summarize matters: "[Giancana's] Outfit friends knew he never would have divulged damaging information; the CIA, rampant with spies and counterspies, crosses and double crosses, may not have been so certain of his loyalty."[357]

All of this, of course, is speculation, but it does suggest that there were secrets that the CIA and its collaborators—such as Israel's Mossad—did not wish be revealed.

## ROSSELLI EXECUTED

In any case, Johnny Rosselli never lived long enough to tell the true story of the CIA-Meyer Lansky Crime Syndicate operations in the Caribbean—and in Dallas. On July 28, 1976, Rosselli disappeared in Miami. On August 7, the flamboyant mobster's butchered corpse bobbed up in a drum from the bottom of the ocean.

Charles Rappleye and Ed Becker note that there have been suspicions that it was indeed Trafficante, again, who may have even arranged the hit on Rosselli. However, they point out that there are many in the Mafia who do not believe this necessarily to be the case.

In the judgment of Rosselli's biographers, "The CIA certainly had the contacts in Cuban Miami to pull off Rosselli's execution, and as it had demonstrated by enlisting him in the first place, it had the will. Even the evidence pointing to Trafficante did not rule out collaboration by the spy agency." [358]

## LANSKY, TRAFFICANTE & THE CIA

As the authors point out, Trafficante did indeed have very close connections with the CIA—connections that went above and beyond his dealings with the spy agency in anti-Castro operations.

In Chapter 12 we shall see, indeed, that Trafficante, as Lansky's primary lieutenant in the Southeast Asian drug smuggling racket, developed even closer and more intimate ties to the CIA following the JFK assassination.

Thus, Rosselli and Giancana—two of the three key "Mafia" participants in the CIA-organized crime operations against Castro (and against JFK)—were silenced.

Only Santo Trafficante, Jr., Meyer Lansky's subordinate, remained alive and, as the Giancana family notes, "conducted business without so much as a whisper of legal difficulty." [359]

The Giancanas point out: "One had only to read the newspapers to see that the focus of underworld crimebusters was not on Tampa, Florida, but on its highly visible New York and Chicago cousins to the north." [360]

And by this time—the mid-1970's—Lansky himself was ailing and almost infirm. Trafficante himself died of kidney failure in 1987—just four years after Lansky.

## MORE THAN 'THE MAFIA'

Whatever Trafficante knew about the CIA assassination plots, Lansky certainly knew. Likewise in regard to the murders of Giancana and Rosselli. There is no question however that it was Meyer Lansky, in particular— primarily because of his over-riding influence—who was central to the joint CIA-Organized Crime operations not only in the Caribbean, but elsewhere

In Chapter 12 we shall learn how Lansky and his subordinate partner, Santo Trafficante, Jr. went above and beyond their CIA dealings in Cuba and extended those CIA connections into Europe and Southeast Asia. And, as we shall see, it was Lansky's drug-money laundering banking connections in Switzerland that bring the Israeli Mossad-CIA-Lansky connection full circle.

The "Mafia" was indeed intimately tied into the JFK assassination conspiracy, but those who refuse to look beyond the Mafia are not prepared to look at the truth. It is the Lansky connection which points further toward the proof that Israel and its Mossad played a key role in the assassination of John F. Kennedy.

# Chapter Twelve

## An Opiate for the Masses:
## The Lansky-CIA-Southeast Asian Drug Pipeline
## and the Mossad Connection

Tampa, Florida Mafia boss Santo Trafficante, Jr. has frequently been mentioned as a possible mastermind behind the assassination of John F. Kennedy. The media has also portrayed Trafficante as the prime mover behind the international heroin racket operating out of Southeast Asia. However, the truth is that it was Meyer Lansky who was the primary architect of the global drug operations. Trafficante was his immediate underling.

The Lansky heroin pipeline was conducted through the CIA-backed French Corsican Mafia in Marseille and used the CIA's covert activities in Southeast Asia during the Vietnam War as a cover for its operations. In fact, all the evidence suggests that the drug smuggling was a joint CIA-Organized Crime venture. What's more, Lansky's chief drug money laundering bank in Switzerland was a Mossad operation. Thus, the Lansky Crime Syndicate/Mafia connections with Israel's allies in the CIA are even deeper and more intimate than we have been led to believe.

Veteran JFK assassination researcher Peter Dale Scott has suggested that "[the flood] of drugs into this country since World War II was one of the major 'unspeakable' secrets leading to the ongoing cover-up of the Kennedy assassination."[361]

Scott is correct, for any careful, in-depth examination of the global drug racket shows conclusively that Israel's allies in the Lansky crime syndicate and the CIA are very much a part of the international drug racket.

Students of the global drug trade are indebted to Professor Alfred McCoy of the prestigious University of Wisconsin at Madison for his ground-breaking expose of the real origins of the modern-day drug crisis.

First published in 1972—despite the strongest efforts of the CIA to block its publication—McCoy's classic work, *The Politics of Heroin in Southeast Asia,* has withstood the test of time.

In 1992 McCoy re-issued the work under the title *The Politics of Heroin: CIA Complicity in the Global Drug Trade.* The new edition is an equally remarkable work which not only includes additional findings uncovered in the subsequent 20 years since its initial publication, but also a valuable preface in which McCoy outlines the CIA operations against his research and the publication of the book.

## THE DRUG BOSS

Although the Establishment media has repeatedly pinpointed Santo Trafficante, Jr., Mafia boss of Tampa, as the brains behind the Southeast

Asian drug traffic, McCoy makes it very clear that Trafficante was simply operating as Lansky's underling. McCoy describes the origins of the Lansky-Trafficante relationship:

"During the 1930's Meyer Lansky 'discovered' the Caribbean for northeastern syndicate bosses and invested their illegal profits in an assortment of lucrative gambling ventures. In 1933 Lansky moved into the Miami Beach area and took over most of the illegal off-track betting and a variety of hotels and casinos. He was also reportedly responsible for organized crime's decision to declare Miami a 'free city' (that is, not subject to the usual rules of territorial monopoly).

"Following his success in Miami, Lansky moved to Havana for three years, and by the beginning of World War II he owned the Hotel Nacional's casino and was leasing the municipal racetrack from a reputable New York bank.

"Burdened by the enormous scope of his holdings, Lansky had to delegate much of his responsibility for daily management to local gangsters. One of Lansky's earliest associates in Florida was Santo Trafficante, Sr., a Sicilian-born Tampa gangster. Trafficante had earned his reputation as an effective organizer in the Tampa gambling rackets and was already a figure of some stature when Lansky first arrived in Florida. By the time Lansky returned to New York in 1940, Trafficante had assumed responsibility for Lansky's interests in Havana and Miami.

## TRAFFICANTE THE FRONT MAN

"By the early 1950s Trafficante had himself become such an important figure that he delegated his Havana concessions to Santo Trafficante, Jr., the most talented of his six sons. The younger Santo's official position in Havana was that of manager of the Sans Souci Casino, but he was far more important than his title indicates.

"As his father's financial representative, and ultimately Meyer Lansky's, Santo Jr. controlled much of Havana's tourist industry and became quite close to the pre-Castro dictator, Fulgencio Batista. Moreover, it was reportedly his responsibility to receive bulk shipments of heroin from Europe and forward them through Florida to New York and other major urban centers, where the distribution was assisted by the local Mafia bosses."[362]

## LANSKY MOVES TO THE TOP

Lansky biographer Hank Messick makes it very clear that it was Trafficante Jr. who played a key role in ensuring Lansky's dominance over syndicate gambling in Cuba. It was Trafficante who helped orchestrate the assassination in 1957 of Lansky rival, New York Mafia figure Albert Anastasia, the most vocal Italian Mafia critic of Lansky's growing influence in the Cuban gambling rackets. Anastasia's removal from the scene was vital to Lansky's ultimate dominance.

Messick notes that Trafficante got caught in the middle between Albert Anastasia and Lansky over the Havana gambling. Not only did Trafficante opt to abandon his fellow Italian Mafia figure, but Trafficante also swore a blood oath Mafia-style, assuring Lansky of his support.

"So long as the blood flows in my body," he intoned solemnly, "do I, Santo Trafficante, swear allegiance to the will of Meyer Lansky and the organization he represents. If I violate this oath, may I burn in hell forever."[363]

He signed it in his own blood. It was shortly thereafter, on October 25, 1957, that Anastasia was shot dead after what he wrongly believed to have been a friendly meeting in New York with Trafficante. Anastasia should have known what was coming. After all, according to Messick, he had, shortly before, told his fellow Mafia figures what he thought of them: "You bastards have sold yourselves to the Jews."[364]

(Interestingly enough, Lansky's friendly biographical cheerleader, Robert Lacey, never mentions the Lansky-Anastasia stand-off that led to the Lansky rival's murder.)

Organized crime authority Dan Moldea summarized the Lansky-Trafficante relationship best and most succinctly: "Trafficante was deeply devoted to Lansky."[365]

## THE MAFIA UNDER FIRE

It was shortly after Albert Anastasia's murder that public attention began focusing on Organized Crime as a result of media publicity. It was not, in fact, until the infamous Mafia conclave at Appalachian, New York, in 1957 that the media began hyping "the Mafia" as a major force in organized crime.

Americans had long been aware of legendary mobsters such as Al Capone and Lucky Luciano, but general awareness that a national crime syndicate did indeed exist was not commonplace.

Following a police raid of the Appalachian conference—attended exclusively by top Mafia figures from around the country, Trafficante included—public attention began focusing on "the Mafia"—thanks to the media.

The official story has always been that a local policeman just happened to stumble upon the conclave at the home of Mafia figure Joseph Barbara. The officer called in reinforcements and a major "bust" took place, following a heated chase of the Mafia figures through the briars and brambles of the rural countryside.

However, according to Hank Messick, the police had been tipped off by a Lansky associate that the meeting was about to take place. Messick described the consequences of the Appalachian raid:

"The delegates were scattered before any alliance could be reached. And the publicity caused the greatest heat since the 1930's. It focused not only on the men who attended the session but on the entire Mafia. What's more, it continued for well over a year as state and federal officials tried to find some charge to stick against the delegates they had captured or identified. Not only were Mafia leaders immobilized by the continuing publicity, but also they were demoralized. Almost instinctively they rallied to Lansky and other non-Mafia syndicate leaders for advice and assistance."[366]

(Perhaps not coincidentally, one of the attorneys who played a key role in the Appalachian investigation was one Justin Finger. It was Finger who later went on to become chief of the "civil rights division" of the Lansky-financed Anti-Defamation League of B'nai B'rith, the primary intelligence and propaganda arm of Israel's Mossad in the United States.)

Despite all this, as Messick notes, Trafficante himself stood to benefit. According to Messick: "Trafficante was a little annoyed at the publicity he received—after being picked up with the rest—but was soon mollified when he discovered he was now being hailed as the Mafia boss of Florida by the press. Glory was as important as loot to the Mafia mind."[367]

## RETIREMENT

Clearly, a close working relationship between Lansky and Trafficante had been cemented. It continued for many years, up to and including—and beyond—the critical year of 1963. It was in 1970, however, that Lansky, preparing to take refuge in Israel, turned over most of his responsibilities to his subordinate, Santo Trafficante, Jr. By this time Lansky was aging and in ill health. He was ready to move into retirement.

In 1968—just two years earlier—Trafficante had journeyed to Saigon, Hong Kong and Singapore. It was there in the exotic East that he was solidifying the longtime relationship between Lansky and the CIA in the international drug racket.

## WHO'S THE BOSS?

Here we turn once again to Professor Alfred McCoy for an elucidation of Lansky's ties with the CIA in the Southeast Asian drug racket and the covert part it played in the CIA's involvement in the Vietnam conflict. McCoy writes:

"[After Mafia kingpin Charles "Lucky" Luciano, was deported from the United States in 1946], he charged his longtime associate Meyer Lansky with the responsibility of managing his financial empire. Lansky also played a key role in organizing Luciano's heroin syndicate: he supervised smuggling operations, negotiated with Corsican heroin manufacturers, and managed the collection and concealment of the enormous profits

"Lansky's control over the Caribbean and his relationship with the Florida-based Trafficante family were of particular importance, since many of the heroin shipments passed through Cuba or Florida on their way to America's urban markets. For almost twenty years the Luciano-Lansky-Trafficante partnership remained a major feature of the international heroin traffic."[368]

McCoy notes further: "There is reason to believe that Meyer Lansky's 1949-1950 European tour was instrumental in promoting Marseille's heroin industry. After crossing the Atlantic in a luxury liner, Lansky visited [Lucky] Luciano in Rome, where they discussed the narcotics trade. He then traveled to Zurich and contacted prominent Swiss bankers through John Pullman, an old friend from the rumrunning days.

"These negotiations established the financial labyrinth that organized crime used for decades to smuggle its enormous gambling and heroin profits out of the country into numbered Swiss bank accounts without attracting the notice of the U.S. Internal Revenue Service.

"Pullman was responsible for the European end of Lansky's financial operation: depositing, transferring, and investing the money when it arrived in Switzerland."[369]

## THE MOSSAD DRUG LINK

As we noted in Chapter 7, Lansky biographer Hank Messick himself pointed out that, ultimately, Pullman's chief Swiss depository for Lansky's drug money was the Banque de Credit International (BCI), established in 1959. This bank, as we have seen, was the brainchild of longtime Israeli Mossad officer Tibor Rosenbaum. In Chapter 15 we shall examine the Lansky-Rosenbaum-BCI link to the JFK assassination in detail.

According to Messick, "Once safely deposited in numbered accounts [at BCI and other banks], it could be invested in the stock market or returned in the form of loans to individuals and corporations controlled by the National Crime Syndicate." [370] (Pullman, who had moved from Lansky's base in Miami beach to Montreal was Lansky's lieutenant in charge of that phase of the international drug operations.)

## THE CORSICAN MAFIA

McCoy describes Lansky's European sojourn further: "After making the financial arrangements with Pullman in Switzerland, Lansky traveled through France, where he met with high-ranking Corsican syndicate leaders on the Riviera and in Paris. After lengthy discussions, Lansky and the Corsicans are reported to have arrived at some sort of agreement concerning the international heroin traffic.

"Soon after Lansky returned to the United States, heroin laboratories began appearing in Marseille. In future years, U.S. narcotics experts were to estimate that the majority of America's heroin supply was being manufactured in Marseille."[371]

McCoy notes that the European phase of the Lansky drug operations gradually began moving out of the hands of Lansky's associates in the Sicilian Mafia to the Marseille area in France, under the domination of the Corsican Mafia.[372]

All of this took place at the same time Israel's friend in the American OSS (and later the CIA), James Angleton was engaged in the region, assisting the emigration of European Jews to Palestine. (In Chapter 8 we examined Angleton's role in these affairs further, including his links to the Corsican Mafia and to BCI founder Tibor Rosenbaum.)

## LANSKY, THE CIA AND THE CORSICAN MAFIA

McCoy explains how the CIA had developed ties with Lansky's partners in the Corsican Mafia: "The CIA . . . had sent agents and a psychological warfare team to Marseille, where they dealt directly with Corsican syndicate leaders through the Guerini brothers [Antoine and Barthelemy, leaders of the Corsican Mafia]."[373]

The CIA's operatives supplied arms and money to Corsican gangs for assaults on Communist picket lines and harassment of important union officials. The communists had amassed much political clout in the region and the CIA utilized the Corsican Mafia to shatter the communists' strength.

"The Guerinis gained enough power and status from their role in smashing the 1947 strike to emerge as the new leaders of the Corsican underworld. While the CIA was instrumental in restoring the Corsican underworld's political influence, it was not until the 1950 dock strike that the Guerinis gained enough power to take control of the Marseille waterfront.

"The combination of political influence and control of the docks created the ideal environment for the growth of Marseille's heroin laboratories—fortuitously at the same time that Mafia boss Lucky Luciano was seeking an alternative source of heroin supply."[374]

## THE VIETNAMESE DRUG LINK

As McCoy notes further, the CIA had also began flexing its muscles in Southeast Asia, where the drug trade originated. McCoy describes the CIA's relationship with the indigenous drug racketeers:

"[In Laos] from 1960 to 1975, the CIA created a secret army of 30,000 Hmong tribesmen to battle Laotian Communists near the border with North Vietnam. Since the Hmong's main cash crop was opium, the CIA adopted a complicitous posture toward the traffic, allowing the Hmong commander, General Vang Po, to use the CIA's Air America to collect opium from his scattered highland villages.

"In late 1969, the CIA's various covert action clients opened a network of heroin laboratories in the Golden Triangle. In their first years of operation, these laboratories exported high-grade no. 4 heroin to U.S. troops fighting in Vietnam. After their withdrawal, the Golden Triangle laboratories exported directly to the United States, capturing one-third of the American heroin market."[375]

Thus it was that the Meyer Lansky Organized Crime Syndicate had developed a close working relationship with the CIA.

Sam Giancana's family biographers stated flatly that Giancana claimed that in exchange for the underworld services of the Organized Crime

Syndicate, "the CIA looked the other way—allowing over $100 million a year in illicit drugs to flow through Havana into the United States.

"It was an arrangement similar to all the rest they'd made, he said. The CIA received 10 percent of the take on the sale of narcotics, which they utilized 'for their undercover slush fund.' Such illegally earned monies were stashed away by the CIA in Swiss, Italian, Bahamian, and Panamanian accounts."[376]

Further, according to the Giancanas, when Sam Giancana was engaged in various and sundry rackets he conventionally shared his profits with other Organized Crime bosses depending on the region or activity in question. "Largely," they pointed out, "[Giancana's] international deals involved Lansky and whomever else they needed to take care of at the time."[377]

### SHACKLEY, CLINES & LANSDALE, AGAIN

The two primary CIA figures in Southeast Asia during the time of the Lansky-CIA drug smuggling collaboration were, interestingly enough, Theodore Shackley and Thomas Clines. Shackley was chief of station for the CIA in Laos. Clines served as Shackley's immediate deputy. [378]

As we saw in Chapter 11, it was Shackley and Clines who had supervised the CIA's Operation Mongoose, the code name for the CIA-Lansky Crime Syndicate assassination plots against Castro, operating at a headquarters on the University of Miami campus. It was this operation that came to be known as JM/Wave.

Operation Mongoose, it turns out, was under the direction of General Edward Lansdale whom, assassination researcher Bernard Fensterwald notes later "reportedly cultivated a close relationship with the Corsican Mafia during his controversial service in Vietnam."[379]

Interestingly enough, it was Shackley and Clines—upon "retiring" from the CIA who set up an arms dealing agency—the Egyptian Transport Service Company.[380] This firm worked closely with Israel's Mossad figure Shaul Eisenberg's Aviation Trade and Service Company.[381] Eisenberg, in fact, was a major player in Israel's nuclear arms development program—the very operation that created the crisis between John F. Kennedy and Israel. The plot clearly comes full circle.

The role of Lansky in all of these activities, however, has been carefully ignored, even by writers—Alfred McCoy, the notable exception—who have exposed the CIA's role in the global drug racket.

### COVERING UP THE LANSKY CONNECTION

In *Endless Enemies: The Making of an Unfriendly World*, journalist Jonathan Kwitny takes several pages to outline the CIA-backed drug trafficking networks operating out of Southeast Asia and using the CIA-allied Corsican crime families as a central distribution source.

Kwitny points out the role of Charles "Lucky" Luciano in establishing the initial networks which also utilized the Sicilian crime families in the Mediterranean. Kwitny even acknowledges Alfred McCoy's work as "the best published documentation of all of this." [382]

However, interestingly enough, Kwitny does not once mention Meyer Lansky's pivotal role in formally establishing the Luciano-launched global drug network, despite the fact that Kwitny cited McCoy as "the best published" source on the history of the drug network. Nor does Kwitny make reference to Santo Trafficante, Jr., Lansky's chief lieutenant and primary heir in the global drug racket.

This is all particularly interesting when one realizes that in the recent furor over the JFK assassination conspiracy (resulting from the release of Oliver Stone's JFK film) that Kwitny himself is one of the primary promoters of the theory that "The Mafia Killed JFK," According to Kwitny, the principal architect of the crime was, by his estimation, more than likely New Orleans Mafia boss Carlos Marcello—who, as we have seen, was one of Lansky's local front men.[383] Evidently Kwitny—like others who claim that "The Mafia Killed JFK"—doesn't want to acknowledge that Meyer Lansky even existed.

## NOT GUILTY?

It is also worth mentioning as well that Lansky's friendly biographer, Robert Lacey, writing in his 1991 biography of Lansky goes to great lengths to suggest that Lansky had no part in the international drug racket. This, as we have seen, is par for the course as far as Lacey's attitude toward Lansky is concerned.

However, Rachel Ehrenfeld, one of the world's leading experts on the drug combine and its connections with global terrorism, writes in her book *Evil Money* that "there exists reliable evidence to the contrary."[384]

She cites an interview she conducted with a former congressional special investigator for organized crime. She reports that she was "reassured that the evidence for Lansky's illegal dealings was ample and that Lacey must have been the victim of his close dealings with Lansky's former associates and family."[385]

## FRENCH ASSASSINS?

Considering the CIA's alliance with Lansky's allies in the Corsican Mafia, it is interesting to consider here that there are those who believe that the Corsican Mafia or other French elements may have played a role in the assassination of John F. Kennedy. There is evidence, indeed, that at least one French mercenary did show up in Dallas the day JFK was slain.

Writing in *Reasonable Doubt*, Henry Hurt explores one aspect of the so-called "French connection" in some detail. He describes the possible role of a French OAS terrorist in the assassination.

As we saw in Chapter 6 and in Chapter 9, the OAS was comprised of CIA-backed French forces who opposed granting independence to the French colony in Arab Algeria. This led them into direct confrontation with French President Charles DeGaulle who granted Algerian independence.

As a member of the Senate, as we saw in Chapter 4, John F. Kennedy had called for Algerian independence, in opposition to the OAS. Israel itself had a stake in continued French domination of Algeria in that French occupation of Algeria was a direct obstacle in the path of Arab nationalism. (In Chapter 15 we will examine Israel's covert ties to the OAS.)

Hurt cites a CIA document discovered in 1977 by Mary Ferrell, Dallas researcher: "The document, dated April 1, 1964, reported that the French intelligence service wanted help in locating one Jean Souetre, a French OAS terrorist considered a threat to the safety of French President Charles DeGaulle.

"The document asserted that Jean Souetre was in Fort Worth, Texas, on the morning of November 22, 1963. That morning President Kennedy also was in Fort Worth.  A few hours later, John F. Kennedy was in Dallas, where, at 12:30 p.m. he was assassinated. Also in Dallas that afternoon was Jean Souetre.

"Within forty-eight hours of Kennedy's death, according to the query from the French, Jean Souetre was picked up by U.S. authorities in Texas. He was immediately expelled from the United States. French intelligence wanted to ascertain whether he was expelled to Canada or Mexico.

"The French also wanted to know why the U.S. authorities had expelled Souetre. The simple purpose was to ensure the safety of President DeGaulle on his pending trip to Mexico."[386]

Hurt notes that the original document also noted that Souetre used the names Michel Roux and Michel Mertz.  Roux happened to be in Fort Worth on November 22, having entered the country on November 19 and leaving at Laredo, Texas on December 6. He was not expelled. When questioned later, Souetre said that Mertz was an old enemy who often used **his** name and may have been trying to implicate him in misdeeds.

## THE HUNT CONNECTION

Interestingly enough, it was CIA man E. Howard Hunt (whom we first met in Chapter 9) who was one of the CIA's point men in the dealings with Souetre and OAS intelligence.[387] That the two may have been in Dallas—perhaps even together—during the time of the JFK assassination is intriguing, to say the very least and yet another of the details that, taken together, demonstrate continuing intimate connections between persons and institutions that have (elsewhere) been repeatedly linked to the JFK assassination conspiracy.

In Chapter 15  and Chapter 16 we shall see that Israeli Mossad/Lansky-linked elements in New Orleans and elsewhere funnelled money to the OAS for a 1962 assassination attempt against Charles DeGaulle and that, indeed, these same elements are tied directly to the JFK assassination.

## TWO SIDES OF THE SAME COIN

Professor Alfred McCoy summarizes the covert links between the CIA and organized crime around the world:

"Since prohibition of narcotics in the 1920s, alliances between drug brokers and intelligence agencies have protected the global narcotics traffic. Given the frequency of such alliances, there seems a natural attraction between intelligence agencies and criminal syndicates . . . Both are practitioners of what one retired CIA operative has called the 'clandestine arts'—the basic skill of operating outside the normal channels of civil society. Among all the institutions of modern society, intelligence agencies and criminal syndicates alone maintain large organizations capable of carrying out covert operations without fear of detection."[388]

Chicago Mafia boss Sam Giancana's family biographers have written of Giancana's own elaboration on this relationship. They described how Giancana showed his brother an ancient Roman coin and declared: "Look, this is one of the Roman gods. This one has two faces . . . two sides. That's what we are, the Outfit and the CIA—two sides of the same coin."[389]

## ISRAEL, THE CIA AND THE DRUG COMBINE

All the evidence we have covered here suggests that the CIA and the Meyer Lansky Organized Crime Syndicate were indeed partners in many areas of mutual concern—not only in Cuba and in the Southeast Asian drug racket—but also in the assassination of John F. Kennedy.

And as we saw in Chapter 6, Lansky's allies in Israel stood much to benefit from American involvement in Southeast Asia.

While Israel was using America's engagement in and preoccupation with the Vietnam conflict as a means whereby Israel could flex its muscle in the Middle East, the Lansky narcotics network was using its partnership with the CIA during the Vietnam War as a cover for its drug-smuggling.

And as we have seen in Chapter 8, the CIA and Israel itself had long and close ties equally as incestuous of those of the Lansky Organized Crime Syndicate and Israel. That Israel had its own difficulties with John F. Kennedy we have already seen. Likewise with the Mafia and the Lansky Syndicate. In Chapter 9 we reviewed the CIA's own problems with John F. Kennedy. Clearly, this alliance of forces against JFK was such that there was really no way John F. Kennedy could have ever completed his first term in the White House.

## Chapter Thirteen

## Israel's California Connection:
## Mickey Cohen and the JFK Assassination Conspiracy

**The role of Meyer Lansky's West Coast henchman—longtime Israeli loyalist Mickey Cohen—in the JFK assassination conspiracy is one of history's little-known stories. Cohen—who was one of Jack Ruby's idols—apparently had a direct hand in the initial stages of Israeli machinations against John F. Kennedy. Evidence suggests also that the death of film actress Marilyn Monroe was linked, in fact, to the Israeli connection in the JFK assassination conspiracy.**

When Mickey Cohen's name has appeared in numerous books and monographs relating to the JFK murder, it has only been in passing. Cohen, it would appear on the surface, deserves mention if only because of his involvement in Organized Crime which figures so prominently in JFK conspiracy theories.

However, Cohen's intimate involvement with Israel and its international intrigue, and Cohen's dedication to advancing Israel's interests—even at the expense of his own criminal money-making activities—needs to be examined further.

The evidence we shall examine here suggests that even the death of film actress Marilyn Monroe is indeed linked to the John F. Kennedy assassination in a way never imagined.

Cohen, as we shall see, was using Miss Monroe—one of John F. Kennedy's illicit liaisons—as a conduit to learn Kennedy's intentions toward Israel. There is a lot more to the story of Marilyn Monroe's affair with JFK than the tabloids have told us.

### COHEN'S MEMOIRS

The primary source on Mickey Cohen is the Los Angeles mobster's own colorful memoirs. Cohen's memoir—*Mickey Cohen: In My Own Words*—is one of the more fascinating first-hand accounts of life in Organized Crime. The memoir is particularly interesting for three specific reasons:

(a) it is one of the few autobiographical accounts of life in Organized Crime written by a non-Italian. Virtually all of the popular accounts of life in the mob come from former "Mafia" members or associates. Cohen—with the exception of Michael Milan, whom we first met in Chapter 7—is perhaps the only other non-Italian, non-Mafia Organized Crime leader to put his experiences in writing.

(b) Cohen, as Hollywood's rackets boss, was a central player in that unique underworld that links the entertainment industry to Organized Crime. A friend and associate of the prominent and of the rich and powerful, Cohen knew where Hollywood's bodies were buried, in more ways than one.

(c) Cohen's "ghost-writer,"—the man who put Cohen's sometimes inelegant ramblings together and edited them for publication—was John Peer Nugent.

## THE CIA CONNECTION

A former correspondent for *Newsweek*, Nugent was—on one occasion—taken into custody while in Africa on suspicion of being a CIA agent. He was released through the personal intervention of then-Secretary of State Dean Rusk. However, according to organized crime authority Art Kunkin, Nugent did have CIA connections. [390]

Interestingly enough, Nugent himself once participated in a debate with JFK assassination investigator, A. J. Weberman, co-author of *Coup d'Etat in America*, where he—Nugent—sought to refute CIA complicity in the JFK assassination.

In this context, one can't help but wonder if Cohen's memoirs weren't a laundered version, CIA-style.

Both what does appear in Cohen's reminiscences—and what doesn't appear—are equally intriguing. Cohen's memoirs are a gold-mine of often fascinating information, particularly in regard to the Hollywood mobster's early links to Israel and its birth struggle.

## SUCCESSOR TO SIEGEL

Cohen was the West Coast successor to Meyer Lansky's ill-fated boyhood crony, Benjamin Siegel, Organized Crime's top man on the West Coast until his bloody assassination on June 20, 1947. Remembered best as "the man who invented Las Vegas," the handsome Siegel was shot dead in the Beverly Hills home of his second wife, mob playgirl Virginia Hill.

Lansky and Siegel were longtime friends and early partners in Brooklyn at the beginning of their initial reach into the upper echelons of Organized Crime. The oft-told tales of New York's "Bug and Meyer Mob" are legendary in the annals of Organized Crime. "Bug and Meyer" were treacherous killers in those early years. There's no reason to think that Lansky mellowed with age.

Believed by Organized Crime's ruling commission of looting  funds earmarked for the casino network he was establishing in Las Vegas on behalf of the syndicate, Siegel was slain in retribution for his betrayal. This was said to be a great personal loss for his friend, Lansky.

## LANSKY ORDERS THE HIT

Yet, Lansky himself apparently agreed to the decision that Siegel had to be executed. Lansky even agreed to handle the arrangements if necessary.

Apparently he did. "I had no choice," Lansky later said, reflecting upon his friend's betrayal and its consequences.[391]

(The best accounts of Siegel's role in the development of the Las Vegas front for the Lansky Crime Syndicate appear in *The Green Felt Jungle* by Ed Reid and Ovid Demaris and *We Only Kill Each Other*, a biography of Siegel written by Dean Jennings).

## HOOVER SENDS HIS SYMPATHIES

In Chapter 7 we explored the FBI Director J. Edgar Hoover's seeming inability to acknowledge the existence of the Lansky Organized Crime Syndicate as well as Hoover's connections to Israel's American-based intelligence and propaganda agency, the Lansky Syndicate-financed Anti-Defamation League (ADL) of B'nai B'rith. (We shall discuss the ADL in further detail in Chapter 17.)

Michael Milan (whom we first met in Chapter 7 as a mutual associate of both Hoover and Lansky) says that when the hit was ordered on Ben Siegel, "Even [J. Edgar Hoover] himself had to concur and told everybody to stand away. He sent Meyer Lansky his personal condolences, however, because he had liked Benny, and Benny had showed him a good time whenever he went to the Coast."[392]

Whatever the circumstances, it was, in fact Mickey Cohen who assumed Siegel's position as Lansky's West Coast representative upon Siegel's assassination.

## LANSKY'S 'EYES AND EARS'

According to Lansky's biographer, Hank Messick, it was Cohen who was Lansky's real "eyes and ears" in Southern California—not his good friend Siegel. One of Cohen's primary responsibilities was keeping an eye on the free-wheeling and reckless Siegel on Lansky's behalf.

When Siegel was removed from the scene it was Cohen who stepped in and took charge of Lansky's West Coast affairs—quite a fortuitous set of circumstances for the simian thug who could —by no means—ever have competed with Siegel in a beauty contest. No wonder then that Cohen recalled in his memoirs, "I have a great love and respect and a complete high regard for Meyer Lansky."[393]

## COHEN & ISRAEL

Aside, however, from his direct ties to Lansky, and his own intra-mob machinations, Mickey Cohen was in the State of Israel's camp from the very beginning of its existence—even before. By his own admission, Cohen was engaged in arms smuggling and fund-raising for Israel even before Israel had become a state.

In his memoirs Cohen recalls his first encounter with an agent of Israel's international fund-raising and arms-smuggling operations and how he came to identify with Israel's cause.

Speaking of his crony, Mike Howard, Cohen recounted the day that Howard introduced him to an Israeli operative. (In his memoirs Cohen does not name the Israeli in question.) Howard, he says, "knew that I would do anything for a cause that was right, and particularly Jewish causes." [394]

At first, Cohen says, he was hesitant to become involved. He changed his mind, though. "So they come back," Cohen recalled, "and we sit down to talk. And the guy tells me this story about the Haganah, which was organized by the David Ben-Gurion guy. And he tells me especially about the Irgun and the type of war they're fighting against the British, and the type of guys they are and all this. And I got high on him.

"But you know when you're kinky [i.e. criminally-oriented] your mind runs kinky. I still figured this must be a racket thing. So I says to the guy, 'Lookit, I don't know nothing about these things. I didn't even know there was a war going on in Israel. Let me think it over.'"[395]

Cohen made no decision, one way or the other, but after Hollywood screenwriter, publicist and playwright Ben Hecht—an ardent advocate of the Zionist cause—came visiting, Cohen began to see the light. Hecht appeared at Cohen's headquarters accompanied by a representative of the bloody terrorist Irgun gang. The individual, once again, Cohen did not name. "I could see that I was dealing with a real man, no con guy," [396]remembered Cohen.

## MENACHEM BEGIN COMES TO TOWN

In his own memoirs Jimmy ("the Weasel") Fratianno, a top West Coast Mafia figure-turned-government informant, gives us a hint as to who Cohen's Irgun friend may have been. Fratianno described a benefit for Israel at an exclusive Bel Air home:

"After [Cohen's] little speech, we start moving around the room and Mickey's rabbi introduces us to a guy called Menachem Begin, who's the boss of the Irgun, an underground outfit in Palestine. This guy's wearing a black armband and he tells us he's wanted back there for bombing a hotel that killed almost a hundred people. He's a fucking lamster [i.e. on the run].

"Anyway, he makes a speech, and after him just about everybody made a speech. It just goes on and on. Afterwards these other guys from the Haganah, another underground outfit, start arguing with Begin about who's going to handle the money. So Mickey chirps in and it's agreed that his rabbi will handle the money and Mickey will buy guns and ammo and ship them over there."[397]

[This, as we shall see, would not be the last time that Menachem Begin would be spotted in the company of Mickey Cohen, however.]

Fratianno frankly doubted Cohen's sincerity and suspected that Cohen was in "the cause" for the money to be made. However, in his own memoirs, Cohen was insistent about his dedication to Israel. In fact, he goes on at length about his devotion.

"I got engrossed with the goddamn thing pretty strong see. Through my connections I made everybody throughout the country–the Italians, the Jews, the Irish—set up whatever positions there were to be helpful to the Israel cause."[398]

## DEDICATED TO ISRAEL

Cohen's dedication was inestimable. He was so devoted to Israel, indeed, that he allowed his criminal activities to go by the wayside. Cohen says:

"Now I got so engrossed with Israel that I actually pushed aside a lot of my activities and done nothing but what was involved with this Irgun war. It's a nature of mine, see. Either I go whole hog or nothing. So I got involved with this goddamn Israel war for three years. I started to have relationships with Irgun members back in Israel. They got to understand me better and I got to understand them better.

"Well, I had raised considerable money, not particularly myself, but through me, throughout the country. There were dinners held in Boston, Philadelphia, Miami. And plenty of armament and equipment was collected that you couldn't possibly get.

"It was only God's will that Harry Truman was President. He couldn't openly allow it to be known that he was okaying stuff to be shipped back there or that stuff was being stolen from the ships that were coming back from the Second World War.

"But it was only with Truman's looking the other way, or with his being in favor, that it was done. To me, he was the greatest man in the world, Harry Truman, because of what he done for Israel and because he made it available for us to do.

"We were able to get on ships that were being put into mothballs. I had access to all that stuff on the docks. Some of the stuff and equipment like machine guns that we got back to Israel had never got a chance to be used in the Second World War. They weren't even put together. They were still in the cases, in the straw, in the oil and everything. We shipped them right over."[399]

## JACK RUBY COMES TO TOWN

It was during this same time that Cohen was also making the acquaintance of another thug, Jack Rubinstein, who ultimately changed his last name to Ruby.

Gary Wean—whose business it was to keep an eye on Cohen's activities—later put his fascinating experiences down in an informal memoir entitled *There's a Fish in the Courthouse.*

Wean's contributions to Kennedy assassination research, however, have not received the widespread recognition they deserve.

A detective sergeant for the Los Angeles Police Department, Wean got to know Mickey Cohen well. What's more, as a Criminal Intelligence Investigator for the Los Angeles District Attorney's Bureau of Investigation, Wean was privy to much "inside" information about Cohen and his activities in Hollywood.

(Wean was also—later—chief investigator for the Ventura County Public Defenders Office until 1970. He is now retired.)

In his memoirs, Wean says he saw Ruby twice in Hollywood in 1946 and in 1947. The first time Ruby was riding with Cohen in Cohen's big black limousine, although, on that occasion, they were not introduced.[400]

The second time Wean encountered Ruby was a year later. According to Wean, he and his partner went to a nightclub known as Harry's Place. Ruby was there, and Wean introduced himself and informed Ruby that he was a police officer.

In turn, Ruby introduced himself. He said: "My name is Jack Ruby. I just came out from Chicago to get with Harry. Since the war's over the West Coast is dead, so is Chicago, We're moving 'everything' to New Orleans and Miami. That is where all the action is going to be from now, between the United States and Cuba."[401]

(A New Orleans chief assistant district attorney has essentially confirmed Ruby's claim that the Crescent City had become a hub of syndicate financing and activity. According to the prosecutor, "There is too much money here. We feel that it's flowing in from other Cosa Nostra [Mafia] organizations in other parts of the country for investment by the local mobs. This could be their financial center, with a lot of nice safe places where campaign contributions and outright bribery have pretty well insulated them from the law.") [402]

In any case, as we shall see, this was just the beginning of Jack Ruby's relationship with Mickey Cohen and Cohen's West Coast associates. It wasn't until 1963, however, that the relationship came full circle, as we shall see in Chapter 14.

## COHEN'S SPECIAL RACKET

By 1960, Cohen was an established power in the West Coast syndicate operations of Meyer Lansky. And Cohen was also a key figure in Hollywood, nurturing his relationships with the film colony there—for his own insidious purposes.

As author John Davis notes: "One of Cohen's rackets was sexually compromising Hollywood stars for the purpose of blackmail. It had been Cohen who engineered the torrid affair between his accomplice, Johnny Stompanato, and [film star] Lana Turner, in the hope of getting pictures of the two in bed together." [403] [Miss Turner's daughter later killed Stompanato in an event that became a major Hollywood scandal.]

But Cohen's activities went further. Cohen was also manipulating beautiful screen star Marilyn Monroe for yet another purpose—one which had international implications.

Now as the legend goes, it was ostensibly the Frank Sinatra connection that led to the introduction of Marilyn Monroe to John F. Kennedy. However, according to Gary Wean, it was in fact the Mickey Cohen connection that brought the handsome Massachusetts Senator and the Hollywood sex symbol together.

Wean reveals that Cohen's close friend, entertainer Joey Bishop—who also happened to be a member of Sinatra's famous clique known as "the rat pack"—was the one who actually set up the circumstances that led to the initial liaison between JFK and Miss Monroe during the 1960 presidential campaign.

"It was Joey Bishop that came up with the 'idea of a wild party' for Kennedy. He talked [Peter] Lawford [JFK's brother-in-law] into it."[404]

## MARILYN MONROE

According to Wean, there was a reason for all of this—beyond satisfying JFK's notorious appetite for beautiful women: "Bishop knew Kennedy would be taken by the Monroe sex appeal. Bishop was a Jew and real tight with Cohen.

"At that time the rabbis were pushing them hard as hell to squeeze every bit of dough they could get out of Hollywood for Israel. [Menachem] Begin was spending more time hanging around Cohen in Hollywood than in Israel. Begin desperately wanted to know what Kennedy's plan was for Israel if he became president.

"Cohen figured if they could duke Marilyn into Kennedy, [Cohen's pimp Georgie] Piscitelli would be able to manipulate her and tell them everything Kennedy told her. Also they'd work a [blackmail] squeeze [against JFK] if a romance blossomed.

"Cohen also had something going on with Jack Ruby. His girl friend, [a stripper by the name of] Candy Barr, was making a lot of trips between Ruby in Dallas and Cohen in Hollywood."[405]

According to what Wean uncovered during his surveillance, Cohen's pimp Piscitelli was also sleeping with Miss Monroe. Wean learned this from a young lady named Mary Mercandante who was jealous of Piscitelli's relationship with Miss Monroe. Miss Mercandante, it seems, was a prostitute and Piscitelli was her pimp.

## JFK'S VIEWS TOWARD ISRAEL?

It was from Miss Mercandante that Wean learned something which he came to describe as "the really weird stuff."[406] Miss Mercandante told Wean that Piscitelli's job was to pump Miss Monroe for information about JFK's views toward Israel. (As we have seen in Chapter 4 and Chapter 5,

Israel and its American lobby were uneasy, to say the very least, about Kennedy.)

However, according to Wean, Piscitelli told Miss Mercandante that Marilyn would get upset when he began pressing her, saying she didn't know anything about politics. Wean reports that Miss Mercandante told him that: "Cohen got mad and told Georgie to stick with Marilyn and pour drinks or pills down her, whatever it takes and find out what John Kennedy intended to do about financing Israel."[407]

## ANGRY WITH KENNEDY

According to Wean's source: "Cohen and Begin were plenty upset over Kennedy's plans to give billions of dollars to the Peace Corps, and the South American and African countries."[408]

Miss Mercandante began threatening to reveal all she knew about Cohen's manipulation of the film actress and the affair with Kennedy. Wean, however, had already reported his findings to his superiors.

## TWO MURDERS?

Miss Mercandante was later murdered. She appears to be yet another of the many victims of what ultimately evolved into the JFK assassination conspiracy and cover-up.

Now although there has long been widespread suspicion that Marilyn Monroe was herself perhaps murdered, the tabloids would have us believe that she was murdered by the Kennedy family to keep silent about her affair with the President and—allegedly also—his brother, Attorney General Robert Kennedy.

The evidence we have seen here, however, suggests that if Miss Monroe was murdered it indeed was to keep her silent—but for an entirely different reason.

If Miss Monroe ever revealed that Mickey Cohen had used her to find out Kennedy's stance toward Israel, it would have opened a Pandora's Box that could have exposed Israel's uneasy relationship with JFK—something that Israel and its American lobby could not afford.

What is interesting is that in his memoirs—which are filled with Cohen's incessant name-dropping and accounts of his friendships with a bevy of Hollywood figures—Cohen never once mentions Marilyn Monroe. Nor does he mention Jack Ruby, for that matter either.

There were evidently certain things that Cohen and his co-author did not see fit to mention. It is more than interesting to note, at least in passing, that Meyer Lansky himself had "inside" knowledge on the extra-marital affairs of Attorney General Robert Kennedy at the very least.

According to J. Edgar Hoover biographer Curt Gentry, Lansky was overheard on a federal wiretap on August 1, 1962 telling his wife, Teddy, that Robert Kennedy was carrying on an affair with a woman in El Paso, Texas.[409]

## WHAT WERE THEY UP TO?

In any event, Mickey Cohen's strange activities were of continuing particular interest to Gary Wean.

Wean described in his memoirs how he first discovered the close working relationship between Cohen and Israeli terrorist-turned-roving diplomat (and later Israeli Prime Minister) Menachem Begin, whose Hollywood activities we reviewed earlier in this chapter:

"[My partner] and I'd been watching Mickey Cohen from a distance. We knew he was up to something out of the ordinary. He spent a lot of time with a weird-looking little guy at the Beverly Wilshire Hotel lunch counter and drug store area.

"What got our curiosity most was Mickey seemed to be taking orders from the stranger. We got photos with our telescopic lens of Cohen and his friend. The office checked it out. We learned his name: Menachem Begin."[410]

To find out further what Cohen and Begin were involved with, Wean deployed a Yiddish-speaking spy to listen in on Cohen and Begin's conversations. Wean notes: "He reported that the two in a deep discussion were very excitable. There was a lot of talk about Cuba and military operations and the Kennedys."[411] According to Wean's operative: "We've really got something going. Mickey sounded like a politician. They were going on about war and billion dollar appropriations, cursing JFK about his crazy Peace Corps and wasting money."[412]

## MELVIN BELLI

According to Wean, after this coffee shop conference, Cohen and Begin departed. Wean and his partner followed Cohen to an elegant home in Los Angeles. There, Wean says, Cohen and Begin met with high-priced lawyer Melvin Belli, Cohen's longtime friend and attorney. [413]

Belli, we shall see in Chapter 14, came to play an important role in the tangled web of intrigue surrounding the Kennedy assassination. Belli served as attorney for Jack Ruby.

Interestingly enough, according to Wean, Cohen, Ruby and Menachem Begin shared one other thing in common: Cohen was sharing his girlfriend, stripper Candy Barr, with not only Ruby (then operating in Dallas), but also with Begin, Israel's man in Hollywood.[414]

However, Mickey Cohen had a lot more on his mind than his criminal activities and his sexual pursuits. Cohen was interested in the survival of Israel, the nation he had helped establish.

## COHEN'S MISSION

Cohen's peculiar interest in JFK's Middle East policy, coupled with his unfortunate manipulation of Marilyn Monroe, along with his longtime devotion to the Zionist cause, places him squarely in the midst of the Lansky Organized Crime Syndicate's central part in the JFK assassination conspiracy.

The simian-like Los Angeles thug was very much privy to the circumstances of what really took place in the JFK assassination. What Cohen may have known, however, was lost forever when the Lansky henchman died suddenly of a heart attack. He had no known history of heart trouble. In Chapter 14 we shall examine Cohen's connection with Jack Ruby in more detail.

Years after his encounter with Cohen and Begin, Gary Wean received what he described as "a strange call." It was from a writer named Ed Tivnan who said he was looking into Begin's alleged association with American gangsters.

## COVERING FOR ISRAEL

"My book's purpose is to deny, dispel and silence the accusations of Begin's criminal associations with them," [415]said Tivnan. Tivnan was not interested in Wean's account of Begin's very real association with the Lansky Organized Crime Syndicate. It was something that Israel did not want told.

There is another interesting sidelight to all of this. When author Anthony Summers was preparing his book *Goddess*, a life of Marilyn Monroe, he contacted Wean for information and Wean provided Summers with all of the details we've reviewed in these pages.

However, when Summers' biography of Miss Monroe finally hit the bookstores, the author had nothing to say about Cohen and the Israeli connection. Instead, the book suggested that Miss Monroe's death was a proximate result of her affair with the Kennedy brothers.

Indeed, the book led the reader to believe that it was the Kennedys who were, one way or the other, responsible—directly or indirectly—for the young woman's tragic death. The Mickey Cohen-Israel connection went unmentioned.

There is something else interesting. This same Anthony Summers is the Anthony Summers who wrote an exhaustive study of the JFK assassination entitled *Conspiracy*. (This was before he met with Wean.) *However, when Summers released an up-dated edition of his book in 1992, he never reported the information that Wean provided him about the Israeli connection.* It is likely, in all fairness to Summers, that he probably did not understand the significance of what he had learned. However, it is very clear, considering everything that we have already examined in these

pages—and what we are about to examine—that Wean's discovery was a
key to understanding what really happened on November 22, 1963.

## THE COHEN CONNECTION

Today, there are those, as we have seen, who continually cite Jack
Ruby's connections with organized crime as proof that "The Mafia Killed
JFK." Some have even pointed out that one of Ruby's first telephone calls
he made immediately after the JFK assassination (just shortly after Lee
Harvey Oswald had been arrested) was to Al Gruber, a Mickey Cohen
associate in Hollywood.

Gruber, it also turns out—perhaps not surprisingly—was associated
with Lansky's Mexico City syndicate drug-smuggling connection, "Happy"
Meltzer, with whom, as we shall see in Chapter 14, Ruby had his own
connections.[416]

In fact, although Ruby had not seen Gruber in some ten years, Gruber
came to visit Ruby in Dallas in November of 1963, just shortly before the
assassination.

Other than this, the Cohen-Ruby link is given little play—perhaps
precisely because it points not in the direction of the Mafia, but instead,
more directly to Israel and the Meyer Lansky Organized Crime Syndicate.

As it stands, ironically enough, Mickey Cohen was already incarcerated
in federal prison by the time of the JFK assassination. Lansky's West Coast
lieutenant was one of many "big names" snared in the Kennedy war against
the Lansky crime syndicate. There was clearly no love lost between Mickey
Cohen and the Kennedy brothers.

It seems likely—and Gary Wean believes, as he told this author—that
Cohen's henchman Gruber was the intermediary for the Lansky syndicate in
the delicate matter of how to silence the patsy—Oswald—who had
somehow escaped being killed and was then in the custody of the Dallas
police.

Mickey Cohen and Menachem Begin very clearly were involved in the
intial stages of what ultimately evolved into the JFK assassination
conspiracy precisely because of Kennedy's difficult foreign policy struggle
with Israel which sparked the plot against the American president.

Perhaps this might explain why Jack Ruby—in his final days—was
fearful that if the truth about the assassination of John F. Kennedy ever
came out that, as Ruby put it, "the Jews" would be blamed for the crime.[417]

In the next chapter we will examine Jack Ruby's role further and
consider his connections with the Lansky syndicate—and with Israel.

## Chapter Fourteen

## The Errand Boy:
## Jack Ruby, Lansky & the CIA

Jack Ruby's connections to the criminal underworld are well-documented. However, what is often ignored is Ruby's integral link to the Meyer Lansky Organized Crime Syndicate—not "the Mafia"— and to Israel's allies in the CIA.

In fact, the lawyer who came to Ruby's defense following the killing of Lee Harvey Oswald was Melvin Belli, longtime associate of Lansky's West Coast henchman (and Israel's arms-smuggling contact) Mickey Cohen.

Organized crime historian Stephen Fox has called Dallas nightclub operator Jack Ruby "the smoking gun, the Rosetta stone, the trout in the milk" in the JFK assassination conspiracy.[418]

Ironically, not only did Ruby silence Oswald and help perpetuate the JFK assassination conspiracy and cover-up, but he also added fuel to the fire of speculation as a consequence. Had Lee Harvey Oswald died of a heart attack in the Dallas jail, rather than at the hands of a mob-linked thug named Jack Ruby, suspicion of a conspiracy might not have evolved so quickly. Yet, when Jack Ruby stepped into the public limelight and eliminated Oswald, attention was focused on the strange background on the Chicago-born underworld figure who had killed the alleged assassin.

Ruby's criminal ties are legendary. As a youth in Chicago, Ruby worked for Al Capone himself. His other organized crime connections, in Chicago, Dallas and elsewhere have been documented time and again.

However, as we shall see in this chapter and as we already determined in Chapter 13, Ruby was more than a low-level Jewish henchman in the employ of the Italian wing of organized crime.

Ruby, in fact, was very much a part of the Meyer Lansky Crime Syndicate and, what's more—the Warren Commission's conclusions notwithstanding—was also working for Lansky's longtime collaborators in the CIA, itself tied closely with Israel's Mossad (documented in detail in Chapter 8.)

### THE LANSKY-RUBY CONNECTION

The late Bernard Fensterwald, one of the leading JFK assassination researchers, documented Ruby's Lansky connection in his encyclopedic work, *Coincidence or Conspiracy*:

"Ruby told the Warren Commission on June 7, 1964 about his 1959 visit to [Lewis] McWillie in Havana, and also spoke of knowing McWillie's bosses. Interestingly enough, McWillie's bosses at that time were Meyer and Jake Lansky. Ruby mysteriously spoke of meeting two brothers who'd owned the Tropicana Casino which McWillie managed. Ruby said he was unsure of their last name but thought it had been Fox. It has long been known that Meyer and Jake Lansky were in fact the two key Tropicana owners. The Tropicana had been a cornerstone of their Cuban holdings.

"Ruby also described 'the Fox brothers' as 'the greatest that have been expelled from Cuba,' and said they were then living in Miami. Meyer and Jake Lansky were known as the most prominent Syndicate men expelled by the Castro government and were in fact then living in Miami. Ruby said he thought one of the 'Fox brothers' first names may have been Martin.

"Ruby further testified that one of the 'Fox brothers' had later visited him in Dallas, accompanied by Lewis McWillie. Ruby claimed that they had dined at the Dallas airport together. Ruby further testified that Fox and McWillie had also subsequently dropped by his nightclub, where they posed for photographs with him. Ruby later took the photos with him when he visited McWillie in Cuba:

"'Evidently the Foxes were in exile at that time, because when I went to visit McWillie . . . [Cuban officials] looked through my luggage and they saw a photograph of Mr. Fox and his wife.

"'They didn't interrogate but they went through everything and held me up for hours . . . Evidently in my ignorance I didn't realize I was bringing a picture [of someone] they knew was a bitter enemy."[419]

There is some question, however, as to whether or not the "Fox brothers" were, in fact, the Lansky brothers.

Ruby biographer Seth Kantor notes that there were brothers named Martin and Pedro Fox who were Cuban nationals and involved in the Tropicana. (Nonetheless, the Tropicana was owned by the Lansky brothers.)

Kantor writes: "The significance of all this marching up and down the hill about the Fox brothers is that Ruby was a rational man at the time of the Warren Commission's June 7, 1964 interview with him.

"He was telling them the truth, and begged to be taken out of Texas so he could tell them more. But no one listened, on one of the sorriest days in the Warren Commission's history." [420]

It is interesting to note that at the time of the JFK assassination Ruby's good friend McWillie was working at the Thunderbird Hotel in Las Vegas, owned in part by Meyer Lansky and his brother Jake. As Peter Dale Scott succinctly summarizes it: "In other words, McWillie was working for the Lanskys when Ruby made seven phone calls to him in 1963."[421] These were among the phone calls made to organized crime-related figures that authors David Scheim and John W. Davis and G. Robert Blakey have used to promote the theory that "The Mafia Killed JFK."

Ruby did indeed call some seven or eight mob-linked individuals in the period just before the JFK assassination, but, according to Peter Dale Scott, "only one of these was Italian."[422] Yet, as Scott points out, Blakey's House Assassinations Committee preferred to cast Ruby as a "Mafia" figure and to ignore his positioning in the Lansky sphere.

"Only from officials," Scott notes wryly, "can logic like this be encountered."[423] In general Scott describes this as a form of "conscious bias, or what might be called contrived bias, the purpose of which is to deceive others."[424]

Whatever the direct link between Lansky and Ruby in this regard, however, JFK assassination researcher Jim Marrs states flatly that Ruby had a share in a gambling house in Hallandale, Florida along with Meyer and Jake Lansky, among others, in the early 1950s. [425]

There is no doubt that Ruby and Lansky's world of intrigue intersected in several arenas, as we shall see—whether the two actually ever were personally acquainted or not.

## RUBY AND THE LANSKY DRUG RACKET

Peter Dale Scott has scored G. Robert Blakey and his House Assassinations Committee for its dismal failure to explore and to expose Ruby's Lansky connections which are very strong indeed. Scott, who has studied Jack Ruby's criminal antecedents, has outlined Ruby's critical positioning in the Lansky syndicate.

According to Scott: "It is certain that Ruby was investigated [in the mid-1940's] for his role in [an] international drug-trafficking syndicate, involving corruption of government officials in Mexico City."[426] The top syndicate representative in Mexico City was one Harold "Happy" Meltzer, but, in fact, it was Meyer Lansky who was "the key figure in the Meltzer syndicate."[427] According to Scott, "Right after World War II this was probably the biggest drug-smuggling channel into the United States."[428]

The House Assassinations Committee, in Scott's judgment, failed to note that "Ruby was in some way an important figure"[429] in the linkage between organized crime and the political arena in Dallas and "on a federal level."[430] Ruby, in short, was no mere mob hanger-on as some have tried to suggest and he was not, by any stretch of the imagination, part of "the Mafia" as G. Robert Blakey and some others have suggested.

## RUBY WAS NOT 'MAFIA'

According to Scott, the House Committee investigation of Ruby and his underworld associates chose to focus on what Scott describes as an "ethnic model of organized crime as 'La Cosa Nostra'"[431]—that is, focusing on the so-called "Mafia," the popularized media sobriquet for Italian elements in the organized crime underworld, rather than upon the more substantially predominent Jewish elements personified by Meyer Lansky and those in his sphere of influence.

According to Scott, these descriptions of organized crime "are bureaucratically distorted to the point of falsehood . . . [and that] this distortion involved systematic distortion of the facts, not just about Ruby, but about other aspects of the Kennedy assassination."[432]

In Scott's assessment, the House Assassinations Committee investigation of Jack Ruby omitted any reference to what he delicately

describes as "the ongoing, drug-fueled, intelligence-mob connection"[433]—
what we, in the pages of *Final Judgment*, more correctly and precisely call
the Lansky Organized Crime Syndicate.

As Scott has concluded (and rightly so): "The so-called Cosa Nostra
has been systematically misrepresented by law enforcement investigators
and prosecutors. For this active misrepresentation has deformed the two
official investigations into the Kennedy assassination itself, not in marginal
ways, but so as to conceal central truths about the assassination, truths that
were embarrassing to those conducting the investigation.

"In the end one comes to recognize that the history of organized crime
and the history of the investigation and prosecution of organized crime are
closely intertwined processes affecting one another. Processes, one must
add, which mutually affect the truth, but concealed, seats of political power
in this country."[434]

"To sum up: official investigations of the Kennedy assassination have
failed, not because the case is inherently insoluble, but because both the
case and the investigations have been governed by deeper political
processes, which have not yet been discerned."[435]

In short, Jack Ruby was not a "Mafia" hireling, but, instead, a key point
man in Dallas for the Meyer Lansky Crime Syndicate and, ultimately, as
Stephen Fox has said, "the smoking gun, the Rosetta stone, the trout in the
milk" in the JFK assassination conspiracy.

The deeper political processes of which Peter Dale Scott has noted
"have not yet been discerned" are now, however, in the pages of *Final
Judgment*, being bared for the first time.

## RUBY'S ISRAELI CONNECTION

Now although Jack Ruby was long known to be proud of his Jewish
heritage and ready to rumble with anti-Semites, what is little known is that
Ruby himself had an intimate connection with an individual with deep ties
to the world of intelligence and to the pro-Israel lobby in the United States.
This was Ruby's "longtime associate and former lawyer,"[436] Luis Kutner of
Chicago, who had represented Ruby when Ruby was called before the staff
of the Kefauver Senate Rackets Committee in 1950 to discuss underworld
activities in his former home base of Chicago.

According to Kutner, Ruby's offer was contingent upon the condition
that the Kefauver Committee stay away from investigating organized crime
in Dallas where Ruby was by then ensconced. Peter Dale Scott notes that
"The performance of the Kefauver Committee would seem to corroborate
Kutner's claim, for the Committee did give Dallas a clean bill of health."[437]

Although a "mob lawyer," it seems, Kutner did have additional
interesting connections. According to Scott, "Kutner, by his own account,
had known Ruby since 1936, when he had used Ruby to 'run errands' in his
unsuccessful 1936 congressional campaign. Later Kutner had inserted
himself into what can only be described as international intelligence

operations, ranging from Latin American coups to the defense of ousted Congolese leader Moise Tshombe."[438]

But Kutner was himself also active in efforts to advance the interests of Israel. He was among a host of people who formed an organization known as the Center for Global Security, Inc., which he served as "honorary counsel." Serving as "honorary chairman" of this pro-Israel lobbying group was General Julius Klein, an American military figure who not only played a major role in supplying weapons to the Israeli Haganah underground prior to the establishment of Israel, but also assisted in the founding and training of the Israeli Mossad.

What's more intriguing is that Klein also later served as chairman of the Swiss-Israel Trade Bank on whose board of directors was Rabbi Tibor Rosenbaum, the former director for finance and supply for the Mossad and founder of the Banque De Credit International of Switzerland, Meyer Lansky's chief money laundry on the European continent.

In Chapter 15 we shall see further that the Rosenbaum connection is indeed central to the JFK assassination conspiracy.

Clearly, Jack Ruby's friend and lawyer, Kutner, was a man with important and powerful ties to Israel and its global power networks. So, what Peter Dale Scott says regarding Ruby's association with Kutner is not an overstatement: "[Kutner's] involvement with Ruby confirms that Ruby should not just be thought of as a man with local influence with the Dallas police, but as a player in international deep politics."[439]

Yet, when G. Robert Blakey and the House Assassinations Committee were looking into Jack Ruby's connections and when Blakey later wrote about his findings, Blakey never once mentioned Kutner—surely a significant Ruby connection indeed, and particularly in light of what we have already outlined—and will examine further—in the pages of *Final Judgment*.[440]

## RUBY AND THE CIA

Jack Ruby's own covert activities were evidently well-established, his connection to Kutner notwithstanding—or perhaps precisely because of his longstanding relationship with the CIA- and Israeli Mossad-linked Chicago lawyer. The Giancana family, in their biography of Chicago Mafia chieftain Sam Giancana say that Ruby was an integral figure in joint Gulf Coast operations between the CIA and the Lansky Syndicate.

According to the Giancanas, "Ruby had been . . . running strip joints, gambling rackets, and narcotics for the Outfit and running guns—and . . . narcotics, as well—for the CIA." [441]

All of the evidence of Ruby's gun-running, both to Castro himself and, ultimately to anti-Castro Cuban exiles, has been explored relentlessly, and in detail, by JFK assassination researchers. But his Lansky connection has been repeatedly ignored.

Former CIA contract agent Robert Morrow reports that Ruby's pro-Castro gun-running was done in conjunction with former Cuban president

Carlos Prio Socarras. (Prio, also, had a long history of close association with Meyer Lansky, as we saw in Chapter 7 and Chapter 11 having received lucrative Lansky pay-offs.)

## GUN-RUNNING TO CUBA

According to Morrow: "With the blessing of the syndicate and the guidance of the CIA, Prio made his deal with Castro, arranging for the Mafia (which was also supporting Batista) to supply the necessary arms and finances to make Castro's revolution successful—on the condition that Fidel would reinstate him as president once Batista was overthrown.

"Castro agreed, and Prio turned into a high-class gun-runner. One of his partners would be Jack Ruby of Dallas, Texas, then known as Jack Rubinstein. This is supported by a Miami FBI informant named Blaney Mack Johnson who claimed Ruby supplied arms for Castro through Prio, that he had seen Ruby around a private airport, and had known Ruby to run guns by boat.

"There are others who confirm that Ruby was in the gunrunning business in Florida during the late 1950's. One was Eladio del Valle, a former Cuban congressman and a good friend of Mario Kohly . . . " [442]

## LANSKY'S CUBAN FRIENDS

The aforementioned Kohly was one of the primary leaders of the Cuban exiles who turned against Castro after the Cuban dictator turned the tables on his previous allies in the Lansky Crime Syndicate which helped bring Castro to power (as we documented in Chapter 7).

Kohly himself subsequently turned to Meyer Lansky for support and offered to return his casino rights if he, Kohly, were able to assume power in Cuba after Castro was removed.[443]

Thus it was that Jack Ruby was an important errand boy in the strange pro- and anti-Castro dealings of both the CIA and the Meyer Lansky Organized Crime Syndicate. Nonetheless, there is clearly more to the story of Jack Ruby that needs to be explored.

## RUBY, OSWALD AND THE CIA

The late John Henshaw, a crack investigative reporter operating out of Washington, D.C., did some of his own digging into Ruby's background. Henshaw, who worked as an investigator for syndicated columnist Drew Pearson (about whom we shall see more in Chapter 17) uncovered a link between Ruby and Lee Harvey Oswald, tying them together with the CIA.

According to Henshaw, Dallas police officials were actually in the process of investigating Ruby and Oswald in the assassination attempt on retired General Edwin Walker several months before the JFK murder.

A bullet was fired through Walker's window, although the general, a dedicated anti-communist and Castro critic, was unharmed.

However, there is some debate among assassination researchers as to what role Oswald did play—if any—in the shooting at the Walker residence. This is yet another of the many unanswered questions surrounding the JFK mystery.

At any rate, according to Henshaw's account, a secret police investigation of the shooting linked Oswald and Ruby to the incident. Then, according to Henshaw, a high-ranking FBI official was asked by a top official in the Justice Department to intervene and stop the impending arrest of the two Dallas operatives.

Henshaw says that it was the CIA itself that had asked the FBI to intervene. According to Henshaw, the CIA was using Ruby to recruit Dallas men into the anti-Castro movement. However, the FBI official refused to intervene, saying it would be obstructing justice and would therefore be a crime.

The FBI official did say, though, that he would make the request only if he were formally directed to do so in a written communication signed by the Justice Department official. Shortly thereafter, according to Henshaw's account, the FBI official then received a signed directive. He contacted Dallas police and urged them not to arrest Oswald and Ruby.

But the Dallas police also wanted an official signed communication. Thereupon the Justice Department sent the communication to Dallas Police Chief Curry asking that Oswald and Ruby be left strictly alone. Justice explained it didn't want Oswald and Ruby arrested because of "reasons of state" and that the department was making the request on the CIA's behalf.[444]

Henshaw's account is yet another of the significant reports which point in the direction of undisclosed covert activities by both Ruby and Oswald together, being carried out under the direction of the CIA.

## THE JUSTICE DEPARTMENT

Henshaw also wrote that Texas Attorney General Waggoner Carr was being kept under surveillance by the FBI because he had undisclosed evidence:"The evidence includes a copy of the missing film taken moments before Jack Ruby shot and killed Lee Harvey Oswald. The film covers Ruby's progress through the FBI and police screens guarding the entrance of the Dallas Police headquarters. Two cameramen had been assigned by a Dallas TV station to cover the entrance, but were ordered by federal agents to knock off film footage which showed a high official of the Justice Department escorting [Ruby] through the two security screens."[445]

According to Henshaw, high-level federal pressure stopped Carr's investigation after it was learned that he had an uncut copy of the entire film. He allegedly kept a copy for himself. Henshaw also provides us with this interesting tidbit:

"On the day of the JFK assassination, Justice Department counselor Abram Chayes and Nicholas Katzenbach got together in a midnight conference and jointly agreed that Oswald was the lone assassin and that there must not be any international overtones in the upcoming investigation.

"On that same day, Lyndon Johnson telephoned his attorney, Abe Fortas, a prominent leader in the Jewish community and asked him to assume charge of coordinating the investigation into Kennedy's death. Fortas concurred in the recommendations of Chayes and Katzenbach and then sold LBJ on the idea of setting up the Warren Commission, which came up with a report proving exactly what Katzenbach, Chayes and Fortas had agreed upon."[446]

Whatever the case, Henshaw died some years later, never having fully recovered from the injuries inflicted during what was investigated as a "mugging" but which Henshaw's friends believe was actually a failed murder attempt.

## OTHER OSWALD-RUBY CONTACT

There is evidence of other possible contact between Ruby and Oswald—even in New Orleans. This evidence has never been published to this author's knowledge.

This author received access to a private letter written on February 20, 1967 during the controversy in New Orleans over District Attorney Jim Garrison's inquiry into the JFK assassination.

The author of the letter was describing the fears of his aunt, a New Orleans woman, who was a neighbor of Lee Harvey Oswald's during his sojourn in the Crescent City. "She is terrified to the point that she will not cooperate," he said. "She stated that her fear was based upon the possibility that 'Garrison would get me for withholding evidence' and the possibility that 'someone will put a bullet in my back.'

"She made the following points to me: (1) She observed Oswald having visitors three times (a) two "Cuban looking" men visisted him twice and (b) a man and woman came and picked up Oswald one weekend. 'This man had the same profile as pictures of Ruby.' she said. 'Every time I see a picture of Ruby, this visitor of Oswald pops into my mind, but I am afraid to say anything about it. I could not swear that it was Ruby, but I couldn't swear that it wasn't.'"[447]

Ruby apparently did visit New Orleans during the time Oswald was there, ostensibly trying to find a stripper for his nightclub. Could it be that the woman seen with the Ruby-lookalike was one of these strippers?

## THE RUBY COVER-UP

That Jack Ruby did indeed have ties to both the Lansky Syndicate and to the CIA involving Cuba is, today, not in doubt. However, during the period of the Warren Commission investigation, the official government "investigation" preferred to look the other way. According to Ruby biographer, Seth Kantor:

"After the Ruby trial ended, Leon Hubert and Burt Griffin, the Warren Commission's two Ruby experts, tried to convince Commission members in memorandums on March 19 and April 1, 1964, that there was "substantial evidence" showing Jack Ruby had maintained unexplained Cuban associations. But the efforts of Hubert and Griffin were blocked by the CIA and discouraged by others on the Commission staff." [448]

Kantor suggests that "Ruby and Oswald probably didn't know each other; yet both could have been used as separate parts of a conspiracy to commit murder in Dallas on the weekend of November 22-24, 1963. Oswald on Friday. Ruby on Sunday. Two men separately manipulated by the same power.

"After they were arrested and jailed, both men said they had been manipulated. "I'm a patsy," said Oswald. "I've been used for a purpose," said Ruby. [449]

Despite Kantor's observations to the contrary, we have seen evidence (in Chapter 11, for example) that Ruby did almost assuredly know Lee Harvey Oswald and that Ruby did indeed participate in matters relating to the assassination.

Whether Ruby—and Oswald—did, in fact, know that the assassination of Kennedy was in planning is another story.

## A CONSPIRACY AGAINST CONNALLY?

Michael Milan, who has written of his role in working as part of a secret U.S. government team collaborating with organized crime—the Lansky Syndicate in particular—says that there were at least several people operating in Dallas who believed that they were not involved in a conspiracy to kill John F. Kennedy, but, instead, in a conspiracy to kill Texas Governor John B. Connally.

According to Milan, he (Milan) played a part in the JFK assassination cover-up, Milan claims that following the assassination he was dispatched to Dallas by J. Edgar Hoover himself. Milan's assignment was to kill a cab driver named Brinkman. Milan met with Brinkman and began questioning him.

When Milan asked who set up the shooting, Brinkman said, "I never met the guy before I was introduced to him by this broad at [Jack Ruby's] Carousel Club. And I didn't shoot nobody. There was me and two other guys. We weren't even after the president. We were supposed to shoot the governor, but things happened too fast. They were gone before anybody did anything."

"I think there were two other guys doin' what I was supposed to do. But I don't know who they are or where they was when the shooting started. We was just supposed to shoot at the governor when they passed and get out of there. That's all. But nuthin' happened. I mean, everything happened and I just got outta there fast."[450]

Milan completed his assignment and killed Brinkman. When he returned to Washington he was met at the airport, he says, by Hoover who said, "You already know too much. So I'll just say: Johnson. No doubt. We stand away. Do you get it?" [451]

Is it conceivable, perhaps, that Jack Ruby was not consciously involved in a plot that he believed was aimed at John F. Kennedy, but at John B. Connally instead? Can the same thing be said for Oswald?

Is it possible that the two men were being manipulated as part of an even bigger conspiracy that they knew nothing about? This is all speculation, but it is something to consider. In Chapter 16 we shall ponder this question in some detail.

The Lansky connection to Ruby's role in the JFK assassination conspiracy and cover-up goes much deeper than we have explored thus far.

## LANSKY'S COURIER IN DALLAS

One day prior to the JFK assassination one of Meyer Lansky's longtime personal couriers, one Jim Braden, was visiting in Dallas. He was also on the scene in Dealey Plaza when JFK was assassinated, actually being taken into custody by the Dallas police, and then released.

Standard accounts of the role of organized crime in the JFK assassination conspiracy have frequently pointed out Braden's strange doings in Dallas. What has been ignored, however, is his close relationship to Meyer Lansky.

## COVERING UP THE LANSKY LINK

David Scheim, writing in *Contract on America*, provides his readers a lengthy discussion of Braden, but never once mentions his connection with Lansky. Scheim prefers to leave the reader with the impression that Braden was a "Mafia" courier—not a Lansky courier. [452]

Even G. Robert Blakey and Richard Billings (Scheim's chief source) acknowledge in their own book that Braden was, reportedly, a "personal courier" for Lansky.

"In the end," say Blakey and Billings, "we reached no firm judgment on Braden's mob connections or on whether his activities in Dallas were in any way related to the assassination." [453]

What Blakey does not mention, however, is that Braden was so much a key figure in the Lansky Organized Crime Syndicate that he was a charter member of the Lansky Syndicate-financed La Costa Country Club.

In Chapter 10, as we have seen, it was Blakey who was on the payroll of Lansky associate, Morris Dalitz, one of the founders of La Costa, after Dalitz and his partners sued *Penthouse* magazine for publicizing the mob links of the Carlsbad, California resort.

Blakey, in fact, served, in effect, as a character reference for the Lansky Syndicate defending the resort against the accusations—something Blakey, for obvious reasons, would not be inclined to brag about when proclaiming himself a crime-buster.

## BRADEN, RUBY & FERRIE

The late Bernard Fensterwald supplies us some of the interesting details about the activities of Lansky's courier: "Braden also had some other startling connections which were also never discovered by the Warren Commission. Jim Braden had visited the same Dallas office of the H. L. Hunt Oil Company that Jack Ruby visited on November 21, 1963—the afternoon before the assassination—and at approximately the same time.

"Braden was also staying at the Cabana Motel in Dallas—a reported "mob hang-out" that was frequented by Jack Ruby and various Ruby associates. Ruby visited the Cabana Motel sometime around midnight on the night before the assassination—November 21, 1963—while Jim Braden was a guest there.

"Braden also has a possible connection to the late David Ferrie. According to information documented by Peter Noyes, Braden worked out of an office suite—Room 1701—in the Pere Marquette Building in New Orleans in the fall of 1963, in the weeks immediately preceding the assassination.

"During this same period in late 1963, David Ferrie was working for Mafia leader Carlos Marcello on the same floor . . . in the same building . . . just down the hall from Braden—in Room 1707. [454]

[Fensterwald notes further that Noyes has found additional evidence that Braden once listed his address as Room 1706--right next to Ferrie!]

(In Chapter 11 we examined the role of CIA contract agent David Ferrie and his connection to the JFK assassination conspiracy in some detail. The evidence cited by Fensterwald only draws the circle more closely.)

That one of Meyer Lansky's chief couriers would be in Dallas and moving in Ruby's sphere of operations is evidence that the fine hand of Meyer Lansky himself was in motion in Dallas and, more than likely, this is a direct link between Lansky and Ruby.

## SECRET MESSAGES

According to Lansky's West Coast henchman, Mickey Cohen (Ruby's role model) couriers such as Braden were very important in the Lansky Syndicate.

"Important messages never came by phone. Anything to do with a hit, a gambling operation, to go somewhere or to see somebody, was by courier. See, we worried about wiretaps thirty years ago. Even money was only transacted person to person. If anybody had money coming or going, you put a man on a plane.

"But my messages went strictly by Neddy [Herbert]. He was tried and tested. He would bring a proposition from Charlie the Jew or a message from Chopsie or Frank Costello or Meyer Lansky. He may have been in town only overnight. He'd have dinner with me, deliver the proposition or

message verbally, and go right back with the answer. He was a solid Jew."
455

Another Lansky associate, Michael Milan, has also written of the importance of mob couriers and the need for secrecy. "Whenever he came to a sitdown, Mr. Lansky always had his percentage figured out in advance. He kept it all in his head, too. 'Never put anything on paper,' he said to me once. 'That way they never know what you got.'" 456

There is evidence, however, that Ruby and Braden did indeed have a very close connection. Lansky's courier Jim Braden was also a "friend"457 of Lansky's Mexico City representative,"Happy" Meltzer," whom we met earlier in this chapter as the head of a drug-smuggling operation in which Ruby was evidently involved.

Obviously, Lansky's courier, Jim Braden, may have indeed been bringing a message from Lansky to Ruby. But whatever his role in Dallas, there's no question but that he was there for a purpose. This was not a case of coincidence, but indeed, conspiracy.

All of this, taken together, suggests, as we have said, that the Lansky-Ruby connection is much deeper than might be perceived and far more than some "crime solvers" would have us realize.

What is especially interesting, further, is an additional Lansky connection to Ruby that surfaced after the assassination of JFK and after the murder of Lee Harvey Oswald.

## MELVIN BELLI COMES TO TOWN

In Chapter 13 we examined the strange—and little known role—of Meyer Lansky's West Coast henchman, Mickey Cohen, in the JFK assassination conspiracy.

Cohen—himself a longtime Ruby associate and the Dallas mobster's role model—was obviously a key figure in the network of conspiracy. It was Cohen's longtime friend—and attorney—Melvin Belli who stepped forward as Jack Ruby's defense attorney.

(In Chapter 13, of course, we learned of at least one meeting between Belli, Cohen and Israeli terrorist-turned diplomat Menachem Begin, around the time when Cohen and Begin were apparently engaged in some sort of conspiracy against the Kennedy administration's foreign policy-making, the nature of which is now clear.)

Belli and Cohen had known each other for years. In fact, Belli was a regular at the Los Angeles nightspot, Rondelli's, of which Cohen was the secret owner. And, as we've noted, he was also Cohen's lawyer.

The two were so close that Belli even once had Cohen introduced as "Professor O'Brien from Harvard who's going to give you a talk on tax laws,"458 to a meeting of the American Bar Association in Miami.

According to Cohen, writing in his memoirs, the Los Angeles mobster assumed the platform and then began rattling on for some time, essentially saying nothing. He then concluded, "My advice to all of ya is to be sure to pay your goddamn taxes right to the letter."459

Belli's little attempt at humor did not go over well when the audience realized whom their "tax expert" really was, and there was even talk of disbarring the California attorney. Nonetheless, the incident illustrates the nature of the Belli-Cohen relationship.

## DIFFERENT STORIES

Blakey and Billings, in *The Plot to Kill the President*, addressed the circumstances in which the Lansky henchman's attorney came to represent Jack Ruby:

"How Melvin Belli, a nationally known trial lawyer, was brought in to handle the Ruby defense was a matter of some dispute. We heard a report that Seymour Ellison, a lawyer associated with Belli, got a phone call from 'a Las Vegas attorney' who said, 'Sy, one of our guys just bumped off the son of a bitch that gunned down the President. We can't move in to handle it, but there's a million bucks for Mel if he'll take it.'

"Ellison confirmed to us that he received the phone call, but he said he did not remember the name of the Las Vegas attorney and nothing developed from the call. Belli told us a different story. He said Earl Ruby came to California three days after his brother was arrested; he watched Belli sum up a murder defense in a Los Angeles courtroom and he asked him to take the case.

"Belli said he declined at first. He had learned that his fee would be paid by the sale of Ruby's story to newspapers, and he did not care to be involved in that sort of exploitation. Nevertheless, Earl Ruby talked him into it, Belli told us, and he took the case with five goals in mind: to save Jack Ruby, to strengthen the law; to show that current legal tests for insanity were inadequate; to wed modern law to modern science; and to help Dallas 'solve its problem.'" [460]

Interestingly, Blakey and Billings report further that Ruby's brother Earl had told yet another version of the "official" story. They also make passing reference to the Ruby-Cohen relationship.

Noting that "Ruby liked to tell friends that he knew Mickey Cohen," they concluded: "We could not be certain just how well Ruby knew Cohen, who also grew up in Chicago, but he admired him and tried to emulate him." [461] As far as Belli's decision to defend Ruby, Blakey and Billings said: "We found it difficult to believe that Belli did not receive a substantial fee for his defense of Ruby." [462] The two also noted that "We considered the possibility that Belli went to Mexico to pick up a fee for the Ruby defense, but we found no proof that he did." [463]

Whatever the case, Belli's defense of Ruby failed. Ruby was convicted and sentenced to death. Ruby's family formally fired Belli as Ruby's attorney. But Ruby's death was announced just shortly before he was scheduled to be retried for his murder of the alleged assassin.

As a consequence, any final determination of just what role Ruby actually played in the JFK assassination scenario became another mystery in an endless series of mysteries related to the president's murder. Jack Ruby could never tell what he knew.

## BELLI AND THE COVER-UP

This was not the end of Melvin Belli's role in the JFK controversy, however. As pioneer JFK assassination investigator Mark Lane noted in his second book on the assassination, *A Citizen's Dissent*, Belli emerged as one of the leading defenders of the official Warren Commission version of the assassination.

According to Lane, ABC-TV's Les Crane show wanted to stage a debate between Lane and Belli. "I was less sanguine, for, although I was confident in my knowledge of the facts, Belli's almost legendary oratorical accomplishments had preceded him to the East coast."[464]

Lane points out that he subsequently received a call from the producer telling him that the debate was canceled. According to the producer: "It's the ABC brass. They have just said no. Period. They say you have the facts and the affidavits and that would just confuse the audience."[465]

But the show itself was not, in fact, canceled—only the debate between the well-informed Lane and Belli. "It's just that we can't have you on." Lane was told. There's going to be a debate anyway. We're getting Oswald's mother."[466]

Lane summarized the situation in this way: "And so it came to pass that the first network broadcast presenting both sides of the controversy found splendiferous Melvin Belli, conqueror of a thousand juries, opposed by a poorly educated widow.

"Mrs. Oswald's visceral responses were meritorious, but her lack of command over the facts, together with Belli's bully tactics, reduced the program to the low level of entertainment that the network apparently sought." [467]

## BELLI ON STAGE

After some negotiations, according to Lane, Belli finally agreed to debate on stage under one condition--that both wear tuxedoes. There would be three debates. It was during the first debate, in San Francisco, that Belli came on stage, wearing a cape over his tuxedo, and in his concluding remarks made his final judgment on the JFK assassination conspiracy. He declared, "If we cannot trust the FBI, the CIA and Earl Warren, then God pity us."[468]

However, the Establishment media did not see fit to publicize the circumstances of this debate, despite the fact, as Lane points out, that Belli himself is somewhat of a celebrity.  As Lane noted: "In San Francisco, if Belli's office is burglarized or if he agrees to represent a topless dancer, he is on the front page of the newspapers and may be seen repeatedly on television screens.  Perhaps those assembled that evening constituted the largest paying audience to witness a debate in many years in San Francisco.

Yet not one word appeared in any of the three daily newspapers the morning after the debate."[469]

## MEDIA COVER-UP

The subsequent New York debate between Lane and Belli was jam-packed with the press. However, according to Lane, "Not one daily newspaper in New York, and possibly in the nation, even mentioned that the event had occurred." [470]This despite the fact that there were half a dozen papers in New York at the time.

Lane commented: *"The New York Times* refers to itself as a newspaper of record. That which is not found within its many pages ostensibly did not happen. For this reason the Belli encounter in New York is known to some as the debate that never occurred."[471]

The Establishment media in the United States was determined to quash any open inquiry or debate into the JFK assassination, even when a celebrity attorney such as Melvin Belli was one of the featured players.

(In Chapter 17 we shall see, further, how the media has played a part in the JFK cover-up and we shall further trace the role of an intelligence and disinformation arm of Israel's Mossad in helping orchestrate that cover-up.)

That a prominent attorney who represented Mickey Cohen, a key figure in Meyer Lansky's international crime operations (and also an important cog in Israel's global machinations), later came to represent Jack Ruby is clearly significant.

## A WELL-PLACED ERRAND BOY

Although Jack Ruby's actual role in the planning stages of the JFK assassination conspiracy will probably never be fully known, there is no question that, in the end, Ruby became a critical factor in the cover-up. His murder of Lee Harvey Oswald silenced the one man who could no doubt fill in at least some of the missing pieces of the puzzle.

Jack Ruby was a well-placed errand boy, not only for Meyer Lansky and his global crime syndicate, but also, it appears, for the covert arm of the CIA as well. Ruby did his job and he did it well.

## RUBY MUZZLED

Although Ruby sought to speak freely, the Warren Commission refused his entreaties to be allowed to come to Washington to tell his story. The story of how Chief Justice Earl Warren refused to give Ruby the opportunity to leave Dallas and tell his story is a famous part of JFK assassination folklore. As a consequence, Ruby never did have the chance to give his version of what really happened. We can only speculate as to what Jack Ruby would have had to say.

For all  his unpleasantness, Ruby—on the whole—is a pathetic figure. One cannot help but believe that Ruby himself never knew precisely just how he was being used in the JFK assassination conspiracy.

Jack Ruby was indeed "the smoking gun, the Rosetta stone, the trout in the milk." He also may have even been—as even Lee Harvey Oswald proclaimed himself—a "patsy."

Just one player—albeit, in the end, an important one—Ruby played a starring role in a drama orchestrated far beyond his seamy Carousel Club in Dallas. Ruby was an errand boy in a high-stakes operation—the assassination of an American president—that was being undertaken by the joint alliance of the Mafia, the Meyer Lansky Organized Crime Syndicate, the CIA and Israel's Mossad.

## A STRANGE STORY

As this book was being completed, a very strange story about Jack Ruby came to this author's attention that bears repeating, if only for the reason that it should be part of the permanent record, particularly considering our contention that Israel did indeed have a hand in the assassination of John F. Kennedy.

Before relating the story itself, a few words should be mentioned about the credibility of the source.

The original source was a now deceased Idaho woman named Grace Pratt who related the story to a friend  (now living in Oregon) whose name must remain anonymous.

This author has spoken with the Oregon man, an elderly retiree, and has concluded that he believes very strongly in the reliability of Mrs. Pratt.

He has provided this author with a written summary of  what Mrs. Pratt told him about her connection with Jack Ruby. The memorandum reads—in pertinent part—as follows:

"In Idaho in the 1960's I met George and Grace Pratt, who had moved to Nampa from California upon retirement.  The Pratts became very good friends of  mine.  George had worked in the Navy yard and Grace had cooked for many years in many of the big restaurants in San Francisco.

"For a longtime she had worked for 'Tiny's.' Tiny's had a side-by-side restaurant and bar with a door between, opening into the anteroom between the dining room and the kitchen.

"The bar was run by Jack Ruby. He also had charge of the ladies in the basement. The bar was a place for the 'underworld' to meet. After the dinner rush was over, Grace would fix her plate and one for Jack Ruby, and they would eat in the anteroom.

"One day she heard a shuffle and looked up just in time to hear the zip of a gun with a silencer. A man had rushed through the door and fallen dead on the floor. A big husky man came back, gripped her by the arm until she thought he would crush it and said, 'You didn't see anything, did you. You didn't hear anything, did you?'

"She answered, 'No, I was in the back of the kitchen. I did not see anything. I did not hear anything.' From then on she had their confidence. Jack shared a lot of the things that went on in the bar with her. Anyone who knew Jack Ruby that well would always be able to recognize him going or coming.

## BOUND FOR ISRAEL?

"Six days after Jack Ruby's funeral was publicized in the press, Grace called me very excited and said, "I was just now watching the news. They turned the TV camera on a ramp up to a plane loading for Israel from New York, and who do you think went up the ramp? I screamed to George in the other room, calling him and saying, 'Come quickly! Jack Ruby is boarding that plane!'

"At the top of the ramp he stopped, turned around, and looking straight into the camera he tipped his hat and entered the plane. She said she thought he was giving the message to someone that he had made it and was on his way. The Pratts were shocked. She said there had already been a number of JFK assassination witnesses who had mysteriously died. Two years after seeing him board for Israel, she heard through the underground that Ruby had gone to Brazil.

"She made me promise not to tell anyone what she told me until after her death. Grace has been gone about ten years now. Knowing Grace and her credibility, I believe every word. If someone had the clout to check the grave to have the 'body' exhumed, this might be very revealing."[472]

So ends the strange memorandum received by this author. The words speak for themselves.

Ruby did indeed spend time in San Francisco (along with time spent in Los Angeles as we have seen). The source who provided the author with this unusual memorandum firmly believes that Mrs. Pratt did indeed know Jack Ruby well and that Mrs. Pratt herself was convinced that she had seen Ruby boarding the plane for Israel.

Another individual who knew Mrs. Pratt told this author that she was a highly credible individual not given to tale-spinning and that she had indeed mentioned her acquaintance with Ruby (although she had not told him the story that she wanted kept under wraps).

Is this story the product of one woman's imagination? Or did Mrs. Pratt indeed see just what she believed she saw? Is is possible that Mrs. Pratt has provided us yet another key tying Israel to the most intimate levels of the JFK assassination conspiracy?

## A MORE RECENT PRECEDENT

It is worth remembering that even as these words arc written, many leaders in Israel and leaders of the Israeli lobby in the United States are working tirelessly for the pardon of American-born Israeli spy, Jonathan Jay Pollard, sentenced to life in prison for passing U.S. defense secrets to Israel.

Is it possible, perhaps, that a similar, secret arrangement was made on Jack Ruby's behalf?

Is it possible that, on "humanitarian" grounds, Ruby was quietly released from prison and permitted to go to Israel? (After all, it could be argued, it was Ruby who had become a hero by killing "the man who killed President Kennedy.")

Is it possible that the decision was made to usher Ruby quietly out of the country so that there would be no widely publicized trial in which Ruby's motivations—and sinister connections—would be bared?

## SOMEBODY WAS HELPING RUBY

It is interesting to note that on October 6, 1966, at the time Ruby was granted a new trial, the *Washington Daily News* carried a story proclaiming that "It's Possible for Ruby to Go Free," as a result of a second trial. The story quoted his lawyer as saying the case was so simple that "Somebody just out of law school can handle it."[473]

What's more, it's interesting to note a little-noticed column by veteran crime reporter Dorothy Kilgallen who had an abiding (and perhaps fatal) interest in the JFK case.

In her column datelined DALLAS, February 21, reporting on the Ruby trial, Miss Kilgallen reported that "one of the best kept secrets of the Jack Ruby trial is the extent to which the federal government is cooperating with the defense. The unprecedented alliance between Ruby's lawyers and the Department of Justice in Washington may provide the case with the one dramatic element it has lacked: MYSTERY."

Miss Kilgallen revealed that a deal between Ruby's lawyers and the FBI, "provides Ruby's side with reams of helpful information that they would never have been able to get without the G-Men—on the condition they do not ask for anything at all about Ruby's alleged victim, Lee Harvey Oswald.

"It appears that Washington knows or suspects something about Oswald that it does not want Dallas and the rest of the world to know or suspect.

"Why is Oswald being kept in the shadows, as dim a figure as they can make him, while the defense tries to rescue his killer with the help of information from the FBI? Who was Oswald, anyway?"[474]

Perhaps Miss Kilgallen found out the answer to the questions. She reportedly told several friends, shortly before her "accidental" death from a combined drug overdose and alcohol, that she was about to crack the Kennedy case wide open.

That Ruby's path to possible freedom was being assisted by the FBI (during his first trial) does raise questions. Then, coupled with his reported "death" prior to a second trial—especially considering the story told by the late Grace Pratt—the mystery deepens.

Did Jack Ruby really die in prison or did he secretly emigrate to the Jewish homeland of Israel? *The answer to that question has no direct bearing on the thesis of Final Judgment, but it may be a mystery that deserves further scrutiny.* Perhaps some enterprising researcher may answer the question: "What did happen to the 'corpse' of Jack Ruby?"

A NOTE FOR THE RECORD: Following the release of the first edition of *Final Judgment,* the author came across an obscure volume entitled *The Ruby-Oswald Affair,* published in 1988. The author was the late Alan Adelson who had served as the attorney for Jack Ruby's family in the probate of Ruby's will. Adelson died just shortly before his book was published. At the beginning of the book Adelson describes how he attended Ruby's funeral in the company of Ruby's brother, Earl:

"The funeral had been a closed-casket affair. I realized immediately that the closed casket would raise questions. Who was to know if Jack was really in the casket? I had heard rumors that Kennedy was not really dead, but was hidden away in South America. 'Earl,' I said, 'let them see. I know it sounds grisly, but let's put it to rest.' The lid of the casket was opened, and for the first time I saw Jack, the man I would learn to know almost as well as I knew myself."[475]

To the best of my knowledge, this is the only known reference to anyone actually having seen Jack Ruby in the casket. In this case, the reference came from someone who had not actually known Jack Ruby in person. Although photographs of Lee Harvey Oswald (both during his autopsy and in his coffin) as well as photographs of John F. Kennedy (during his autopsy) have been widely circulated, there are no known such photographs of Ruby.

Frankly, I do not find Adelson's posthumously-published proclamation of having seen "Jack" (a man he never saw while Ruby was alive) as any substantive refutation of the story told by Grace Pratt. For the record, however, it seems appropriate to record the comments attributed to Adelson in his posthumously-published book.

## THE TWAIN SHALL MEET

We have examined the players. We have examined the motives. We have examined their interplay.

Let us now move forward and determine the critical point of contact which ties together the diverse—yet closely connected—elements behind the conspiracy that took the life of John F. Kennedy. This is vital to recognizing and understanding the central role of Israel's Mossad in the crime of the century.

## Chapter Fifteen

### The Twain Shall Meet—
### The Permindex Mystery:
### Israel, the CIA, the Lansky Crime Syndicate
### and the Plot to Kill John F. Kennedy

**Central to understanding the joint Mossad-CIA-Lansky Organized Crime Syndicate nexus in the plot to assassinate John F. Kennedy is to recognize the importance of a little-explored corporate entity based in Rome and known as Permindex. New Orleans businessman Clay Shaw, indicted by Jim Garrison for conspiracy in the JFK assassination, served on the Permindex board of directors.**

**Many assassination researchers, over the years, have contended that Permindex was a covert CIA money laundering operation. Shaw, of course, in fact did have intimate ties with the CIA. Other researchers have propounded the theory that Permindex was a front for a Nazi remnant left over from World War II—perhaps even a front for Hitler's SS. This theory, exciting though it may be, falls far off the mark. All of the firm evidence indicates that Permindex was, in fact, a joint CIA-Mossad operation—one tied inextricably with the Meyer Lansky Organized Crime Syndicate.**

**Unraveling the mystery of Permindex explains the web of intrigue that ties all of the key players in the conspiracy together. The Permindex connection is also the famous "French connection" to the JFK assassination. And as we shall see, the French connection is, actually, the Israeli connection.**

In Oliver Stone's explosive film, *JFK*, actor Kevin Costner (portraying Jim Garrison) confronts actor Tommy Lee Jones (portraying Clay Shaw) and displays Italian newspaper articles exposing the activities of a Rome-based operation known as Permindex. Shaw, an international trade executive, served on the board of Permindex.

The film audience is left with the impression that Permindex was a covert CIA operation—the purpose of which—at least in the film—is never defined. However, as we have noted, Permindex was, instead, a joint Mossad-CIA venture operating in conjunction with the Lansky Organized Crime Syndicate.

Therein lies the key to the mystery behind the JFK assassination. Therein lies the explanation as to why Jim Garrison's investigation of Clay Shaw, a director of Permindex, had to be scuttled.

Not only had Garrison stumbled upon a definitive CIA link to the JFK assassination, but he had also (inadvertently) discovered Israel's link as well. Garrison himself probably never even suspected how deeply the Permindex nexus went. His CIA theory was correct, but he had only come across the tip of the iceberg.

Israel and its Mossad was a key force behind Permindex. In fact, one of the chief shareholders in the Permindex holding company was the Banque De Credit International of Geneva,[476] established by Tibor Rosenbaum, the longtime Director for Finance and Supply of Israel's Mossad. It was BCI, as we saw in Chapter 7 and Chapter 12, which served as Meyer Lansky 's chief money laundering bank in Europe. BCI also served as a depository for the Permindex account.

**That Tibor Rosenbaum's BCI was a controlling force behind the enigmatic Permindex entity places Israel and its Mossad in the very center of the conspiracy behind the assassination of John F. Kennedy.**

Clay Shaw's positioning in New Orleans, site of one operational rung of the conspiracy, resulted in Shaw's implication in the invesigation conducted by Jim Garrison. But obviously the conspiracy went much deeper.

## THE SECRET ABOUT PERMINDEX

If Jim Garrison had uncovered the origins of Permindex he would have uncovered the unsuspected truth about the assassination of John F. Kennedy: that Israel's Mossad was intimately involved in the events in Dallas on November 22, 1963.

Garrison himself probably never even suspected it. He had no reason to do so. Kennedy's secret war with Israel was a hidden factor in the geopolitical events of the decade and the war in Vietnam had begun to emerge as the big issue of the day.

Israel was hardly an issue in the public mind at all in the period of the Kennedy assassination and the subsequent controversy over the Warren Report. And it wasn't until the later period of the 1960's that the Vietnam conflict rose to prominence in the American public agenda.

## 'TRANSNATIONAL CONNECTIONS'

In examining the JFK assassination conspiracy, according to researcher Peter Dale Scott, "a first step is to suggest that one ingredient in the complex, multi-centered intrigues that climaxed in the Kennedy assassination was the participation of diverse unaccountable transnational connections, each transcending the limits of American political society, and each with distinctive motives for the murder of the president . . .

"To now recognize a transnational dimension to the case is . . . to recognize that the American political system is of necessity an open one, and thus increasingly susceptible to the growing influence of money and **intelligence penetration from abroad** [our emphasis] . . .

"Transnational connections are common modes of interaction between intelligence agencies, often in intrigues of which heads of government may be, at best, only dimly aware. Sometimes they may give rise to more overt, structured arrangements or forums such as the World Anti-Communist League, a forum, financed over the years by countries like Nationalist China and Saudi Arabia, with recurring links to the international drug traffic."[477]

Scott notes additionally that "It is well known that in the 1950s and 1960s the Israel Lobby and the Taiwan Lobby were both powerful in Washington and sometimes collaborated on common projects . . . There was also a Nicaragua Lobby, or perhaps more accurately, a Somoza Lobby, which also overlapped with the Israel, China, and Cuba lobbies."[478]

(Scott points out, for example, that a Washington lobbyist who was close to New Orleans Mafia chief Carlos Marcello also served as a registered lobbyist for both Nicaragua and the Israeli Aircraft Industries.)

It is clear, based upon the evidence that we shall review in these pages, that Permindex, which played so central a role in the JFK assassination conspiracy, was indeed one of these transnational "overt, structured arrangements or forums" of which Scott speaks.

### WHAT WAS PERMINDEX?

What exactly then was Permindex? How did Permindex fit into the center of the international conspiracy that resulted in the assassination of John F. Kennedy?

Author Paris Flammonde's 1969 account of the Garrison investigation, *The Kennedy Conspiracy,* contains valuable information on Permindex, although, unfortunately, Flammonde didn't pursue the matter as far as he could have. Had he done so he would have unearthed the Israeli-Lansky Organized Crime Syndicate connection.

Flammonde cites several articles that appeared in the foreign press, specifically Italy's *Paesa Sera* (March 4, 1967) and the Canadian publication, *Le Devoir* (March 16, 1967) as his source for much of the information he provides his readers on Permindex.

These articles appeared just shortly after Clay Shaw's status as the primary figure in the Garrison investigation first came to public attention and were, in fact, the articles highlighted in Oliver Stone's *JFK.* These articles provide the unusual background of Permindex and point toward the direction of the affinities of this shadowy entity.

"There was established in Rome an organization named the Centro Mondiale Commerciale." reported *Paesa Sera.* [Centro Mondiale Commerciale is Italian for "World Trade Center."] "Its origins, functions, rotating presidency, geographical displacements, sub-, subsequent, and alternate designations were so complex and labyrinthine as to make a comprehensive and comprehensible description of it in anything less than a modern-sized book impossible." [479]

### A MYSTERIOUS OPERATION

The CMC was founded in 1961 by one Giorgio Mantello.[480] The Italian name, however, was an affectation. Mantello was an Eastern European Jew originally named Georges Mandel.

At the time CMC was established, it was asserted that CMC would function as an international commercial organization, that it would aid in the establishing of a permanent worldwide network of trade expositions, and generally assist concerns involved in trade matters.

Permindex was a subsidiary of CMC. The name Permindex is an acronym which stood for PERmanent INDustrial EXpositions.[481]

Clay Shaw, of course, was the founder and director of the International Trade Mart in the key port city of New Orleans. Thus, his connection with an international trade entity seems logical. However, there was a lot more to the story, as the foreign press revealed:

"Actually it was soon to become evident that the seemingly vast, mighty structure was not a rock of solidarity, but a shell of superficiality; not constructed with mass, supporting promise, but composed of channels through which money flowed back and forth, with no one knowing the source or the destination of these liquid assets." reports Paris Flammonde.[482]

## CLAY SHAW'S LITTLE-KNOWN SPONSORS

What about Clay Shaw? How did this New Orleans socialite come to become involved in the strange world of the international entity known as Permindex? Who were Clay Shaw's sponsors?

What few JFK assassination researchers—even those who cite Clay Shaw's now widely-known CIA connections—seem to have noted is yet another Shaw connection that places him further into the net of the CIA-Mossad-Lansky Crime Syndicate nexus.

We refer to Shaw's tie to Seymour Weiss who ran New Orleans, alongside Carlos Marcello, for the Lansky syndicate and was Lansky's contact man with Louisiana's famed "Kingfish," Huey P. Long.[483]

In Chapter 10, as we have seen, it was Lansky who installed Carlos Marcello as the Mafia boss of New Orleans. It was Weiss, however, who emerged as the Lansky syndicate bagman and political operative working in conjunction with Marcello.

In fact, Lansky's man Weiss was purportedly the prime target of the IRS investigation of Long—referenced in Chapter 10—that was initiated the day before Long's assassination, and, according to Peter Dale Scott, "Long's murder in 1935, some say, was arranged to prevent men like Weiss from going to jail."[484]

Scott has noted additionally that House Assassinations Committee director G. Robert Blakey has omitted "all reference to the role of Seymour Weiss"[485] in his account of Carlos Marcello's rise to power in New Orleans. To do so, of course, as we noted in Chapter 10, would point in the direction of Meyer Lansky.

## SEYMOUR WEISS AND THE CIA

Now although Weiss ultimately did serve time in prison on other racketeering charges, this did not prevent Weiss from eventually serving on the board of Standard Fruit and Steamship[486] which maintained strong ties with the CIA in its activities in Latin America.[487]

In this context it is interesting to note that there have been suggestions that Weiss, in fact, may have been the CIA station chief in New Orleans or was, at the least, a key CIA contact in the Crescent City.

As many JFK assassination researchers have pointed out, one New Orleans-based CIA contract agent investigated by Jim Garrison—the ubiquitous and colorful Gordon Novel—is known to have written a letter to a "Mr. Weiss" in which Novel discussed the dangers of the Garrison investigation. The letter surfaced at the time that Garrison's inquiry was in full swing and Novel was seeking to avoid giving testimony.

Most researchers have opined that the Mr. Weiss in question—never identified beyond that—was probably Novel's CIA superior. It is not stretching the imagination to suggest that this Mr. Weiss was, in fact, our own Seymour Weiss discussed in these pages.

Whatever the case, there is no question but that Seymour Weiss—a prime figure in the Lansky syndicate—was indeed tied closely to the intelligence community and undoubtedly worked on its behalf during his heyday, particularly in the context of his role with Standard Fruit.

The major fruit companies, as numerous documented works can attest, had extensive interplay with the CIA and other intelligence agencies throughout the 20th century, inasmuch as their vested interests in the so-called "Banana Republics" of Latin America were directly affected by the governments therein. And needless to say, the CIA itself has played a major role in the revolutions and counter-revolutions in Latin America from almost its very inception.

Where then do we find a tie-in between the scholarly and erudite Clay Shaw, a seemingly respectable trade executive, and the Lansky syndicate henchman—and intelligence contact—Seymour Weiss? In fact, it is a very close connection indeed.

## THE MEN BEHIND SHAW

You see, it was during the time that Weiss served as a director of the CIA-linked Standard Fruit that the powerful corporation was under the management of one Rudolph Hecht, a leading figure in the small and tightly knit but highly influential Jewish community of New Orleans.

Hecht, in fact, had become chairman—by the time of his death in 1956—of the executive committee of the International Trade Mart[488] of which Clay Shaw was managing director. It was Hecht and his associates, Ted Brent and Herbert O. Schwartz, who were Shaw's sponsors.

In short, Hecht was Shaw's superior. Shaw maintained the high public profile with the Trade Mart that won him his place in New Orleans society, while Hecht and his associates were the real powers behind the scenes.

And among those who likewise served on the board of the International Trade Mart was another powerful figure in the Jewish community, Edgar

Stern, Jr., whose father Edgar and his mother Edith were among the most prominent and leading financial angels for the Israeli lobby in America.

As we shall see in Chapter 17, the Sterns—perhaps Shaw's closest friends—were the forces behind the WDSU media empire that played a key role in laying the groundwork for Lee Harvey Oswald's ultimate portrayal as a "lone nut assassin" with ties to Castro.

Thus, we see that there is indeed much more to Clay Shaw than what we have been told. It was perhaps inevitable that this "respectable businessman" would, in time, emerge as a central figure in the complex web of international intrigue which we now know as Permindex and which did indeed have multiple ties to the forces that conspired to end the life of President John F. Kennedy.

Let us explore the Permindex connection further. As we do, the reality of what Permindex was—and how it was intimately tied to the JFK assassination—will become more apparent.

## LOUIS M. BLOOMFIELD

Above all, the Permindex connection to Israel and its global intelligence network is best personified by the individual who served as chairman of the board of Permindex: Major Louis M. Bloomfield of Montreal, Canada, himself a devoted and influential supporter of the Israeli cause.

It was Bloomfield who held half the shares of Permindex and its parent company "for party or parties unknown."[489] In fact, Permindex had its headquarters in Bloomfield's base of operations in Montreal until 1961 at which time it was relocated to Rome. [490]The facts about Bloomfield indicate, beyond doubt, that Bloomfield was a major player in Israel's international network.

Our first introduction to Bloomfield was in Chapter 7 where we examined Bloomfield's role in Operation Underworld during World War II, working directly under the supervision of Sir William Stephenson whose connections to both Israeli intelligence and the Lansky Crime Syndicate we explored in that same chapter.

Bloomfield had been recruited into Britain's Special Operations Executive [counter-intelligence] in 1938, the year that his immediate superior—another Canadian—the aforementioned Sir William Stephenson—set up British intelligence activities in the United States in the period leading up to World War II.

## THE BRONFMAN CONNECTION

Bloomfield, however, was a man of many parts. He was reputed to control Le Credit Suisse [bank] of Canada, Heineken's Breweries, Canscot Realty, the Grimaldi Siosa [shipping] Lines, Ltd—and, interestingly enough—the Israel Continental Company.[491]

A very busy man, Bloomfield's other ties were equally interesting. He was a founding partner in the Phillips, Vineberg, Bloomfield and Goodman firm which represents the Canadian-based Bronfman family interests.[492] This rather intriguing detail suggests, perhaps, that Bloomfield's wide-ranging financial interets were, in fact, those of the Bronfman family and the the Montreal lawyer was, essentially, the Bronfman's front man.

The Bronfman family, which built its fortune working with the Lansky Organized Crime Syndicate in the illegal liquor trade, have been key backers of Israel and leaders in the Zionist cause. Edgar Bronfman most recently served as president of the World Jewish Congress.

But there is yet another intriguing Bronfman family link to the JFK assassination conspiracy. When a Russian translator was needed for Lee Harvey Oswald's Russian wife, Marina, it was Texas oilman Jack Crichton, a former military intelligence officer who made the arrangements.

According to JFK assassination researcher Peter Dale Scott, Crichton, until 1962, "was also a Vice-President of the Empire Trust Company, a firm whose leading shareholders, the inter-related families of Loeb, Lehman and Bronfman, are said by Stephen Birmingham to have maintained 'something like a private CIA . . . around the world' to protect their other investments such as in Cuba, in Guatemala, and in General Dynamics."[493]

So it was that another Bronfman family intimate was in a key position in the days following the assassination of John F. Kennedy. It is no stretch of the imagination, then, to conclude that Crichton himself worked closely with Bronfman family henchman, Louis M. Bloomfield.

## ISRAEL

Bloomfield also, naturally, maintained close links with Israel in his own Canadian business and social affairs. The director of the Israeli-Canadian Maritime League, Bloomfield also served as Chairman of the Histadrut Campaign in Canada. [494]

(The Histadrut, Israel's national labor federation, at one point owned over one-third of the gross national product of Israel and controlled the second largest bank in Israel, the Bank Hapoalim. This bank, as we shall see in this chapter, was implicated in Permindex-linked intrigue in Europe that, ultimately, comes full circle back to New Orleans and the Clay Shaw connection to the JFK asssassination.)

## BLOOMFIELD AND THE FBI

And, as we have already seen, the intelligence connections of Permindex chief Bloomfield were impeccable. Although a Canadian by birth, Bloomfield was hired by J. Edgar Hoover to serve as a recruiting agent for the FBI's counterespionage division, Division Five

Through this position Bloomfield became a working partner of Division Five chief William Sullivan, a close friend of James J. Angleton, the Mossad's CIA ally. Sullivan was Angleton's "man inside" the FBI.

## BLOOMFIELD AND SHAW

Bloomfield was also given an officer's rank in the U.S. Army during World War II and assigned to the Office of Strategic Services (OSS)—just as had been the American who ultimately became his fellow Permindex director, Clay Shaw. It was the OSS, of course, that worked closely with the Corsican Mafia and Italian Mafia in anti-communist and anti-Nazi operations during World War II.

(A witness uncovered by Jim Garrison claimed to have seen a meeting in Winnipeg airport between Permindex board member Clay Shaw and CIA contract agent David Ferrie with another individual who may have been Bloomfield. [495] It is known that Shaw and Ferrie journeyed in a plane flown by Ferrie to Bloomfield's home base in Montreal at some time in 1961 or 1962.) [496]

There is an additional interesting Bloomfield-Shaw connection in this regard. Both Bloomfield and Shaw were intimately involved in setting up international trade arrangements and expositions. It will be remembered—indeed—that John F. Kennedy was on his way to speak at the newly-established Dallas Trade Mart. The primary way of access to the Dallas Trade Mart from downtown Dallas was through Dealey Plaza where the fatal shots were fired that killed Kennedy. (It is likely that Shaw and/or Bloomfield may have manipulated the making of these arragements.)

Obviously, Louis Bloomfield was a key figure in the Permindex network—a vital link between Clay Shaw's operation in New Orleans and other forces operating through Permindex—most especially Israel.

## BLOOMFIELD, SHAW AND ANGLETON

It is conceivable that not only did Bloomfield first come across Shaw during his service with the OSS during this same period, but also even another OSS man, James Jesus Angleton, who later went on to become Israel's ally in the CIA.

Angleton himself may have had contact with Shaw during that same period, although there is no firm evidence to prove that. However, there is no question, as the evidence suggests, that the two men were certainly moving in the same intimate circles.

In fact, when Shaw was later arrested for his involvement in the JFK assassination conspiracy, it was discovered that his address book contained the private telephone number of the Principessa Marcelle Borghese. [497] The principessa was a relative of Prince Valerio Borghese who was rescued during World War II by Angleton whose exploits with the OSS in Italy as its station chief in Rome won him a decoration from the Vatican. [498]

It will be recalled, of course, that one facet of the OSS-orchestrated campaign against the Nazis and the Italian fascists was known as Operation Underworld.

As we saw in Chapter 7, it was Meyer Lansky who was the middle man between the OSS and organized crime and who helped arrange for Sicilian Mafia support for the invading Allied troops when they landed in Italy. Angleton, of course, would have been the point man in Europe for this Lansky project.

(That Permindex just happened to be based in Rome, may thus be no small coincidence, considering Angleton's long-standing connections with the Italian city, even including family business connections:  his father held the National Cash Register franchise for Italy.)[499]

Angleton, of course, later went on to become chief of counter-intelligence at the CIA and the primary link between the Israeli-CIA alliance as we have seen in Chapter 8. (And in Chapter 16 we will see the key role that Angelton played in the JFK assassination conspiracy and in its ultimate cover-up.)

## MORE STRANGE CONNECTIONS

That Clay Shaw and Guy Banister's contacts in the Mossad-linked Permindex entity had a wide-ranging array of international interests in the world of intrigue is further evidenced by some of the other personalities involved. Among those who were either investors in Permindex or who shared seats on the board of Permindex alongside Clay Shaw and Louis M. Bloomfield were several interesting characters with equally interesting connections. Among them were:

• Ferenc Nagy. The former premier of Hungary was a fierce anti-communist who maintained close connections not only to Israel's allies in the America CIA, but also to the anti-Castro Cuban colony in Miami, itself practically a joint operating subsidiary of both the CIA and the Lansky Organized Crime Syndicate. (Nagy himself later settled in Dallas, Texas and was residing there at the time of the Kennedy assassination.)[500]

• Hans Seligman. A member of the family which controlled the Seligman Bank of Basel and whose extended family were, in America, part of the famous "Our Crowd" (German Jewish elite) in New York City during the latter period of the 19th century. Seligman was intimately involved with the Israel-oriented Zionist agency known as the Jewish Colonization Association.[501]

• Morris Dalitz. The former Cleveland bootlegger-turned-Las Vegas casino gambling czar. Dalitz was a longtime Lansky intimate who was Benjamin Siegel's successor as Lansky's point man in Las Vegas. [502]

As we saw in Chapter 10, Dalitz later employed "racket buster" G. Robert Blakey  as a consultant/character witness in a libel action in which Dalitz was contesting charges that his La Costa Country Club in Carlsbad, California was linked to organized crime. It was shortly thereafter that Blakey was placed in charge of the House Assassinations Committee investigation of the JFK murder.

Dalitz himself, as noted in Chapter 10, was also a longtime fund-raiser for the Israeli lobby in the United States and honored by the aforementioned Anti-Defamation League (ADL ) for his services.

• Carlos Prio Socarras. The President of Cuba from 1948-1952, Prio Socarras had been a front-man for Meyer Lansky's partner-in-crime, Cuban strongman Fulgencio Batista. In fact, it was Lansky who persuaded Batista with a hefty bribe to "step down" in favor of Prio Socarras. [503] And as we saw in Chapter 14 Prio was engaged in gun-running with a business partner whose name is now more than a footnote in history: Dallas nightclub operator Jack Ruby.

No wonder then, that the Italian journal, *Paesa Sera*, would be moved to comment: "It is a fact that the CMC is nevertheless the point of contact for a number of persons who, in certain respects, have somewhat equivocal ties whose common denominator is an anti-communism so strong that it would swallow up all those in the world who have fought for decent relations between East and West, including Kennedy."[504]

CMC/Permindex—it might also be added even more particularly—is nevertheless the point of contact for a number of persons who, in certain respects, have somewhat equivocal ties whose common denominator is a devotion to the cause of Israel.

## ISRAEL'S ROLE COMES FULL CIRCLE

As we have noted, however, it is the Tibor Rosenbaum-BCI connection with Permindex that points most definitely toward the Israeli Mossad interest in Permindex. BCI, as we have seen, was very much a creature of Israel and its Mossad.

Among the directors of Rosenbaum's BCI was Ernest Israel Japhet, also chairman and president of the Bank Leumi, the largest bank in Israel. BCI and Bank Leumi were involved in the diamond trade and tied into Far East drug trafficking.[505]

(We have already examined, in Chapter 6 and Chapter 12, Lansky's central role in global drug-trafficking in Southeast Asia, all of which was made further possible—under CIA cover—as a consequence of American involvement in the Vietnam conflict.)

Two other directors of BCI—as we noted in Chapter 7—were Ed Levinson, front man at the Fremont Casino in Las Vegas for Lansky's close friend, Joseph "Doc" Stacher, who died in exile in Israel and John Pullman, Lansky's international money courier.

Rosenbaum's other operation, the Swiss-Israel Trade Bank owned one-third interest in the Paz group, which had been a Rothschild family entity, maintaining control over Israel's oil and petrochemical industry. [506]

## EISENBERG AND FEINBERG—AGAIN

As we noted in Chapter 7, associates of Rosenbaum in the Swiss-Israel Trade bank included Shaul Eisenberg, a key figure in Israel's nuclear bomb development—the central point of conflict between JFK and Israel—and New York businessman, Abe Feinberg.

In Chapter 8 we learned that Eisenberg later became a business associate of CIA figure Theodore Shackley. Shackley, as we discovered in Chapter 11 was the CIA's chief of station in Miami during the CIA-Lansky Crime Syndicate plots against Fidel Castro. And, in Chapter 12, we learned, it was Shackley who was the CIA's chief of station in Laos during the period of the close working relationship between the intelligence agency and the Lansky syndicate in the global drug racket.

It was Feinberg, as we saw in Chapter 4, who was the American Jewish fund-raising contact of the 1960 Kennedy for President campaign. Feinberg's heavy-handed tactics so infuriated Kennedy that he privately told a close friend that he, as president, intended to enforce changes in presidential campaign fund-raising regulations that permitted powerful groups such as the American pro-Israel lobby to wield so much influence.

Feinberg additionally, of course, was close to Israeli Prime Minister David Ben-Gurion and, in fact, helped arrange the bitter meeting between Kennedy and Ben-Gurion recounted in Chapter 5.

The manager of Rosenbaum and Feinberg's Swiss-Israel Trade Bank was Gen. Julius Klein, a U.S. army counterintelligence officer.

Klein had engaged in illegally re-routing whole shiploads of medical supplies, construction equipment scheduled to go to post-war Germany to the Haganah in Palestine. (The Haganah was the self-defense forces of the Jews in Palestine and the forerunner of the Israeli Defense Force.) Klein conducted this enterprise during the period when he served as chief of the U.S. Army Counterintelligence Corps responsible for Western Europe at the end of World War II.

## ANOTHER MOSSAD LINK

However, Klein's services on behalf of the state of Israel were even more significant. It was Klein who had been involved in setting up Israel's Mossad and in training its officers. Klein worked alongside Sir William Stephenson in this particular venture.[507]

In Chapter 7, as noted earlier, we learned of Sir William's clandestine alliance with Meyer Lansky and his crime Syndicate in the so-called Operation Underworld apparatus aimed against Axis intelligence during World War II.

## ANOTHER LANSKY CONNECTION

Stephenson, of course, had been the chief of British intelligence operations in the United States in the years preceding and during World War II and in this capacity served as the aforementioned Major Louis M. Bloomfield's immediate operating superior.

It was during his days working with the American OSS and Naval Intelligence—and the Lansky Crime Syndicate—that Stephenson had cemented his ties with the Jewish anti-Nazi underground.

According to intelligence historian Richard Deacon: "Stephenson received a great deal of intelligence from Jewish scientists. This particular operation, though seemingly far removed from the story of Palestine, in the long run greatly helped Israeli Intelligence in the early days of the state of Israel.

"Some of these scientists who had become friends with Stephenson were encouraged to develop their talents in the cause of Allied intelligence and they not only worked for Britain in World War II, but later assisted the Israeli Secret Service."[508]

What's more, it might be noted, interestingly enough, Stephenson was a close personal advisor to British Prime Minister Winston Churchill. Here, almost certainly, Stephenson had contact, during those early days, with a young American who became a friend of Churchill—Clay Shaw, an American Army officer detailed to the Office of Strategic Services.

## THE PERMINDEX PLOT

Obviously, the connections (at an intimate level) between Tibor Rosenbaum's Israeli Mossad banking operation, the Banque de Credit International, and a wide-ranging array of figures tied closely to the Lansky Organized Crime Syndicate and—even—to Clay Shaw, a member of the Permindex board of directors, brings the conspiracy full circle. That BCI was one of the primary shareholders of the Permindex entity clearly points toward a Mossad role in the Permindex plot that ended the life of John F. Kennedy. However, there is much, much more as we shall see.

## LANSKY'S MIAMI-GENEVA COURIER

Research by former CIA contract agent Robert Morrow not only sheds light on the connections between Lansky's Miami banks and Mossad officer Tibor Rosenbaum's BCI, but also provides us evidence of a role by Meyer Lansky in the assassination of John F. Kennedy.

Shortly after Morrow had published his first book, *Betrayal*, in which he described his own connections through the CIA with a number of the figures involved in the JFK assassination conspiracy, he was contacted by a young man with an incredible story he wanted to tell.

According to Morrow, "In our initial conversation, the young man claimed his father, an ex-Air Force colonel, and others working for the CIA had prior knowledge that President Kennedy was going to be assassinated in Dallas on November 22, 1963 . . .

"The intelligence officer's son then made a wild accusation. He asserted that his father had been tied into organized crime and had been a bagman for at least one of the payoffs relating to the presidential assassination, transporting a large sum of money to Haiti for payoff purposes during the summer of 1963." [509]

This young man told Morrow that his father was associated with a mob courier. The courier in question was Mickey Weiner. Pursuing the Weiner lead further, Morrow learned from another source that tape recordings had been uncovered in which Weiner had participated in conversations relating to the circumstances of the Kennedy assassination.

According to Morrow's source, Albert Moakler, "The tapes were indicative that there was a conversation going on which was more than idle gossip. It definitely concerned Jersey and Miami . . . the areas, people in the areas. Something concerned with the assassination." [510]

(Miami, of course, was Meyer Lansky's base of operations. New Jersey, as we saw in Chapter 7, was the base of Lansky's Mafia associate, mobster Jerry Catena who was responsible for distribution of "skim" money from Lansky's Las Vegas gambling operations to Lansky's organized crime associates in the northern states.)

Morrow also determined that Weiner made regular runs between Switzerland and Miami where he would visit the Bank of Miami Beach. [511]

The aforementioned Mickey Weiner, obviously, was one of Lansky's couriers between his banking operations in Miami and those of the Israeli Mossad's Tibor Rosenbaum and the Banque de Credit International in Switzerland.

Based upon the findings of Robert Morrow, it's clear that Lansky's courier definitely had "inside" information about the JFK assassination. We may even go so far as to speculate that it was Lansky's courier who was providing funds from Permindex to the assassination conspirators stateside.

## ANOTHER ISRAEL CONNECTION

A "high level financial backer" of the Permindex operation, according to *Paesa Sera*, was one Dr. David Biegun, national secretary of the National Committee for Labor Israel, Inc., based in New York. This committee was the American affiliate of the Israeli Histadrut for which Permindex board chairman Louis M. Bloomfield was a chief fundraiser. [512](Flammonde, despite his excellent research, failed to carry this connection further.) [Ex-CIA man Philip Agee has said that the Committee for Labor Israel is often used as a CIA cover.][513]

Biegun's role in Permindex was explicitly important—even central to the operation of Permindex. In fact, it was Biegun who oversaw the liquidation of CMC/Permindex after the company was expelled from Switzerland and Italy in 1962, subsequently relocating the operation to Johannesburg, South Africa.[514] (South Africa, it might be noted, has long been engaged in intimate international intrigues in conjunction with Israel.)

*Paesa Sera* speculated that [CMC/Permindex] "was a creature of the CIA . . . set up as a cover for the transfer of CIA . . . funds in Italy for illegal-political-espionage activities."[515]

## A PERMINDEX ASSASSINATION PLOT

Public controversy surrounding Permindex, resulting in its expulsion from Switzerland and Italy, involved the role of Permindex in assassination plots aimed at French President Charles DeGaulle. And as we shall see, it is here that we find even more intriguing connections between Permindex and the JFK assassination.

Earlier in these pages, as we have seen, the rebel Secret Army Organization—known by its acronym OAS—was bitterly opposed to DeGaulle's decision to grant independence to Arab Algeria. (It was, as we noted in Chapter 4, John F. Kennedy who, as a young senator, riled the Israeli lobby by calling for Algerian independence in 1957.)

The OAS launched numerous assassination attempts against DeGaulle, none of which were successful, of course, but they did later inspire Frederick Forsythe's famous novel (later turned into a popular motion picture), *The Day of the Jackal.*

Following an investigation of one attempt, in 1962, French intelligence (the SDECE) charged that Permindex laundered money into the OAS coffers to finance the attempt on DeGaulle's life. [516]

According to DeGaulle's biographer, Jean Lacouture, "for moral as well as political reasons, [the OAS leadership] considered it necessary to sacrifice the Head of State, either physically or politically, so that Algeria would remain French."[517]

### 'A MUNIFICENT CONTRIBUTOR'

One of the French leaders who was a particularly bitter opponent of DeGaulle's decision to grant Algerian independence was a Jewish-born convert to Christianity, Jacques Soustelle, who had served as governor-general of Algeria. Soustelle himself went into exile saying, "The present regime in France is a dictatorship tempered by anarchy. At its summit, a single man exercises an unlimited, unimpeded tyrannical power . . . The present regime is based on a huge deception. DeGaulle has systematically betrayed those who had trust in him . . . ."[518]

Although Soustelle himself denied any contacts with the OAS,[519] he served as one of its primary political supporters, winning the plaudits of OAS supporters around the globe who believed the OAS propaganda line (echoed by Israel and its lobby in America) that Algerian independence would establish a Soviet foothold in the Middle East. (In fact, Israel's primary fear was that a strong new independent Arab republic would be a threat to Israel's survival.)

Interestingly enough, according to *Paesa Sera*, the Italian journal which publicized the role of Permindex in the plots against DeGaulle, former Hungarian premier and Permindex board member Ferenc Nagy was a "munificent contributor"[520] to Jacques Soustelle and the OAS.

(What's more, we now know, one of the key bases of financial support for Rabbi Tibor Rosenbaum's BCI—the key force behind Permindex and the plots against DeGaulle—were "clandestine deposits of undeclared funds from French Jews,"[521] not to mention, of course, the criminal funds from the Lansky crime syndicate.)

One French military leader who emerged as an OAS leader, General Antoine Argoud said, "the physical elimination of the Head of State poses no moral problem for any of us . . . We are all convinced . . . that DeGaulle has deserved the supreme punishment a hundred times over."[522]

## INTERNATIONAL SUPPORT

However, there were other elements that proved supportive of the French rebels within the OAS. According to historian Alexander Harrison: "Factors that seemed to favor the success of the [OAS] efforts to keep Algeria French [included]:

• The complicity of the 'old boy' networks within the various intelligence agencies, most notably [the French secret service, the SDECE] and the Direction de la Surveillance du Territoire [responsible for internal counterespionage] both of which at times placed loyalty to a former comrade-in-arms . . . above loyalty to the government; and

• Possible logistical help from countries [such as] the United States that had been hostile to DeGaulle since the first days of the Resistance in world War II and viewed his pro-Soviet stance as a threat to Western hegemony in the Mediterranean."[523]

(In Chapter 9 and in Chapter 12 we learned of apparent CIA support for the OAS, despite opposition by John F. Kennedy. This, of course, however, did not prevent the CIA from providing covert support to the OAS, JFK's opposition notwithstanding.)

## ISRAEL AND THE OAS

Not surprisingly, according to historian Harrison, whose OAS sympathies are apparent, "Some of the most ardent supporters of the OAS in Algeria were Jews."[524] What's more, notes Harrison, "a Jewish branch of the OAS was created."[525]

Another historian, Paul Henissart, has also noted an Israeli connection with the OAS. According to Henissart, "[The OAS] attracted hotheads including some Jews who belonged to Irgun Zvai Leumi, the Israeli underground military organization. They were recruited by the OAS as specialists in clandestine warfare."[526]

He notes additionally that while there were Jewish defense groups established in Algeria, "official Israeli delegations in Algeria to organize emigration of Jews from the coastal cities were not averse to aiding these self-defense groups. The Israeli government, however, never confirmed any connection with them."[527]

Nonetheless as Israeli historian Benjamin Beit-Hallahmi has pointed out, there is evidence of official Israeli support of the OAS: "During 1961 and 1962, there were numerous reports of Israeli support for the French OAS movement in Algeria."[528]

He notes that the Israelis had assisted the French in the Algerian war of independence between 1954 and 1962. Then, when Algeria was finally independent and sought admission to the UN, only Israel voted against it. Beit Hallahmi quotes another historian, Stewart Steven, as saying, "When in 1961 the OAS was created, it was a natural development that Israel, as keen on [French retention of Algeria as a colony] as the OAS themselves, should lock themselves into the [OAS]."[529]

So it was that Israeli intelligence—and its allies in the American CIA— had formed a close working alliance with the very forces that were attempting to destroy French President Charles DeGaulle. At the same time, in fact, these same elements were using their Permindex connection in yet another plot, this one aimed at the life of John F. Kennedy.

## THE OAS, PERMINDEX AND NEW ORLEANS

There is, interestingly, a New Orleans connection here. According to a report later issued by DeGaulle's secret service, the SDECE Israel's Bank Hapoalim supplied funds to the OAS through Guy Banister in New Orleans.[530] Banister's agent, Maurice Brooks Gatlin, carried the money to the OAS in Paris.[531] (Several years later Gatlin died in Panama when he fell—or was pushed—from a hotel balcony.)

Gatlin, evidently, had many interesting international affairs. When a Latin American regional conference of a global anti-communist confederation was set in place, organized by CIA operative and Banister contact, E. Howard Hunt, the chairman of that conference was Antonio Valladares. This same Valladares, based in Guatemala, also happened to serve as an attorney for New Orleans Mafia chief Carlos Marcello whom, as we have seen, was assisting in financing Banister's anti-communist activities. In attendance at the conference, which ultimately merged into the World Anti-Communist League, was Maurice Brooks Gatlin,[532] suggesting that the New Orleans connection to the the CIA and other worldwide intrigue was very strong indeed.

The aforementioned Bank Hapoalim was the bank established by Israel's labor bund, the Histadrut, for which Permindex chairman Louis Bloomfield served as chief fundraiser in Canada. Guy Banister's activities were explored earlier in Chapter 10, Chapter 11 and Chapter 14.

According to Gilbert LeCavelier, an associate of the late Bernard Fensterwald (a leading JFK assassination researcher), Banister's office also served as a New Orleans headquarters for OAS-connected mercenaries.

Among those OAS mercenaries was Jean Souetre who, we noted in Chapter 12, was reported to have been picked up in Dallas on November 22,

1963 and expelled from the United States.[533] In Chapter 16 we will explore Souetre's activities further.

Banister, the former FBI and Naval intelligence operative oversaw CIA-backed anti-Castro gun-running and intelligence operations out of an office at 544 Camp Street in New Orleans. Closely linked to the anti-Castro Cuban movement, Banister's operation functioned with the support of the CIA. Former CIA contract agent Robert Morrow asserts in his book, *Betrayal*, that Permindex board member Clay Shaw was, in fact, Banister's immediate superior in coordinating CIA operations out of New Orleans.

Among others, Banister was associated with former CIA pilot and anti-Castro adventurer David Ferrie (one of the key figures in Jim Garrison's case against Clay Shaw). Ferrie, as we have seen, also had a long-standing connection with Lee Harvey Oswald and, by all accounts, was associating regularly with Oswald in New Orleans in the summer of 1963.

Former CIA man Morrow also reports that during his activities with the CIA, working in conjunction with David Ferrie, he and Ferrie visited a warehouse in Europe where vast amounts of arms were stored—arms intended for the anti-Castro Cuban underground. The warehouse was a Permindex operation. [534]

Banister's secretary, Delphine Roberts, has been quoted as having said that Oswald was a regular visitor to 544 Camp Street engaged in some sort of "intelligence" work. [535] In fact, as is now generally acknowledged, it appears as though Oswald was being set up as a "pro-Castro" patsy.

## BANISTER'S ISRAELI CONNECTION

However, interestingly enough, there is yet another Israeli connection to the New Orleans scenario that set up Lee Harvey Oswald as the fall guy in the JFK assassination plot.

One of Banister's longstanding friends and fellow anti-communists was one A. I. (Bee) Botnick.[536] Botnick was a key figure in the New Orleans regional office of the Anti-Defamation League (ADL) of B'nai B'rith, which is now acknowledged as an intelligence agency with close ties to the Israeli Mossad.

Botnick, who reportedly considered himself "a super communist hunter," was obsessed with communism and, like Banister, believed communism to be a major force behind the civil rights movement.[537]

(In 1993 it was reported that the ADL had spied extensively on the late Dr. Martin Luther King and then turned its findings over to J. Edgar Hoover, Banister's former superior at the FBI.)[538]

(In Chapter 7 and in Chapter 10 we noted the long and close links between the ADL and the Meyer Lansky Organized Crime Syndicate, itself tied closely to the CIA and to Israeli intelligence, most notably through the Permindex link discussed in this chapter.)

In general, and under Botnick's leadership in New Orleans in particular, the ADL had a history of deploying agents into left-wing groups in order to spy on their activities.

This, of course, fits precisely into the profile of Lee Harvey Oswald's "leftist" and "pro-Castro" activities in New Orleans during the summer of 1963, operating a "Fair Play for Cuba Committee" out of Banister's private detective agency/intelligence operation at 544 Camp Street.

What is additionally intriguing is that, according to former ADL general counsel and intelligence chief Arnold Forster, much of the ADL's "fact finding" (i.e. spying) utilized agents "employed by an outside investigative agency operating as an independent contractor."[539]

In light of the close association between the ADL's Botnick and Banister, it seems quite likely indeed that Botnick channeled ADL contract work out to his anti-communist friend.

What's more, according to the ADL's Forster, many of the ADL's fact-finders were "retired local or federal government investigators"[540]—such as, perhaps, a likely former American intelligence agent named Oswald who had once done covert work in the Soviet Union.

We can only wonder, then, if, in fact, Lee Harvey Oswald's "left wing" activities were actually being financed by the ADL. Was Oswald, indeed, being utilized to infiltrate left-wing groups by Banister as part of what appeared to be a fact-finding mission for the ADL with an ulterior motive?

Does this suggest, then, that the ADL—as part of Israel's American intelligence operations—was itself somehow part and parcel of the JFK assassination conspiracy?

It is not extraordinary, in this context, to suggest that Oswald was being "sheep-dipped" as a "pro-Castro" agitator by the ADL on behalf of its contacts in the Mossad and the CIA in the guise of its standard "fact finding" endeavors.

## A 'THIRD FORCE'?

Although he does not pinpoint the ADL as a force behind Banister's activities, respected JFK assassination researcher Peter Dale Scott has lent credence to the possibility that there was much more to Banister's operations than would seem to meet the eye. According to Scott: "Disagreement arises . . . as to who was paying for Banister's anti-Communist activities: governmental intelligence, the New Orleans Mafia, or **some third force** allied with both together." [emphasis added]

Those stressing the intelligence angle, notes Scott, point to Banister's FBI and CIA and Office of Naval Intelligence connections while those stressing the "Mafia" point to Banister's connections, through David Ferrie and others, to New Orleans Mafia chief Carlos Marcello.

As Scott notes, however, "a third and more likely possibility is that both Oswald and Banister were working for what was in effect a third force: an intelligence-Mafia gray alliance, rooted in the deep political economy of New Orleans."[541]

And as we have seen in this chapter and elsewhere, the ADL did indeed have a strong root in the deep political economy of New Orleans, even indeed in the Clay Shaw connection.

## COINTELPRO AND ADL

"As to the story that Oswald was an FBI informant," writes Scott, "I doubt that Oswald was directly on the FBI payroll. A more likely possibility is that he worked for a **private security agency** which in turn reported to the FBI, the way that ex-FBI and ex-Official of Naval Intelligence agent Guy Banister, according to a CIA document, reported to the FBI in New Orleans."[542] [emphasis added]

That the ADL did, in fact, report back to the FBI, a long-standing relationship cemented by J. Edgar Hoover himself, is now common knowledge, a fact that we shall examine further in Chapter 17.

One prominent Black civil rights leader of the 1960's has told intimates of how his own FBI files, released under the Freedom of Information Act, revealed that it was the ADL which was actually monitoring his public lectures and then turning the information over to the FBI as part of its COINTELPRO operations.

And as we saw in Chapter 7, it was COINTELPRO, carried out by the FBI's Division Five, that was under the direct control of William Sullivan, who was effectively a CIA "mole" inside the FBI for his close friend, the Mossad's CIA ally, James J. Angleton.

(In Chapter 17 we will explore the activities of the ADL further, paying particular attention to the apparent manipulation of media coverage of the controversy over the JFK assassination by the ADL and by ADL-linked sources in New Orleans, the very site of Oswald's contact with Banister.

(And in Appendix Two we shall examine a little-explored link between Lee Harvey Oswald and at least one covert government informant who almost certainly had connections with the ADL.)

Whatever the case, it is very clear that the Israeli Mossad and the CIA had a direct hand in the strange activities of Guy Banister, David Ferrie and Lee Harvey Oswald in New Orleans during the summer of 1963.

Both the Mossad and the CIA were intimately tied with the Permindex plot against French President Charles DeGaulle and with the Permindex plot against John F. Kennedy. In the bloody conflict over Algerian Arab independence both Kennedy and DeGaulle found themselves on the same side of the issue—and on the opposite side of that of the Mossad and its allies in the CIA.

## A VISIT FROM PERMINDEX

That New Orleans District Attorney Jim Garrison was indeed on the right track is illustrated by a strange visit that Garrison got during the early days of his investigation. A Denver oilman, later identified by investigators as John King, appeared in Garrison's office and offered to arrange the district attorney's appointment to a federal judgeship in return for Garrison's abandonment of his investigation.

King very clearly had inside information about the nature of Garrison's inquiry and was obviously interested in shutting it down before it went any further. Garrison would not be bribed, however, and promptly showed the gentleman to the door.

It just so happens that during the very period of King's mysterious visit to New Orleans, the "Denver oilman" was engaged in lucrative international business dealings with Bernie Cornfeld, the Geneva-based head of the Investors Overseas Service (IOS). King's other interests included oil drilling offshore of the Sinai peninsula, Arab territory seized by the Israelis in 1967.[543]

King's partner Cornfeld, as we saw in Chapter 7 and in Chapter 9, was, in fact, the protege and front man of Rabbi Tibor Rosenbaum, founder of the Banque De Credit International (BCI) and a central financial figure behind Permindex.

King's visit was very clearly a friendly offer from Permindex. They hoped to silence Garrison before his inquiry went further—before he made the Clay Shaw connection, before he discovered the real origins of the Permindex plot that led to the murder of John F. Kennedy. Permindex and its backers were determined to stop the investigation in its tracks.

John King's visit to New Orleans is very clear evidence, indeed, that the role of Clay Shaw and his link to Permindex is the key to the JFK assassination mystery.

## MYER FELDMAN'S NEW EMPLOYER

An interesting footnote: By 1967, a key player in the Permindex network of Tibor Rosenbaum, Bernie Cornfeld and the ubiquitous John King, was the super-lawyer who represented IOS interests in Washington— Myer Feldman.[544]

It was Feldman, whom we first met in Chapter 5 as John F. Kennedy's liaison to the American Jewish community and of whom, we learned, the president's brother, Robert F. Kennedy said, "His major interest was Israel rather than the United States."

So it was that the same Feldman, after leaving the White House, who signed on as a highly-paid henchman for the very interests that orchestrated the assassination of John F. Kennedy. A small world indeed.

## THE STRANGE WORLD OF CLAY SHAW

Those who have been most strident in their denunciations of Jim Garrison for his investigation and indictment of Clay Shaw are among those who push the myth that "The Mafia Killed JFK." They suggest that Clay Shaw was some innocent figure whose most notable accomplishment was rehabilitating French Quarter carriage houses.

Yet, despite the link between Permindex and the Lansky Syndicate money laundering Banque De Credit International, those who say that "The Mafia Killed JFK" say absolutely nothing about Shaw's very firm ties—

through Permindex—to this criminal banking entity, very much linked to "the Mafia" through Lansky.

To disregard the Israeli Mossad linkage in the Permindex connection is to avoid the truth altogether. This is why those who seek to point the finger of blame toward "the Mafia," for example, are so determined to vindicate Clay Shaw. To look in the direction of Clay Shaw is to look in the very direction of Israel—and that is why it was so vital that Jim Garrison's investigation had to be scuttled at all costs.

Obviously, there's much more to the Permindex controversy than many people would like to admit. And in this author's judgment it is because of the Permindex link to Israel and its Mossad that some JFK assassination researchers have chosen to ignore the truth before them.

## WHAT ABOUT THE 'NAZI' CONNECTION?

There have been those who have proclaimed Permindex to have been some sort of "Nazi" remnant surviving in the wake of World War II. The leading promoter of this theory was the late Mae Brussell, a somewhat eccentric and perhaps erratic conspiracy researcher who became an icon for many obsessed with the JFK assassination.

Yet, there is something about Miss Brussell's background that has been ignored but what is significant in light of the Israeli role in the Kennedy assassination that we have dissected here in the pages of *Final Judgment*.

Miss Brussell, you see, was the daughter of Rabbi Edgar Magnin, the spiritual leader of Hollywood's politically powerful and immensely wealthy Jewish community—next to the New York Jewish community the most significant force in the pro-Israel lobby in America. For this reason alone Miss Brussell would not be inclined to follow the Permindex connection to its Israeli antecedents.

Be that as it may, Brussell's claim that Permindex was part of a "Nazi" conspiracy behind the JFK assassination is very clearly far off the mark, considering all that we have reviewed in these pages.

However, ironically, there is a bizarre and highly unusual "Nazi" connection to Permindex that is either misunderstood or has been deliberately obscured but which, strangely enough, points further toward our understanding of Permindex as a transnational point of contact for the Mossad and its allies in the CIA and organized crime.

## THE 'FASCIST JEWS'

The fact is that not only Mossad figure Tibor Rosenbaum but also Permindex figures Georges and Ernst Mandel were part of a Zionist operation that had its origins in a multi-layered intelligence venture that laid the groundwork for not only the establishment of the state of Israel but the reported escape of former Nazi leaders out of Europe following the close of World War II.

According to John Loftus and Mark Aarons, writing in *The Secret War Against the Jews*, "During World War II Soviet intelligence used a network of supposedly "fascist Jews," code named Max, to penetrate the inner circles of the Third Reich and to destroy the German army on the Eastern front. The Nazis believed that the Max network was their secret intelligence source inside the Kremlin, and it did in fact give 'good' intelligence to the Germans but it was strictly controlled by the Communists.

"The Jews of the Max network were mostly Communist double agents, but they also were Jews who defected to the Zionist cause toward the end of the war and revealed [future CIA director] Allen Dulles' [pre-war and wartime] secret [financial and intelligenc] deals with the Nazis.

## ANGLETON BLACKMAILED

"The Zionists," according to Loftus and Aarons, "blackmailed Dulles' [CIA] protege, James Angleton, into setting up a parallel smuggling system for Jews and fugitive Nazis."[545]

(That the Israelis were blackmailing Angleton, according to Loftus and Aarons who are undoubtedly pro-Israeli partisans, is an interesting point and something which, in the context of our study of the JFK assassination, explains much about Angleton's behavior throughout his CIA career and in the events which involved Angleton in the circumstances of the JFK assassination, more about which we shall discuss in Chapter 16.)

It was in Chapter 8, of course, that we learned of Angleton's role in the Jewish refugee network that ultimately evolved into the modern-day Mossad.

So it is that we can now understand why Zionist leaders would find themselves in the company of reputed Nazis and Nazi collaborators in the strange transnational entity known as Permindex.

There were—as Peter Dale Scott has said—common modes of interaction between a variety of interests involved in complex, multi-centered intrigues where these diverse elements, each with distinctive motives, collaborated on common projects, each for their own ends.

## A TRANSNATIONAL ARRANGEMENT

There is indeed much more to Permindex than we have been told by some JFK assassination researchers, but ultimately the truth is that Permindex was, more than anything, predominantly a transnational arrangement with Israel's intrigues as its driving force.

Israel's worldwide connections—particularly with the anti-Kennedy forces within the CIA and the CIA-linked Lansky crime empire, along with the French OAS rebels and Charles DeGaulle's enemies within his own intelligence service—made possible the network through which the plan to kill JFK was carried out. Permindex was in the center of it all.

Through the so-called "false flag" technique in which the Mossad is so skilled (as we saw in Chapter 3), "Mafia" figures, anti-Castro Cubans, low-level CIA operatives and an assortment of other strange figures were drawn into the Permindex web of intrigue that resulted in the JFK assassination.

## WHAT DID SHAW KNOW?

In the end, however, it was New Orleans businessman and Permindex board member Clay Shaw who became the one person (aside from the hapless Lee Harvey Oswald) to be charged with having participated in the JFK assassination conspiracy.

Whether Shaw knew in advance of JFK's impending assassination will probably never be known. That Shaw was trafficking with the likes of David Ferrie and Guy Banister—Oswald's immediate handlers—and with Oswald himself was firmly established in the course of Jim Garrison's investigation. Whether Shaw knew that Oswald, ultimately, would be the patsy in the JFK assassination is another mystery that will almost certainly never be solved. Nonetheless, it is the Clay Shaw connection to the assassination—through Permindex—that points directly toward the role of the Israeli Mossad in the JFK assassination conspiracy.

## THE KEY TO THE MYSTERY . . .

Clearly, Permindex is the key to understanding the full nature of the JFK assassination conspiracy. It is the focal point in the Mossad-CIA-Lansky-Mafia linkage which manipulated events in New Orleans and Dallas—and within the anti-Castro Cuban community in Miami and elsewhere—that led to the assassination of John F. Kennedy.

**To ignore the Permindex connection is to ignore the reality about the origins of the plot that led to the assassination of America's thirty-fifth president. Obviously the tentacles of CMC/Permindex reached far and wide and they inextricably intertwined the forces of Israel, the CIA and the international Lansky Crime Syndicate.**

In our next chapter we will review, at last, the most recent, startling and definitive evidence which proves that, indeed, the CIA did have a hand in the JFK assassination and that it was Israel's ally at CIA headquarters in Washington, James Jesus Angleton, who played a key role in the conspiracy cover-up.

What's more, we will examine important new information which suggests that there was much more happening in Dallas, Texas on November 22, 1963 than otherwise might meet the eye.

We will also discover that the so-called "French connection" to the JFK assassination—long suspected by many JFK assassination researchers—is, in fact, the Israeli connection.

## Chapter Sixteen

### Double Cross in Dallas?
### What Really Happened in Dealey Plaza?
### James Jesus Angleton, E. Howard Hunt and the JFK Assassination.
### The Truth About the "French Connection"

It was in a little publicized libel trial conducted in Miami in 1985 that veteran Kennedy assassination investigator Mark Lane proved to the satisfaction of a jury that the CIA played a part in the assassination of John F. Kennedy. Lane's ground-breaking best-seller, *Plausible Denial*, published in 1991, told the whole incredible story.

Evidence from that trial also points toward Israel's connection to the assassination through the offices of Israel's CIA ally, James Jesus Angleton. It was Angleton who assisted in the cover-up of his favorite foreign nation's central role alongside the CIA in the murder of JFK.

There is also strange new evidence that there was much more happening in Dealey Plaza in Dallas than even many of those involved in the events surrounding the JFK assassination really knew.

Mark Lane's *Plausible Denial* proved conclusively that the CIA had a hand in the assassination of President John F. Kennedy. This monumental book was written by the one man who sparked the search for the truth that has preoccupied Americans for nearly three decades.

As we saw in Chapter 9, Lane's book told how the Washington-based *Spotlight* newspaper's libel trial with ex-CIA man E. Howard Hunt brought into a Florida courtroom the first hard evidence linking the CIA to the Kennedy assassination.

As noted previously, Lane agreed to serve as *The Spotlight's* defense attorney after Hunt won a $650,000 libel judgment against the populist weekly. It was Lane who successfully handled *The Spotlight's* defense after the case again went to trial after the initial libel verdict was overturned.

The libel action stemmed from an article published in the pages of *The Spotlight* in 1978.

The article was written by Victor Marchetti, an ex-CIA executive officer who had become internationally famous after he published his best-selling critique, *The CIA and the Cult of Intelligence*, the first book ever censored prior to publication by the CIA.

After leaving the CIA, Marchetti became a journalist, specializing in matters relating to the CIA and the intelligence community in general. As such he was a recognized authority in his field and had done a number of intelligence-related articles for *The Spotlight*, among numerous other publications, both here in the United States and abroad.

As a consequence, when Marchetti approached *The Spotlight* with a rather intriguing article which gave an interesting new slant on the JFK assassination furor (in the midst of the House Assassinations Committee investigation), the editors of the weekly newspaper were interested.

## CIA TO FRAME HUNT?

Marchetti's article suggested that upper echelon executives of the CIA had decided to frame E. Howard Hunt for involvement in the Kennedy assassination. Not that Hunt was involved in the crime--simply that the CIA had decided to frame Hunt for the deed. This distinction is important.

Over the years, several assassination buffs had claimed that the famous photographs taken in Dealey Plaza of three so-called "tramps" being led away from the scene by police officers revealed Hunt as one of those tramps. This story was picked up the tabloids and given wide play.

## A CIA-MOSSAD CONCOCTION?

However, there are those who believe that the "Hunt as a tramp" story was, in fact, deliberately trumped up as part of the CIA's scheme to frame Hunt for involvement in the assassination. It was the CIA's plan to implicate Hunt that Victor Marchetti exposed in *The Spotlight*.

The leading promoter of the theory that Hunt was one of the "tramps" in Dallas is A. J. Weberman who maintains very close ties to the Jewish Defense League.

Weberman has also been closely associated with Mordechai Levi, a known *agent provocateur* of the Israeli's Mossad's propaganda and intelligence arm, the Anti-Defamation League of B'nai B'rith, which we examine in further detail in Chapter 17.

(Levi was also active in the Jewish Defense League (JDL), created by militant Rabbi Meir Kahane. In Chapter 8 we saw that Kahane was a CIA asset and protege of Irving Lovestone who handled CIA liaison with the Meyer Lansky-linked French Corsican and Sicilian Mafias. Lovestone's operation was directed out of James J. Angleton's Israeli desk at the CIA.)

It may very well be that the "Hunt as a tramp" story being touted by Weberman was indeed a CIA-Mossad concoction to further muddy the waters.

What is interesting is that in 1975—precisely at the time when Weberman was publishing and promoting a book that named Hunt as one of the tramps—a strange letter appeared, anonymously, in the mailbox of another (and more reliable) assassination researcher, Penn Jones, Jr.

The letter was written in Spanish and its envelope carried a Mexico City postmark. The letter accompanied another letter which read as follows:
"Dear Mr. Hunt,

I would like information concerding [sic] my position.

I am asking only for information. I am suggesting that we discuss the matter fully before any steps are taken by me or anyone else.
Thank you,
Lee Harvy [sic] Oswald."[546]
Subsequent analyses suggested that the letter may or may not have been Oswald's handwriting (although he was known to misspell even his own

middle name as it was misspelled in the letter. When word of the letter's existence gained circulation, the reference to a "Mr. Hunt" created immediate speculation that the Hunt in question was either Texas oilman H. L. Hunt or, more than likely, E. Howard Hunt.

In light of the then-current rumors about Hunt's alleged role in the JFK affair, coupled with his known connections to the CIA and, in particular, Mexico City, where he had been active during his CIA career, the suspicions about E. Howard Hunt were quite natural.

It is interesting, though, that the letter was sent from Mexico City, Hunt's former base of operations. Whether the letter was real or not, it is obvious that someone wanted to throw further suspicion on E. Howard Hunt—and succeeded.

That the Weberman story of "Hunt as a tramp" and the "Dear Mr. Hunt" letter appeared at the same time are particularly intriguing in light of another matter we are about to consider.

Both the "Hunt as a tramp" story and the "Dear Mr. Hunt" letter appear to be part and parcel of a CIA black propaganda operation run by the Mossad's man at the CIA, James J. Angleton.

## HUNT WAS IN DALLAS

Ironically, as we shall see, the evidence suggests that E. Howard Hunt was indeed in Dallas—on, at the very least, November 21, 1963—and very much involved in strange activities in league with key players in the JFK assassination scenario.

According to Marchetti, widespread public suspicion of CIA involvement in the president's murder was forcing the CIA to play its hand and "admit" that, in fact, one of its more notorious longtime operatives, Hunt, had indeed been in Dallas on the day that Kennedy was killed.

Obviously, Hunt—with his well-known ties to the anti-Castro Cubans, often considered prime suspects in the JFK assassination—would have a difficult time explaining why he had been in Big D on that fateful day—if indeed he had been.

Interesting, Marchetti's article never said that Hunt had, in fact, been involved in the assassination conspiracy. Marchetti's article said only that top-ranking CIA officials had decided to frame Hunt for the crime. Hunt, according to Marchetti's sources, was deemed expendable.

## A STRANGE MEMO

Marchetti's article reported that a strange in-house CIA memo— allegedly written some years previously—had somehow ended up in the hands of investigators for the House Assassinations Committee and that Hunt, as a consequence, would ultimately be forced to explain his reported presence in Dallas (as described in the memo) on November 22, 1963.

The editors of *The Spotlight* felt Marchetti's article served, if anything, as an advance warning to Hunt of what his former employers had in mind.

*The Spotlight's* editors didn't, in fact, feel that the article implicated Hunt in the president's murder.

Inexplicably, however, the ex-CIA man decided to sue, even though he ultimately admitted under oath that when he first read *The Spotlight's* story that Marchetti's contentions seemed plausible indeed. In short, that Hunt did believe that his former colleagues would be willing to throw him to the wolves—for their own nefarious reasons.

Hunt's lawsuit against *The Spotlight* did go to trial. However,*The Spotlight's* management did not take the lawsuit seriously. They did not believe either that the article damaged Hunt's reputation or that Hunt's attorneys could prove that the newspaper had published the article maliciously.

(In fact, *The Spotlight* had invited Hunt to visit the newspaper's editorial offices for an interview to rebut the claims made in Marchetti's article or to even write an article rebutting Marchetti's article.)

## HUNT WINS LAWSUIT

During that trial, *The Spotlight's* attorney unexpectedly stipulated that the newspaper did not believe that Hunt had been in Dallas on November 22, 1963. The trial, however, resulted in a massive $650,000 libel judgment against the newspaper. *The Spotlight* appealed the judgment and the appeals court granted a new trial on the basis that the trial judge's instructions to the jury had been faulty .

## LANE ENTERS THE CASE

It was at this point that famed JFK assassination investigator Mark Lane, an attorney, entered into the case—almost purely by chance, having been introduced to the publisher of *The Spotlight* by a mutual acquaintance shortly before the case was heard on appeal.

Based upon his own decades of intensive research, Lane had long been convinced that the CIA had been instrumental in orchestrating the JFK assassination, but he had never had a legal forum in which to conduct an investigation of this sort.

The new trial—which took place in 1985 (some seven years after the controversial article had first been published) gave him that opportunity. Lane launched *The Spotlight's* defense with a very different approach.

He contended that Hunt had indeed been in Dallas just prior to the president's murder and that he would be able to prove it. This took Hunt's lawyers by surprise, to say the least, but despite their efforts to derail Lane's new approach, they were unsuccessful.

## TESTIMONY IGNORED

The key witness in the second libel trial (conducted in Miami) was Marita Lorenz, a former CIA operative who had testified before the House

Assassinations Committee in 1978, relating what information she had in connection with the president's assassination.

Yet, despite the inflammatory nature of what Miss Lorenz had told the committee, her testimony was discounted by the House Committee director G. Robert Blakey (about whose own connections with the CIA and the Meyer Lansky Organized Crime Syndicate we learned in Chapter 10).

Miss Lorenz, a German-born beauty, had, in fact, been the one-time mistress of Cuban dictator Fidel Castro, but she had ultimately turned on the Cuban leader and had become involved in anti-Castro activities under the CIA's tutelage. Among her key contacts in the CIA during this period was the CIA's chief liaison with the anti-Castro Cuban operatives, E. Howard Hunt.

Mark Lane asked Miss Lorenz to testify in the Hunt trial in *The Spotlight*'s defense, restating—again under oath—what she had told the House Assassinations Committee and what she had told Lane himself years previously.

## HUNT & RUBY IN DALLAS

So it was that during the Hunt libel trial, Miss Lorenz testified in a deposition that just one day prior to Kennedy's assassination, she, along with a handful of other CIA figures, met in Dallas, Texas with not only E. Howard Hunt, but also nightclub operator Jack Ruby who later killed Lee Harvey Oswald, the president's alleged assassin.

According to Miss Lorenz, Hunt was the CIA paymaster for a top-secret operation, the purpose of which she did not know. Miss Lorenz said that he had been told that she was to serve as a "decoy."

However, Miss Lorenz left Dallas on November 22 and never participated in the operation. It was later she learned that President Kennedy had been assassinated and that, of course, Jack Ruby had killed Lee Harvey Oswald, the president's alleged assassin.[547]

## CONTRADICTORY TESTIMONY

As for Hunt himself, his contradictory stories about where he was situated both the day before the Kennedy assassination and the day of the assassination itself were suspicious. Lane took excellent advantage of Hunt's sworn statements (in deposition and during the two trials, as well as several other forums) to show those contradictions. These contradictions alone could have spelled Hunt's courtroom demise.

What's more, the witnesses called in Hunt's defense by the ex-CIA man's attorneys only ended up suggesting Hunt had more to hide than he had to admit. Many of these witnesses, in fact, were an assortment of Hunt's former CIA colleagues, a number of whom were represented during their testimony in deposition by CIA-dispatched lawyers.

However, it was the testimony of Marita Lorenz that convinced the jury, once and for all, that *The Spotlight* (and Lane himself) had a much

more plausible story than Hunt. Thus, the stunning courtroom victory for
*The Spotlight*, vanquishing Hunt's libel action.

## A JURY'S VERDICT

Leslie Armstrong, a Miami resident who was jury forewoman in the
case, issued a statement in conjunction with the release of Lane's written
account of the trial:

"Mr. Lane was asking us [the jury] to do something very difficult. He
was asking us to believe John Kennedy had been killed by our own
government. Yet when we examined the evidence closely, we were
compelled to conclude that the CIA had indeed killed President
Kennedy."[548]

Despite this stunning conclusion, the media remained silent. Very little
about Hunt's courtroom defeat appeared in the media, particularly the sum
and substance of Miss Lorenz's amazing allegations. This, of course, was
real news in every sense but the media chose to ignore what had taken place
in that Miami courtroom.

Interestingly, however, as we shall see, there was yet another
newspaper report (similar in content to that of Victor Marchetti's disputed
article) which—like Marchetti's—suggests that there was a lot more to the
story than meets the eye.

## THE ANGLETON CONNECTION

In fact, the in-house CIA memorandum linking Hunt to the JFK
assassination was the work of Israel's ally at the CIA, James Jesus Angleton,
whose own history we examined in Chapter 8 and whom we have met
repeatedly throughout these pages.

This is not to suggest, though, that Hunt was not in Dallas on either
November 21 or November 22, 1963.

On the contrary, the evidence we are about to relate suggests that
Hunt's presence in Dallas—for whatever purpose—was indeed linked **in
some fashion** to the circumstances surrounding the JFK assassination
conspiracy.

This evidence suggests, as we shall see, that it was Angleton—who was
also responsible for leaking the memo he drafted that linked Hunt to the
JFK assassination.

## WHAT MARCHETTI SAID

Before proceeding further with our exploration of Angleton's deeds and
misdeeds, however, it is important to review Victor Marchetti's article
(printed in *The Spotlight* on August 14, 1978) which is published here in
pertinent part:

A few months ago, in March, there was a meeting at CIA headquarters in Langley, Va., the plush home of America's super spooks overlooking the Potomac River. It was attended by several high-level clandestine officers and some former top officials of the agency.

The topic of the discussion was: What to do about recent revelations associating President Kennedy's accused assassin, Lee Harvey Oswald, with the spy game played between the U.S. and the USSR? A decision was made, and a course of action determined. They were calculated to both fascinate and confuse the public by staging a clever 'limited hangout' when the House Special Committee on Assassinations (HSCA) holds its open hearings, beginning later this month.

A "limited hangout" is spy jargon for a favorite and frequently used gimmick of the clandestine professionals. When their veil of secrecy is shredded and they can no longer rely on a phony cover story to misinform the public, they resort to admitting—sometimes even volunteering—some of the truth while still managing to withhold the key and damaging facts in the case. The public, however, is usually so intrigued by the new information that it never thinks to pursue the matter further.

We will probably never find out who masterminded the assassination of JFK—or why. There are too many powerful special interests connected with the conspiracy for the truth to come out even now, 15 years after the murder.

But during the next two months, according to sensitive sources in the CIA and on HSCA, we are going to learn much more about the crime. The new disclosures will be sensational, but only superficially so. A few of the lesser villains involved in the conspiracy and its subsequent cover-up will be identified for the first time—and allowed to twist slowly in the wind on live network TV. Most of the others to be fingered are already dead.

But once again, the good folks of middle America will be hoodwinked by the government and its allies in the establishment news media. In fact, we are being set up to witness yet another cover-up, albeit a sophisticated one, designed by the CIA with the assistance of the FBI and the blessing of the Carter administration.

A classic example of a limited hangout is how the CIA has handled and manipulated the Church Committee's investigation [of the CIA] two years ago. The committee learned nothing more about the assassinations of foreign leaders, illicit drug programs, or the penetration of the news media than the CIA allowed it to discover. And this is precisely what the CIA is out to accomplish through HSCA with regard to JFK's murder.

Chief among those to be exposed by the new investigation will be E. Howard Hunt, of Watergate fame. His luck has run out, and the CIA has decided to sacrifice him to protect its clandestine services. The agency is furious with Hunt for having dragged it publicly into the Nixon mess and for having blackmailed it after he was arrested.

Besides, Hunt is vulnerable—an easy target as they say in the spy business. His reputation and integrity have been destroyed. The death of his wife, Dorothy, in a mysterious plane crash in Chicago still disturbs many people, especially since there were rumors from informed sources that she was about to leave him and perhaps even turn on him.

In addition it is well known that Hunt hated JFK and blamed him for the Bay of Pigs disaster. And now, in recent months, his alibi for his whereabouts on the day of the shooting has come unstuck.

In the public hearings, the CIA will 'admit' that Hunt was involved in the conspiracy to kill Kennedy. The CIA may go so far as to 'admit' that there were three gunmen shooting at Kennedy. The FBI, while publicly embracing the Warren Commission's 'one man acting alone' conclusion, has always privately known that there were three gunmen. The conspiracy involved many more people than the ones who actually fired at Kennedy, both agencies may now admit . . .

Now, the CIA moved to finger Hunt and tie him to the JFK assassination. HSCA unexpectedly received an internal CIA memorandum a few weeks ago that the agency just happened to stumble across in its old files. It was dated 1966 and said in essence: Some day we will have to explain Hunt's presence in Dallas on November 22, 1963—the day President Kennedy was killed. Hunt is going to be hard put to explain this memo, and other things, before the TV cameras at the HSCA hearings.

Hunt's reputation as a strident fanatical anti-communist will count against him. So will his long and close relationship with the anti-Castro Cubans, as well as his penchant for clandestine dirty tricks and his various capers while one of Nixon's plumbers. E. Howard Hunt will be implicated in the conspiracy and he will not dare to speak out—the CIA will see to that.

[Marchetti noted, at this juncture, that Fidel Castro's former mistress, Marita Lorenz had alleged that Hunt was part of a CIA hit squad aiming for President Kennedy.]

Who else will be identified as having been part of the conspiracy and/or cover-up remains to be seen. But a disturbing pattern is already beginning to emerge. All the villains have been previously disgraced in one way or another. They all have 'right wing' reputations. Or they will have after the hearings.

The fact that some may have had connections with organized crime will prove to be only incidental in the long run. Those with provable ties to the CIA or FBI will be presented as renegades who acted on their own without approval or knowledge of their superiors.

As for covering up the deed, that will be blamed on past Presidents, either dead or disgraced. Thus, Carter will emerge as a truth seeker, and the CIA and FBI will have neatly covered their institutional behinds.[549]

Marchetti's article is very interesting in many respects. First of all, as noted previously, Hunt himself initially admitted that he believed that the story had a basis in truth—that it was plausible, that indeed his former colleagues in the CIA did consider framing him for involvement in the JFK assassination.

The origin of the memorandum linking Hunt to the JFK assassination is interesting as it is presented by Marchetti. He describes it as a memorandum that "the agency just happened to stumble across in its old files."

In other words, one might presume from Marchetti's flippant reference, the CIA had, instead, perhaps concocted the memo. That the agency "just happened to stumble across" the memo at a time when public suspicion of CIA involvement in the JFK assassination was growing is, of course, interesting, to say the least.

## A LIKELY SUSPECT

If Hunt were indeed in Dallas either on the day JFK was killed—or even the day prior—it would look suspicious. Hunt's long-standing involvement with anti-Castro Cubans through the egis of his CIA activities—would make Hunt a likely suspect were he, in fact, proved to have been in Dallas at the critical time.

As Marchetti points out, linking Hunt to the JFK assassination would be a cover story that the public would easily accept. The CIA, as an institution, would absolve itself of any responsibility, having thrown Hunt to the wolves as a independent operator out of the CIA's control. Indeed, the CIA could then lay claim to having "solved" the JFK assassination at long last. Hunt's alleged involvement would also draw in a number of other false flags—not only the anti-Castro Cubans, but also "right wingers" in general.

## TARNISHED IMAGE

What's more, considering Hunt's involvement in Watergate (and with Richard Nixon having left the presidency in shame), Nixon himself may have taken some of the heat with many of the public suspecting the very worst—that perhaps Nixon might have had a hand in arranging the JFK assassination.

Not only had Nixon been involved in the earliest high-level anti-Castro planning, alongside Hunt and the CIA, but Nixon himself had been vanquished in the 1960 presidential campaign by Kennedy. That one of Nixon's Watergate burglars was being implicated in the JFK assassination would do no service to Nixon's already tarnished image.

Marchetti also pointed out that "The fact that some [of Hunt's to-be-alleged co-conspirators] may have had connections with organized crime will prove to be only incidental in the long run."

## THE LANSKY CONNECTION

This "limited hangout" by the CIA would have, as a consequence, covered up the role of the Israeli-linked Meyer Lansky Organized Crime Syndicate. To delve too deeply into the real origins and linkage of the crime network would have dragged the Israeli connection into the open—if pursued to its logical conclusion.

Now, obviously, the scenario presented in Marchetti's article—the framing of Hunt by the CIA—never, in fact, took place. That it had a basis in truth—that Hunt was being pondered as a "fall guy"—however, seems apparent.

This is supported by the fact that a similar article, based on relatively the same fact situation, appeared during the same period in another newspaper.

While the claims made in the second article are somewhat different than those which appeared in Marchetti's article, it is clear that the similarities, in general, are what are most significant.

The article appeared in the Wilmington, Delaware *Sunday News Journal* on August 20, 1978. The authors were Joe Trento and Jacquie Powers. The article reads [in pertinent part] as follows:

WASHINGTON—A secret CIA memorandum says that E. Howard Hunt was in Dallas the day President John F. Kennedy was murdered and that top agency officials plotted to cover up Hunt's presence there.

Some CIA sources speculate that Hunt thought he was assigned by higher-ups to arrange the murder of Lee Harvey Oswald.

Sources say Hunt, convicted in the Watergate conspiracy in 1974, was acting chief of the CIA station in Mexico City in the weeks prior to the Kennedy assassination. Oswald was in Mexico City, and met with two Soviet KGB agents at the Russian Embassy there immediately before leaving for Dallas, according to the official Warren Commission report.

The 1966 secret memo, now in the hands of the House assassination committee, places Hunt in Dallas Nov. 22, 1963.

Richard M. Helms, former CIA director, and James J. Angleton, former counterintelligence chief, initialed the memo according to investigators who made the information available to the *Sunday News Journal.*

According to sources close to the Select Committee on Assassinations, the document reveals:

• Three years after Kennedy's murder, and shortly after Helms and Angleton were elevated to their highest positions in the CIA, they discussed the fact that Hunt was in Dallas on the day of the assassination and that his presence there had to be kept secret.

• Helms and Angleton thought that news of Hunt's presence in Dallas would be damaging to the agency should it leak out.

• Helms and Angleton felt that a cover story, giving Hunt an alibi for being elsewhere the day of the assassination "ought to be considered." . . .

. . . Helms could not be reached for comment. A secretary said that he was out of town and would not be available. When Angleton was questioned by committee staffers, he was "evasive," according to a source who was present. Angleton could not be reached for comment.

Asked to explain why a potentially damaging cover-up plot would be put out on paper, one high-level CIA source said, "The memo is very odd. It was almost as if Angleton was informing Helms, who had just become director, that there was a skeleton in the family closet that had to be taken care of and this was his response."

One committee source says the memo "shows the CIA involvement in the Kennedy case could run into the CIA hierarchy. We are trying not to get ahead of ourselves but the mind boggles." . . .

. . . Hunt's appearance on the scene in Dallas and Mexico City at the time of the murder adds strength to a theory shared by some internal CIA investigators. They believe Oswald was working for U.S. intelligence, that he was ordered to infiltrate the KGB, and that this explains his life in Russia. They also believe that Oswald proved to be so unstable that he was "handled" by the KGB into becoming a triple agent, and assigned for the Dallas job.

The same investigators theorize that Hunt was in Dallas that day on the orders of a high-level CIA official who in reality was a KGB mole. Hunt allegedly thought he was to arrange that Oswald be murdered because he had turned traitor. Actually he was to kill Oswald to prevent him from ever testifying and revealing the Russians had ordered him to kill Kennedy, the CIA sources speculate.

CIA investigators are most concerned that either Helms or Angleton might be that mole.

Hunt first detailed the existence of a small CIA assassination team in an interview with the *New York Times* while in prison in December 1975 for his role in Watergate. The assassination squad, allegedly headed by Col. Boris Pash, was ordered to eliminate suspected double agents and low-ranking officials.

Pash's assassination unit was assigned to Angleton, other CIA sources say .. . It was also learned from CIA and committee sources that during the time that the Warren Commission was investigating the Kennedy assassination, Angleton met regularly with a member of the commission—the late Allen Dulles, then head of the CIA and Angleton's boss.

Dulles, on a weekly basis, briefed Angleton about the direction of the investigation. Angleton, according to sources, in turn briefed Raymond Rocca, his closest aide and the CIA's official liaison with the commission.[550]

This article is interesting in many ways. First of all, one of the co-authors, Joseph Trento, admitted under oath during the E. Howard Hunt-*Spotlight* libel trial that he had actually seen the controversial memo in question. Trento also noted that he knew James Jesus Angleton of the CIA and had utilized him as a source on occasion.

## ANGLETON AND HUNT

That Angleton was the author of the memo addressed to his CIA superior (and longtime patron) Richard Helms is also of interest, considering Angleton's close working relationship with Israel's Mossad (documented in Chapter 8).

What's more, as we have seen in Chapter 12, Angleton also was intimately engaged in CIA-sponsored intelligence dealings in Europe with the underworld associates of the Meyer Lansky Crime Syndicate. It was Angleton who coordinated the CIA's dealings with the Corsican Mafia— Lansky's European contacts in his joint global drug smuggling activities with the CIA.

While the Trento story claims that the CIA memo was ostensibly drafted in 1966, the actual date the memo first appeared is subject, of course, to question, as is the actual intent of the memo itself.

## A 'VERY ODD' MEMO

The article itself notes that a "high-level CIA source" considered the memo to be "very odd" in that it recorded—in writing—the alleged presence in Dallas of longtime CIA operative, Hunt, at the time of JFK's murder.

The evidence suggests that the reason why Angleton's memo was put on paper—and then subsequently released—was that Angleton wanted the story to be leaked to the press—as part of a continuing cover-up of the real origins of the JFK assassination. Hunt—a lower level CIA operative (already tarnished by Watergate) was being hung out to dry and the real conspirators at the top were washing their hands of the matter.

## WAS THE MEMO LEAKED DELIBERATELY?

Did Angleton and Helms really worry, as the article suggests, that the agency would be damaged by the revelations, or did they, instead, arrange for the memo to be leaked so that there would be, as Victor Marchetti's aforementioned article suggested, a "limited hangout" which would absolve the CIA as an institution of any involvement in the crime?

Joe Trento has subsequently revealed that Angleton did in fact leak the memo to the House Assassinations Committee. However, according to Trento, "It was all handled in such a way that Angleton was not the source."[551]

That the Trento article suggests that Hunt was in fact in Dallas and that he was there on an assignment involving Lee Harvey Oswald is significant as well.

## WAS HUNT ORDERED TO DALLAS?

Could it be that Hunt had somehow been manipulated into involvement in the JFK assassination conspiracy, not knowing that there were bigger and more insidious things going on in the strange world of Lee Harvey Oswald?

Was Hunt indeed sent to Dallas on a CIA-sponsored pretext, orchestrated by one of his superiors—namely James Jesus Angleton—only to discover, after the fact, that the assassination of John F. Kennedy was in the works?

According to Trento, Angleton told him that Hunt had been sent to Dallas by a high-level Soviet KGB mole working in the CIA. However, says Trento, "I later came to conclude that the mole-sent-Hunt idea was, to use his phrase, disinformation; that Angleton was trying to protect his own connections to Hunt's being in Dallas . . . My guess is, it was Angleton himself who sent Hunt to Dallas, because he didn't want to use anybody from his own shop."[552]

All of this is interesting, to say the least, and pinpoints Angleton as a key player in the events linking the CIA and Hunt to Dallas. Yet, as we shall see, there is much more to the story of the role played by the CIA's Mossad ally James J. Angleton in the JFK assassination and cover-up.

In fact, Angleton had a hand in the very part of the assassination conspiracy that involved the frame-up of Lee Harvey Oswald as a "pro-Castro agitator" guilty of associating with the Soviet KGB.

## THE CIA & THE MEXICO CITY SCENARIO

The Trento article accepts, as its basis, the story that Lee Harvey Oswald had been in Mexico City meeting with the Soviets and the Castro Cubans.

However, as Mark Lane demonstrated in *Plausible Denial*, the story that Oswald had been in Mexico City meeting with the communists was an outright fraud—a concoction of the CIA itself.

Lane summarized the situation: "At the outset it should be understood that almost all of the information regarding Oswald's alleged visit to Mexico and his contact with the Soviets and Cubans while there had been fabricated by the Central Intelligence Agency. In its report, the [Warren] commission cited the CIA as the primary source for the Mexico City scenario, declining to seek independent corroboration for the CIA's version of events.

"Nevertheless, the Mexico City scenario constitutes the conventional wisdom as promulgated by the CIA and accepted by the Warren Commission. It remains an article of faith for those who subsequently endorsed the Warren Report, including journalists and official investigating committees. One of the central tenets of the lone assassin theory is Lee Harvey Oswald's presence in Mexico City.

"Soon after the commission was created, the CIA informed Earl Warren that Oswald had been in Mexico from September 26 to October 3, 1963 and that he had spent most of that time in Mexico City.

"According to the CIA, Oswald had visited the Cuban Embassy in Mexico City on September 27 and the Soviet Embassy on October 1. Proof that Oswald had been in the Cuban Embassy, the CIA reported, came from Senora Silvia Duran, a Mexican employed at the Cuban Embassy. Proof that Oswald had been to the Soviet Embassy, the CIA claimed, came from the observations of its own agents."[553]

## OSWALD AND THE KGB?

The CIA told the Warren Commission that Oswald had met with a Soviet KGB officer named Valeriy Kostikov who was a specialist in assassination and sabotage; that Kostikov was in charge of Soviet-orchestrated assassinations in the United States. Clearly, the CIA's implication was that Oswald had been meeting with the KGB officer to plan JFK's murder.

However, even the Warren Commission was suspicious and asked for evidence of Oswald's activities in Mexico City. Some four months went by before the CIA could provide anything other than the testimony of the aforementioned Miss Duran.

Yet, as the evidence shows, Miss Duran only identified Oswald as a visitor to the Cuban Embassy after she had been arrested by the Mexican police at the direction (unknown to her) of the CIA. She was forced into making the statement that the CIA wanted: that Oswald had been to the Cuban Embassy.

After she was released from custody, she spoke out about her experience and the CIA cabled the Mexican police to re-arrest the young lady, but cautioned the police to make sure that Miss Duran knew nothing about the CIA's involvement in her imbroglio.

Finally, under pressure to provide further corroboration of Oswald's activities, the CIA managed to come up with recordings of a telephone conversation between someone alleged to be Lee Harvey Oswald and someone at the Soviet Embassy.

However, even the FBI, having reviewed the recording, concluded that its agents were of the opinion, "was NOT Lee Harvey Oswald."[554]

Despite this provocative conclusion, the FBI report never reached the Warren Commission. Warren and company had only to rely upon the reports from the CIA. (The FBI report only became public some years later when Mark Lane obtained it through the Freedom of Information Act.)

## A CONFESSION ...

In 1977 David Atlee Phillips, former head of the Western Hemisphere for the CIA, admitted publicly that Oswald had not been to the Soviet Embassy in Mexico City.

Phillips, if anybody, should have known inasmuch as he had been CIA station chief in Mexico City at the time of Oswald's alleged visit.

(There have been allegations also, incidentally, that Oswald may have been spotted in Dallas with a CIA operative known as "Maurice Bishop" whom many believe, in fact, was Phillips.)

In a rather fierce debate with Mark Lane at the University of Southern California, a somewhat distressed Phillips confessed: "I am not in a position today to talk to you about the inner workings of the CIA station in Mexico City ... but I will tell you this, that when the record comes out, we will find that there ... is no evidence to show that Lee Harvey Oswald visited the Soviet Embassy."[555]

## WARREN 'HELD HOSTAGE'

According to Mark Lane: "The magnitude of this CIA misconduct can be fully understood only when its conspiracy to cover up is traced to its origin. For the CIA charade, which evidently included employing an imposter for Oswald, began no later than October 1, 1963.

"One month and twenty-two days before President Kennedy was assassinated, the CIA had set into motion a series of events apparently designed to prevent any American institution from ever daring to learn the truth about the assassination, an assassination that had not yet taken place.

"More than seven weeks before President Kennedy was murdered, the CIA was dramatically and falsely establishing a link between Lee Harvey

Oswald and a Soviet diplomat, whom the CIA would later designate as the KGB authority on assassinations in the United States." [556]

As a consequence, the Warren Commission, confronted by the CIA with what appeared to be possible Soviet involvement in the Kennedy assassination, moved to suppress what it mistakenly believed to be "the truth."

The fate of the world was in the hands of Chief Justice Earl Warren and his fellow commission members. If the public learned that Oswald was a pawn of the Soviets, a nuclear war could break out. As Mark Lane commented, Warren was "held hostage"[557] by the CIA's provocative lie.

During his debate with David Atlee Phillips, Mark Lane exposed all of this before the audience. When confronted and following his confession that Oswald had not been at the Soviet Embassy, Phillips suggested essentially that he didn't want either the CIA or himself to be held responsible for "some CIA guy that I never saw [who] did something that I never heard of."[558]

Now while Phillips was being disingenuous at best, the fact is that it was indeed someone whom he certainly knew who was behind the Mexico City scenario. It was none other than his CIA colleague, James J. Angleton.

## ANGLETON & MEXICO CITY

Assassination researcher Bernard Fensterwald reported in 1977 that, "Angleton had handled several controversial CIA matters relating to the assassination, such as the mysterious series of CIA photographs taken in Mexico City in September and October, 1963, in which a man identified by the CIA as Lee Harvey Oswald turned out not to be Oswald at all." [559]

What's more, as pointed out by Peter Dale Scott, a report by the House Assassinations Committee "established that, on the death of Win Scott, the by-then retired Mexico City station chief who had sent out the Kostikov cable, CIA counterintelligence chief Angleton flew immediately to Mexico City, retrieved a photograph of 'Oswald' from the family safe, and destroyed it . . . ."[560]

What is particularly interesting, in light of all that we have seen in relation to Angleton's ties to the Mossad, Scott adds further: "Angleton may have undertaken this mission on behalf of the agency. Another possibility is that he undertook it on behalf of a cabal within the government who had conspired to create the 'Oswald'-Kostikov story."[561]

The Mexico City-Oswald scenario was clearly part of the groundwork for the ultimate framing of Lee Harvey Oswald as a communist sympathizer—perhaps even a KGB operative—who had killed the American president.

And in light of the mysterious appearance of the "Dear Mr. Hunt" letter (ostensibly from Lee Harvey Oswald] mailed from Mexico City, we can only speculate as to whether Angleton himself may have been the mastermind behind the leak of that hitherto unknown document as well.

Was the "Dear Mr. Hunt" letter also part of Angleton's tangled web of intrigue?

## ANGLETON & THE COMMUNIST COVER STORY

It was Angleton who was so determined to bury any evidence that proved that Oswald was not, in fact, a KGB operative (as we have already seen in Chapter 8.)

It was Angleton who most vociferously accused Soviet defector Yuri Nosenko of being a KGB plant. Nosenko had come to the United States following the JFK assassination and claimed insistently that Oswald had not worked for the Soviet KGB, that the KGB had vetoed any idea of attempting to recruit Oswald after the young American had "defected" to the USSR (whether Oswald's "defection" was genuine or not).

The story told by Nosenko disproved Angleton's thesis entirely—which perhaps explains why Angleton dealt so harshly with Nosenko. That Trento's story—leaking the Angleton memo on Hunt—would incorporate a major portion of Angleton's JFK cover story is interesting, to say the least.

## WHAT MOTIVATED ANGLETON?

Pointing toward the intra-CIA turmoil which, in fact, had resulted in Angleton's ouster from the CIA, is the interesting suggestion in Trento's story that sources within the CIA had suggested that Angleton was suspected by some of being a KGB mole.

This, of course, is part of the great irony of Angleton's complex life in that it was Angleton who was the prime mover behind long-term internal CIA inquiries into possible infiltration of the agency at the highest levels.

However, Angleton's fiercest critics, as we have seen, have suggested that Angleton was indeed a mole—but not for the Soviets; that instead, Angleton was a full-fledged co-opted agent for Israel.

In the context in which we have examined Angleton's role in the CIA, working for—Israel and its Mossad, this appears to be the real driving force behind Angleton's dealings insofar as the JFK assassination was concerned.

## ANGLETON'S SPECIAL INTEREST

That Trento's story notes Angleton's interest in the Warren Commission investigation only displays part of the picture, however. JFK assassination investigator Bernard Fensterwald detailed how very much interested Angleton was in the JFK assassination.

"The extent of Angleton's involvement in the CIA's end of the assassination investigation first became underscored in 1974, when Senator Howard Baker (R-Tenn.) released some information that he had originally secured while serving on the Senate Watergate Committee.

"Senator Baker disclosed that he had come across at least two CIA 'dossiers' indicating that the Agency may have been involved in domestic affairs. He disclosed that one of these CIA files, on Warren Commission critic Bernard Fensterwald, Jr., contained copies of several high-level internal CIA memos which clearly showed that James Angleton was the key CIA official in dealing with matters related to the Kennedy assassination.

"In a memo dated January 13, 1969 to FBI Director J. Edgar Hoover, Angleton noted that Fensterwald was setting up a Washington-based Committee to Investigate Assassinations. In this confidential memo, Angleton . . . went on to request that Hoover run some kind of vaguely defined identification check on Fensterwald and three other Warren Commission critics associated with him. In June, 1976, new information became available regarding Angleton's key role in dealing with the Warren Commission investigation.

## THE CIA'S IN-HOUSE JFK EXPERT

"The Senate Intelligence Committee reported that at a meeting in late December of 1963, Angleton had requested that he be allowed to take over CIA responsibility for dealing with the Warren Commission probe.

"The Senate Committee's Final Report noted that, 'Angleton suggested that his own Counterintelligence Division take over the investigation and [Richard] Helms acceded to this suggestion.' Thereafter, Angleton's staff became responsible for all CIA dealings with the Commission. "[562]

So it was that Israel's chief advocate at the CIA became that agency's number one in-house handler for JFK assassination investigation—some would call it a "cover-up"—during the Warren Commission's botched inquiry into the president's murder.

What's more, Angleton's close friend (and FBI source), William Sullivan, number three man at the FBI, was detailed as the FBI's liaison with the Warren Commission.

(In Chapter 17 we shall learn more about how another prominent friend of Israel helped shape Chief Justice Earl Warren's views about the JFK assassination—pointing the finger, like Angleton, in the direction of "the communists.")

## THE MURDERED MISTRESS

Angleton's interest in the affairs of John F. Kennedy were evidently broad-ranging. For example, *The Washington Post* reported on February 23, 1976 that after Washington socialite Mary Pinchot Meyer was shot to death (in what was said to be a robbery) on October 12, 1964, it was Angleton who obtained Mrs. Meyer's diary and destroyed it at CIA headquarters.

Mrs. Meyer, in fact, had been a longtime lover of President Kennedy's—one of many, apparently—and her diary contained much information about her relationship with the president. It was her sister, Toni Bradlee, wife of *Post* editor Ben Bradlee (himself a reported former CIA asset) who provided Angleton Mrs. Meyer's diary for his disposal. [563]

What the diary contained is anyone's guess, but it does suggest that Angleton was very much involved in intrigue involving the late president. There have been those who have speculated that the diary may have contained secrets about the CIA-Organized Crime plots to assassinate Castro that JFK may have told Mrs. Meyer about. However, of course, it is just as easy to speculate that perhaps the diary also contained Mrs. Meyer's written memories of President Kennedy's musings about his most unpleasant relationship with the state of Israel.

Angleton's own relationship with Hunt is also quite mysterious to say the least. If indeed Angleton did sign off on a 1966 memo pinpointing Hunt as having been in Dallas, the CIA's shadowy counterintelligence chief seemed to have forgotten by 1972 at the time of the Watergate break-in.

## WHAT DID HE KNOW AND WHEN DID HE KNOW IT?

According to investigative reporter Jim Hougan, Angleton, on June 19, 1972 denied ever having seen Hunt, following revelations that Hunt had been involved in the Watergate burglary. Hougan quotes Angleton as having said, "I'd never seen [Hunt] before in my life."[564]

This suggests that Angleton was proclaiming ignorance of Hunt's existence, although this, of course, is highly unlikely, especially since we now know of the existence of the memo from Angleton which was evidently drafted in 1966—six years before the Watergate affair.

Or, logically, we could also suggest that the memorandum itself was not, in fact, drafted in 1966 as we have been told. It could, instead, have been drafted at a much later time and then given the earlier date.

What's more, of course, Angleton was knee-deep in the Bay of Pigs invasion planning and it is inconceivable that he would not be aware of the existence of Hunt, the chief political liaison to the anti-Castro Cuban exiles involved in that operation.

Whichever the case, it strongly suggests that there was a lot more to the Angleton-Hunt relationship than meets the eye.

## ANGLETON, HUNT & THE JFK ASSASSINATION

What we can glean from all of that which we have considered thus far is this:

• That it was James Jesus Angleton, Israel's ally at the CIA, who was particularly interested—from the very beginning—in overseeing any investigation of the CIA's links to the JFK assassination.

• That Angleton's interest in the furor over the JFK assassination was long-standing and continued well into the years beyond the Warren Commission investigation.

• That Hunt was, in some way, connected to events linked to the assassination and that he was, in fact, in Dallas—if not on the day of the murder, at least one day prior.

• That when public attention began focusing on the CIA's presumed complicity in the president's murder (during the period of the House Select Committee on Assassinations investigation), a memo (written by Angleton and linking Hunt to the JFK murder) was leaked by Angleton to the House Assassinations Committee.

• That Angleton's relationship with Hunt was murky, to say the least, and subject to some suspicion.

• That Victor Marchetti's disputed article (subject of E. Howard Hunt's libel suit) was acknowledged by Hunt himself to have some apparent plausibility.

• That despite his admission that Marchetti's article might have a basis in truth, Hunt did not choose to challenge his former colleagues in the CIA who may have been intent on implicating him in the assassination conspiracy.

• That Joe Trento's similar article shed unusual light on internal CIA intrigue involving Lee Harvey Oswald, E. Howard Hunt and the circumstances surrounding the JFK assassination.

• That Hunt insisted that he was not guilty of complicity in the president's murder and chose to use a libel suit against *The Spotlight* to prove his innocence, however unsuccessful he may have been.

• That when Hunt prepared his case against *The Spotlight* (and his own defense against the charge that he—if not the CIA itself—was involved in the president's murder) that he turned to the CIA for help, relying upon high-ranking ex-CIA colleagues for their assistance.

## A PRIVATE ACCORD?

This final point is interesting, especially in light of Hunt's initial suspicion that the CIA intended to frame him as he admitted in testimony.

Could it be that somehow Hunt and his CIA colleagues reached a private accord following the publication of *The Spotlight* article by Victor Marchetti—the publication of which, in effect, frustrated the until-then secret, internal CIA plot against Hunt?

Could it be that both Hunt and the CIA determined that, whatever really happened in Dallas involving Hunt, Oswald and any other CIA-connected figures, was better left alone?

## WHAT WAS ANGLETON UP TO?

We can only speculate as to the motivation of Hunt and the CIA in this regard. What we do know, however, is that it was Israel's friend at the CIA, the enigmatic James Jesus Angleton, who was the prime mover behind the memorandum that would have been used to frame Hunt for involvement in the assassination.

Was Angleton simply looking out for the interests of the CIA? Or was he also looking out for his own interests? And if so, what were those interests? What did Angleton know about the JFK assassination?

Angleton sent E. Howard Hunt to Dallas just prior to the assassination. What was Angleton's purpose in doing so?

And why was Angleton involved in the sensitive, top-secret CIA Mexico City intrigue which took place over a month prior to the JFK assassination, linking Lee Harvey Oswald to the Soviets and Castro's Cuba?

Angleton's link to Israel and its Mossad is the key to understanding Angleton's unusual behavior that we have outlined.

The Mossad loyalist, James J. Angleton, was the central player in the intrigue between the CIA and the Mossad in the JFK assassination.

Never-before-published information that we will be reviewing later in this chapter confirms our contention that Angleton was indeed the primary high-level CIA collaborator in the JFK assassination conspiracy.

Angleton was the CIA figure involved with the Mossad—if not in the actual planning of the JFK assassination itself—then certainly in key aspects of the subsequent cover-up. E. Howard Hunt, indeed, may have been Angleton's fall-guy—another patsy—from the beginning.

## HUNT'S SILENCE

What role did E. Howard Hunt play in Angleton's game of intrigue? Hunt himself is not saying. He has, instead, chosen to deny any responsibility or involvement—for whatever reasons—and bitterly contests any suggestions of his connection to the events in Dallas.

Perhaps he does so for several reasons. One reason may be that Hunt—like many of his colleagues in the CIA—did not necessarily regret the assassination of JFK. Hunt was bitter toward Kennedy for the president's moves against the CIA and Hunt himself probably felt then (as perhaps he does today) that Kennedy was getting a taste of his own medicine.

What's more—and perhaps most importantly, in a personal sense for Hunt—the ex-CIA man cannot fail to note that many of the key JFK assassination witnesses over the years have met early—and violent—deaths. And like all people Hunt wants to live.

Whatever Hunt does know, we will probably never find out—and Hunt intends to keep it that way.

## HUNT'S 'ACCIDENT'

In the February 1, 1992 edition of his newsletter, *New American View*, a monthly critique of the Israeli lobby and its power in America, Marchetti recently commented on the renewed furor over the JFK assassination. Marchetti's words speak for themselves:

"As for my personal views on the CIA's involvement in JFK's assassination, I do not (repeat do not) believe that the CIA had anything to do with the young president's murder.

"But it was and still is involved with the government's cover-up of the conspiracy . . .

"Finally, E. Howard Hunt had nothing to do with JFK's assassination. Hunt was in Dallas that day by accident. He was working on another case. But his presence there was an embarrassment to the CIA and a potential threat to the government's cover-up of the conspiracy."[565]

Marchetti's earlier controversial article in *The Spotlight*, as we have pointed out, never suggested that Hunt had actually been in Dallas or that he played a part in the assassination—only that the CIA was considering the option of framing Hunt for the president's murder.

And, as we have seen, it was Israel's contact at the CIA, James J. Angleton who was behind the impending operation against Hunt. However, Marchetti's final comment about Hunt's possible appearance in Dallas is interesting, particularly in light of what we are about to consider.

## WAS HUNT A FALL GUY?

There is evidence that Hunt, in fact, may have been inadvertently caught up in intrigue involving the JFK assassination conspiracy—intrigue beyond his own control. There have been suggestions that perhaps Hunt was not actively involved in a genuine assassination plot against Kennedy— as indeed as suggested in Trento's aforementioned article—and that he was in Dallas for another purpose entirely.

Our source for this little-known information is Gary Wean, formerly of the Los Angeles Police Department's criminal intelligence squad. It was in Chapter 13 that we first became acquainted with Wean who detailed his own dealings and surveillance of Meyer Lansky's Hollywood henchman, Mickey Cohen.

(Wean, it will be recalled, learned that Cohen, along with his Israeli contact, Menachem Begin, later prime minister of Israel, was especially concerned with JFK's Middle East policy and that, in fact, Cohen was using JFK's mistress, actress Marilyn Monroe, as a conduit in an attempt to learn the president's intentions toward Israel.)

## THE COP, THE MOVIE STAR & THE SHERIFF

It was shortly after the JFK assassination that Wean stumbled upon information relating to the president's murder—information that sheds new—and interesting—light on how E. Howard Hunt may have come to be implicated in the crime of the century.

According to Wean, it was just several weeks after the president's murder that he (Wean) happened to become acquainted with Dallas Sheriff Bill Decker through their mutual friend, Audie Murphy, the ex-war hero-turned-film star. Decker was visiting in Los Angeles and the three men got together along with another friend of Wean's and the talk turned to the JFK assassination.

(Decker, it might be noted, appears to be one Dallas law enforcement official who is definitely in the clear as far as any involvement in the assassination is concerned. It was Decker, in fact, who had ordered his men to investigate the railroad yard behind the picket fence on the grassy knoll from where shots at the president's motorcade appeared to have originated.[566] Were Decker a co-conspirator he certainly would not have assisted in the capture of the president's assassins.)

Decker told Wean that he was certain that Lee Harvey Oswald was innocent of the president's murder. The three gentlemen, all of whom were familiar with firearms, didn't believe that Oswald could have carried out the crime with the weapon he was alleged to have used.

### 'A TERRIBLE DOUBLE CROSS SOMEWHERE'

However, Wean reports that Sheriff Decker proceeded to elaborate further, saying, "I have another reason, much stronger, for knowing Oswald never shot JFK. There's a man in Dallas I've known a longtime. He knows the entire truth about Oswald's involvement.

"He's scared to death to go to the Dallas P.D. or FBI. There has been a terrible double cross somewhere and everybody is scared shitless of everybody else. You wouldn't believe the crazy suspicions and accusations heaped on all law enforcement in the south by the imbeciles in D.C. and the chaos it has created."

"There was no conspiracy in my sheriff's department involving the assassination nor in the Dallas P.D. I've known all these people too long. I would have known it. Believe me, something as 'crazy' as this I'd feel it in my bones."[567]

Wean remembered this conversation and later, during a trip to Dallas in the company of Audie Murphy, Wean was introduced to Decker's source in that city, whom Wean says was named "John."

### ASSASSINATION INTRIGUE

According to Wean's source, CIA man E. Howard Hunt was indeed involved with Lee Harvey Oswald—but not in planning the president's assassination. Wean reports that John told him that Hunt had something else in mind altogether.

Essentially, according to Wean's source, Hunt—like other leaders in the anti-Castro movement—was becoming frustrated with the Kennedy' administration's moves to achieve at least an informal detente with Castro. Hunt, of course, had devoted much energy to the drive to undermine Castro and now all of his work was being undone.

Wean quoted his source as describing what happened: "Hunt's festering frustration conceived what's become the most bizarre political assassination intrigue of all time. His scheme was to inflame American people against Castro and stirring patriotism to a boiling point not felt since Pearl Harbor. Enraged Americans would demand that our military invade Cuba wiping out the two-bit dictator for his barbarous attempt to 'assassinate' President Kennedy."[568]

## FOOTPRINTS TO CASTRO'S DOORSTEP

"There was to be an attempt on the life of President Kennedy so 'realistic' that it's failure would be looked upon as nothing less than a miracle. Footprints would lead right to Castro's doorstep, a trail that the rankest amateur could not lose. Unfortunately for Oswald he fit the bill perfect for Hunt's operation."[569]

"At first Hunt did not tell Oswald what his exact mission was, except it was of the highest National Security priority . . . It was only two months before the 'fake assassination' when Hunt gave Oswald the rifle, explaining his part in the plan. Oswald was to fire three shots from his rifle 'in the air.' He was to abandon it and empty cartridges at the scene and quickly leave the building for a rendezvous with agents who'd transport him to a secret destination." He'd remain in hiding until after Cuba was invaded by the U.S. A fake trail to Mexico City ending at the Cuban Embassy would lead investigators to think he'd fled to Cuba, the belief that 'Castro planned the assassination' of President Kennedy [which failed] and [that] the [attempted] 'assassin' was being harbored under [Castro's] protection in Cuba would stir the Americans to a feverish pitch of anger . . ."[570]

## SOMETHING WENT WRONG

According to Wean's source, Hunt told Oswald that President Kennedy himself was not aware of the plan, but high-ranking cabinet officers were in on the deal. Oswald would be free to come back and live as a free man after Castro was dealt with.[571]

Wean was also told that the famous "attempted assassination" of General Edwin Walker, the outspoken anti-Castro leader in Dallas, was also part of the plan to establish a pattern of violent activity by a suspected "pro-Castro activist."[572]

However, Wean reports, John told him that in the course of the planning for the fraudulent assassination attempt, something went wrong—there was interference from outside—from a power beyond E. Howard Hunt's immediate influence.

John noted: "Of course, all covert operations have inherent dangers and are subject to break-downs. By my God, this was no break-down or neglect of performance, or even bad luck. What happened is incomprehensible. "[573]

## KENNEDY IS KILLED

In short, according to the source in Dallas, Hunt's plan backfired. Shots were actually fired at JFK's motorcade and the president was indeed killed. However, John did not believe that the blame lay at the hands of either the Mafia or the anti-Castro Cubans. He believed that another force had intervened.

"It can't be that the Mafia or Cuban exiles [did] it," noted John. "They had no motive, as they'd already been given inside tips an operation was underway that would return them to Cuba. It would have been totally stupid for them to interfere . . .

## 'SOMETHING SINISTER'

According to John: "Only a few of Hunt's most trusted men knew all of his plans down to the last detail. It is impossible to believe any of them is a traitor. Still it's clear, whoever shot Kennedy had to know all these minute details to pull it off the way they did. Something frightening, horribly sinister had interposed Hunt's mission."[574]

## THE COVER-UP

Wean and Audie Murphy listened in shock at what they had been told and, at the time, John gave Murphy a packet of what he described as evidence which backed up his story. However, it was just several days later that John asked that they forget what they had been told.

According to Wean, Murphy informed him that he had been advised from Dallas that "Hunt and his agents have regrouped from their horrified panic and sprung back into action. Hunt's machinations and connection with Oswald had to be covered up at all costs." According to Murphy, military intelligence, the FBI and the CIA were all in a panic.

"If their secrets were to be exposed they'd be rooted out in an eruption of calamitous national anger. In their nightmares all they can see is a firing squad. In fact they have solemnly determined that national security is at stake. That's their justification for a cover-up." [575]

To assuage the fears of John in Dallas, he assured John that the documents he had received from him had been destroyed.

Murphy himself may well be one other on the long list of additional victims of the JFK assassination conspiracy. The actor died in a plane crash in 1971. Gary Wean, however, has lived to tell the story of what he was told.

Quite accurately, Wean himself has described how Hunt and Oswald both must have reacted if the story that John told Wean and Murphy was indeed true.

## 'A DOUBLE CROSS OF FANTASTIC DIMENSIONS'?

According to Wean's assessment of what may have then happened, "Hunt and Oswald salvaging their senses from the paralyzing shock of Kennedy being murdered most certainly had identical thoughts: 'I have been framed.'

"A double-cross of fantastic dimensions. The consequences were too devastating, and terrifying to grasp. It was the end for them. Regardless of Hunt's convictions that his closest men were beyond suspicion, one of them was a spy—a mole in deep, deep cover."[576]

It is up to E. Howard Hunt to provide us the missing pieces of the puzzle. It does not seem likely that he will.

## JOHN'S IDENTITY?

There is additional documentation about the activities of an individual named "John" who was active in the Dallas area and in Miami (Hunt's base of operations with the anti-Castro Cuban exiles) immediately before and after the JFK assassination.

In his book *Conspiracy*, Anthony Summers describes one John Martino who was known to have connections to both the Mafia, Meyer Lansky's lieutenant, Santo Trafficante, Jr., in particular, and the Central Intelligence Agency. In fact, Martino admitted in 1975 that he had been a CIA contract agent and that he had inside knowledge about the circumstances surrounding the JFK assassination.

Summers quotes Martino as having said, "The anti-Castro people put Oswald together. Oswald didn't know who he was working for—he was just ignorant of who was really putting him together."[577]

After Martino died in 1978, Summers notes, his widow claimed that "the Company" (i.e. the CIA) picked up his body to determine the cause of death, which was established to have been a heart attack.[578]

Martino and film star Audie Murphy unquestionably had at least one connection, indirect, at the least, that can be documented.

Murphy was employed for a period during the mid-1960s by New Orleans businessman, D'Alton Smith.[579] Smith was an intimate personal associate of Meyer Lansky's Louisiana front man, Carlos Marcello.

## THE REAL 'JOHN'

The story told by John Martino, at the very least, has a ring similar to the story told by the "John" whom Gary Wean met in Dallas. However, shortly before *Final Judgment* went to press, Wean revealed to this author the identity of the gentleman named John who told him what had really happened in Dallas.

According to Wean when he wrote his book describing his meeting with John, he deliberately did not reveal John's last name, although he knew exactly who John was. What's more, according to Wean, he slightly altered his physical description of John in order to protect his identity.

At the time Wean's book was written, John was alive. However, on April 5, 1991 John died, like Audie Murphy, in a bizarre airplane explosion that made national headlines. He was John Tower who, in 1961 had been the first Republican in this century to win a Senate seat from Texas.

A stalwart ally of the CIA throughout his career, it was Tower who took many of the secrets of the Iran-Contra scandal to his grave, having headed the commission which critics contend was a CIA whitewash of the events, particularly those involving Israel's role in the affair.

## A 'THIRD FORCE'?

Veteran JFK assassination researcher, Dick Russell himself has pondered the possibility that the CIA's relationship with Lee Harvey Oswald—whatever the nature of that relationship—was "usurped by another group."[580]

As Russell notes, "Many people in the CIA had reasons to cover up their own relationship to Oswald, even if this had nothing to do with an assassination conspiracy. In considering this plethora of possibilities . . . what cannot be overlooked is that a 'third force' was aware of the counterspy web [surrounding Oswald] and seized on it to their own advantage."[581]

Russell has also pointed out that the anti-Castro Cuban exiles now believe that there was much more going on behind the scenes than even they realized at the time.

## CUBANS MANIPULATED?

According to Russell, "[legendary longtime CIA contract agent] Gerry Patrick Hemming, who still keeps his ear to the ground in Miami's Little Havana, maintains that some of the exiles who thought they knew the score in 1963 have today become convinced that they were being used. They were incited to an anti-Kennedy fervor by being let in on the secret knowledge that Kennedy was seriously exploring accommodation with Castro. They were told that their dream of retaking their homeland was dead—unless something drastic was done. They took the bait.

"Should it have become necessary in the design of the behind-the-scenes planners, the exiles were also expendable. Implicating a few Cuban refugees in the assassination was not desirable, but it would not come at a high cost, especially if . . . they had worked diligently to build a cover as Castro agents.

"Small cogs in the wheel, they could also be made to disappear. So Cuban exiles were merely the base of the pyramid. They had no power to initiate the cover-up that followed. And neither did organized crime."[582]

## WHO HAD THE POWER?

Hemming himself has spoken of at least one faction of anti-Castro Cuban exiles who seemed to be out of the conventional loop. According to Hemming: "It's hard to say exactly who this select group of Cuban exiles was really working for.

"For a while they were reporting to Bill Harvey's ex-FBI CIA guys. Some were reporting back to [J. Edgar] Hoover, or the new [Defense Intelligence Agency].

"There was a third force—pretty much outside CIA channels, outside our own private operation down in the [Florida] Keys—that was doing all kinds of shit, and had been all through 1963.

"Then after the assassination, a lot of us presumed that somewhere down the line, the KGB was orchestrating with Fidel to do the Dallas job. not until later did we figure out that most of the exiles being approached were being set up as patsies themselves.

"And not by Castro or the Russians. It was domestic. Somebody like J. Edgar Hoover. Who else had the power?"[583]

## AN ANSWER TO THE QUESTION . . .

Dare we suggest an answer to Hemming's question—"Who else had the power?" Obviously, the answer is this: Israel, its Mossad and Israel's powerful domestic American lobby and its contacts at all levels.

## OTHER SIMILAR SCENARIOS

Interestingly enough, there have been several widely-read works relating to the JFK assassination which have indeed suggested that Oswald, at least, was roped into some sort of operation which he was led to believe was of the nature described by Gary Wean's source in Dallas.

*Executive Action*, the book loosely based on the film of the same name, presents Oswald as being manipulated in this fashion. Likewise with former CIA contract agent Robert Morrow's work, *Betrayal*, which Morrow based on his own "inside" information from his involvement with figures involved in the conspiracy.

More recently, Don DeLillo's novel, *Libra*, presents Oswald at the center of a fraudulent assassination attempt which, for a variety of reasons, went awry. (One CIA character in the novel bears a striking resemblance, in several ways, to E. Howard Hunt.)

However, there is yet one last piece which may fit into the puzzle—a story doubted by some JFK assassination researchers but accepted by others—that is interesting, at the very least.

This story also suggests that some sort of "dummy assassination attempt" or instance of provocation to be blamed on the Cubans was utilized in Dealey Plaza as a cover for the assassination.

## WAS HOLT A 'TRAMP'?

This is the story told by one Chauncey Holt who claims to have been the "old tramp" in Dealey Plaza in Dallas (who was often mistaken for being E. Howard Hunt.) It was in the wake of the furor over Oliver Stone's *JFK* that Holt came forward and told his story.

## THE LANSKY-CIA CONNECTION, AGAIN

Holt, a native of Kentucky, claims that through organized crime connections in Detroit he was introduced to Meyer Lansky, for whom he eventually became an accountant. Later, Holt says, he was sent by Lansky to work at the Florida-based International Rescue Committee, which he said he soon learned was nothing more than a front for the CIA. By 1963, Holt claims that he was working in Los Angeles operating three "proprietary interests" for the CIA, including a document-forging mill.

He also had become a pilot and, as a result of his Army training, a weapons expert. According to Holt, his CIA contact instructed him to go to Dallas with a packet of false identifications.

According to Holt, he and another operative flew to Tucson, where they picked up two other people and continued the trip in an Oldsmobile station wagon with several Goldwater stickers on it. (A similar station wagon was reportedly seen in Dealey Plaza the day of the assassination.)

Holt said they arrived early on the morning of November 22, 1963, and dropped off their passengers at the Adolphus Hotel in downtown Dallas.

After going to Red Bird Airport outside Dallas to check out the plane he and his colleagues were supposed to fly out of Dallas, he delivered the documents—all except two—to his contact.

## IN THE RAILROAD YARD

Those two other sets went to Richard Montoya and Charles Harrelson, the men who joined him as the "tramps" in the railroad yard behind the picket fence next to Dealey Plaza's famous "grassy knoll." Holt said the fake identification prepared for Montoya included a pilot's license and a ham radio operator's license.

He had been told to stay in the parking lot near the railroad yard as 'support,' According to Holt he had been told that an anti-Castro protest rally was going to be conducted as President Kennedy's motorcade went through the Plaza.

## AN 'ANTI-CASTRO' OPERATION?

"I was told that there was going to be some sort of incident that would be laid at the door of the Castro Cubans and would breathe life back into the Cuban movement. I realize now that I was very naive. I was a patsy."

Holt says he was supposed to monitor the progress of the presidential motorcade on a police radio scanner he was carrying in a paper bag."I never asked any questions,' he said. 'I wondered about it, but you don't ask questions. That's just the nature of the business."

It was as the motorcade went by that he heard the shots being fired at the motorcade

"I should have just walked out through Dealey Plaza,' he said. 'I could have done that. But I'd been told that if anything happened I should go to a boxcar [in the railroad yard] that would be open. When I got there Montoya and Harrelson were already there, so they couldn't have been the shooters."

"Inside the boxcar, ' he said, 'we were surprised to see that it was partially loaded with explosives. Looking back on it, I think they had a contingency plan. If anything went wrong, they were going to blow up the railroad car with us in it—three of the best shooters in the country, case closed."[584]

It was at this point that Holt says he and his colleagues were apprehended by the police and led through Dealey Plaza, at which point their photographs were taken. According to Holt they were carrying phony United States Bureau of Tobacco, Alcohol, & Firearms identification and that they were subsequently released.

Holt's alleged associate, Charles Harrelson, now in prison for the murder of a federal judge, had previously admitted to having been the so-called "younger tramp" in the famous photograph in which Holt claims his own visage was captured, but Harrelson has since changed his story.

There is also evidence that there was a Charles Rogers, believed to have been associated with the CIA, who appears to be Richard Montoya, although this individual has since disappeared.

## WHO WAS 'THE ARCHITECT OF THE THING'?

Since Holt came forth with his story, however, there has been widespread controversy among assassination researchers who dispute the validity of his claims.

Was Chauncey Holt really in Dallas as he claims? Again, we'll probably never know. However, one thing Holt has said, in an effort to back up his own story, bears repeating.

According to Holt, "Dallas that day was flooded with all kinds of people who ended up there for some reason. It's always been my theory that whoever was the architect of this thing—and no one will ever know who was behind it, manipulating all these people.

"I believe that they flooded this area with so many characters with nefarious reputations because they thought, 'Well, if all these people get scooped up it'll muddy the waters so much that they'll never straighten it out." [585]

## OTHER CONSPIRACIES IN DALLAS?

That there were people in Dallas on the day JFK was killed who may not have known the real reason they were there is also buttressed by other sources.

Michael Milan, whose book *The Squad* outlines his role in working as part of a secret U.S. government team collaborating with the Lansky Syndicate says that there were at least several people operating in Dallas who believed that they were not involved in a conspiracy to kill John F. Kennedy, but, instead, in a conspiracy to kill Texas Governor John B. Connally. (We first considered Milan's claims in this regard in Chapter 14)

According to Milan, he (Milan) played a part in the JFK assassination cover-up. Milan claims that following the assassination he was dispatched to Dallas by J. Edgar Hoover himself. Milan's assignment was to kill a cab driver named Brinkman. Milan met with Brinkman and began drilling him for information. When Milan asked who set up the shooting, Brinkman said, "I never met the guy before I was introduced to him by this broad at [Jack Ruby's] Carousel Club. And I didn't shoot nobody."

"There was me and two other guys. We weren't even after the president. We were supposed to shoot the governor, but things happened too fast. They were gone before anybody did anything. I think there were two other guys doin' what I was supposed to do. But I don't know who they are or where they was when the shooting started. We was just supposed to shoot at the governor when they passed and get out of there. That's all. But nuthin' happened. I mean, everything happened and I just got outta there fast."[586]

Milan completed his assignment and killed Brinkman. When he returned to Washington he was met at the airport, he says, by Hoover himself who said, "You already know too much. So I'll just say: Johnson. No doubt. We stand away. Do you get it?" [587]

As we documented in Chapter 3, the use of "false flags" by Israel's Mossad is a standard method of operation. Manipulation of evidence, false clues and other tactics are used to disguise the Mossad's activities.

Could some of those involved in the JFK assassination been manipulated into believing that they were involved in a plot against Connally (when in fact the ultimate target was Kennedy)?.

In his biography of Connally, James Reston, Jr. suggests that Oswald had been recruited by Jack Ruby as part of an organized crime plan to kill Connally, rather than Kennedy. Reston suggests, however, that Oswald's operation failed and that Kennedy was the victim, purely by chance.

The overall picture (which Reston ignores) shows that Oswald (whatever his role) had been the pre-determined "patsy" as Oswald himself finally concluded, and that Ruby—wittingly or unwittingly—was part of the scheme to frame Oswald as the "lone gunman"—the "lone nut."

Reston also disregards the CIA connections of both men, thereby damaging his overall thesis. Nonetheless, it does suggest that there might be more to the story we have been told than meets the eye.

## WHAT THE MOSSAD CLAIMS . . .

The unusual contention that Connally was the target and that Kennedy was an unintended victim has some very interesting support.

Former Mossad operative Victor Ostrovsky writes in his book *By Way of Deception* that part of his Mossad training included an in-depth review of the JFK assassination which was part of the required course of study for all new Mossad recruits.

According to Ostrovsky: "One particularly intriguing aspect of the course was a movie called, "A President on the Crosshairs," a detailed study of the November 22, 1963 assassination of John F. Kennedy.

"The Mossad theory was that the killers—Mafiosa hit men, not Lee Harvey Oswald—actually wanted to murder then Texas Governor John Connally, who was in the car with JFK but was only wounded.

"Oswald was seen as a dupe in the whole thing and Connally as the target of mobsters trying to muscle their way into the oil business.

"The Mossad believed that the official version of the assassination was pure, unadulterated hokum.

"To test their theory, they did a simulation exercise of the presidential cavalcade to see if expert marksmen with far better equipment than Oswald's could hit a moving target from the recorded distance of 88 yards. They couldn't.

"It would have been the perfect cover. If Connally had been killed, everyone would have assumed it was an attempt on JFK. If they'd wanted to get Kennedy, they could have got him anywhere."

He writes: "According to what we found, the rifle was probably aimed at the back of Connally's head, and JFK gestured or moved just at the wrong moment—or possibly the assassin hesitated."[588]

## THE MOSSAD IN DEALEY PLAZA

Now what Ostrovsky notes further is particularly of interest, especially in the light of the theory presented in *Final Judgment*. According to Ostrovsky, the Mossad had every film taken of the Dallas assassination, pictures of the area, the topography, aerial photographs—everything.

Is it possible that the reason that the Mossad had so much information about Dealey Plaza was not because the Mossad studied the area AFTER the Kennedy assassination but BEFORE the assassination? This, we must conclude, seems likely considering all the evidence we've assembled in the pages of this work.

That the Mossad would go to the length of calculating an extensive cover story (presented to its own recruits) is interesting in itself and perhaps further evidence that the Mossad had a very particular—one might say "peculiar"—interest in the JFK assassination.

There were clearly many forces at work in Dealey Plaza, perhaps beyond the comprehension of any one conspirator—be it Lee Harvey Oswald or Jack Ruby—or any of the others involved. Some of the conspirators may have indeed been led to believe this was a Mafia hit on Connally and that it, in fact, turned out to be a hit on Kennedy.

## MOSSAD COVER STORY

The Mossad story that it was a botched operation aimed at Connally and resulting in the accidental killing of Kennedy sounds like nothing less than—to borrow a phrase from Ostrovsky—"pure, unadulterated hokum"— coming from the Mossad itself.

And then there is the question of the manner in which Lee Harvey Oswald was being made to appear as though he were a pro-Castro/pro-Soviet agitator through the Mexico City Scenario (as we saw in this chapter) and of his manipulation in New Orleans by the Clay Shaw-Guy Banister apparatus.

Did Oswald think that he was, in fact, operating on behalf of the CIA—even on behalf of John F. Kennedy himself—setting up a "phony" assassination attempt that could be blamed on Castro, igniting international fury at the Cuban leader?

The bottom line is this: at all critical times when Oswald was being set up as the patsy—and following the assassination itself—the fine hand of Israel's Mossad and its allies in the CIA is evident.

## MISLEADING THE PATSIES

Is it possible that some of the other conspirators at the lowest levels were led to believe that the whole operation was designed to kill the two proverbial birds with one stone: that is

(1) eliminate Connally, who was allegedly perceived to be a roadblock in the way of the mob, and, in turn

(2) force Kennedy—or otherwise give him the incentive—to take action against Fidel Castro who had shut down organized crime operations in Cuba?

Could, for example, some of the conspirators been told that the plan was to kill Connally and make it appear as though it were a Castro-sponsored bullet intended for the president which missed—and thereby force Kennedy into retaliating against Castro?

One can only imagine, for example, the surprise of a hidden gunman firing at John Connally when he realized that another gunman was firing at John F. Kennedy.

The possibilities are endless, of course, and one could spend hours concocting a variety of scenarios. However, all of the evidence we have seen suggests that the JFK assassination conspiracy was multi-leveled and ranging out in a variety of directions.

## 'FALSE FLAGS' IN DEALEY PLAZA?

Were all of these "characters with nefarious reputations" simply "false flags" being utilized by what Chauney Holt called "the architect of this thing"?

Were these JFK assassination "suspects" brought there by a force which wanted, as Holt suggested, to "muddy the waters."?

If so, we cannot help but be reminded of the Mossad's famous use of false flags in its various and sundry international criminal endeavors.

## WHO INTERVENED?

One investigator, Scott Thompson, who believes in the dummy assassination theory has gone so far as to charge that the provocation was being carried out with the full knowledge of Attorney General Robert F. Kennedy.

Thompson alleges that E. Howard Hunt was, in fact, in charge of coordinating the fraudulent assassination attempt and that one of his immediate collaborators was the enigmatic Russian nobleman (and fellow intelligence operative) George DeMohrenschildt.

(In Chapter 9, of course, we examined the apparent long-term links between Hunt and DeMohrenschildt.)

Thompson notes, however, that "it remains unclear to this day who intervened into the dummy assassination set-up and turned it into the real thing."[589]

Former CIA contract agent Robert Morrow has lent credence to the "dummy assassination attempt" scenario. Morrow has reported that he had been told that CIA operatives, working with Cuban exiles, "had some kind of test they were doing, a fake assassination attempt against Kennedy."[590]

## WHAT DeGAULLE SAID . . .

Writing in *Farewell America* under the pseudonym "James Hepburn," veteran French intelligence officer Herve Lamarr suggests: "Oswald was probably told that he had been chosen to participate in a new anti-Communist operation together with [David] Ferrie and several other agents.

"The plan consisted of influencing public opinion by simulating an attack against President Kennedy, whose policy of coexistence with the Communists deserved a reprimand. Another assassination attempt, also designed to arouse public feeling, had been simulated on April 10 against General (Edwin A.] Walker."[591]

Lamarr's book, according to assassination researchers Warren Hinckle and William Turner, was prepared under the direction and imprimatur of French President Charles DeGaulle, who was, as we noted in Chapter 15, a victim of assassination attempts financed by the Permindex operation that played the central part in the JFK assassination conspiracy.[592]

## THE FRENCH CONNECTION . . .

In a private communication to this author after he read the first draft of *Final Judgment*, a former high-ranking retired French diplomat and intelligence officer stated (based on his own inside knowledge) that a French team—professional assassins—were the actual shooters in Dealey Plaza, committing the crime at the behest of the Israeli Mossad.

(In the Postscript to this volume we review the remarkable story of this Frenchman and his own astounding experiences with the Mossad.)

According to the French intelligence officer: "Never the Prime Minister of Israel would have involved Mossad people, American Jews or CIA personnel in the execution part of the conspiracy.

"Even the CIA contract the services of other members of the intelligence community (they like the French style) to wash dirty linens. The right hand does not know what the left did. The cover-up team doesn't know who execute. And the executioners are not interested in the aftermath of their mission. They don't care less."[593]

## ANGLETON AGAIN ...

According to the French intelligence officer, then-Mossad assassination chief Yitzhak Shamir (later Israeli prime minister) arranged the hiring of the assassination team through the good offices of the deputy chief of the French intelligence service (the SDECE), Colonel Georges deLannurien.

"It was no coincidence," he wrote, "that on the very day of the execution of the president by the French team that [deLannurien] was at Langley meeting with James Jesus Angleton, the Mossad mole."

According to the diplomat, "There are no coincidences in the suspicion business—just cover-ups. The case of communist infiltration of the French secret service was an appropriate cover-up to justify the presence of Colonel deLannurien at Langley, Virginia."[594]

Obviously, Angleton and deLannurien were together for a very specific purpose: damage control—making sure that the assassination cover-up fell into place after the crime itself had been committed.

Angleton himself told the House Assassinations Committee that de Lannurien had come to his office for just that purpose: seeking assistance in routing out communist moles in the SDECE.[595]

## MANIPULATING THE FRENCH

This controversy—alleged KGB infiltration into French intelligence—was a direct result of Angleton's machinations. It was Angleton (often prodded by his Mossad allies) who had a history of fingering alleged Soviet infiltrators in other nations' intelligence services, creating mass disarray, confusion, bitterness and resentment in their ranks.

Following World War II, it just so happens, Angleton served as American intelligence liaison with the SDECE and maintained close friendships with a number of French intelligence officials throughout his career. And undoubtedly these were Frenchmen who shared Angleton's devotion to Israel.

One particularly embittered high-ranking SDECE officer, Leonard Houneau, who had been caught in Angleton's web and was ultimately cleared of the slander that he was a Soviet mole, later said, "The whole story was invented. Angleton was a madman and an alcoholic. He was trying to set us against one another."[596]

## THE OAS MERCENARY

Interestingly enough, it was OAS mercenary, Jean Souetre, who approached the CIA in June of 1963 with information on alleged communists in the DeGaulle government and in French intelligence—one of Angleton's widely-documented preoccupations.[597] Angleton would have been very much "in the know" as to Souetre's activities (and, indeed, may have been actively collaborating with Souetre).

In Chapter 12 we noted that it was Souetre who was picked up in Dallas on November 22, 1963 and expelled from the United States and who was also CIA man E. Howard Hunt's OAS liaison.

It was Souetre who also maintained an informal OAS outpost at Guy Banister's office at 544 Camp Street in New Orleans. What's more, Souetre maintained ties with Meyer Lansky's allies in the Corsican Mafia. All of this, certainly, suggests a very clear pattern which spells more than coincidence.

The plot thickens, however. As we saw in Chapter 12, there is some question as to whether the individual picked up in Dallas was, in fact, Souetre or someone using his name.

### AN ASSASSIN IN DISGUISE?

Souetre has suggested that it was another Frenchman, one Michael Mertz, who may have been the guilty party who was actually in Dallas and using Souetre's name.

What makes this allegation most provocative is that Mertz was a former French SDECE officer who had actually infiltrated the anti-DeGaulle OAS and foiled a plot against DeGaulle's life.[598]

(There is firm evidence that in at least one instance Israeli Prime Minister David Ben-Gurion "foiled" an OAS "plot" against DeGaulle, bringing the conspiracy to DeGaulle's attention. As a consequence, according to Ben-Gurion's biographer, "Ben-Gurion now received [DeGaulle's] gratitude."[599]

(In this particular instance, however, the alleged conspirator was ultimately released since there was not enough evidence to keep him in custody.[600] Was this "plot" perhaps—in reality—an Israeli operation designed to bring Israel back into DeGaulle's good graces? We can only speculate. We can only speculate, likewise, that perhaps Michael Mertz's rescue of DeGaulle from yet another "plot" may have also been a similar Israeli-orchestrated operation.)

In any case, Mertz's connections went much further. Mertz was also—interestingly enough—engaged in the illegal drug racket, said to be the Paris connection man for the Lansky-Trafficante-Corsican Mafia network examined in Chapter 12.[601]

Just shortly after the JFK assassination, Dr. Lawrence Alderson, a Houston dentist, found himself being questioned by the FBI. Alderson, who had struck up a friendship with the real Jean Souetre while both were in their respective country's armed services, said that he was told that "The FBI felt Souetre had either killed JFK or knew who had done it."[602] And that could have included the aforementioned Mertz.

Former CIA insider Robert Morrow, who was enmeshed in much of the intrigue surrounding the activities of the Clay Shaw-Guy Banister operation in New Orleans, contends that it was Mertz who was on one of the assassination teams that struck down John F. Kennedy in Dallas.[603] According to Morrow, in fact, Mertz was on the Angleton-supervised CIA ZR/Rifle Team of foreign mercenaries where he was known by his code name, QJ/WIN.

There have been other possible candidates put forth as a possible participant in the events in Dealey Plaza. Two in particular are worthy of note: one is Robert Blemant, a known narcotics trafficker who was an intermediary between the Corsican Mafia and the CIA; the second is Joe Attia, a heroin financier and assassin for the SDECE.[604]

Although there is some debate over this question, both of these men have also been suspected of having been the operative QJ/WIN. Nonetheless, it is apparent that of the primary suspects named, all have very firm ties to not only the CIA and organized crime, but also French intelligence.

## ISRAEL'S FRENCH CONNECTIONS

Although the SDECE was DeGaulle's own service, the agency was as much apparently out of DeGaulle's actual hands-on control as the CIA was out of JFK's control. As DeGaulle's biographer said of the fight between DeGaulle and the OAS, the conflict was "within the State itself."[605]

In fact, at least one assassination attempt against DeGaulle by the Permindex- and Israeli-backed OAS came as a direct result of "inside" information.[606] What's more, there was one high-ranking SDECE official, Louis Betholini, later discovered to be "an OAS sleeper [secret agent]."[607]

And according to historian Paul Henissart, there was—within the SDECE—a high percentage of anti-DeGaulle officers who were, in fact, sympathetic to the OAS. Like its self-centered American counterpart, the CIA, "the SDECE's main worry, according to well-informed sources, was to protect its own personnel and interests during [the] difficult period [of conflict between DeGaulle and the OAS]."[608]

Intelligence historian Richard Deacon has noted, for his own part, that in France, during this difficult period, there was "a good deal of unofficial support for Israel, notably in the [SDECE]"[609] pointing further toward the role of SDECE officers in arranging the assassination of John F. Kennedy on behalf of its allies in the Israeli Mossad.

According to Stewart Steven, an authority on the history of the Mossad, "Brilliant in many respects, the SDECE had the reputation internationally of being the rogue elephant of the world's intelligence circus. The CIA regarded it as being 'leaky as a sieve,' and probably with some justification, for few services had so many departmental heads constantly at loggerheads with one another, all serving different masters, either within France itself or in some cases abroad.

"The Israelis, however, had always got along with the French service very well. As an ally in the tricky world in which the Mossad was obliged to operate, the SDECE had proved itself extremely useful, principally because its officers did not feel obliged to necessarily receive political authority for its operations. This gave the service a freebooting quality very much like the Israelis themselves but without Israeli discipline and order.

"Mossad's contacts within the service," said Steven, "tended to be with the ex-OAS elements, those opposed to DeGaulle for what they believed to be his sell-out of French interests in the Algerian war of independence."[610]

## DEALING WITH DEVILS

To complicate matters, DeGaulle himself had reached a truce with the OAS in early 1963 and had helped arrange for its members to set up operations elsewhere.[611]

One or more of these "former" enemies of DeGaulle, now operating under the auspices of his own intelligence service, or at least within its sphere of influence, may have been brought into the JFK assassination conspiracy.

The likelihood that an Israeli-linked faction of DeGaulle's intelligence service, the SDECE, might have recruited an assassin—particularly a Corsican assassin—for the hit against JFK is very strong.

## JACKAL OR JACL?

The SDECE was divided into five "services." Service Five was known as "Action" and was dominated by Corsicans. According to Frederick Forsyth's background account of the conflict between DeGaulle and the OAS (the subject of his novel, *The Day of the Jackal*) these Corsicans, "had been professional thugs from the underworld before being enlisted, kept up their old contacts, and on more than one occasion enlisted the aid of their former underworld friends to do a particularly dirty job for the government.

"It was these activities that gave rise to talk in France of a 'parallel' (unofficial) police, supposedly at the orders of one of President de Gaulle's right-hand men, M. Jacques Foccart.

"In truth no 'parallel' police existed; the activities attributed to them were carried out by the Action Service strong-arms or temporarily enlisted gang-bosses from the 'milieu.'"[612]

In light of Forsyth's famous "Jackal," it might be noted that active in Europe during the period of the joint plots against JFK and Charles DeGaulle was a Jewish terrorist group known as the Jewish Anti-Communist League—or JACL.

This JACL in fact, collaborated with the OAS. So it seems Frederick Forsyth knew whereof he spoke when he described a fictional OAS-sponsored "Jackal" seeking to destroy DeGaulle.

Noting the SDECE's involvement with the Corsican underworld, Professor Alfred McCoy has written that "informed observers were convinced that some of SDECE's top intelligence officers had been organizing narcotics shipments to the United States to finance [its] operations, using SDECE's counterintelligence net to protect their shipments."[613]

(In Chapter 12, of course, we examined the CIA's own collaboration with these same Lansky Crime Syndicate-linked elements through Angleton's Israeli desk at the CIA.)

In fact, according to McCoy, one Corsican gangster tipped off one of his drug smugglers in the United States that a presumed American contact was really an undercover narcotics agent. His source was a high-ranking colonel in the French SDECE.[614]

Who was that high-ranking colonel of whom McCoy wrote, choosing to delete his name? Could it have been the aforementioned Colonel Georges deLannurien? This is speculation, of course, but certainly food for thought in light of the facts we have seen in these pages.

## THE PLOT COMES FULL CIRCLE

However, there is even more evidence substantiating that the so-called "French connection" to the JFK assassination is indeed, instead, the Israeli connection reaching all the way to Dallas.

In 1965 a bizarre crime took place which exposed the close ties between certain elements in DeGaulle's intelligence agency, the Israeli Mossad and the French Corsican Mafia underworld.

And, incredibly enough, this same crime implicated individuals whose names have been linked with the JFK assassination as a consequence of subsequent revelations.

The crime in question was the murder of a Moroccan political figure, one Mehdi Ben-Barka who was a critic of the ruling regime in his native country. (Although an Arab regime, the Moroccan government maintained covert intelligence cooperation with Israel and its Mossad.)

Israeli historian Benjamin Beit-Hallahmi assessed the parameters of Ben-Barka's demise as follows:

"The Mossad became involved in the kidnapping of Ben-Barka in Paris. He was later murdered in cold blood. Since the affair took place on French soil, and involved collaboration with right-wing [i.e. pro-OAS] elements in the [SDECE], it led to a major political crisis, to a purge of the service by DeGaulle."[615]

## A FURIOUS DeGAULLE

The irony for DeGaulle was immense. According to historian Stewart Steven, "As always . . . one arm of the SDECE didn't know what the other was doing. As one department [of the SDECE] was arranging for Ben Barka's assassination, another [arm of the French intelligence agency] was organizing a regular monthly paycheck paid [Ben Barka] through a French scientific research center, one of the covers for the extensive SDECE operation in Africa."[616]

Dan Raviv and Yossi Melman, Israeli historians, commented on the crisis as follows: "De Gaulle, who suspected that his secret agency might be plotting against him, was absolutely furious. He immediately ordered that the secret service's house be put in order. He also directed his anger at Israel."[617]

The French president "ordered that the Mossad's European command be removed from Paris, and he also ordered a cessation of all intelligence cooperation between the two nations."[618]

According to historian Stewart Steven, "As far as President DeGaulle was concerned, the implications were that Israel was dealing with the OAS in France, which was still active, still bent on revenge, and indubitably involved through its supporters in the SDECE in the killing of Ben Barka. It meant that Israel was involved in illegal activites on French soil, an affront to French nationalism, and it meant that he himself, whose support for Israel had never been challenged, had been dealt with treacherously."[619]

According to Steven, Israeli Mossad expulsion from Paris was "a severe blow, perhaps the most severe the Israeli secret service has ever suffered . . . DeGaulle was never to forgive Israel."[620]

## CHRISTIAN DAVID

It just so happens that a chief suspect in the Ben-Barka murder was one Christian David, a French gangster who was a known associate of the aforementioned Michael Mertz, alleged participant in the JFK murder.

Ex-Army intelligence officer William Spector told JFK assassination researcher Jim Marrs that David was part of the CIA's ZR/Rifle Team which was under Angleton's supervision. David was reportedly known by his code-name WI/ROGUE.

What makes this all the more intriguing is that David has claimed knowledge of a French team of assassins being involved in the JFK murder.[621] David himself claims to have been offered a contract to kill JFK by the Lansky-connected Guerini brothers, the leaders of the CIA-backed French Corsican Mafia in Marseille. [622]

WI/ROGUE—whoever he really was—was apparently recruited to the ZR/Rifle Team by another operative known as QJ/WIN. And QJ/WIN is generally believed, as we noted previously, to be Michael Mertz who is alleged to have been one of the assassins in Dallas.

## THOMAS ELI DAVIS III

Incredibly, the plot comes full circle. It was QJ/WIN who used his influence to secure the release of one Thomas Eli Davis III from an Algerian jail after Davis was arrested in North Africa for supplying arms to the OAS. As we noted in Chapter 5, a group of foreign mercenaries—led by Israeli operatives—were taken captive by the Algerians in August of 1963. Davis was almost certainly one of those involved in that incident.

Although Davis was thus in jail on the day of the Kennedy assassination, a letter found on Davis during his incarceration made references to Lee Harvey Oswald and the JFK assassination. (Davis later admitted that he used the name "Oswald" while in North Africa.)

And it was Jack Ruby (who killed Oswald) who mentioned to his lawyers his connection with a Thomas Eli Davis III. Ruby said that he and Davis had run guns and jeeps to Cuba.[623]

All of this taken together explains the so-called "French connection" to the JFK assassination, although, as we have seen, the origin of the conspiracy to kill the American president was not, in fact, French in origin.

## COVER-UPS WITHIN COVER-UPS

That Charles DeGaulle would have had an interest in getting to the bottom of the JFK assassination is evident, inasmuch as there were multiple French connections to key players in the conspiracy.

DeGaulle clearly discovered that elements of French intelligence and/or agents of his sworn enemies in the OAS had been brought into the JFK assassination conspiracy by the Mossad.

It seems apparent that it was one or more of these French assassins who played a role in the events in Dallas, having been recruited by the Mossad through its allies within DeGaulle's own intelligence service. A complex web indeed, but one which is evident indeed.

There is no doubt, however, that the New Orleans faction of the assassination conspiracy—those framing Lee Harvey Oswald as a pro-Castro agitator—had direct ties to not only the OAS network but also to the Mossad's Permindex operation that had conspired against DeGaulle.

The New Orleans faction was also closely connected to the CIA's anti-Castro operations and to the inner circles of Meyer Lansky's organized crime empire.

At CIA headquarters at Langley, Virginia there was the Mossad's devoted friend and longtime associate of top SDECE officials, James J. Angleton. He was engaged in intrigue both before and after the assassination that clearly points to his own involvement in some fashion, either at his own initiative or under the manipulation of the Mossad.

Even the CIA's E. Howard Hunt himself was tied directly to the French connection—not to mention his own work with the anti-Castro Cubans. His apparent visit to Dallas just prior to the assassination—evidently at Angleton's behest—put him squarely in the middle of the intrigue. The later attempt to frame Hunt for involvement in the assassination reaches directly back to Angleton.

There were, very clearly, many, many people involved in the periphery of the assassination conspiracy—whether as active co-conspirators or not.

French President Charles DeGaulle had a direct interest in finding out how his own intelligence service and/or individuals connected thereto had been manipulated by the Mossad. He also had a direct interest in covering up that embarrassing fact.

## DeGAULLE STRIKES BACK

DeGaulle's inquiries into the activities of the SDECE in the year following the JFK assassination had an interesting consequence. The Mossad's CIA man James J. Angleton's own machinations—his purported discovery of KGB "moles" in the SDECE's ranks—had created havoc in French intelligence forcing the French president to take action.

According to Angleton's biographer, Tom Mangold: "Within the year, DeGaulle finally lost his patience with the CIA. The French president, quietly, without any publicity, issued an order terminating all joint operations between SDECE and the CIA. For the next three years the two services remained estranged, a break without precedent between the two friendly countries."[624]

This, of course, recalls DeGaulle's decision during the same time frame—as noted previously—to expel the Mossad from France. In light of all that we have considered here, it is likely that a large part of DeGaulle's move against Angleton's CIA and Angleton's Mossad allies arose directly from his discovery that his own intelligence service had been directly compromised through its involvement in the JFK assassination.

There clearly is much more to the so-called "French" connection to the assassination of President Kennedy than meets the eye. This is indeed an area that some enterprising JFK assassination researcher of the future should study much more closely. Here in *Final Judgment*, however, we have laid the foundation for that study and outlined the parameters of the French connection as it has never been done.

## THE DRIVING FORCE

Pinning down the truth of precisely what happened in Dealey Plaza will never be possible, but we believe that in the pages of *Final Judgment* we have come closer to the truth than ever before.

The information supplied by the retired French intelligence officer relative to Israeli Mossad orchestration of the JFK assassination through the egis of other intelligence networks, specifically James J. Angleton's CIA, and with pro-Israel forces in the SDECE, meshes with other facts assembled in this chapter and in the pages of this volume.

The final judgment is inescapable . . .

***Israel was indeed the driving force behind the assassination of President John F. Kennedy. The role of Israel was the unsuspected "missing link" in the JFK assassination conspiracy.***

Let us now move forward and examine the manner in which the media maneuvered and/or was manipulated by the CIA and the Mossad in covering up the truth about the president's murder. We will also examine the murder of Sen. Robert F. Kennedy. His death was indeed a critical part of the cover-up of his brother's assassination in Dallas.

## Chapter Seventeen

## They Dare Not Speak Out:
## The Media's Silence—
## Why Israel's Role in the JFK Assassination Could Not Be Exposed

The influence of Israel and its lobby over the American media would have made it difficult for anyone who even suspected that Israel had a hand in the JFK assassination to get the word out. The media promoted the conclusions of the Warren Commission and savaged its critics. And when the media did place the blame it was on Fidel Castro.

The reporting of syndicated columnist Drew Pearson and the sensational Oliver Stone film *JFK* are classic case studies of how Israeli-linked media sources have manipulated public perception of the murder of President Kennedy.

"The Kennedy assassination cover-up has survived so long only because the press, confronted with the choice of believing what it was told or examining the facts independently, chose the former. Unless and until the press repudiates that choice, it is unlikely that we shall ever know the truth."[625]

These are the words of longtime JFK assassination researcher Jerry Pollicoff summarizing the attitude of the Establishment media toward its coverage of the crime of the century.

The media was content to churn up virtually every theory imaginable—up to a point—except one: that Israel was behind the assassination, a theory widely held in the Arab world at least.

However, as we have seen, in Chapter 5, in particular, very little was in fact known about JFK's secret war with Israel and the major Middle East foreign policy turn-about that came on the heels of JFK's assassination.

Thus, even the harshest critics of the Warren Commission which ostensibly "investigated"—most would say "covered up"—the assassination conspiracy had no reason to suspect that there might be an Israeli connection to JFK's murder. The final conclusions of the Warren Commission hardly satisfied anybody—except, of course, for the friends of Israel and the CIA in the Establishment media who gave the Report's conclusions wholehearted support.

### A CITIZEN'S DISSENT

New York attorney Mark Lane made great headway with his clinical dissection of the Warren Report in his best-selling *Rush to Judgment*. A flurry of other books followed. Lane's second book on the subject of the JFK assassination, *A Citizen's Dissent*, is most illuminating, however, on the Establishment's reaction—particularly the media—to the furor caused by the publication of *Rush to Judgment*.

Without question—and this is significant—the media almost unanimously sided with the Warren Report, despite all of the evidence which proved the report a fraud. The media would not tolerate dissent. As far as the media was concerned, the JFK controversy was closed. Period.

## GARRISON AND THE CIA-MOSSAD LINK

The media certainly went into a frenzy with its hysterical coverage of New Orleans District Attorney Jim Garrison's 1967-1969 inquiry into the JFK murder and his prosecution of Crescent City businessman Clay Shaw.

At the time Garrison began pursuing Shaw, the facts that we now know today about Shaw and his connections with the Lansky-Mossad-CIA-linked Permindex operation based in Rome, were not so obvious.

It wasn't, in fact, until 1975 that former CIA official Victor Marchetti acknowledged publicly that Shaw had ties to the CIA and that the CIA was very much interested in assisting Shaw during the period of his prosecution in New Orleans.[626]

Former CIA Director Richard Helms himself subsequently admitted under oath that Shaw had CIA connections. If Jim Garrison had had that proof at the time of Shaw's trial, the verdict indeed may have been different.[627]

## ANGELTON'S INTERVENTION

There is yet additional evidence of attempts by the CIA to undermine Garrison's investigation. This evidence directly implicates the CIA's director of counterintelligence, James J. Angleton, whose own unique ties to the Mossad and whose central role in the JFK conspiracy cover-up we examined in Chapter 8, Chapter 15 and Chapter 16.

Author Anthony Summers, in his recently-released biography of former FBI Director J. Edgar Hoover, described how the alleged compromising photos of Hoover engaged in homosexual activities (described in Chapter 7) managed to surface in relation to the Garrison investigation.

According to Summers, he was told by former CIA contract operative Gordon Novel that he (Novel) was shown such photos by James J. Angleton.

Novel, who operated out of New Orleans, had popped up in Jim Garrison's investigation as a possible suspect and, as a direct consequence, he (Novel) had filed a lawsuit against Garrison.

Novel said that he was being urged to pursue his lawsuit against the New Orleans district attorney by his associates in the CIA, but that Hoover was opposed to the lawsuit. It was then that Angleton contacted Novel, displayed the compromising photos, and suggested that Novel discreetly advise Hoover that he had seen the photos which Novel says he did, much to the FBI director's dismay.[628]

Clearly, Garrison was on the right track. When he launched his investigation of Shaw, Garrison thought he was doing his patriotic duty. He was trying to prosecute a man he believed was connected to the JFK assassination conspiracy. Garrison was trying to bring our president's killers to justice. However, the New Orleans district attorney was greeted with a hurricane onslaught by the media—and, in particular, a media outlet with close ties to elements in the pro-Israel lobby.

## THE 'STERN GANG'

The evidence indicates, in fact, that the fine hand of pro-Israel propagandists were at work, orchestrating the attack on Garrison. Leading the assault on the district attorney was NBC's New Orleans television (and radio) affiliate, WDSU.

The owner of WDSU was Edgar Stern, of the powerful New Orleans Stern family, major contributors to not only the American Jewish Committee and the American Jewish Appeal, but also the Anti-Defamation League (ADL) of B'nai B'rith. [629] Additionally, a close friend of Clay Shaw was Edgar Stern's wife, Edith Stern, whose support for Shaw in the face of his prosecution was prominently noted in James Kirkwood's account of the Shaw trial, *American Grotesque*.[630]

As we shall see in this chapter, the ADL not only functions as a foreign intelligence operation for Israel, but it also works closely with American intelligence. More importantly—the ADL uses its influence to play a major role in shaping American media news coverage. This was critical to covering up the truth about the JFK assassination.

WDSU's malicious attack on Garrison, however, was a much bigger project than it might have appeared. In fact, NBC national news in New York was the prime mover behind the propaganda campaign against the district attorney.

NBC's coordinator for the project was a former Justice Department official, Walter Sheridan, who had also previously worked for the National Security Agency. According to Sheridan, Edgar Stern was "a courageous, liberal man who shared our views concerning Garrison and his probe. WDSU was the only voice in the Louisiana wilderness speaking out against what Garrison was doing."[631]

However, how courageous and liberal the Stern family may have been is subject to question, in light not only of their attack on Garrison, but also in light of their widely known support of the ADL and its activities, particularly in New Orleans.

In 1968, during the midst of the Garrison-Shaw controversy, it was the ADL's New Orleans office that provided $36,500 of its own funds toward an FBI operation designed to entrap Ku Klux Klansman Tommy Tarrants and a young woman named Kathy Ainsworth. In a shoot-out which erupted, Miss Ainsworth was slain.[632]

Interestingly enough, the ADL official in New Orleans who was the prime player in this bizarre conspiracy was A. L. (Bee) Botnick. It was in Chapter 15 that we noted Botnick's close relationship to Guy Banister, the ex-FBI official-turned-CIA coordinator of anti-Castro Cuban exile activities in New Orleans.

It was, of course, out of Banister's office at 544 Camp Street that Lee Harvey Oswald carried out apparent intelligence activities at Banister's instruction and portrayed himself as a pro-Castro agitator.

## SABOTAGE

The aforementioned Walter Sheridan's involvement in the Garrison case went far beyond being a reporter who was simply out to do a hatchet job. Instead, Sheridan was actually trying to sabotage Garrison's investigation by interfering in the actual course of the inquiry.

As Garrison pointed out, Sheridan and his associates were "going far beyond word games. They were engaged in an organized effort to derail an official investigation of a major city's district attorney's office. They were attempting to persuade witnesses to alter their testimony, even attempting to move major witnesses permanently to another part of the country." [633]

## MORE FROM 'THE STERN GANG'

What is additionally interesting is that the ADL-linked Stern family-run WDSU media had actually played a primary part in helping promote Lee Harvey Oswald's image as a "pro-Castro" activist both before—and after—the assassination of President Kennedy.

It was on August 16, 1963 that Oswald and a colleague appeared outside Clay Shaw's International Trade Mart distributing pro-Castro leaflets. Researcher Dick Russell points out two intriguing facts: "The leafleteers were there for only a few minutes, yet the demonstration was filmed by WDSU-TV, which happened to be on hand--apparently alerted in advance. Jessie R. Core III, the public relations man for the International Trade Mart, also attended the leafleting and alerted the FBI immediately afterward." [634]

So it was that not only did the Stern family's television cameras just happen to be there to capture Oswald, the "pro-Castro" activist, but Permindex board member Clay Shaw's Trade Mart associate took the effort to report the young "communist" to the FBI, thus cementing Oswald's leftist image further.

This, however, was not the end of WDSU's involvement in promoting Oswald's public image as a pro-communist agitator prior to the assassination of President Kennedy.

On August 17 William Stuckey of WDSU Radio arranged for a radio interview with Oswald in which the young man proclaimed his leftist views. Then WDSU turned a copy of the tape over to the FBI.

There's more. On August 19 WDSU's Stuckey again contacted Oswald and arranged for Oswald to appear in a debate with an anti-Castro activist over his radio station. It was at this time that Oswald proclaimed himself a

Marxist. The next day WDSU turned a copy of the debate transcript over to the FBI office in New Orleans.[635]

In fact, then, on a second occasion—on August 30—WDSU Radio again made the transcript of the Oswald radio debate available to the FBI.[636] WDSU was very public spirited indeed.

## OSWALD'S 'FREE PUBLICITY'

The ADL-connected WDSU television and radio had thus provided "one lone nut"—Lee Harvey Oswald—with more free publicity than any other single leftist in the city of New Orleans could have dreamed about.

But WDSU wasn't finished with Oswald. Immediately after Oswald was arrested in Dallas on November 22, it was—once again—WDSU that played a part in portraying Oswald, now to a national television audience, as a pro-Castro agitator.

According to Warren Hinckle and William Turner: "The NBC Network scored a coup, thanks to its New Orleans affiliate WDSU. Early in the evening it played a tape of Oswald's voice professing admiration for Fidel Castro and declaring, 'I am a Marxist.'"[637]

An interesting footnote. The young WDSU cameraman who filmed Oswald's demonstration, Johann Rush, emerged some thirty years later—in 1993—as an "expert" whose "enhancement" of the Zapruder film of the JFK assassination was hailed as the final proof that Oswald acted alone.

Rush collaborated with author Gerald Posner in the publication of a volume entitled *Case Closed* which was widely hailed in the Establishment media as the ultimate refutation of JFK assassination conspiracy theorists.

*U.S. News & World Report*, published by outspoken Israeli enthusiast Mortimer Zuckerman, devoted an extended special issue promoting the book in its cover story

However, the Posner-Rush book is rife with errors, contradictions, misstatements and distortions of fact. The book is quite disingenous in its thesis that while the Warren Commission was wrong on some points—thus sparking criticism—its basic thesis (that Oswald acted alone) was correct.

The authors ignore critical evidence of CIA and other intelligence connections to Oswald and Ruby and suggest that virtually all of the many witnesses who were able to provide information which pointed toward a conspiracy were either mentally unstable or outright liars or both.

So it is that Johann Rush, a veteran of WDSU's conspiracy to frame Lee Harvey Oswald as a pro-Castro agitator, has once again returned to the center of the media's cover-up of what really happened in Dallas on November 22, 1963.

## SHERIDAN'S ISRAEL CONNECTION

It was later, of course, that Walter Sheridan, on the payroll of NBC news, came to New Orleans and, aided by WDSU, launched the effort to undermine Jim Garrison to a national television audience, WDSU already having done so much to lay the groundwork for the portrayal of Lee Harvey Oswald as a lone communist agitator.

In later years, it should be noted, it was Sheridan who set up shop—although he was not a lawyer—at the law firm of Miller, Cassidy, Larroca and Lewin in Washington, D.C. This was the firm of a former Justice Department colleague of Sheridan's named Nathan Lewin who, by this time, had emerged as one of the Israeli lobby's most prominent legmen in the city of Washington.

It was from his office in Lewin's firm that Sheridan laid the groundwork for the establishment of a security firm that provided exclusive services to the Caribbean resort empire known as Resorts International.[638] As we noted in Chapter 7, Resorts International, not surprisingly enough, is generally perceived as a joint intelligence operation linking the CIA and the Meyer Lansky Crime Syndicate alongside the Israeli Mossad.

It is fitting, in this context, to note that JFK assassination researcher Peter Dale Scott has pointed out that Walter Sheridan's account of his work in fighting organized crime in the Kennedy Justice Department "omits such obviously relevant names as those of Meyer Lansky."[639] This is not surprisingly, of course, in light of all that we have seen regarding Sheridan and the forces behind the effort to destroy Jim Garrison's investigation of Clay Shaw and the JFK assassination conspiracy.

## GARRISON PILLORIED

In any case, it is very clear that forces with close ties to the Israeli lobby were among those leading the assault on Garrison.

Garrison was pilloried on national television time and again. He was ruthlessly savaged in the press. His integrity was questioned and his methods of inquiry were called into judgment.

So it was with anyone who questioned the "official" word on the JFK assassination. The CIA even went to the trouble of preparing a review of Warren Commission critic Mark Lane's best-selling *Rush to Judgment* that was distributed to CIA friends and assets in the media

This was all part and parcel of the campaign to discredit those who were on the brink of uncovering the real truth about the JFK assassination, something that neither Israel nor its allies at the CIA could permit.

## SABOTAGE FROM WITHIN

In his own memoirs, Garrison notes how, time and again, he and his fellow investigators in the New Orleans District Attorneys office discovered evidence that their work was being sabotaged from within. Government infiltrators and others were not only spying on Garrison's activities, but they were attempting to undermine the whole investigation. To Garrison's dismay, even some seemingly dedicated volunteers who had offered to help the professional investigators turned out to be saboteurs.

One "volunteer" helper was a chap whom Garrison describes as "a young Englishman."[640] This young Englishman, in fact, was one Tom Bethell, who later "broke" with Garrison—if he had ever really been working on the same side as Garrison to begin with—and became a source for Garrison's critics. Perhaps we now know what Bethell's reward was, now that time has passed.

Former CIA man William F. Buckley, Jr. later hired on young Bethell as an editor for his *National Review* magazine, touting him as one of the great young conservative writers of the era. Thanks to Buckley's patronage, Bethell's career as a journalist moved along quite nicely.

(In Chapter 9, of course, we reviewed the extensive and repeated connections of Buckley and his family to a wide variety of key players in the JFK assassination conspiracy—in particular to E. Howard Hunt whose own role we discussed in further detail in Chapter 17.)

## MORE CIA INTERVENTION?

There is other evidence of apparent CIA meddling in the Garrison investigation. When, in 1968, Garrison critic, author James Kirkwood, published his book *American Grotesque*, he inadvertently let the cat out of the bag regarding an intelligence community-linked effort to sandbag Garrison's prosecution of Clay Shaw.

Describing how journalist James Phelan had provided him (Kirkwood) with his own account of how he (Phelan) was trying to disprove Garrison's case against Shaw, Kirkwood published a transcript of a taped interview he conducted with Phelan.

Phelan described how he had arranged to meet with Garrison in Las Vegas (during a vacation interlude by the tired and worn district attorney). At this point Garrison was unaware that Phelan was hostile. Phelan told Kirkwood how Garrison provided him a number of key documents, in confidence, which he was supposed to return the next morning.

According to Kirkwood's transcription, here is what Phelan said: "When [Garrison] gave them [the documents] to me he did not put any restrictions on them. He knew I was writing a piece. He said, 'You'll now understand my case when you read them." So I got up early and made a call to Bob Mayhew at the Desert Inn and told him I needed a Xerox and needed it fast. I had to have two documents Xeroxed and I did not want anyone else reading them or knowing they were being copied. They Xeroxed the copies for me and I returned the originals to Garrison and made no comment about the thing. I wanted to wait for the trial."[641]

What is significant, particularly in the context of the time in which Kirkwood first published this interview (1968) is this: it was not until some years later that it first came to light that it was former FBI man-turned-CIA contract agent Robert Maheu who was the primary intermediary between the CIA and organized crime in the joint plotting against Fidel Castro. When Kirkwood first revealed the Phelan-Maheu machinations, Maheu's behind-the-scenes activities were still a deep, dark secret.

It was this same Robert Maheu (misspelled as "Mayhew" by Kirkwood) who was assisting Phelan in the attempt to scuttle the Garrison investigation--an investigation that would, if pursued to the ultimate, have exposed the very CIA-organized crime conspiracy against Castro that also implicated many of those involved in the JFK assassination itself.

In Chapter 11 we examined Maheu's involvement with the CIA and such organized crime figures as Johnny Rosselli, Sam Giancana and Meyer Lansky lieutenant Santo Trafficante in detail.

It will also be recalled that the aforementioned Desert Inn (by this time the property of billionaire Howard Hughes) was initially established by Meyer Lansky's trusted associate, Morris Dalitz, whose activities and strange connections we examined in Chapter 10 and Chapter 15.

So it was that the CIA did have its collaborators in key positions to undermine the Jim Garrison investigation.

## GARRISON & MARCELLO

Some of Garrison's more creative foes in the media cleverly came up with a new way to discredit the New Orleans prosecutor. Instead of really seeking the truth about the JFK murder, they said, Garrison was, in fact, trying to cover it up. Garrison—so they said—was a willing tool of Mafia chieftain Carlos Marcello.

By pointing his finger in the direction of the CIA, the Garrison critics claimed, the D.A. was trying to take the heat of suspicion off Carlos Marcello who, they said, was the more likely suspect.

This claim is illogical at best. If Garrison were deliberately trying to cover up any Marcello connections—if any—to the assassination conspiracy, he was going about it in the wrong way.

(It was in Chapter 10 where we learned of the campaign against Garrison led by *Life* magazine's Richard Billings, who promoted the Garrison-Marcello scenario. It was Billings, of course, who later served as a top advisor to the House Assassinations Committee which pointed the finger of blame for the JFK assassination on "The Mafia,"—and Marcello in particular. )

If Garrison was trying to protect Marcello, the last person that he should have picked on was David Ferrie, the Mafia kingpin's sometime-personal pilot and occasional legal researcher. Ferrie himself was standing alongside Marcello in a federal courtroom in New Orleans at the very moment JFK was shot.

By first inquiring into Ferrie's activities, Garrison was practically walking right into Marcello's office itself. This fact alone nullifies the creative (but very much flawed) "Mafia cover-up" critique of Garrison that continues to hang over Garrison's memory to this day. Yet, those who push the theory that "The Mafia Killed JFK" ignore this fact.

Evidently the people of New Orleans didn't buy the Establishment's heavy-handed assault on Garrison. He won re-election to the district attorney's office, despite—or perhaps precisely because of—the media barrage. This is all the more remarkable in that it was the very newspapers of New Orleans who were Garrison's fiercest at-home critics.

Garrison clearly was on the right track. He was looking in the right places. It was Garrison who linked Clay Shaw to the JFK assassination conspiracy and it was Shaw who sat on the board of Permindex, the shadowy Israeli Mossad-linked entity that played so central a role in the murder of the American president. How much Shaw actually knew about the impending murder of the president will probably never be known, but there is no question that his activities played a part in the conspiracy.

## THE FEDS VERSUS GARRISON

No wonder then that the full force of the federal government came down on Garrison's head. He was hit with a wholly-concocted indictment on bribery charges but subsequently—and rightly—was acquitted. The key witness against him, a former friend named Pershing Gervais, admitted in a press interview (with journalist Rosemary James, herself a Garrison critic) that the charges against Garrison were a Justice Department concoction. Gervais said, "They wanted to silence Jim Garrison. That was their primary objective . . ." It was, according to Gervais, "a total, complete political frame-up, absolutely." He said "the entire thing" was a whole lie.[642]

Despite the vindication, the Internal Revenue Service jumped into the picture and brought a tax evasion indictment against Garrison for not paying taxes on the alleged bribes that he had been acquitted of having accepted. This, of course, seems incredible, but it is absolutely true. Garrison beat that charge, but his Establishment critics continue to allege (in a last desperate effort to pummel Garrison) that the jurors in that case—as in the previous case—may have been bribed to bring in a not guilty verdict.

## THE MEDIA TRASHES THE KENNEDY IMAGE

What's more, thanks to the media, the image of John F. Kennedy had been repeatedly savaged—indeed tarnished—in the years following the assassination. It virtually became a form of ritual defamation.

Kennedy's reputed sex life became the subject matter not of just the tabloids, but of the Establishment press itself. Kennedy, we were being told, was not all that he was cracked up to be. His affair with Marilyn Monroe became the subject of conversation at every dinner table. (The strange role of Meyer Lansky's man in Hollywood, Mickey Cohen, in the Kennedy-Monroe liaison—which we examined in Chapter 13—however, was not a staple of the continuing coverage.)

The antics of John Kennedy's brother Edward did little to help things. The media eagerly pounced on the Massachusetts senator's every mistake and as the 30th anniversary of the JFK assassination approached in 1993 began hyping several malicious book-length attacks on Ted Kennedy with what many people might accurately assume was the purpose of preventing the youngest Kennedy brother from ever reaching the White House.

Even the late Jaqueline Kennedy—subsequently married to Greek billionaire Aristotle Onassis—was held up to ridicule by the media in subsequent years. Not even she was free from the media's defamation.

## THE HUNT-CIA CONNECTION SUPPRESSED

Despite all the media's interest in trashing the Kennedy family, the media was strangely silent about the astounding revelations that came forth in the E. Howard Hunt-*Spotlight* newspaper libel trial in Miami in 1985.

It was then, as we saw in Chapter 16, that the jury concluded that the CIA had indeed played a part in John F. Kennedy's assassination.

The CIA's friends at *The Washington Post* had barely a word to say about Hunt's stunning loss during the trial. Was this by accident—or by design? At this juncture the conclusion is all too obvious.

## THE CIA AND THE MEDIA

That the CIA, of course, has had a major role in subverting the First Amendment and influencing the American media is now a widely accepted truth. According to David Wise, writing in *The American Police State*, which examined, in part, the role of the CIA in manipulating the media:

"The CIA's contacts with the publishing world were not confined to attempts to suppress books. Through the U.S. Information Agency as a 'cut-out,' the CIA subsidized major publishers to produce books, some of which were then sold in the United States bearing no government imprint to warn the unsuspecting purchaser.

"In 1967 publisher Frederick A. Praeger conceded he had published 'fifteen or sixteen' books for the CIA. By the mid-sixties, more than $1 million had been spent by the government on its 'book development' program. The Senate intelligence committee estimated that by 1967, the CIA had produced, sponsored, or subsidized 'well over 1,000' books' here and abroad."[643]

(One of Praeger's volumes is interesting in light of the "French connection" to the JFK case. In 1989 Praeger issued *Challenging DeGaulle: The OAS and the Counterrevolution in Algeria*. Former CIA Director William Colby wrote the introduction to Harrison's book which was described as the first fully documented history of the OAS.)

Wise continues: "The CIA also planted stories in the foreign press, some of which were played back to American audiences. [CIA Director William] Colby assured the House intelligence committee that the CIA would never manipulate [the Associated Press], since it was an American wire service. In addition, the CIA operated two news services of its own in Europe. These 'proprietaries,' or CIA cover companies, serviced American newspapers; one had more than thirty U.S. subscribers."[644]

However, there is one other significant force in American life which plays an even bigger part in shaping the media.

## ISRAEL AND THE AMERICAN MEDIA

The real key to understanding the media's part in the JFK assassination cover-up is to recognize the incredible influence of the Israeli lobby in the United States on the American media. It is a subject that deserves far more consideration than we can provide in these pages.

However, there are four volumes in particular which give the reader an in-depth look at the way Israel and its lobby in this country have had such a powerful impact on the way news relating to Israel is reported. Each volume deserves careful study:

• *Split Vision: The Portrayal of Arabs in the American Media*, edited by Edmund Ghareeb, published in 1983 by the American-Arab Affairs Council;

• *They Dare to Speak Out: People and Institutions Confront Israel's Lobby* by former Congressman Paul Findley, published in 1985 by Lawrence Hill & Company.

• *A Changing Image: American Perceptions of the Arab-Israeli Dispute* by former diplomat Richard H. Curtiss, published in 1986 by the American Educational Trust;

• *Conspiracy Against Freedom*, issued in 1986 by Liberty Lobby, the Washington-based populist institution which publishes *The Spotlight*, the newspaper that sparked the lawsuit by E. Howard Hunt (described in Chapter 16) which proved the complicity of the CIA in the JFK assassination.

This volume is of particular interest in that it displays documents from ADL files which prove the role of the pro-Israel Anti-Defamation League (ADL) of B'nai B'rith in seeking to silence critics of Israel through wide-ranging techniques including threats, economic boycott and other measures of a less than savory nature.

It is the activity of the ADL, in particular, which seems to have had a recurring role in the JFK assassination conspiracy cover-up by the media.

## THE MOSSAD'S TENTACLES

Intelligence historian Richard Deacon, writing in his history of Israel's Mossad, has commented on the pervasive role of the Israeli lobby and the manner in which it has exercised its influence:

"For years the tentacles of the Israeli Secret Service had reached out into all walks of American life, not in any sinister way, as was sometimes alleged by her enemies, but in a quietly persistent manner which embraced making friends and influencing people, establishing opinion lobbies and gathering intelligence.

Deacon continued: "This influence extended into the U.S. [House] and the Senate, the Pentagon, the defense and electronic industries, the research laboratories and such Jewish-oriented organizations as the Anti-Defamation League, the Jewish Defense Committee, Bonds for Israel and the Federation of Jewish Philanthropies.

"Some of these bodies have served as fronts for intelligence-gathering and there are few of the important congressional committees which do not possess one member or staff-assistant who does not feed the Israeli network relevant material." [645]

## THE ANTI-DEFAMATION LEAGUE

It is significant that Deacon has made specific reference to the Anti-Defamation League (ADL) of B'nai B'rith. Perhaps above any other organization, it is the ADL which has consistently had a major impact on the America media. And in the case of the media's coverage of the JFK assassination, the Warren Commission investigation, and the subsequent critiques of the commission, the ADL's fine hand is, as we shall see, quite visible.

That the ADL, as a voice for Israel, would have an interest in stifling any suggestion that Israel—and for that matter, Israel's allies at the CIA—had a hand in the JFK assassination cannot be disputed.

After all, the ADL has adopted as its mission the defense of Israel and the defamation of its critics—both real and perceived.

## THE ADL AND THE LANSKY SYNDICATE

What's more, the ADL has—to this day—very close ties to the remnants of the Meyer Lansky Organized Crime Syndicate and has throughout its history. Many top Lansky associates were longtime high-level financial backers of the ADL.

According to a 1968 study by Father Dan Lyons, a Jesuit priest, at that time fully $5,500,000 of the ADL's total budget of $6,183,000 came from contributions from the liquor industry. The liquor industry was a virtual fiefdom of powerful Jewish families known for their devotion to Israel, most notably the family of ex-bootlegger Samuel Bronfman. [646]

(As we saw in Chapters 7 and 15, the Bronfman family—along with liquor baron Sam Rothberg, head of the U.S. Israel Bonds campaign, were key backers of Israel and tied closely with the Lansky Organized Crime Syndicate.)

In fact, as we noted in Chapter 10, the ADL is so close to the Lansky Syndicate that in 1983 Lansky's longtime associate, Morris Dalitz, was honored by the ADL with its prestigious annual "Torch of Liberty Award." (Dalitz's service to the cause of Israel was apparently deemed more significant than his activities in the underworld.)

All of this is, of course, significant when we consider the ADL's activities in the context of the media's assault on those who ponder the possibility of a conspiracy behind the JFK assassination.

However, the ADL has—as we shall see—connections above and beyond the organized crime interests that stood to benefit from the JFK assassination. The ADL has long-standing ties to American intelligence.

## THE ADL & AMERICAN INTELLIGENCE

Writing in *American Jewish Organizations and Israel*, Lee O'Brien provides an informative capsule study of the ADL's method of operation:

"In its early decades, the ADL would approach persons or institutions considered to be anti-Semitic and privately attempt to persuade or reason them into retracting abusive statements and correcting offensive behavior.

"In later years, ADL has turned to more public and aggressive measures, which it classifies as "Educational," "Vigilance Work," and "Legislation." In fact, "Vigilance Work" has become outright surveillance of individuals and groups, the results of which are fed into both the Israeli intelligence-gathering apparatus, via their consulates and embassy, and American domestic intelligence, via the FBI. Top ADL officials have admitted the use of clandestine surveillance techniques."[647]

## THE ADL AND THE MEDIA

O'Brien's summary of the ADL's method of operation is quite interesting in that it pinpoints the ADL's influence on the media and on public debate over the role of Israel vis-a-vis American Middle East policy making:

"Today the ADL is much more active than other community relations organizations in the use of its regional offices and constituency for information gathering, and dissemination.

"The central headquarters in New York City provides regional offices with analysis sheets, sample letters to the editor to be placed in local media, biographies of Israeli leaders and anti-Zionist speakers, and directives on how to deal with topical issues.

"The regional offices in turn monitor all Israel-related or Middle East-related activities in their areas, such as the media, campus speakers, and films. By bringing the local events to the attention of the central headquarters, they play a pivotal role in ADL's overall supervision of the national scene." [648]

## OPERATING AGAINST ISRAEL'S CRITICS

O'Brien describes one instance which is typical of the ADL's activities in defense of Israel: "One Jewish activist critical of Israeli policies discovered in 1983 that the ADL maintained a file on him going back to 1970; it included information on the subject gathered from local newspapers, talks on campuses, interoffice memos (from the institution where the subject teaches), business meetings, talk on radio and TV, and press and other miscellaneous materials.

"As the file revealed, specific individuals had been assigned to monitor this person's lectures, either by tape recordings and verbatim transcriptions, or by detailed summaries of what the subject spoke about, the context of the lecture, other participants, size of audience, questions from the floor, mood of the audience, and so forth.

"In some cases, these observers successfully penetrated closed meetings in which the subject participated. Subsequently, the ADL prepared and disseminated a short primer on this person, following the 'myth" and "fact' format, and distributed it to their agents for use at future speaking engagements." [649]

This, of course, is but one example (of many) which demonstrates the pervasive influence of Israel's ADL and its clandestine efforts to control public discussion of U.S. Middle East policy on all fronts—particularly in the American media.

## SPY SCANDAL

At the beginning of 1993, however, the ADL's history of covert—and illegal—domestic spying finally became the topic of widespread public controversy.

A spy scandal erupted in San Francisco, enveloping the ADL, one of its longtime paid informants, and a San Francisco police officer who had been selling classified police intelligence information to the ADL.

A raid by the San Francisco Police Department on the offices of the ADL in both San Francisco and Los Angeles revealed that those offices of the ADL were maintaining surveillance on some 12,000 individual Americans and on the activities of some 950 social and political organizations of all political persuasions.

It was subsequently revealed that the ADL was conducting similar spying operations in other major cities around the country, utilizing a network of paid informants who were charged with the responsibility of infiltrating organizations targeted by the ADL.

(In Chapter 15 we considered the likelihood that the ADL's New Orleans spymaster, A. L. (Bee) Botnick, had utilized the good offices of his fellow anti-communist extremist, ex-FBI man, private detective and CIA asset Guy Banister, to spy upon left wing groups in New Orleans, taking advantage of the talents of a young man named Lee Harvey Oswald.)

Ironically, among the targets of the ADL's spying included organizations that had, over the years, cooperated with the ADL in a number of joint ventures, including the National Association for the Advancement of Colored People and the American Civil Liberties Union.

## SPYING ON EVERYBODY

Contrary to popular perception, the ADL was not spying only on so-called "right wing" or "anti-Semitic" groups. Instead, the ADL appears to have maintained constant surveillance of a wide variety of groups and individuals.

Although the ADL sought to maintain silence about the ongoing investigation, hard-hitting and fact-filled investigative reports by the *San*

*Francisco Examiner* and the *Los Angeles Times*, in particular, received nationwide distribution, doing immense damage to the ADL's long-standing pose as a "civil rights" organization.

## THE ANGLETON CONNECTION

The chief of the ADL's spy network (euphemistically called its "fact finding division") is one Irwin Suall who operates out of ADL headquarters in Manhattan. Formerly active in the labor movement, Suall was a protege of Jay Lovestone, whom we first met in Chapter 8.

Suall's mentor, it will be recalled, was Mossad-allied CIA spymaster James J. Angleton's point man in the CIA's dealings with the Lansky Syndicate-linked Corsican and Sicilian crime organizations.

These foreign crime elements (which handled the Lansky-run drug racket in Europe) were also utilized by the CIA in its campaign against left-wing labor movements in the Mediterranean during the post-war period.

Since James J. Angleton was dismissed from his CIA post after revelations of his involvement in illegal domestic spying by the CIA, we cannot help but speculate that, in light of revelations about ADL spying, Angleton almost certainly relied upon the good offices of his friends at the Mossad-linked ADL for much information.

(In Chapter 15 we pointed out that the FBI also utilized the ADL as a spy asset, noting, in particular the ADL's spying operations aimed at civil rights leader, Martin Luther King, Jr.)

## THE ADL AND THE JFK ASSASSINATION

That the ADL would have a hand in shaping JFK assassination news coverage was inevitable, particularly in light of the revelations we have put forth in the pages of this volume.

In fact, on the first occasion when the Establishment media put forth a theory that perhaps Lee Harvey Oswald was indeed part of a much bigger conspiracy, it was in a news story leaked by two major columnists who were very close to not only the ADL but also to key figures in the Meyer Lansky Crime Syndicate. The case study we are about to examine is highly significant and illustrates the point all too well.

## THE PEARSON/ANDERSON COVER STORY

On March 3, 1967, syndicated columnist Drew Pearson and his understudy, Jack Anderson, floated a story which suggested that Fidel Castro had been behind the JFK murder. (This column appeared during the time that New Orleans District Attorney Jim Garrison was in the earliest stages of his own controversial assassination inquiry.)

Interestingly, Pearson and Anderson even slanted their column to suggest that somehow then-Attorney General Robert Kennedy, the president's younger brother who was elected to the Senate from New York in 1964, had a hand in setting what became the alleged Castro-sponsored assassination plot in motion.

Pearson and Anderson claimed that: "President Johnson is sitting on a political H-bomb, an unconfirmed report that Sen. Robert Kennedy may have approved an assassination plot which then possibly backfired against his late brother." The assassination plot alleged was one of those hatched between the CIA and "the Mafia."[650]

According to what can most charitably be described as the fanciful account by Pearson and Anderson, Castro had captured a number of CIA-Mafia hitmen who were gunning for him and then "turned" them; in short, that the anti-Castro hitmen then had a change of heart and returned to the United States and killed Kennedy.

It was some years later that Anderson revealed that Mafia figure Johnny Rosselli had, in fact, been the alleged initial source of the story which Anderson said had been told to CIA-linked Washington lawyer, Edward P. Morgan.

(In Chapter 11 we reviewed Rosselli's involvement in the Castro assassination plots upon which the Pearson/Anderson story relied, in part, as a basis for its theory.)

## WHY THE COVER STORY DOESN'T WASH . . .

With good reasons which they cite, Rosselli's biographers, Charles Rappleye and Ed Becker, don't believe the Pearson/Anderson story in the least. They write:

"Not mentioned in the column was the simple, powerful argument against Cuban sponsorship of the Kennedy assassination—the powerful risk Castro would run if a plot against the American president was discovered. As the [U.S. Senate's] Church Committee [investigating CIA assassination plots] noted, such a blunder would have 'exposed Cuba to invasion and destruction.'

"Later, it was learned that Castro had opened new channels of diplomacy, at the time of the shooting in Dallas, showing himself, in the words of one diplomat, 'anxious to establish communications with the United States.' Finally, with the benefit of hindsight, Rosselli's story of CIA marksmen being 'turned' seems highly implausible, a product of Korean War recruiting films.

"Nor did Anderson note his own close relationship to his source; that Morgan had no evidence, beyond Rosselli's statements, to back up the Castro retaliation theory; nor that Rosselli may have been pursuing his own, independent agenda."[651]

Mafia enforcer and one-time "acting boss" of the Mafia families in California, Jimmy Fratianno, told of a meeting with Rosselli in 1976, around the time that Rosselli was providing congressional investigators with details of CIA-Organized Crime assassination plots aimed at Fidel Castro.

Fratianno's memory of the event suggests that Rosselli himself was never being straightforward about the events as they had really unfolded. Fratianno recalls Rosselli's words as follows:

"They had me up at the Carroll Arms Hotel . . . for a secret session and I really fixed their fucking wagon. All hot, you know, about who killed Kennedy. Sometimes I'd like to tell them the mob did it, just to see the expression on their stupid faces. You know, we're supposed to be idiots, right?

"We hire a psycho like Oswald to kill the President and then we get a blabbermouth, two-bit punk like Ruby to shut him up. We wouldn't trust those jerks to hit a fucking dog.

"Anyway, they start questioning me about this bullshit I'd told Morgan years ago. You know, Castro retaliating against Kennedy because of our attempts on his life. I said, 'I have no recollection of receiving or passing on such information.'

"Well, Jimmy, it's not my fault if Morgan has a vivid imagination. I've also been dropping by Jack Anderson's office and we're getting pretty chummy, having lunch and dinner together. Nice guy, but he's always trying to pump me, but he's cool about it."[652]

## THE CIA CONNECTION

Rosselli's biographers believe that "more intriguing than Rosselli's motivation [in creating the story told by Pearson and Anderson] is the question of who actually sponsored the bogus lead that Castro killed Kennedy."[653]

According to Rappleye and Becker, "Santo Trafficante seems the most likely party."[654] They go even further, however. They believe that the CIA was behind Trafficante's actions in this regard:

"Might the CIA have floated the Castro theory, again to deflect the [Jim] Garrison investigation [in New Orleans]? If the CIA were actually involved in the Kennedy assassination, as some leading researchers believe, the scenario would fit.

"Considering his intimate association with the Agency, Rosselli would have accepted their directive as well as Trafficante's. And Ed Morgan himself had close ties to the Agency, both through [CIA contract operative Robert] Maheu and from a prior stint as counsel to the Senate Foreign Relations Committee."[655]

(As we saw, particularly in Chapter 12, Trafficante was not the major crime boss he has been portrayed by the Establishment media. Instead, he was the immediate deputy of the CIA's longtime collaborator—and Israel's loyalist—Meyer Lansky.)

## PEARSON, JOHNSON & THE LANSKY SYNDICATE

Warren Commission critic, Peter Dale Scott notes, additionally, that Pearson, himself, was close to then-President Lyndon B. Johnson and that

Pearson was backing Johnson's CIA-backed plans to expand the war in Vietnam (the issue over which JFK and the CIA had been at loggerheads leading to a final showdown). [656]

Floating an anti-communist story (i.e. linking a communist dictator to the murder of the martyred president) then, would also have the side effect of whipping up anti-communist hysteria which would have been helpful to the "anti-communist" offensive in Vietnam that proved so beneficial, as we have seen, not only to the CIA, but also to the Meyer Lansky Crime Syndicate and its allies in Israel.

The Pearson-Johnson relationship had other implications as well. According to Scott, Pearson had used his column to leak government information about a key witness, one Don Reynolds, who was providing evidence against Johnson's longtime crony and reputed bag-man, Bobby Baker.[657]

(Baker, as we saw, in Chapter 6, was not only an independent operator on his own, but a front man for a variety of LBJ's corrupt business ventures. Baker conducted more than a few deals with close associates of Meyer Lansky, most notably Ed Levinson, a director of Mossad operative Tibor Rosenbaum's Banque de Credit International (BCI).

(As we noted in Chapter 15, Rosenbaum's BCI, of course, was one of the chief shareholders in Permindex, the shadowy entity that played so central a role in the CIA-Mossad conspiracy against John F. Kennedy.)

## EARL WARREN CONNED

Drew Pearson's own interest in JFK assassination cover stories was of long standing. In fact, according to Scott's research, it was Pearson himself who told Chief Justice Earl Warren, early in the Warren Commission investigation, that the CIA-Organized Crime plots against Castro had backfired and that Castro had retaliated and ordered the assassination of Kennedy.[658]

According to Pearson's own longtime legman, John Henshaw, Warren and Pearson had traveled together to the USSR shortly after the JFK assassination. There Pearson was introduced to Soviet leader Nikita Khrushchev. Apparently one of the subjects discussed by Pearson and Khrushchev was the assassination of John F. Kennedy. [659]

Henshaw noted that a "top secret" classified document buried in the National Archives in Washington (signed by CIA Director Richard Helms) was designated, "Discussion between Chairman Khrushchev and Mr. Drew Pearson regarding Lee Harvey Oswald."[660]

This was one of the documents that Chief Justice Warren ordered sealed for 75 years. The secret talks between Pearson and the Soviet dictator were never recorded in Pearson's gossip column. It was apparently during this period that Pearson first promoted the Castro conspiracy theory which later came to the public's attention in 1967.

However, at the time of the Warren Commission investigation, the chief justice evidently believed there was a basis for Pearson's story, and thus a consequent need to cover up the truth to prevent the outbreak of war. This apparently was the ruse needed to convince Warren to hide what he mistakenly believed to be the truth. Pearson's biographer charitably described the columnist's actions: "The purpose of the columnist-turned-diplomat was to reduce hysteria, which might upset the delicate balance between the [United States and the USSR]." [661]

Whatever the case, the Pearson-Anderson story about the alleged Castro conspiracy against JFK created a sensation and muddied the waters at a time when JFK assassination conspiracy allegations were gaining widespread credibility. However rational the story may have sounded at the time, the evidence was flimsy at best as we have seen. The fact is that the Pearson-Anderson "revelations" are nothing more than deliberate disinformation.

## SHIFTING THE FOCUS OF CONTROVERSY

The Pearson-Anderson columns, in effect, "cleared" the CIA of involvement in JFK's murder and pointed the finger at Castro.

The Pearson-Anderson columns, likewise, shifted focus away from the Garrison investigation in New Orleans which was focusing on likely CIA involvement and which had stumbled upon the Clay Shaw-Permindex connection bringing the inquiry right onto Israel's doorstep.

That Drew Pearson, in particular, would have an interest in shielding any Israeli involvement as well is beyond doubt.

## ISRAEL'S FAVORITE COLUMNIST

Of Jewish extraction, Pearson was a devoted friend of Israel—from the beginning. In fact, in the period leading up to the establishment of the state of Israel, Pearson functioned as a hitman for the Israeli lobby in the United States, pounding away in his column at those perceived inimical to Israeli interests.

One of Pearson's favorite targets was then-Secretary of Defense James Forrestal. According to Pearson's biographer, "When Forrestal persuaded [President Harry] Truman to take the Arab side against the Jews in Palestine for military reasons, Pearson saw his opportunity. He lathered and shaved Forrestal as a bureaucratic voice for American oil companies with enormous stakes in the Mideast. Walter Winchell and other opinion-makers supported his position."[662]

Pearson's hysterical media attack on Forrestal, some believed, led to the Cabinet secretary's mental instability, resulting in Forrestal's suicide. There are many, though, who believe that Forrestal was in fact murdered—precisely because of his powerful opposition to the Israeli lobby.

Pearson himself had cemented his ties with the Israeli lobby and had engaged in behind-the-scenes intrigue with Israel's intelligence and propaganda arm, the Anti-Defamation League (ADL) of B'nai B'rith for decades.

## PEARSON AND THE ADL

According to Pearson's biographer, "Over the years the ADL had helped Pearson enormously. It had provided information he could not obtain elsewhere, backed his lecture tours, even assisted in the circulation of his weekly newsletter."[663]

Pearson's own former mother-in-law, *Washington Times-Herald* publisher Cissy Patterson, was less charitable in her description of Pearson. In a fiery editorial attack on Pearson she called him "both undercover agent and mouthpiece for the Anti-Defamation League."[664]

What's more, Pearson had a long-standing arrangement with the ADL in which the ADL paid the expenses of his legmen, such as the aforementioned John Henshaw, in return for Pearson floating ADL propaganda in his columns.[665]

## PEARSON'S MOSSAD CONNECTION

Pearson, likewise, had acquainted himself over the years with a number of top-level intelligence operatives close to Israel, in particular, Canadian-born British intelligence wizard, Sir William Stephenson.

Stephenson, as we saw in Chapter 7 and Chapter 15 was not only the the guiding force behind the assembly of Israel's Mossad, but also the brains behind the Allied intelligence operations during World War II which utilized the resources of Meyer Lansky and his organized crime network. He was also a close associate and mentor of Louis M. Bloomfield, president of the Mossad-backed Permindex entity that was central to the JFK assassination conspiracy.

According to Pearson's biographer, "Stephenson had become acquainted during the war with Pearson as a responsible publicist with the largest serious following in the United States." [666] In at least one instance, Pearson published a story that, according to his biographer, "was spoon-fed to him" [667]by Stephenson.

Pearson's other connections were equally interesting and point further toward his interest in covering for Israel and its allies in the JFK assassination conspiracy—both the CIA and the Meyer Lansky Organized Crime Syndicate.

## THE ISRAELI LOBBY AND PEARSON

According to Pearson's associate, John Henshaw, Pearson was engaged in sharp business practices with his partner, attorney Max M. Kampelman, a key figure in the Israel lobby in Washington and a longtime top-level Anti-Defamation League (ADL) director.

Kampelman, the personal attorney for then-Vice President Hubert Humphrey, and Pearson were trying to wrest control of television channel 14 away from a Black-owned station, WOOK, in Washington.[668]

(In Chapter 6, as we have seen, Humphrey was a product of a Minnesota political machine funded, in part, by the notorious Isadore Blumenfeld, a major cog in the Lansky Crime Syndicate.)

The connections between Pearson and the Israeli lobby in Washington were even more intimate. Pearson's stepson (and the editor of his "diaries"), Tyler Abell, an attorney, had been employed by the law firm of David Ginsburg, a registered foreign agent for Israel.

Ginsburg, like several other top figures known for their interest in promoting Israel's interests in Washington, were among those close to Hubert Humphrey. (Ginsburg himself took a leave of absence from his own firm to work on behalf of Vice President Hubert H. Humphrey's unsuccessful 1968 presidential campaign.)[669] In Chapter 6, of course, we examined the vice president's early political successes in Lansky Syndicate-dominated Minneapolis.

### THE MICKEY COHEN DEAL

In 1968 Pearson worked hand-in-glove with Meyer Lansky's West Coast henchman, Mickey Cohen, in an effort to wreck Richard Nixon's presidential campaign in favor of his Democratic opponent, Humphrey. (It was in Chapter 13 where we explored Cohen's connection to the JFK assassination conspiracy in some detail.)

According to Cohen, writing in his memoirs, President Johnson arranged for Pearson to call Cohen who was, by then, in jail. Pearson wanted to uncover dirt about Nixon from the former Vice President's days in California when, according to Cohen, he had provided underworld financial backing for Nixon.

"We're going for Humphrey for president," Pearson told Cohen, "And I assure you that if he becomes our president, you're going to be given a medical parole," in return for providing muck against Nixon.

According to Cohen, "I consented to everything that Pearson wanted to do against Nixon." [670]However, Nixon won the election and Cohen never received his medical parole.

Pearson's relationship with the publishers of the *National Enquirer* newspaper (which has made a speciality out of trashing the Kennedy family and likewise publishing often loony JFK assassination conspiracy stories) is also interesting, particularly in light of the *Enquirer's* CIA and Israeli lobby connections.

### PEARSON AND THE NATIONAL ENQUIRER

As reported by Pearson's legman, John Henshaw, in the July 1, 1969 issue of the *Washington Observer* newsletter, the company which published the *Enquirer*, World Wide Features, Inc. had interesting origins.

It was owned by the three brothers, Anthony, Fortune and Generoso Pope. They were the sons of Generoso Pope, Sr., an Italian leader of New York City's Tammany Hall political machine which was itself inextricably tied to the Meyer Lansky Organized Crime Syndicate.

The Pope family were longtime contributors—through the Generoso Pope Foundation—to pro-Israel causes. The foundation was also widely suspected of being a secret conduit for CIA funds.

Generoso Pope, Jr. owned the *National Enquirer*. Pope, Jr.. had worked for the CIA during the Korean war and was himself famously friendly with Lansky's longtime partner, Frank Costello. In fact, Costello helped finance the *Enquirer* in its infancy.[671]

Pearson had given highly favorable publicity to Generoso Pope, Sr. as the first "prominent Italian American" to oppose Mussolini. In return, Pope promptly gave Pearson a contract to write a weekly column for his *El Progresso*, the leading Italian language newspaper in the country. The $150-a-week contract was more than any other newspaper paid for just one weekly column.

In the mid-1960's Pearson and Fortune Pope, along with Lyndon Johnson's TV-and-radio advisor, Leonard Marks, went into partnership and acquired the Bell-McClure Syndicate and the North American Newspaper Alliance. (Marks was later appointed head of the U.S. Information Agency by Johnson.)[672]

Pearson's biographer dismisses the relationship between Pearson and the controversial Pope family as "puzzling."[673] This relationship, however, further cements Pearson's ties to the Israeli lobby and its allies in the CIA.

## THE JOE TRENTO CONNECTION

It is of more than passing interest to note that for a period, Generoso Pope's Washington bureau chief was journalist Joe Trento, who emerged as an authority on the intelligence community.

It was Trento, as we saw in Chapter 16, who co-wrote a controversial article alleging that former CIA man E. Howard Hunt may have been in Dallas on the day JFK was shot.

Trento, as noted, had excellent CIA connections—James Jesus Angleton, in particular, and we know for a fact that Trento was being used as a media conduit by Angleton for whatever insidious purposes of his own. This, of course, we discussed in some detail in Chapter 16.

## JACK ANDERSON'S CONNECTIONS

Drew Pearson's partner and protege, Jack Anderson, himself had notable ties to not only the Israeli lobby, but also the Lansky Organized Crime Syndicate.

Not only did Anderson once share his offices with at least one registered lobbyist for Israel, who was also close to Lansky's protege, Carlos Marcello,[674] but he also maintained a close working relationship with

Herman (Hank) Greenspun, a longtime Lansky syndicate associate and arms-smuggler for Israel.

Greenspun was a protege of Lansky crony Joseph "Doc" Stacher, a New Jersey mobster who was one of the prime American backers of the Jewish underground in Palestine in the late 1940's. [675]

(Stacher was later permitted to go into exile in Israel following his conviction in the United States on income tax evasion charges. According to Lansky's friendly biographer, Robert Lacey, Stacher's death affected Lansky greatly. They were very close friends and longtime associates.)[676]

Greenspun also functioned as a public relations man for Lansky's boyhood friend—later killed at Lansky's direction—Benjamin Siegel.

According to *The Washington Observer*, "Early in the Palestine War, Hank Greenspun was dispatched by the Jewish underground to Hawaii to buy surplus U.S. Army arms and equipment.

"By bribing security guards at the U.S. Naval Air Station on Oahu, he raided a stockpile of armaments and stole 15 tons of .30- and .50- caliber aircraft machine guns. The contraband machine guns were packed in 58 crates marked 'engine parts' and shipped to Los Angeles, then transshipped to Mexico and on to Israel.

"Greenspun ran the British blockade in a ship delivering arms to Israel. Later he pleaded guilty to violating the U.S. Neutrality Act, and was given a 3-year suspended sentence. He was never prosecuted for theft of Federal government property."[677]

Greenspun, who became a major figure in Las Vegas, went on to establish a chain of newspapers in Nevada and Colorado, publishing *The Las Vegas Sun*.

As we have seen in Chapter 7, the Israeli arms-smuggling underworld of which Greenspun was a part, was a very tightly knit little clique. It was, of course, Louis Bloomfield (later chief executive officer of the Permindex entity) who was one of the key coordinators for the Israeli arms smuggling ventures, working with the Lansky Syndicate and, Anderson's associate, the aforementioned Greenspun.

Anderson and Greenspun were themselves intimately involved in yet another venture linked to the Lansky Syndicate. The two operators, along with CIA-linked attorney Edward Morgan (the alleged conduit for the Castro conspiracy story floated by Pearson and Anderson) were middlemen in the sale of Lansky associate and ADL "Torch of Liberty" winner, Morris Dalitz's Las Vegas gambling palace, the Desert Inn, to billionaire Howard Hughes.[678]

## A CASE STUDY IN DISINFORMATION

That Drew Pearson and Jack Anderson maintained such intimate ties with all of the prime movers behind the JFK assassination—Israel, the CIA and the Meyer Lansky Organized Crime Syndicate—not only casts real doubt about the Castro assassination plot story that the two columnists sensationalized, but it points toward the real motivation behind the release of the tale: to cover for the real conspirators.

The case of Pearson and Anderson exemplifies, above all, the insidious nature of Israel's influence over the American media and provides a clear-cut case study of how the media has been manipulated to distort the truth about the JFK assassination conspiracy.

## KEEPING THE TRUTH HIDDEN

Although the media in general had initially backed the Warren Commission cover-up, public dissent about the conclusions—stirred on largely by the work of pioneer commission critic Mark Lane and his friend, New Orleans District Attorney Jim Garrison—forced Israel's friends in the media to play their hand.

Stories that "The Mafia Killed JFK" and about "Castro" plots against JFK suddenly began emerging. Pearson and Anderson were just two players in the continuing cover-up. And Pearson himself (as we have seen) actually had a hand in convincing Earl Warren that there had been a conspiracy (plotted by Castro) that made it necessary, for the public good, to cover up the truth. In fact, Pearson and his Israeli and CIA allies were seeking to keep the real truth hidden.

## MORE DISINFORMATION?

One rather interesting JFK assassination story appeared in the form of a book by former CIA contract agent Hugh McDonald, co-written with prolific author Geoffrey Bocca. The McDonald-Bocca book, *Appointment in Dallas*, received wide distribution.

The book featured an interview with an international hitman named "Saul" who confessed to McDonald that he was the real murderer of President Kennedy. The hitman said that he was hired by a private group, and not by the CIA for whom he had done contract work in the past.

While many JFK assassination critics were highly skeptical about the book, looking upon it as some form of disinformation (perhaps from the CIA itself)—although not necessarily questioning McDonald's sincerity—it would have been more instructive to consider Geoffrey Bocca's role in the writing of the book.

Bocca, in fact, was a propagandist for the CIA-backed and Israeli-financed French Secret Army Organization (OAS) and was known to have "translated some OAS tracts into English at a time when the organization was thinking of appealing to the United Nations for help."[679] Bocca also later wrote a heroic account of the OAS history entitled *The Secret Army*.

Needless to say, in light of the "French connection" to the JFK assassination conspiracy, the appearance of an OAS propagandist as the co-author of a book which effectively "cleared" the CIA of involvement in the crime is interesting, to say the least.

An odd footnote: several years after publishing *Appointment in Dallas*, McDonald wrote another JFK assassination book. His co-author, who had solid links to the CIA, Robin Moore, was best known, interestingly enough, for his famous book, *The French Connection*—on the French intelligence- and Lansky Syndicate-linked international heroin racket.

McDonald and Moore's book was entitled *LBJ and the JFK Conspiracy*. This volume elaborated on the theme of McDonald's first book, saying that the alleged hitman, Saul, had been hired by the Soviet Union to kill President Kennedy.

The theory that the Soviets were behind the assassination conspiracy, of course, falls right in line with the CIA's initial scheme, through its Mexico City Scenario, concocted by James J. Angleton, to pin the crime on the KGB. Whatever the case, McDonald's second book received little, if any, recognition—and perhaps rightly so.

## A PRO-ISRAEL 'CRITIC'

The tell-tale hand of Israeli sympathizers within even the ranks of the "critics" of the Warren Commission's conclusions has also now become apparent. When a group of Warren Commission critics formed an organization known as the Assassination Information Bureau, one of them included liberal journalist Jack Newfield, a devout and outspoken supporter of Israel.

## THE 'HOFFA KILLED JFK' COVER STORY

In 1992, when public interest in the JFK assassination conspiracy was at a fever pitch as a result of the concurrent release of Mark Lane's best-seller, *Plausible Denial*, and Oliver Stone's film, *JFK*, it was Newfield who floated yet another ridiculous JFK assassination conspiracy story—a new angle on the theory that "The Mafia Killed JFK."

"Hoffa had JKF killed" screamed the headline on the front page of the January 14 edition of the sensationalist *New York Post*.

It was the New York tabloid that "broke" the story that Teamster boss, Jimmy Hoffa had arranged the JFK murder through his Mafia contacts. Not surprisingly, the author of the *Post* article was Jack Newfield.

The *Post*, of course, has been one of the media's primary pro-Israel voices—almost to the point of obsession. Any conspiracy that might somehow link Israel—or its allies in the CIA—could not be tolerated.

Almost immediately, the rest of the Establishment media picked up the scandal sheet's "exclusive" and began hyping it. The purpose was to discredit the conspiracy that was finally being exposed to millions of Americans.

In response to Newfield's concoction, even Dan Rather, on CBS, felt compelled to tell the world that the evidence was in: longtime Teamsters' Union leader Jimmy Hoffa had ordered "the Mafia" to kill John F. Kennedy.

*The Washington Post,* long a CIA disinformation source, also published the story. As did the staunchly pro-Israel conservative weekly, *Human Events* which consistently maintained, otherwise, that any conspiracy in the JFK assassination—particularly involving the CIA—was a madman's fantasy.

Newfield's article quoted a longtime alleged associate of organized crime, attorney Frank Ragano, as having claimed that Teamster boss Jimmy Hoffa told him to order "the Mafia" to assassinate President John F. Kennedy.

According to Ragano's unlikely story, Ragano took the message to New Orleans rackets boss Carlos Marcello and to Tampa mob chieftain Santos Trafficante, both of whom, we have seen, were immediate underlings of Meyer Lansky.

Presumably they complied with Hoffa's order, in Ragano's version of the story, because, after all, Kennedy was indeed shot dead.[680] However, as Mark Lane has commented, "Hoffa didn't give orders to the Mafia. The Mafia gave orders to Hoffa." [681]

## WHY THE HOFFA STORY DOESN'T WASH

Ragano's primary "evidence" that Trafficante was involved in JFK's murder was a comment made by Trafficante to the effect that "We should have killed Bobby," referring to then-Attorney General Robert F. Kennedy. Not that Trafficante admitted that "we" killed JFK—only that "we should have killed Bobby."

Now all of this is most peculiar in that Ragano says that he—a top-level criminal lawyer with high-ranking connections—managed to "suppress" these memories until just recently.

Ragano says that he is "guilty and ashamed" because of his association with organized crime; according to Ragano, his guilt feelings caused him to suppress those memories. However, he might also have been interested in adding some spice to his memoirs which he is also writing.

What's more, Ragano, who is appealing a second federal income tax evasion conviction, might also have something else in mind by telling this story which clears the CIA and any other federal agencies that may have been involved.

## WHO KILLED HOFFA?

Hoffa biographer Dan Moldea shed some interesting "inside" information regarding the truth about Hoffa—and his murder. Moldea reports: "Ironically enough, attorney William Bufalino . . . may have inadvertently pointed a finger in the right direction. He was attempting to suggest that the mob had nothing to do with Hoffa's murder, preferring to shift the blame on the government, but he put it this way:

'Tell the FBI to look into the CIA. And tell the CIA to look into the FBI. **Then** you'll have the answer [to the Hoffa case.]' And he added that it was his belief that Hoffa's murder was related to those of [Sam] Giancana and Johnny] Rosselli.[682]

(In Chapter 11, of course, we examined the strange deaths of Sam Giancana and Johnny Rosselli and concluded, contrary to popular myth, that the two Mafia figures were not, in fact, the victims of "Mafia" hits at all— but were, instead, snuffed out if not by the CIA itself, certainly at its behest.)

Interestingly enough, it was yet another dedicated pro-Israel polemicist, Max Lerner, writing in *The Washington Times*, who also came to the defense of the Hoffa-Mafia cover story. According to Lerner, "The Mafia has always figured among the major possible scenarios for the killing, along with the KGB and Cuba's Fidel Castro. But not until the Ragano account had the pieces of the puzzle begun to fall together. Marcello headed the Mafia operation in New Orleans, Trafficante in Tampa and Cuba. They had time to work out their plan. They had an army of skilled killers to draw on."[683]

Lerner, of course, was playing fast and loose with the facts. He ignored the central part Meyer Lansky played in manipulating the activities of both Marcello and Trafficante.

## SUN MYUNG MOON, ISRAEL & THE CIA

That *The Washington Times* would have an interest in promoting the Hoffa-Mafia story is no surprise. After all, the *Times* itself has close links tc the intelligence community and is a strident editorial supporter of Israel.

*The Washington Times* is funded by the bizarre global conglomerate of Korean cult figure Sun Myung Moon.

Moon himself has been repeatedly linked to the Korean CIA which is, of course, intimately tied with its American counterpart. Additionally, Moon has forged a close working alliance with Israel and its American lobby and has pushed a pro-Israel agenda on the so-called "conservative movement" in the United States.

Moon's editor at *The Washington Times*—and its guiding force—is Arnaud deBorchgrave, a former top correspondent for the CIA-linked *Newsweek* (owned by the Washington Post Company) and himself a reputed "former" intelligence operative. What's more, deBorchgrave himself is closely connected by marriage to the Rothschild family. The Rothschilds, as we have seen, have been longtime financial backers of the state of Israel.

## THE CONSERVATIVE COVER-UP

The response to JFK conspiracy allegations from another "conservative" source is equally interesting. The organization, quaintly named Accuracy in Media, a self-styled conservative "media watchdog" took great umbrage with suggestions that there might have been a conspiracy behind the president's assassination.

At the time Mark Lane's *Plausible Denial* and Oliver Stone's *JFK* were released, AIM chairman Reed Irvine, seemingly inexplicably, signed on with the rest of the media in denouncing the conspiracy theories presented in the book and the motion picture.

Writing in the pages of the conservative weekly, *Human Events,* media critic Irvine actually paid tribute to the Establishment media for its attack on the theories.

According to Irvine, "The mainstream media, to their credit, have been nearly unanimous in denouncing Stone as a lying charlatan." [684]

Irvine went on to dismiss Lane as a "leftist" and announced emphatically that anyone who believes that there was any kind of domestic conspiracy behind the JFK murder was being taken in by Soviet propaganda. The AIM response was interesting, particularly in the context of the background of some of AIM's leading lights.

## WHO'S BEHIND AIM?

Irvine himself was a former economist for the big bank controlled Federal Reserve System. Irvine's AIM co-founder, Bernard Yoh, was a Vietnam-era underling of CIA asset, General Edward Lansdale.[685] It was Lansdale, as we saw in Chapter 11, who was in charge of the anti-Castro operations being conducted under the name Operation Mongoose in league with the Meyer Lansky Crime Syndicate.

It was during his service in Vietnam, as we noted in Chapter 12, that Lansdale worked closely with the Corsican Mafia—an integral part of the Lansky drug smuggling operations conducted in league with the CIA. That Lansdale's former Vietnam era associate would come out swinging against JFK conspiracy theories, then, is no big surprise.

## AIM'S ISRAELI CONNECTION

The aforementioned Yoh is also affiliated with the International Security Council (ISC), a think tank notable for its central devotion to the advancement of Israel's interests in U.S. foreign policy-making.

The founder of the ISC is the ubiquitous Dr. Joseph Churba, an ordained rabbi whom we first encountered in Chapter 8 as a protege of Irving Lovestone who coordinated CIA contacts with the Corsican and Sicilian Mafias on behalf of the CIA's James J. Angleton.

Interestingly enough, Churba is also a key figure in the Jewish Institute for National Security Affairs and in an entity known as Americans for a Safe Israel (ASI) established in the United States as an outgrowth of the Israeli underground terrorist group, the Irgun.

Among those intimately collaborating with the forerunners of ASI was the Romanian Jewish emigre, Ernst Mantello, whose brother Giorgio, along with Major Louis M. Bloomfield, was one of the founders of the shadowy Permindex entity examined in detail in Chapter 15.[686]

## ANOTHER CIA-LANSKY CONNECTION

Another AIM figure is equally interesting in light of the organization's critique of JFK assassination conspiracy theories. AIM's president is Murray Baron, not only a former official with the Lansky Organized Crime Syndicate-dominated International Brotherhood of Teamsters, but also a member of the CIA-funded Citizens Committee for a Free Cuba and the co-founder of the Citizens Committee for Peace With Freedom in Vietnam.[687]

It might be added, in passing, that AIM has consistently also been a strident defender of Israel and its interests. To even hint at any conspiracy which might involve Israel and its allies in the CIA would be an outrage, insofar as AIM would be concerned. So much, then, for accuracy in media from Accuracy in Media.

## OLIVER STONE

What about Oliver Stone's *JFK*? Where does this controversial film fit in the lore of JFK assassination conspiracy theories? What of the media's response to the film?

Writing in the *New York Times* on December 20, 1991, Stone asked a rather simple question: "When a leader of any country is assassinated, the media normally ask: 'What political forces were opposed to this leader and would benefit from his assassination?'"

The irony, as we shall see, is that although Oliver Stone himself seemed to have asked that very question in a big, big way—through the egis of his controversial film *JFK*—the fact is that Stone himself has, in a sense, proven, in the end, to have become a major factor in the continuing cover-up of the real truth about the assassination of John F. Kennedy.

It is ironic indeed that although Stone's film *JFK* has focused widespread international attention on the JFK assassination conspiracy, there has been quiet speculation that the media's furor might be part of a high-level plan to further cover up the truth about the conspiracy.

Many JFK assassination researchers, Mark Lane in particular, are deeply concerned that Stone's film presents a strange admixture of both fact and fiction. The facts about the assassination conspiracy are sensational enough without fictional details being added, he and others have pointed out. Lane, has summarized it best: "It was **good** that Stone called the attention of teenagers and others to the unsolved murder. It was **bad** that he did so by falsifying the record." [688]

## POINTING IN THE WRONG DIRECTION

Although Stone's film referenced, in passing, the CIA connections of David Ferrie and Clay Shaw of Permindex, the film's primary thrust was that the conspiracy originated in the so-called "military-industrial" complex.

The primary conspirators were presented as high-level military men and their allies among the multi-billion-dollar defense contracting companies. The intelligence community's role was understated, to say the very least.

This, in itself, lead some of Stone's critics to suggests that perhaps the ultimate purpose behind the film was not, in fact, to pinpoint those truly responsible for the JFK assassination, but to point the finger in another direction. *The evidence for this, as we shall see, is compelling indeed.*

## STONE'S LANSKY-ISRAEL CONNECTION

That distribution for Stone's film was handled by Warner Brothers is somewhat unsettling in light of the conclusions reached in *Final Judgment*. In fact, Warner Brothers, a subsidiary of the giant Time-Warner media empire, evolved from a film production company established by longtime Meyer Lansky associate, Louis Chesler, a Canadian of somewhat dubious reputation.

It was in 1956 that Chesler, a Lansky front man, established Seven Arts Productions in Montreal, Canada. Although ostensibly a film production company, Seven Arts functioned as a money-laundering facility for Lansky and others among his associates.[689]

By 1955, Seven Arts had gone into partnership with a New York-based banking consortium and was flush with money within a decade.

In 1967 Seven Arts shook Wall Street and stunned Hollywood when it gained control of the famous Warner Brothers Studios—in short, a Lansky take-over. The move was a mystery to many at the time, but little did they know of the behind-the-scenes Lansky Syndicate dealings which made the wheeling and dealing possible.

The new operation was dubbed Warner-Seven Arts Studios and, by 1968, was known as Warner Communications.[690] Not surprisingly, it just so happens, it was Bernie Cornfeld's Investors Overseas Service (IOS) which "owned major blocks of stock"[691] in Warner-Seven Arts.

Cornfeld of IOS, as we saw in Chapter 15, was a front man for Tibor Rosenbaum, former Mossad official and the prime mover behind the Lanksy-linked Permindex operation that was so central to the JFK assassination conspiracy.

## THE 'ISRAELI MAFIA'

It was in 1981 that a major scandal rocked Warner Communications. Several of its top figures—Solomon Weiss, Stephen Ross and Jay Emmett—were caught up in tax fraud, bribery, and assorted other racketeering charges brought by the Justice Department. Warner's links to organized crime were being investigated.[692]

However, what is particularly significant about the case is that much of the evidence against the aforementioned Weiss, who was senior assistant treasurer of Warner Communications, emerged from records gleaned from the files of the United Jewish Appeal and other pro-Israel philanthropies that were seized by the Justice Department.[693]

What's more, the Warner Communications investigation repeatedly stumbled upon links to the so-called "Israeli mafia,"—the domestic elements of organized criminal activity operating in Israel.

And, to draw the circle even tighter, the Warner investigation of the aforementioned Stephen Ross by Justice uncovered close links between the media giant and the American Bank and Trust (ABT) scandal.[694]

## TIBOR ROSENBAUM, AGAIN

In Chapter 7 we first learned that the New York-based ABT was an American subsidiary of the Swiss-Israel Trade Bank, upon whose board served none other than the Israeli Mossad's Tibor Rosenbaum, sponsor of the aforementioned Bernie Cornfeld of IOS.

It was, as we have seen, ironically enough, on November 22, 1963, that Swiss Israel assumed management of American Bank and Trust. The latter firm, however, ultimately went belly up, having been looted by financier David Graiver, himself a longtime Mossad operative.

One of those tarnished by the ABT scandal—and ultimately linked to the Warner Communications affair—was New York financier Abraham Feinberg who not only served as a director of ABT, but who had also been the individual who arranged John F. Kennedy's first unpleasant meeting with the key money men in the pro-Israel lobby in America (described in Chapter 4).[695]

Warner Communications survived the series of scandals and then, ultimately, merged with Time-Life, Inc., the other great media giant which, itself, has been scored by JFK assassination researchers for lending itself to the JFK assassination cover-up.

## THE GANG AT TIME-LIFE

It was in Chapter 10, for example, that we learned how *Life* correspondent Richard Billings went to New Orleans and sabotaged Jim Garrison's investigation into the JFK assassination. Billings and his team used *Life* magazine as a forum to portray Garrison as a tool of "the Mafia." Billings and company presented Garrison as a shill for New Orleans Mafia boss Carlos Marcello, but, of course, ignored Marcello's secondary positioning to Marcello's sponsor, Meyer Lansky.

Billings himself later served on the staff of the House Assassinations Committee which blamed the JFK murder on "the Mafia," working alongside the committee's director, G. Robert Blakey, who several years previously had been employed as a character witness on behalf of longtime Lansky confidant Morris Dalitz, ostensibly "proving" that Dalitz was not linked with the underworld.

So it was that Time-Life and Warner Communications merged, becoming Time-Warner. And, of course, it was one of Time-Warner's subsidiaries, Warner Brothers, which ultimately became the distribution company for Oliver Stone's *JFK*—which blamed "the military-industrial complex"—not Israel's Mossad, not the Mafia, not even the CIA itself—for the JFK assassination.

(The same company, through its subsidiary, Time-Warner Books, also handled distribution for the biography of Chicago Mafia boss Sam Giancana that suggested that it was strictly a CIA-Mafia plot against JFK, orchestrated almost solely by Giancana himself.)

## THE BRONFMANS, AGAIN

Interestingly enough, in early 1993 the Lansky syndicate-linked Bronfman family, through their Seagram Company, purchased a substantial controlling interest in Time Warner, further cementing the media giant into the tightly-knit circles of the CIA-Lansky Syndicate-Israeli Mossad connection that have swirled around the company since its inception.

It was, as we saw in Chapter 15, Major Louis M. Bloomfield, chief executive operative of the Permindex entity, who had been longtime personal attorney for the Bronfman interests and a major figure in the Israeli lobby in Canada.

That a company which has been intimately tied from its earliest years not only with the inner circles of Meyer Lansky and his international crime syndicate, but also with Israel and its Mossad, should be the sponsor of Oliver Stone's grand conspiracy theory is enough to make one wonder, to say the least. But there's more.

It is somewhat interesting to note that when Stone hired on a public relations agency to handle the publicity and controversy which emerged when the film was released, it was the powerful Washington, D.C. firm of Hill & Knowlton. After all, it was Hill & Knowlton that orchestrated major propaganda in favor of American involvement in the Persian Gulf War against Iraq—and in favor of Israel.

## STONE'S ADL CONNECTION

What's more, the Hill & Knowlton executive who handled his firm's efforts on behalf of Stone, Frank Mankiewicz, got his start in the public relations business working on behalf of the pro-Israel Anti-Defamation League (ADL) of B'nai B'rith in Los Angeles. (In Chapter 18, we shall see, Mankiewicz himself had a curious role in the circumstances surrounding yet another Kennedy assassination.)

## STONE REACTS TO FINAL JUDGMENT . . .

In Washington, D.C., on February 16, 1994, an associate of this author attempted to present Oliver Stone with a copy of the first edition of this book, *Final Judgment*. This came several months after the book was first advertised in the program of the annual symposium on the JFK assassination sponsored by the JFK Assassination Information Center in Dallas, Texas.

Although Stone hadn't been in attendence at the symposium, he was represented there by one of his associates and it is certain that Stone was aware of the release of *Final Judgment*. After all, a full-page advertisement promoting a book featuring an introduction by Stone appeared opposite a full-page advertisement for *Final Judgment*.

When Stone was presented his copy of the book, however, his face froze when he saw the book's cover and he refused to accept the book, saying, "Please send it to me in the mail." The "maverick" self-styled free-thinker, Stone, turned his back and walked away, moments later accepting another package of material presented to him by another individual.

Why was Stone so hesitant to accept this book? Perhaps we have information that provides the answer. Stone did, in fact, know of the so-called "French connection" to the JFK assassination documented in *Final Judgment* and referenced in the advertisement in the program of the JFK forum in Dallas.

## STONE AND 'THE FRENCH CONNECTION'

You see, shortly after *Final Judgment* went to press, Ron Lewis, who was a friend of Lee Harvey Oswald in New Orleans and who also worked in Guy Banister's "French"-connected operation, revealed something very interesting about Stone and the "French" connection.

When Lewis, who served as a consultant to Stone during the filming of *JFK*, assised Stone in setting up the movie sets recreating Banister's New Orleans office, Stone included a number of boxes, ostensibly containing arms, that were stenciled in Spanish.

Lewis objected to the Spanish, saying, "The writing on the boxes was in French,"—the arms having been linked to the OAS rebellion, backed by the Israeli-sponsored Permindex operation, against French President Charles DeGaulle. But Stone responded to Lewis by saying, "Spanish serves the theme of the movie better." So, as Lewis commented, "Spanish it was."[696]

So it also was that Oliver Stone ignored the "French" connection—a connection which, in turn, brings forth the Israeli connection to the assassination of John F. Kennedy. A wise move indeed for a film-maker whose sponsors had intimate ties to the guilty parties involved in the crime that Stone brought to grisly life on film.

However, there is one last rather intriguing fact about Oliver Stone and his widely-promoted film that deserves mention. Although Stone was, beyond question, the undeniably talented creative genius responsible for *JFK*, one must always remember that in the motion picture arena, it is ultimately money—pure and simple—that determines whether or not a film will be made. The all-important task of arranging financing falls into the lap of the film's producer. If one checks the credits for Stone's *JFK*, one will find the name "Arnon Milchan" listed as "executive producer."

## STONE'S MOSSAD CONNECTION

Who is Arnon Milchan? Why is his name relevant in our examination of the facts about Israel's role in the JFK assassination conspiracy and the manner in which Oliver Stone has suppressed that critical factor?

According to liberal journalist Alexander Cockburn, writing in *The Nation* on May 18, 1992, Milchan, the executive producer of *JFK*, "was identified in one 1989 Israeli report as 'probably [Israel's] largest arms dealer.' A company he owned was once caught smuggling nuclear weapons fuses to Iraq. As part of a joint Israeli-South African government operation— 'Muldergate'—he acted as launderer to money scheduled to quell liberal publications opposing apartheid."[697]

As a consequence of his status, Milchan, very clearly, is an international wheeler dealer who—if not actually a Mossad officer himself—has certainly worked closely with the Mossad in its global intrigue. It would not be a stretch of the imagination, indeed, to suggest then that it was actually Mossad money, in the end, that helped finance Oliver Stone's interpretation of the JFK assassination conspiracy.

## A 'LIMITED HANGOUT' HOLLYWOOD STYLE?

The question then arises: was the wide media hype given Stone's film some form of "limited hangout" on behalf of Israel and its allies in the CIA? Was the widespread promotion of Stone's film a way of finally attempting to put an end to the controversy and give the public what it wanted: some form of explanation as to "what really happened" in Dallas? This, of course, we will never know.

## WHERE STONE FAILED . . .

As we noted earlier, Stone himself asked this question in the *New York Times*: "When a leader of any country is assassinated, the media normally ask: 'What political forces were opposed to this leader and would benefit from his assassination?'"

As we have seen, one political force that was opposed to John F. Kennedy and would benefit from his assassination was Israel, yet Stone himself evidently prefers not to name that particular force.

Despite all the criticisms we have aimed at Stone—and they are very much deserved—Stone's film has still led the way for new popular perceptions about the obvious fact that it was a conspiracy that ended the life of John F. Kennedy.

Stone failed to nail down the source of that conspiracy but in the pages of *Final Judgment* we have done just that. What a shame indeed that Oliver Stone could not have told the entire story of the JFK assassination conspiracy. That story in itself would have been far more chilling than even that which appeared in his film.

## THE MEDIA REJECTS A FINAL JUDGMENT

Clearly, the media's coverage—or be it non-coverage—of the JFK assassination was critical to the cover-up of the real origins of the conspiracy that resulted in the president's assassination. That the media played a major part in perpetuating the cover-up is unquestioned and that Israel and its lobby has a major influence in shaping the American media can likewise not be questioned.

Although the media initially supported the Warren Commission's conclusions, public skepticism forced the media to bring forth a wide variety of cover stories and limited portions of the truth. But the Israeli connection has never been considered—until now.

## Chapter Eighteen

## The Heir to the Throne
## The Assassination of Robert F. Kennedy
## Israel, Iran, Lansky & the CIA

**The murder of Sen. Robert F. Kennedy, younger brother of the slain president, was vital to the continuing cover-up of the truth about the JFK assassination.**
**If RFK had made it to the White House he would finally have had the power to bring his brother's killers to justice.**
**The slaying of Robert F. Kennedy links not only Israel and its allies in the CIA and the Meyer Lansky Organized Crime Syndicate, but also SAVAK, the secret police of the Shah of Iran.**

On its face, the "official" explanation of the circumstances surrounding the death of former Attorney General Robert F. Kennedy is as simple as the Warren Commission Report on the assassination of John F. Kennedy. In both instances, so the story goes, "one lone nut" was responsible for the crime. There was no conspiracy.

Robert F. Kennedy's assassination in Los Angeles in 1968 came just after RFK (elected to the Senate from New York in 1964) had won the critical California Democratic presidential primary. This put the younger Kennedy in the lead for his party's presidential nomination and thus potentially in line to move into the White House following the general election.

It was in the ballroom of the Ambassador Hotel where RFK delivered his California victory speech to an assembled crowd of supporters. After concluding his speech, the triumphant Kennedy wanted to work his way through the crowd in the ballroom to make his exit from the hotel.

However, according to one campaign volunteer who was on the scene, one of Kennedy's handlers repeatedly insisted that Kennedy exit through the hotel kitchen behind the ballroom. The handler who was so insistent that RFK exit through the kitchen was Frank Mankiewicz, who had started his career in the public relations business at the Los Angeles office of the Anti-Defamation League (ADL) of B'nai B'rith, and who, as we saw in Chapter 17, handled publicity for Oliver Stone's *JFK* extravaganza.[698]

It was there in that kitchen where Mankiewicz steered Senator Kennedy that a young Arab-American\ named Sirhan Sirhan was waiting. According to the late William Sullivan, longtime assistant FBI director, "We could never account for Sirhan's presence in the kitchen of the Ambassador Hotel."[699] However, we now know why Bobby Kennedy left through the hotel kitchen, rather than the way he himself wanted to leave, although Mankiewicz has said that it was RFK's decision to go through the kitchen— against the former ADL man's wishes.

## 'AN ARAB DID IT'

What really happened in those few short seconds is still the subject of controversy, although the bottom line was this: shots were fired at Robert F. Kennedy. The presidential hopeful was critically wounded. He died shortly thereafter. The Arab-American assailant was pummeled to the floor, arrested, convicted and sentenced to prison.

The public was somberly told that Sirhan was dissatisfied with Kennedy's strong pro-Israel stand and that this was one of the driving motivations that led him to commit the crime. So it was that an Arab-American was held up to the world as the killer of a martyred American president's younger brother, himself a popular public figure.

## RFK AND ISRAEL

What an irony that it was an Arab-American who would happen to be the assassin of the Kennedy brother who was perceived by "insiders" to be, at least in private, an anti-Semite in the mold of his father.

That Kennedy did indeed take a strident pro-Israel stand during his years in the U.S. Senate is not in doubt. As a senator from New York State (which, of course, has a heavily Jewish voting population), that was a political necessity for Robert Kennedy, who was, if nothing else, a pragmatist, at least.

(However, as we saw in Chapter 5, it was RFK himself who believed that the loyalties of his own brother's top advisor on Jewish affairs, Myer Feldman, were suspect. "[Feldman's] major interest," said RFK, "was Israel rather than the United States."[700]

If anybody knew of President John F. Kennedy's secret war with Israel (which we examined in detail in Chapter 5) it was his brother and confidant, Robert F. Kennedy. Thus it was that an Arab patsy took the fall for RFK's murder—a crime that had evolved from a conspiracy that was decidedly not Arabic in its origins.

## THE RFK CONSPIRACY

In this chapter we shall explore the source of the conspiracy that removed Robert Kennedy from the political arena and thereby precluded him from ever having the power to investigate the conspiracy that ended his brother's presidency.

And as we shall see, the RFK assassination conspiracy comes full circle with the conspiracy that killed JFK: the same powerful, close-knit sources were connected, but in a uniquely different way.

Unlike Lee Harvey Oswald who proclaimed himself a "patsy," Sirhan Sirhan responded almost without protest, with a certain passivity. This, among other things, led some to suspect that Sirhan, in fact, was a patsy, too, that he had been programmed—perhaps through drugs, or by hypnosis, for example—to kill RFK.

Yet, in the weeks and months of investigation—official and unofficial—that followed, it soon became apparent that there was evidence that more than one gun had been fired in the kitchen of the Ambassador Hotel.

Was it Dallas all over again? Was there more than one gunman involved in RFK's killing? Was there a conspiracy? Did the same people who killed JFK also arrange the assassination of his brother?

These were the kinds of questions that people were asking. Yet, perhaps precisely because of the continuing doubts over the first Kennedy assassination, public awareness of the serious questions arising from the second Kennedy assassination did not reach the same level.

What's more, the turmoil of the year 1968 was such that there were many other things capturing the public's attention: the Vietnam War, racial violence and rioting, and the heated three-way presidential campaign between Richard Nixon, Hubert Humphrey and George C. Wallace.

Ironically, also, it was during this period that New Orleans District Attorney was preparing his case against Permindex board member, Clay Shaw(whom we examined in Chapter 15). This, in itself, was beginning to capture the headlines, too.

Although many believed that the murder of Bobby Kennedy was directly linked to the murder of his brother five years earlier, no one seemed able to fit the pieces of the puzzle together.

## ENTER SAVAK

In fact, as former CIA contract agent, Robert Morrow, has demonstrated in his little-noticed (but very important) book, *The Senator Must Die*, there are connections between the two events—deeper than one might have imagined.

Simply put, Morrow's thesis is this: that the murder of Robert F. Kennedy was a CIA contract hit, carried out through the CIA's long-standing ally in international intrigue, the SAVAK, the secret police of the Shah of Iran—an intelligence agency created, in part, by Israel's Mossad itself and tied closely to the Mossad.

(And as we noted in Chapter 15, information uncovered by Morrow ties the Meyer Lansky Organized Crime Syndicate and its Swiss-based Israeli connection to the conspiracy that snuffed out the life of John F. Kennedy.)

According to Morrow's own extensive investigation, during the final weeks of Robert F. Kennedy's ill-fated presidential campaign in 1968, one Khyber Khan, a high-ranking member of the Shah's SAVAK, had infiltrated RFK's California campaign headquarters.

Khan additionally brought in other SAVAK agents to work on the campaign. This infiltration was part of the assassination conspiracy. Khan was in charge of coordinating the hit on RFK.

RFK allowed Khan into his inner circle because he believed Khan to be an opponent of the Shah of Iran. This conclusion was based upon his previous dealings with Khan.

In the early 1960's Khan had become embroiled in a feud with the Shah over a business deal gone sour and in revenge had come to Washington where he provided then-Attorney General Robert Kennedy with evidence of the Shah's misappropriation of U.S. foreign aid to Iran. The resulting bad blood further strained relations between the Kennedy administration and the Shah which had never been stable.

However, Khan and the Shah had made amends shortly thereafter and an alliance had been cemented. Khan, in fact, set up SAVAK operations on the West Coast in 1963—all of this, of course, unbeknownst to Robert F. Kennedy.

## THE SECOND 'GUN'

As part of Khan's scheme, the decision was made to have the actual assassination carried out by Sirhan Sirhan, a Jordanian-American, and another participant, a Pakistani-American. The two belonged to foreign student organizations, the General Union of Jordanian Students and the National Union of [Pakistani] Students, both of which had large contingents in Southern California.

According to Morrow's account, both Sirhan and the Pakistani were on the scene when RFK was assassinated. Both men fired weapons. Sirhan was using the .22 caliber pistol that was taken from him after the assassination. The Pakistani, however, was carrying a CIA-manufactured .22 caliber gun disguised as a Nikon SLR camera.

(In *The Senator Must Die,* Morrow reproduces a photograph of the Pakistani with the "camera" on a strap around his neck, standing beside Senator Kennedy shortly before the fatal shots were fired.)

After Kennedy gave his final address and made his way into the kitchen of the Ambassador Hotel, Sirhan, of course, thrust his own weapon out and began firing toward the senator. This resulted in Sirhan being the focus of attention, although one witness said that he had told the authorities that Sirhan never got close enough for a point-blank shot.

The other gunman, meanwhile, was also firing his weapon and probably delivered the fatal shot. In the midst of the melee, he escaped with his "camera." (It would not have done the assassination conspiracy good to have the other gunman captured with a CIA-manufactured weapon.)

## THE THANE CAESAR STORY

Many RFK assassination conspiracy theorists have pointed in the direction of a character named Thane Caesar who was on the scene at the time of the senator's murder, employed at the last minute by the Ambassador Hotel as a replacement for another security guard. There are those who suggest, without much real evidence, that Caesar was the "second gun."

Although Caesar has been popularly described as a "bodyguard for Howard Hughes" (the reclusive billionaire), his real connections are far more interesting. Caesar, evidently, had more firm ties to the Meyer Lansky Organized Crime Syndicate through his Las Vegas connections.

## THE INVESTIGATION IS SCUTTLED

In any event, as Robert Morrow notes, later attempts to investigate Ahmand further were frustrated by two CIA operatives on the Los Angeles Police Department's "Special Unit Senator" set up to look into the assassination. Morrow says that the operatives were officers Manny Pena and Enrique Hernandez, both of whom were known to have worked for the CIA.

This, in essence, is the reconstruction of the RFK assassination conspiracy which Morrow documents so precisely and so factually in his book *The Senator Must Die*.

Much of Morrow's research was supported by information he gleaned in an interview with one Alexis Goodaryi of Washington, D.C. Although in his public persona he was the popular *maitre de* of the exclusive Rotunda Restaurant on Capitol Hill, Goodaryi was also the immediate SAVAK superior of Khyber Khan, the West Coast SAVAK operative who coordinated the RFK murder.

Goodaryi himself was murdered in early 1977—just one month after he spoke with Morrow. However, although the media described Goodaryi's murder as a "mob hit," Morrow's sources told him otherwise: it was a SAVAK operation.[701]

## THE LANSKY CONNECTION

All of this is quite interesting, particularly in that Morrow notes that Goodyari told him that during their association, he (Goodyari) introduced Khyber Khan to a number of his Washington associates in organized crime: in particular, one C. H. "Jim" Poller. Mr. Poller, according to Morrow, was the "Washington mob liaison man for [Meyer] Lansky and Santo Trafficante." [702]Thus, we once again see the specter of Meyer Lansky in the murky background in the assassination of a Kennedy.

We might even take one further step. During the time that Sirhan Sirhan was being groomed for his role in the slaying of Robert F. Kennedy, the young Arab-American worked in the stables of the Santa Anita racetrack.

Santa Anita, in fact, was one of the primary profit-centers for Lansky's West Coast henchman, Mickey Cohen, rackets boss of Southern California. We can only speculate that Cohen and his underlings may have had a hand in some aspect of the RFK assassination.

However, it is not speculation that Iran's SAVAK (which handled the killing of Robert F. Kennedy) was closely allied with the American CIA. The record on this is all too clear. The CIA's role in toppling a nationalist Iranian ruler, Mohammed Mossadegh, and restoring the Shah of Iran to his throne in 1953 is well-known and widely documented.

## ISRAEL AND IRAN

What is less-known, however, is the close working relationship between Iran's SAVAK and the Israeli Mossad. Although Iran, a Persian nation, and Israel might be perceived to be hostile to one another, this was not the case at all.

In 1958 Israeli Prime Minister Ben-Gurion proposed to American President Dwight D. Eisenhower a united front against Egyptian leader Gamal Abdel Nasser. According to Ben-Gurion, "With the purpose of erecting a high dam against the Nasserist-Soviet tidal wave, we have begun tightening our links with several states on the outside perimeter of the Middle East. Our goal is to organize a group of countries, not necessarily an official alliance, that will be able to stand strong against Soviet expansion by proxy through Nasser." [703]

Iran was one of those countries that Ben-Gurion proposed be part of this new alliance. Ben-Gurion had it in mind that Iran could be utilized to keep the Arab countries of Iraq and Syria under control. [704]

In fact, Israel had been actively engaged in attempting to interfere in Iran's domestic affairs for some time. According to Andrew and Leslie Cockburn, writing in *Dangerous Liaison: The Inside Story of the U.S.-Israeli Covert Relationship*, "Israeli agents had been at work encouraging friendly forces in Iran since the early days of the state." [705]

The results paid off: in June 1950, for example, Iran had given Israel 'de facto' diplomatic recognition—(a designation just short of full diplomatic recognition).

Although, according to the Cockburns, the relationship between Iran and Israel was uneasy and involved much international intrigue "the connection between the Shah's Iran and Israel rested on firm foundations. The two countries shared a strong suspicion and dislike of the Arab nations on their borders. Both had strong connections to the United States, in particular the CIA."[706]

## IRAN AND THE ISRAELI LOBBY

Additionally, note the Cockburns, "Each [country] had something to offer that the other needed. In Iran's case it was oil, which it began to ship to Israel in 1954. Israel, for its part, could offer valuable expertise in the fields of intelligence, and domestic security. In the eyes of the Shah, Israel had something even more valuable to bestow on its friends: the pervasive influence of the Jews in the United States and indeed the world over.

"[Israeli official] David Kimche recalls with amusement how 'if there'd be any anti-Iranian article in any newspaper in the United States or even in Europe, the Shah would call us and say, 'Why did you allow this to happen?' We would in vain plead innocent [reported Kimche] 'saying that we don't control the whole of world media [and] we don't control the banks as some people think we do.'

"Chaim Herzog [president of Israel] who had many dealings with the Iranian monarch while head of [Israel's] Military Intelligence, later said that [the Shah of Iran] saw every Israeli as a link to Washington." [707]

## SAVAK'S ISRAELI ORIGINS

Mansur Rafizadeh, the former SAVAK chief, who later broke with the Shah, has also provided us additional light on the close relationship between SAVAK, the CIA and the Mossad. Writing in his memoirs, Rafizadeh reveals that SAVAK was set up at the joint urging of Israel, the United States and Britain. [708]

The initial contacts between SAVAK and Mossad appear to have been established in the fall of 1957 at a meeting between General Taimour Bakhtiar and Mossad chief Isser Harel in Rome. They agreed upon mutual interests. [709]

## ISRAEL TRAINS SAVAK

Not only did Israel provide training for the new SAVAK recruits, but so did the CIA. In charge of the CIA's training of SAVAK operatives was an operation known as the International Police Academy in Washington. This academy also played a major part in training operatives of Israel's Mossad. The academy was run by one Joseph Shimon, a man with additional interesting connections. [710]

Shimon counted among his close friends  Chicago Mafia boss Sam Giancana and the Mafia's roving ambassador, Johnny Rosselli, whose own roles in the JFK assassination conspiracy we reviewed in detail in Chapter 11.

Shimon, in fact, also testified before the Senate Intelligence Committee in 1975 that he participated in meetings between Giancana, Rosselli and CIA operatives in Miami in preparation for CIA-Organized Crime assassination plots against Fidel Castro. [711]

## A DELIGHTED SHAH

That the Shah of Iran was pleased by the murder of John F. Kennedy (and certainly that of Robert Kennedy to be sure) is undoubted. According to former SAVAK chief Rafizadeh: "The assassination of President Kennedy on November 22, 1963 made the Shah jubilant. Kennedy had put pressure on him for social reforms. I learned later . . . that the Shah had had a kind of celebration. When he received the news of Kennedy's death, he asked for a drink to celebrate. [712]

"The Shah had despised Kennedy, who constantly advised him to restore human rights to his subjects and insisted that such a course of action was necessary and unavoidable. The Shah viewed that course as a decided threat to his power and so had refused.

"Now the threat posed by Kennedy was gone; the Shah's relationship with President Johnson was comfortable and he felt no fear of the United States despite the huge demonstrations mounted against him in New York, Washington, and indeed throughout the country [when he came to America on state visits]." [713]

(It should be noted, significantly, that Robert Morrow flatly states in his account of the RFK murder that Rafizadeh was, in fact, the SAVAK official in Iran who directed the aforementioned Khyber Khan to orchestrate the RFK assassination plot. Morrow contends that Rafizadeh was promoted to his post as SAVAK chief as a reward for the successful assault on RFK. [714] Thus it is interesting, to say the least, that we find Rafizadeh commenting on the Shah's reaction to JFK's assassination. In his own book, of course, Rafizadeh does not discuss the circumstances surrounding RFK's murder at the hands of the CIA-Mossad-backed SAVAK.)

## PERPETUATING THE COVER-UP

The murder of Robert F. Kennedy by the Shah's SAVAK was a re-affirmation of a long-standing hostility between the Kennedy brothers and the Shah. RFK's murder helped perpetuate the cover-up of the role that SAVAK's allies in the CIA and the Mossad had played in the previous Kennedy assassination. It was again—as in the JFK assassination—a case of mutual interests coming into play.

## RICHARD HELMS AND THE SHAH

There is yet another interesting personal connection between the Shah of Iran and the CIA worth noting.

In fact, in the early 1930's Richard Helms (who later became director of the CIA in 1966) and the Shah had been best friends and schoolmates together as children at the LeRose school in Switzerland. [715] It was Helms who was later the CIA coordinator of the very coup that installed the Shah on the throne in 1953. [716] It was a lifelong relationship which culminated with Helms later becoming U.S. Ambassador to Iran.

Thus it was that through his relationship with Iran and SAVAK, as Robert Morrow notes, that Helms "suddenly would have at his beck and call a worldwide, covert strike-force of dedicated, trained, professional agents and assassins." [717]

It was during his tenure at the CIA, as we have seen in Chapter 8, that Helms was the "chief patron" of the CIA's Mossad liaison, and devoted supporter of Israel, James Jesus Angleton.

And it was after Helms became director that he and Angleton became entangled in a little-noticed controversy involving a CIA memorandum that ostensibly fingered CIA operative E. Howard Hunt as having been in Dallas the day that John F. Kennedy was assassinated. (In Chapter 16, we analyzed that memorandum in detail.)

## THE SECOND KENNEDY

That there was a role by Israel's allies in the CIA and SAVAK in the assassination of Robert F. Kennedy seems clear, based on the information brought forth by Robert Morrow.

SAVAK's role in the assassination of RFK played a major part in the cover-up of the joint Israeli-CIA-Meyer Lansky Crime Syndicate assassination of John F. Kennedy.

# CONCLUSION

## Operation Haman?
## The Theory That Works.
## A Summary

### "Conspired All of Them Together." Nehemiah 4:8

The State of Israel had integral links with all of the major power groups that wanted John F. Kennedy removed from the American presidency.

Israel's global network had the power to orchestrate not only the assassination of Kennedy, but also the subsequent cover-up. Israel was indeed a key player in the JFK assassination conspiracy and, the evidence suggests, the primary instigator of the crime.

All of Israel's co-conspirators—and those who had an interest in seeing Kennedy dead—had good reason to assist in the cover-up. They were protecting their own interests.

By 1963, John F. Kennedy had made many enemies. His brother Attorney General Robert Kennedy's prosecutions of Mafia and Meyer Lansky-bossed Organized Crime figures had many in the crime syndicate very angry, to say the least. The early stages for the prosecution of Meyer Lansky himself were already underway. A case had already been made against Lansky's New Orleans front man Carlos Marcello. Lansky's West Coast henchman Mickey Cohen had been targeted as well.

## LANSKY

Lansky was the ultimate target: the enmity between the Kennedy family and Meyer Lansky went back decades. Not only was the President's father, Joseph P. Kennedy, considered an enemy of the Jewish people, but he was also believed by Lansky to hold a grudge against him (Lansky) because of a Lansky-orchestrated hijacking of one of Kennedy Sr.'s illicit whiskey-running deals. Considering John F. Kennedy's secret alliance with the mob during the 1960 campaign, his war against Lansky's underworld syndicate was a double-cross that could not be tolerated.

## LYNDON JOHNSON

The president was also planning to drop his Vice President, Lyndon Johnson, from the 1964 ticket. It was possible that Johnson—long financed politically by Lansky and his New Orleans Mafia henchman, Carlos Marcello—could end up spending the remainder of his years in prison. The Kennedy brothers were interested in Johnson's deals conducted through his front man, Bobby Baker, who later did end up in prison. Baker, of course, conducted several of his major deals with Lansky associates, including Ed Levinson, a director of the Mossad-linked Banque de Credit International, founded by former Mossad official Tibor Rosenbaum.

## THE ANTI-CASTRO CUBANS

What's more, Kennedy was preparing for a rapprochement with Castro's Cuba and therefore the Lansky syndicate would not be able to re-invigorate its massive gambling interests there as a consequence. The change in Cuban policy was also distressing to the anti-Castro Cuban community in Miami, New Orleans and elsewhere. The anti-Castro Cubans had, of course, been cooperating closely with the Lansky syndicate in anti-Castro activities. Likewise, the new Cuban policy enraged the CIA which was the primary sponsor of the anti-Castro forces.

## THE CIA

What's more, as we have seen, the CIA had also been cooperating with Lansky and his mob lieutenants in assassination plots against Castro. Kennedy had his own problems with the CIA as well. He was making moves to dismantle the CIA and was engaged in a secret war with that agency stemming from not only the "Castro problem" but also Kennedy's intent to withdraw U.S. forces from Vietnam.

## HOOVER

Ultimately, Kennedy planned to merge all of the American intelligence agencies—the FBI included—into a single entity under his brother Robert's direction. This plan, of course, was not greeted enthusiastically by FBI Director J. Edgar Hoover whom Kennedy also planned to dethrone following the 1964 election.

Hoover, as we have seen, had his own secret arrangements with Lansky, individually, and with organized crime in general. Hoover also had a foundation established in his name with funding from Lansky-linked liquor industries and the Anti-Defamation League (ADL) of B'nai B'rith, which functions as a *de facto* U.S. propaganda and intelligence arm of Israel's Mossad.

If Hoover himself did not actively conspire against the life of John F. Kennedy, he certainly looked the other way if he knew that a conspiracy to assassinate JFK had been hatched.

## VIETNAM & DRUGS

Kennedy's intended change in Vietnam policy—his plan to unilaterally withdraw from the imbroglio—infuriated not only the CIA but elements in the Pentagon and their allies in the military-industrial complex.

By this time, of course, the Lansky syndicate had already set up international heroin-running from Southeast Asia through the CIA-linked Corsican Mafia in the Mediterranean.

The joint Lansky-CIA operations in the international drug racket were a lucrative venture that thrived as a consequence of deep U.S. involvement in Southeast Asia as cover for the drug smuggling activities.

## ISRAEL

John F. Kennedy's bitter behind-the-scenes conflict with Israel brought him into combat with an ally of not only the CIA but also the Lansky syndicate, both of which entities also maintained intimate connections to the anti-Castro Cubans.

Vice President Lyndon Johnson's Lansky-Mafia and defense industry ties, coupled with his close relationship to the Israeli lobby, and his long-standing friendly dealings with both the CIA and Hoover's FBI made Johnson an acceptable alternative (among these diverse special interests) to a Kennedy dynasty.

Kennedy himself had long been suspect in the eyes of Israel and its allies in this country as we saw in Chapter 4.

## MICKEY COHEN

As early as 1960 (as we documented in Chapter 13), Meyer Lansky's West Coast henchman, Mickey Cohen, was using Kennedy's filmland bed-partner, actress Marilyn Monroe, as a conduit for attempting to learn Kennedy's intentions toward Israel. Kennedy's introduction to Miss Monroe by one of Cohen's associates, we have learned, was for this very purpose, and also, perhaps, for ultimately blackmailing JFK.

Although "official" history acknowledges the president's stormy affair with Miss Monroe, its real origins—and the intent for which it was orchestrated—have been covered up and forgotten. ("Official" history would have us remember—instead—Kennedy's other widely-publicized illicit relationship with Judith Campbell, mistress of Chicago Mafia boss Sam Giancana.)

Cohen, a long-standing disciple of Israel and one of its earliest adherents, had more than a passing interest in the Middle East state. According to one account, we have discovered, Cohen was less than happy with Kennedy's stance toward Israel.

## BEN-GURION

By April 1963, Kennedy's relationship with Israeli Prime Minister David Ben-Gurion and the state of Israel was at a dangerous impasse, particularly over Israel's determination to develop a nuclear bomb.

At Kennedy's last official press conference, he bemoaned the Israeli lobby's deliberate sabotage of his own efforts to build bridges to the Arab world. Little did JFK know that the seeds of his own destruction had been sown as a consequence of his efforts to bring peace to the Middle East

Israeli leader David Ben-Gurion had developed an intense personal distrust—even hatred and contempt—for Kennedy. He believed that Kennedy's presidency was a danger to the very survival of the state of Israel—the nation that Ben-Gurion had helped create.

Ben-Gurion, by this time, was consumed with paranoia. He believed that Israel might be destroyed. It was because of his contempt for Kennedy and the American president's stance toward Israel that Ben-Gurion left his post as prime minister. It is likely that his last act as prime minister was to order Mossad orchestration of a hit on John F. Kennedy.

We have learned that it was then-Mossad assassination team chief Yitzhak Shamir who took care of the arrangements necessary to set the conspiracy in motion. Shamir knew, of course, that a diverse array of interests—domestic and international—would like to see Kennedy removed from the White House.

There were a variety of components that could be put together to ensure a successful assassination conspiracy: specifically the Mossad-linked Meyer Lansky Organized Crime Syndicate as well as the CIA, and the elements in their spheres of influence.

## CODE NAME 'HAMAN'?

Was there a code name for the conspiracy against President Kennedy? More than likely. But we, of course, will surely never know its name. Did the Mossad, perhaps, call it "Operation Haman"—naming the conspiracy to kill the American president after Haman, the ancient Amalekite conspirator who desired the destruction of the Jewish people? That code name would be as reasonable as any, considering Ben-Gurion's hatred for Kennedy—a modern-day Haman in his eyes.

## THE CONSPIRACY IS SET IN MOTION

A network of assassin recruitment and planning was set in motion through the egis of the  Mossad-CIA-Lansky combine, with the shadowy Permindex entity at the very center of the operation. All stood to benefit from John F. Kennedy's removal from office.

Many people on the periphery of the conspiracy—indeed, perhaps even many of those at the center—did not know how or why they were being directed to undertake many of the actions that they did that advanced the ultimate aim of removing JFK from the White House.

## INSIDE THE CIA . . .

The evidence suggests that it was powerful CIA man, James Jesus Angleton—head of  the CIA's Israel desk—who played the primary role in manipulating the CIA's involvement in the assassination.

Throughout his career, Angleton's activities had intersected with those of the Lansky Organized Crime Syndicate, particularly in the CIA's dealings with the Corsican Mafia.

It was Angleton's Israeli desk at the CIA that coordinated the agency's strange alliance with the Corsican crime figures.

As we have seen, anti-Castro elements in the CIA were involved in setting up the patsy, Lee Harvey Oswald.

In New Orleans, the CIA's assets including Permindex board member Clay Shaw, Anti-Defamation League-linked Guy Banister and David Ferrie were coordinating anti-Castro activities among the Cuban exiles. They were critical to the plot: they were manipulating Lee Harvey Oswald, making him appear as a "pro-Castro agitator."

The inclusion of the eccentric David Ferrie in the plot—a known Kennedy-hater who was on the payroll of New Orleans Mafia boss Carlos Marcello—may well have been a deliberately-staged "false flag" to muddy the waters further and confuse future investigators, perhaps pointing them in the direction of the Mafia.

The WDSU media empire of the Stern family—major backers of Israel's Anti-Defamation League and close friends of Permindex board member Shaw—contributed to the conspiracy by publicizing Oswald's activities and making them available to the FBI, further laying the groundwork for Oswald's identification as a Castro agent.

### THE FRENCH CONNECTION

And as we saw in Chapter 15, there are further indications that CIA-linked French OAS operatives were also utilizing Guy Banister's headquarters in New Orleans.

Many of these same OAS operatives also had ties to the Lansky drug racket. They were also hostile to John F. Kennedy who had supported Algerian independence from France.

What's more, it was the CIA's chief liaison to the anti-Castro Cubans, E. Howard Hunt, who was also liaison to one of the leading longtime OAS operatives, Jean Souetre, whose own alleged presence in Dallas—like that of Hunt—is the subject of some controversy.

As we noted in Chapter 16, a retired French diplomat and intelligence officer contends that it was in fact, a French team that carried out the crime in Dealey Plaza on contract for the Mossad, their presence in Dallas arranged through a faction in the French secret service, the SDECE, under the direction of Col. Georges deLannurien.

### THE 'DUMMY ASSASSINATION'

Evidence suggests that the CIA's E. Howard Hunt may have had his own anti-Castro operation (in the guise of a faked assassination attempt on the president) underway. Oswald, some believe, was part of this operation.

However, it appears that this "faked assassination attempt" was manipulated and/or infiltrated by elements who intended, in fact, to kill the president. Perhaps Hunt himself was as surprised as anybody when those fatal shots were fired in Dallas. Maybe Hunt was, in fact, set up.

Who sent E. Howard Hunt to Dallas in November of 1963? As we have seen it was the Mossad's CIA asset and willing collaborator, James Jesus Angleton. And what was the ostensible purpose of Hunt's dealings in Dallas at that fateful period in time?

Only Hunt can answer these questions—and others—but thus far he has refused to provide the answers. Was Hunt—like Oswald—a patsy?

Hunt himself admitted, under oath, that he believed it possible that his former colleagues at the CIA would consider framing him for the Kennedy assassination. However, Hunt has never explained—at least publicly—what he was doing in Dallas on November 21, 1963, the day before John F. Kennedy's assassination. Instead, Hunt says he was not there.

Did Hunt actually play a hand in the assassination planning? Or was he a not-so-really-innocent bystander who was caught up in events that were bigger than even he realized? We will probably never know the truth.

As we have seen, various sources have suggested that there were at least several people operating in Dealey Plaza on November 22 who believed that they were there as part of a "Mafia" hit aimed not at Kennedy, but instead at Texas Governor John B. Connally who was riding in the president's limousine.

The use of "false flags," has been a classic Mossad tactic, a standard practice of Israel's spy agency. And as we saw in Chapter 16, according to former Mossad operative, Victor Ostrovsky, he and his fellow Mossad trainees were told by their superiors that Kennedy's assassination was, in fact, an accident. The real target, or so the Mossad claimed, was Connally who had been targeted by "the Mafia."

## JACK RUBY

As we saw in Chapter 13, Mickey Cohen appears to have had a important role in the life of Jack Ruby, who admired Cohen and who tried to emulate the California racketeer.

Ruby himself was knee-deep in the CIA's activities in Cuba, alongside the CIA's allies in the Lansky Organized Crime Syndicate. The evidence strongly suggests, of course, that Ruby—in some fashion—was moving in the same circles as Lee Harvey Oswald, although what direct connection there was between the two ill-fated men we will never know.

Just shortly before the assassination, Al Gruber, a Hollywood henchman of Mickey Cohen and a longtime friend of Ruby's (who hadn't seen him in nearly a decade) showed up in Dallas to visit Ruby. And it was just about an hour after Lee Harvey Oswald's arrest was made public that Ruby called Gruber. It is probable that Ruby called Gruber to advise him that the chosen patsy had not been killed before his arrest as planned. It was then that Ruby was told it was his responsibility to finish the job.

Cohen's friend and lawyer, Melvin Belli, of course, assumed a role as Ruby's handler and defense counsel after Ruby killed Oswald, thereby silencing the chosen patsy forever. And as we have seen, Belli himself also emerged as a prominent defender of the Warren Commission cover-up.

Columnist Dorothy Kilgallen discovered that J. Edgar Hoover's FBI was assisting Ruby's defense. Ruby had probably been assured that he would not face prison or the electric chair for killing Oswald. When, in fact, he was convicted, he was granted a second trial on appeal. However, Ruby conveniently "died of natural causes" shortly before the scheduled re-trial.

Many have suspected that Ruby was poisoned or injected with some fast-acting cancer cells. However, as we have seen, there is the distinct possibility that Ruby did not die at that time and was quietly whisked out of the country to Israel. (He may be alive today.)

## ANGLETON & THE COVER-UP

It was James Jesus Angleton of the CIA who attempted to perpetrate the fraud that the Soviet KGB was behind the Kennedy assassination.

Angleton vehemently disputed the reliability of Soviet defector Yuri Nosenko who insisted that he had been Oswald's KGB handler in the Soviet Union and who said that Oswald had not been a KGB agent.

As we have seen, Angleton was—at his own insistence—the CIA's key "point man" in the agency's relationship with the Warren Commission. What's more, Angleton's close friend, William Sullivan, number three man at the FBI, was the FBI's liaison with the commission.

It was, perhaps not coincidentally, Angleton (through a strange in-house CIA memo) who fingered CIA man E. Howard Hunt for possible involvement in the Kennedy assassination, presumably as a "renegade" agent, acting on his own. This frame-up took place at precisely the time when public suspicion of the CIA's institutional involvement was being widely discussed. In Chapter 16 we analyzed that memorandum in detail.

## EARL WARREN

Chief Justice Earl Warren, apprised by the CIA of possible Soviet Communist involvement in the president's murder was pressured into covering up what he mistakenly believed to be the truth about the assassination.

The CIA's "Mexico City scenario"—handled by Angleton's desk at the CIA—was presented to Warren as proof that the Soviets were implicated in the president's murder.

Pinning the assassination on "one lone nut" was Warren's way of protecting America's national security. A war with Soviet Russia, Warren believed, had been prevented. Warren himself probably never had any idea as to the real truth—or even part of the truth—as to what really happened or where the assassination conspiracy originated.

Any effort by Warren to probe deeper would no doubt have been scuttled immediately: after all, one of his fellow commission members was former CIA Director Allen Dulles who had, in fact, been fired by JFK.

What's more, Philadelphia attorney Arlen Specter, a key figure on the commission, would have stood in the way of any probe of any possible Israeli involvement **(had such involvement ever even been considered.)**

Specter, who later won election to the U.S. Senate, has been one of Israel's foremost proponents in Congress. Today, Specter's own American-born sister is living in Israel, having made "aliyah"—as did Meyer Lansky (and perhaps, as we have seen, maybe even Jack Ruby).

Additionally, Warren was also under the influence of his close friend, syndicated columnist Drew Pearson, himself an asset and longtime collaborator of Israel's propaganda and intelligence arm in this country, the Anti-Defamation League of B'nai B'rith. It was Pearson who floated the blatantly fraudulent story that Fidel Castro had been the prime mover behind the JFK assassination.

## FALSE LEADS

False trails and false leads were set in place throughout the chain of events that led up to the assassination—and afterward—a standard Mossad tactic. "False flags" were positioned to point the finger of blame elsewhere.

Even Lyndon Johnson himself may not have known from where the order to kill Kennedy emerged, although there have been allegations (never documented) that Johnson himself was in on the assassination planning. Johnson certainly had no reason himself to intervene or to attempt to stop the assassination from being carried out.

## ROBERT F. KENNEDY

The assassination of Senator Robert F. Kennedy—with an Arab as the "false flag"—the fall guy—was a part of the continuing cover-up of the murder of President Kennedy. In the RFK assassination, as we have seen, the Iranian SAVAK—a joint creature of the CIA and the Israeli Mossad—was responsible for coordinating the hit on the senator. Robert Kennedy's death prevented the younger Kennedy from ever bringing his brother's killers to justice.

## ISRAEL & THE MEDIA

Researchers into the JFK assassination over the past 28 years have not, until just recently, had access to the evidence of Kennedy's secret war with Israel over the nuclear bomb. As a consequence, there has never been any suspicion that Israel—like other often-named suspects in the crime—may have had a reason to collaborate in a conspiracy against John F. Kennedy.

The controlled media with its devotion to Israel, of course, has never pointed in this direction. The media has been content with promoting the theory that "The Mafia Killed JFK"—but the media ignores the Lansky connection. And those who go so far as to suggest that the CIA somehow had a part in the killing and the cover-up are presented as "kooks" and "conspiracy theorists."

Obviously, the full truth—all of the sordid details—will never be known. As a consequence, we must rely upon the information that we do have—information that enables us to make a final judgment.

## THE IMPACT OF THE ASSASSINATION

The assassination of John F. Kennedy had a major political impact, far more profound than the simple elevation of Lyndon Johnson to the presidency. There were several direct consequences of JFK's death—both in the U.S. and abroad:

• Preservation of the CIA's autonomy;
• Protection of J. Edgar Hoover's FBI empire;
• A change in Vietnam policy, resulting in
  (a) a profitable war for Lyndon Johnson's allies in the military-industrial complex; and
  (b) a continuing cover for ever-expanding joint CIA-Lansky drug-smuggling operations out of Southeast Asia.
• An end to the burgeoning crackdown on the Lansky Organized Crime Syndicate; and
• A drastic reversal in U.S. policy toward Israel.

**It is, beyond question, the final result that is the most striking of all, and not subject to debate.**

While there are those who contend that John F. Kennedy would, in fact, have continued American involvement in Vietnam, **one cannot dispute the clear and now widely-documented fact that JFK was engaged in a fierce battle with Israel on several fronts and that upon Kennedy's demise, U.S. Middle East policy took an immediate 180-degree turnabout.**

In the pages of *Final Judgment* we have outlined, for the first time, **the entirety of the conspiracy** that led to the assassination of John F. Kennedy and the cover-up that followed.

We do not pretend to have all of the answers, but we believe that many missing pieces of the puzzle have now been supplied.

Most of the critical information compiled in the pages of this work has been published in a wide variety of independent sources, many of which do not even focus on the assassination of John F. Kennedy. Never before, however, has the evidence been assembled in this fashion.

## A SMALL CIRCLE OF CONSPIRATORS

The close connections between a relatively **small circle** of people and those operating in their immediate spheres of influence is not coincidence. That all of them, in some fashion, were part of the circumstances surrounding the assassination of John F. Kennedy is also no coincidence.

Critics of JFK assassination conspiracy theories contend that a conspiracy so immense would require a vast number of people involved. In fact, the actual mechanics of the conspiracy described in *Final Judgment* involve perhaps less than twenty people at a maximum. Most of the people involved in the actual assassination planning were probably not even aware of the activities of others at other levels of the conspiracy.

Let us name, for the record, those whom we believe had **advance knowledge that John F. Kennedy was going to be killed** on November 22, 1963. They are:

• Israeli Prime Minister David Ben-Gurion;
• Israeli Mossad assassinations chief Yitzhak Shamir;
• Permindex chief executive officer Louis M. Bloomfield;
• Mossad officer and Permindex banker Rabbi Tibor Rosenbaum;
• CIA Counterintelligence chief James J. Angleton;
• French intelligence officer Georges deLannurien;
• Crime Syndicate boss Meyer Lansky;
• Tampa Mafia chief (and Lansky lieutenant) Santo Trafficante, Jr;
• New Orleans Mafia chief (and Lansky lieutenant) Carlos Marcello;
• Mafia "ambassador" Johnny Rosselli;
• Chicago Mafia boss Sam Giancana; and
• The actual shooters in Dealey Plaza. Evidence strongly points toward French mercenary Michael Mertz as one of those gunmen. Cuban exiles Guillermo and Ignacio Novo also appear to have been involved.

**PEOPLE ON THE PERIPHERY . . .**

Here are those persons who were engaged in **some form of activity that tied them to the assassination** (whether or not they were aware that an actual assassination would indeed take place):

• Lee Harvey Oswald;
• CIA operative E. Howard Hunt;
• CIA station chief for Mexico City, David Atlee Phillips;
• CIA contract agent and Permindex board member Clay Shaw;
• CIA contract agent Guy Banister;
• CIA contract agent David Ferrie;
• Maurice Brooks Gatlin; Permindex courier;
• CIA contract agent Robert Morrow;
• Meyer Lansky's West Coast henchman, Mickey Cohen;
• Israeli diplomat (later Prime Minister) Menachem Begin;
• Mickey Cohen's associate Al Gruber;
• Dallas mob associate Jack Ruby; and
• CIA associate, U.S. Senator John Tower.

Various members of the CIA, figures in the Mafia and the Lansky Syndicate, FBI Director J. Edgar Hoover, and some investigators for the Warren Commission and the subsequent House Assassinations Committee may have gleaned some information over the years as to portions of what had happened, but few, if any, would be aware of the entirety of the conspiracy.

Those on the periphery participated in various aspects of the cover-up (for their own reasons) as did certain figures in the media such as Drew Pearson and Jack Anderson, among others.

There is also a final person who learned a part of how the conspiracy was carried out: French President Charles DeGaulle, whose own intelligence service was compromised by the Israeli Mossad.

**A FINAL JUDGMENT . . .**

The evidence we have put forth demonstrates that there is a very strong foundation for the thesis presented in this volume. It is a scenario that does make sense.

This is our final judgment: the government of Israel, through its secret spy agency, the Mossad, orchestrated the conspiracy that ended the life of John F. Kennedy.

Through its own vast resources and through its international contacts in the intelligence community and in organized crime, Israel had the means, it had the motive, and it had the opportunity to carry out the crime of the century—and did.

# APPENDIX ONE

## Where Was George?
### George Bush, the CIA, and the Kennedy Assassination
### Did GHWB Have a Hand in the Murder of JFK?

When Sen. Edward M. Kennedy cynically asked "Where was George?" during a fiery address to the 1988 Democratic National Convention, was the senator hinting, perhaps, that he knew something that we didn't know? Was Kennedy really asking "Where was George Herbert Walker Bush on November 22, 1963?"

Newly-emerging evidence strongly suggests not only that George Bush has been a CIA asset for most of his adult life—since his college days in fact—but that he also has had unusually intimate ties to the circumstances surrounding the JFK assassination and the subsequent high-level cover-up.

In his best-selling *Plausible Denial*, author Mark Lane did a great service to the American public when he re-published, as appendices, two important articles that appeared in *The Nation* magazine, but which received little national notice outside the elite circles who read that journal.

As a consequence, hundreds of thousands of Americans learned something that they might not otherwise know: the evidence strongly suggests that George Herbert Walker Bush was an active CIA operative on November 23, 1963.

The *Nation* articles, written by Richard McBride (published in the July 16/23 and August 13/20, 1988 issues) took note of a declassified FBI memorandum dated November 29, 1963. The memorandum, from FBI Director J. Edgar Hoover, was addressed to the Director of the Bureau of Intelligence and Research at the Department of State. The subject was "Assassination of President John F. Kennedy - November 22, 1963." The memo read as follows:

Our Miami, Florida, Office on November 23, 1963 advised that the office of Coordinator of Cuban Affairs in Miami advised that the Department of State feels some misguided anti-Castro group might capitalize on the present situation and undertake an unauthorized raid against Cuba, believing that the assassination of President John F. Kennedy might herald a change in U.S. policy, which is not true.

Our sources and informants familiar with Cuban matters in the Miami area advise that the general feeling in the anti-Castro Cuban community is one of stunned disbelief and, even among those who did not entirely agree with the President's policy concerning Cuba, the feeling is that the President's death represents a great loss not only to the U.S. but to all of Latin America. These sources know of no plans for unauthorized action against Cuba.

An informant who has furnished reliable information in the past and who is close to a small pro-Castro group in Miami has advised that these individuals are afraid that the assassination of the President may result in strong repressive measures being taken against them and, although pro-Castro in their feelings, regret the assassination.

The substance of the foregoing information was orally furnished to Mr. George Bush of the Central Intelligence Agency and Captain William Edwards of the Defense Intelligence Agency on November 23, 1963, by Mr. W. T. Forsyth of this Bureau.[718]

Copies of Mr. Hoover's memorandum were circulated to a number of individuals including, among others, the director of the CIA (John McCone) and marked to the attention of "Deputy Director, Plans." (This was Richard Helms).

Needless to say, the existence of this memorandum presented a problem for George Bush who had claimed to have had no prior service with the CIA prior to his appointment as director of the agency in 1976. However, Bush's spokesmen suggested that there must have been another "George Bush" working for the CIA at the time in question and that it was he who was referenced in the controversial Hoover memorandum.

Richard McBride, the author of the *Nation* articles, did some checking, only to find out that there was indeed a George William Bush who had worked for the CIA at the time—and for a very short time—and only as a low-level researcher and analyst. George William Bush told McBride that he was never part of any inter-agency briefing and knew neither of the other people referred to in the memorandum. In short, this George Bush was not the George Bush in the memorandum.[719]

## INITIATION

So where was George Herbert Walker Bush on November 23, 1963? Evidently working, as he had been for some time, as an operative for the Central Intelligence Agency. New research suggests that Bush was with the CIA as long ago as his college days at Yale.

Anthony Kimery, an investigative reporter who has been researching George Bush's relationship with the CIA, notes that: "The CIA's full-time salaried headhunter at Yale was crew coach Allen 'Skip' Waltz, a former naval intelligence officer who had a good view of Bush. As a member of Yale's Undergraduate Athletic Association and Undergraduate Board of Deacons, Bush had to have worked closely with Waltz on the university's athletic programs from which the coach picked most of the men he steered to the CIA. It is inconceivable Waltz didn't try to recruit Bush, say former Agency officials recruited at Yale."[720]

It was while a student at Yale, of course, that Bush was a member of the secret Skull and Bones fraternity which has been well-known as a CIA recruiting ground for many years. (One of Bush's fellow "Bonesmen" is Yale man, William F. Buckley, Jr., himself a former CIA man.)

What's more, it was another Bonesman, Henry Neil Mallon, longtime chairman of the board of Dresser Industries, based in Houston, who gave Bush his first job in the oil business. Mallon, a classmate and close family friend of Bush's father, Senator Prescott Bush, set young Bush up as a salesman for International Derrick and Equipment Company (IDECO), a subsidiary of Dresser.

However, as Anthony Kimery comments, "Bush's job, peddling IDECO's services, including behind the Iron Curtain, was a curious responsibility, considering Bush's inexperience in either the oil industry or international relations."[721] All of this, together, of course, suggests that Bush, in fact, was operating as a CIA asset under the cover of Dresser Industries, which, according to Kimery's sources, "routinely served as a CIA cover."[722]

## THE TWO GEORGES

It was Henry Mallon who apparently introduced Bush to an international petroleum engineer who later emerged as one of the genuine "mystery men" in the JFK assassination: Lee Harvey Oswald's friend—and suspected "CIA handler"—George DeMohrenschildt whose CIA connections we examined in Chapter 9.

The two Georges became so well acquainted, in fact, that DeMohrenschildt's address book not only included Bush's home address and telephone number in Midland, Texas where Bush lived from 1953 until 1959, but also the oilman's youthful nickname, "Poppy." Kimery says that his sources contend that Bush and DeMohrenschildt continued to meet secretly in Houston after Bush had left Midland to set up the Houston office of his Zapata Off-Shore Oil Company.

(Kimery points out that in his testimony to the Warren Commission DeMohrenschildt admitted that he made frequent trips to Houston beginning in the late 1950's but that he gave vague explanations as to the purpose of the trips.)

Kimery's research suggests that the Bush-DeMohrenschildt relationship stemmed from not only their mutual interests in the oil business, but also from their mutual background in intelligence work.

According to Kimery, DeMohrenschildt was part of a spy network OSS man (and later CIA Director) Allen Dulles ran inside the Nazi intelligence community and later began working for the CIA "operating under the guise of a consulting petroleum geologist specializing in making deals between U.S. oil companies and the East-bloc nations to which [DeMohrenschildt] was remarkably well-connected."[723]

As a consequence, then, it is not surprising then that CIA asset George Bush, working in the Eastern bloc in the oil business and CIA asset George DeMohrenschildt, working in the Eastern bloc in the oil business, would have ultimately come together. According to former CIA official Victor Marchetti (who specialized in Soviet affairs for the CIA), "It's inconceivable that the CIA didn't debrief Bush after each and every meeting

[Bush had with East bloc representatives]. "Businessmen with dealings like [Bush had] were routinely debriefed."[724]

All of these dealings between Bush and DeMohrenschildt would appear to be innocent behind-the-scenes intrigue between two spies named George if it weren't for the fact that the more one traces Bush's connections, the more one finds that the CIA man is enmeshed all the more deeply in the circumstances surrounding the assassination of John F. Kennedy.

## THE ANTI-CASTRO OPERATIONS

For instance, the evidence strongly suggests that Bush, in fact, was a major player in the CIA's drive to destroy Fidel Castro. According to Anthony Kimery, "Veteran CIA operatives in the war against Castro say Bush not only let the CIA use Zapata as a front for running some of its operations (including the use of several off-shore drilling platforms), but assert that Bush personally served as a conduit through which the Agency disbursed money for contracted services."[725]

Kimery contends that he has several sources who contend, independently, that Bush was indeed deeply involved in CIA operations, particularly in the Caribbean and in the campaign against Castro. This seems to jibe with information provided by Col. Fletcher Prouty who points out that not only was the CIA's top-secret code name for the Bay of Pigs invasion "Operation Zapata" (as in Bush's company) but that two of the ships utilized in the operation were christened the *Houston* (Bush's home base) and the *Barbara* (Bush's wife's name). [726]

## SHACKLEY—YET AGAIN

Bush's connections to the CIA's operations against Castro go even deeper, however. According to Kimery, "There is evidence that prior to Bush's appointment as DCI in 1976, he was well-acquainted with legendary spook Theodore George "Ted" Shackley who joined the Agency in 1951. When Bush arrived on the scene at Langley, it was clear to longtime Agency insiders that there was a bond between these two men that went back many years."[727]

This, of course, is the same Theodore Shackley whom we first met in Chapter 8 as a friend of Israel's secret nuclear development program. It was Shackley who served as CIA Station Chief in Miami, then the largest CIA station in the world, and the base of the CIA's operations against Castro being jointly conducted with Meyer Lansky's syndicate henchmen.

(It is worth noting, if only in passing, that the Israeli Mossad itself maintains one of its largest North American bases in Miami—the longtime headquarters of its organized crime collaborator—Meyer Lansky.)[728]

It was from the CIA's base in Miami, we learned from former CIA operative Marita Lorenz (in Chapter 9 and in Chapter 16) that a two-car caravan carrying anti-Castro Cubans and several CIA figures was dispatched to Dallas, arriving just prior to the assassination of President John F. Kennedy.

Kimery quotes a former CIA operative who was involved in the anti-Castro operations: "You've got ole George baby helping the Company's operation against Castro and here's Shackley in charge of the Miami station that's running that show. Now how do you think they know each other my friend? Their's was a damn close relationship—still is."[729]

And, as we noted in Chapter 12, it was Shackley, again, who was the CIA's chief of station for the CIA in Laos during the Vietnam War—this during a period when the CIA and the Lansky syndicate were jointly engaged in lucrative drug-running operations.

Kimery points out that, "In 1976, shortly after he became DCI, without seeking advice, Bush promoted Shackley to Associate Deputy Director of Operations. In this position, he was second in command to the [Deputy Director of Operations]—the third most powerful position in the CIA and one of the most pivotal in the entire government."[730]

## THE MOSSAD CONNECTION

After leaving the CIA, as we noted in Chapter 12, Bush's friend Shackley later went into the international arms business and worked closely with the Aviation Trade and Service Company, a creation of Israeli Mossad figure Shaul Eisenberg.

Bush himself, however, was also developing intimate ties with Israel, ties which, of course, had been cemented during his service as CIA director. In 1979, then Republican presidential candidate Bush attended the Jerusalem Conference on International Terrorism, an event hosted by the Israeli government and attended by most of Israel's top intelligence officials. The delegates to the conference from the United States were all tried-and-true friends of Israel, Democrat and Republican alike.[731]

Accompanying Bush were Major General George Keegan, former chief of intelligence for the U.S. Air Force, and Harvard Professor Richard Pipes. Keegan and Pipes were part of an elite group formed by Bush while serving as CIA director that operated under the name "Team B." [732]

Bush's Team B was a new, secret supervisory body for the CIA empowered to re-evaluate, criticize or dismiss the CIA's intelligence reports. Significantly, however, Team B was composed of a clique of high-level officials who were bound together primarily by their devotion to advancing Israel's interests.

Among the more notable members included Richard Perle, who ultimately became assistant secretary of defense in charge of international security policy and Perle's longtime associate, Stephen Bryen, a former Senate staff member who was forced to resign his post after it was discovered that he had passed U.S. defense secrets to Israel's Mossad.[733]

That Bush should have been affiliated so closely with this select group of devotees of Israel is intriguing, particularly in light of Bush's subsequent conflicts with Israel's Mossad, which we first examined in Chapter 2.

## THE COVER-UP

For his own part, it was while Bush served as CIA Director that the Senate Intelligence Committee was probing the connections between Jack Ruby, Lee Harvey Oswald, the CIA, organized crime and the anti-Castro operations conducted by the CIA and its mob collaborators. As Anthony Kimery comments: "With his own ties to those operations, Bush was now in charge of what the CIA would and wouldn't divulge."

"As DCI [Bush] frustrated committee investigator's requests for specific information in the Agency's files on Oswald and Ruby and downplayed revelations about CIA involvement. Memoranda written by Bush on the intelligence committee's investigation of Oswald's and Ruby's links to the CIA and organized crime show he was especially interested in the committee's probing not only of what the CIA knew about the events in Dallas and didn't report to the Warren Commission, but to what extent, if any, the Agency was complicit in Kennedy's murder."[734]

Kimery quotes an ex-CIA contract agent and Bay of Pigs veteran who claims to have been associated with Bush in the CIA's anti-Castro operations in the early 1960's: "Bush was worried about something during those investigations when he was DCI, all right. He was worried it was going to be found out that he worked for the Company and was tied right into all the messes the CIA was in during the late 50s and early 60s."[735]

David Robb, writing in *Spy* magazine points out that although Bush was asked in January of 1992 whether or not he had looked into the JFK assassination during the time he was CIA director that Bush said, "No, I didn't have any curiosity . . ."[736] However, Robb has pinpointed a September 15, 1976 memo to the Deputy Director for Central Intelligence which reads as follows:

"A recent Jack Anderson story referred to a November 1963 (?) CIA cable, the subject matter of which had some UK journalist observing Jack Ruby visiting [Santo] Trafficante in jail. Is there such a cable? If so I would like to see it. This is the same cable that Mike Hadigan, Minority Counsel for the SSC [Senate Select Committee] had asked for." [737]

The memo was signed "GB" above the typewritten name "George Bush." Clearly, George Bush was just a bit more curious about the inquiries into the JFK assassination than he would have us believe.

## A THREAT AGAINST JFK?

And, curiously enough, there is this interesting tidbit unearthed by *Spy* magazine suggesting that Bush had an inordinate interest in John F. Kennedy's welfare. According to *Spy*: "Internal FBI memos indicate that on November 22, 1963, 'reputable businessman' George H. W. Bush 'telephonically advised that he wanted to relate some hearsay that he had heard in recent weeks, date and source unknown. He advised that one James

Parrott has been talking of killing the president when he comes to Houston."[738]

Parrott was a 24-year-old Young Republican who regularly picketed Kennedy administration officials when they came to Houston. The FBI also learned that the Secret Service had been told—in 1961—that Parrott had said he "would kill President Kennedy if he ever got near him." Parrott denies the charges. *Spy* asks—not entirely satirically—"Was Bush just being a misguided do-good weenie? Or was he trying to throw the FBI off the trail?"[739]

## ISRAEL AGAIN . . .

It was after George Bush left the CIA in 1977 that he continued to maintain close ties with business interests which had, in turn, intimate ties to Israel and its lobby in this country.

Returning home to Houston, Bush was named to serve as executive committee chairman of the First International Bank of Houston, the family-owned enterprise of the heirs of Texas billionaire H. L. Hunt.

The Hunts were owners of a 15% controlling interest in Gulf Resources and Chemical Corporation, a Houston based company which controlled half the world's supply of lithium, which is an essential component in the production of hydrogen bombs.

Among the board members of Gulf Resources was George A. Butler, chairman of Houston's Post Oak Bank, controlled by one W. S. Farish, III, often described as one of Bush's closest confidants.

Gulf Resources had taken over the Lithium Corporation of America as a wholly-owned subsidiary some years previously. Among the directors of both Gulf Resources and the Lithium Corporation was John Roger Menke, who was also a director of Israel's Hebrew Technical Institute.

All of this is significant in that it was during this period that Israel was continuing in its secret development of nuclear weaponry, the most monumental issue of conflict between John F. Kennedy and Israeli prime minister David Ben-Gurion, discussed in detail in Chapter 5.[740]

## THE ADL AGAIN

Perhaps, then, it is no surprise that Robert Allen, the chairman of Gulf Resources—a non-Jew not known as a contributor to Jewish causes—received the so-called "Torch of Liberty" award from the Anti-Defamation League (ADL) of B'nai B'rith, the self-styled "civil rights" organization that functions as an American intelligence arm for Israel's Mossad.

(It was in Chapter 8 that we first met another Torch of Liberty recipient, gangster Morris Dalitz, a longtime top-level associate of Meyer Lansky and an investor in the shadowy Permindex corporation which, as we saw in Chapter 15, played the central role in the JFK assassination conspiracy.)

It is also probably worth pointing out that another director of both Gulf Resources and Lithium Corp. was Samuel H. Rogers who was, in turn, a director of industrialist Dwayne Andreas' Archer Daniel Midland Corp.[741]

The aforementioned Andreas, it just so happens, has been a major financial backer of the ADL for many years and has been a close associate of two major national ADL officials, Burton Joseph, ADL national chairman from 1976-1978 and Max M. Kampelman, a national ADL honorary vice chairman.[742]

All of this taken together places George Bush in the center of a wide-ranging network of international corporate bodies with long-standing ties to Israel and its major backers—including one corporation with a particular interest in the development of nuclear weaponry.

## THE H. L. HUNT CONNECTION

The Hunt connection, which brings the complex series of inter-relationships full circle, is also interesting, inasmuch as, for years, JFK assassination researchers, have tried, albeit unsuccessfully, to pinpoint the late H. L. Hunt as the mastermind behind the JFK assassination, presumably driven by his hard-line conservative opposition to Kennedy's progressive domestic and foreign policy stands.

What those who have been pointing the finger at Hunt have failed to do, however, is to trace Hunt's connection back to the Gulf Resources Corp. with its own intimate links to Israel.

These facts do not prove or disprove a role by either H. L. Hunt or George Bush—together or alone—in the JFK assassination conspiracy. However, they do pinpoint the strange—and little-noticed—role played by Israel and its high-level backers in the ever-converging circles surrounding the JFK assassination conspiracy. For the record they need to be noted.

## WHERE WAS GEORGE?

In any case, Bush's closest associates during his CIA years, as we have seen, and his activities, have all repeatedly bound Bush to circumstances which tie together the CIA and the Meyer Lansky Organized Crime Syndicate in joint ventures not only in the Castro assassination plots of the early 1960's, but the joint CIA-Lansky drug-running operations in Southeast Asia. Bush's own ties to the Israeli lobby thus cement the circle.

The evidence we have reviewed here suggests that perhaps George Bush does indeed know more about the assassination of John F. Kennedy than he might be willing to admit. Whether Bush will ever tell what he knows is another matter entirely.

Yet, for the record, it seems appropriate to catalogue these intriguing details so that someday, when all is said and done, we can also reach a final judgment about that other matter: "Where was George?"

## APPENDIX TWO

### The Man From the Klan—
### Lee Harvey Oswald's "Nazi" Connection
#### The Alleged Assassin's Little-Known Ties to Undercover
#### Intelligence Operatives in the Neo-Nazi Underground

Among those whose names appeared in Lee Harvey Oswald's address book was one Daniel Burros. In 1963, Burros was national secretary of George Lincoln Rockwell's American Nazi Party. Just two years after the JFK assassination, however, Burros died mysteriously of multiple gunshot wounds. However, despite the strange circumstances of Burros' demise, his death was ruled a suicide.

Burro's strange death took place in the home of his close associate, the ubiquitous and enigmatic Roy Frankhouser, a long-time federal intelligence undercover operative in the Minutemen, the Ku Klux Klan and the Communist Party USA. Frankhauser, it just so happens, claims to have been associated with Lee Harvey Oswald prior to the assassination of John F. Kennedy.

The story of Lee Harvey Oswald's possible connection to Daniel Burros has never been explored in any other work on the JFK assassination. Yet, the evidence, as we shall see, suggests that there is much more to the Oswald-Burros connection than meets the eye.

Although JFK assassination researchers have long been busy compiling, recompiling, editing and re-editing lists of "mysterious deaths" among people with links—both real and perhaps sometimes imagined—to the JFK assassination, Burros' name never pops up.

Burros' name does not even appear in the comprehensive list compiled by Jim Marrs in his mammoth JFK assassination conspiracy overview *Crossfire*, even though, of all things, Marrs includes numerous people who died from what appear to have simply been natural causes. But Burros— who died from three gunshot wounds—does not appear on the list.

The circumstances of Dan Burros' death were quite bizarre. Just one day before the "Nazi" leader died in October of 1965, he had been publicly exposed in the *New York Times* as having been born to Jewish parents. This expose was the ostensible trigger that led to Burro's "suicide" at the Reading, Pennsylvania home of his fellow "Nazi," Roy Frankhauser.

### BURROS AN INFORMANT?

Although Burro's death was trumpeted in the media as the story of a nice Jewish boy gone haywire, the fact is that some members of the American Nazi underground have long felt that Burros was not a Jewish apostate, but, instead, an active informant and agent provocateur of the Anti-Defamation League (ADL) of B'nai B'rith operating within the ranks of the so-called "racist right."

In his short career in the political underworld, Dan Burros is known to have indeed been closely associated with ADL undercover informants and was perhaps such an informant himself, although it is unlikely that the full truth will ever be known.

What is known, however, is that Burros was a key figure in the New York City-based National Renaissance Party, a small neo-Nazi entity founded by the late James H. Madole. Although Madole was apparently a dyed-in-the-wool Nazi, it is an established fact that his organization was infiltrated, funded in part and manipulated by agents of the ADL's undercover spy apparatus.

The ADL's operative inside the NRP was one Emmanuel Trujillo who also went by the name Mana Truhill. In turn, Truhill worked closely with Sanford Griffith, then the ADL's chief spymaster.

Two "right wing" activists of the 1950s era—author Eustace Mullins and businessman DeWest Hooker (referenced in Chapter 4)—have confirmed to this author that the ADL was indeed active in "infiltrating" rightist groups at the time and that the aforementioned Griffith was a familiar figure moving in and out of the right-wing orbit during the period.

During the heyday of Madole's ADL-manipulated organization well-known maverick New York publisher Lyle Stuart publicly accused the ADL of financing American Nazi groups—such as Madole's outfit—for its own insidious ends.

The nature of the allegation—coupled with the prominence and credibility of the source (Stuart was a respected publisher who happened to be Jewish himself)—should have raised eyebrows, although Stuart's explosive charge received no media attention whatsoever.

That Daniel Burros was himself deeply a part of this unusual circle being manipulated by the ADL is an intriguing fact. But there's much more to the story of the Oswald-Burros connection.

## THE MINUTEMEN ...

Some JFK assassination researchers have focused on New Orleans private detective and CIA contract agent Guy Banister's ties to Robert DePugh and the paramilitary group known as the Minutemen as proof that "right wing extremists" were perhaps behind the JFK assassination. As we noted in some detail in Chapter 15, however, there is strong evidence to suggest that Banister was also being deployed by the Anti-Defamation League (ADL) of B'nai B'rith in its own "fact-finding" operations aimed against left-leaning civil rights groups.

The evidence regarding the Minutemen, however, suggests that the Minutemen were, for all intents and purposes, a government-infiltrated—perhaps even government-controlled—"right wing extremist" outfit.

It is the Minutemen link that opens up the door in the Oswald-Burros connection to some highly unusual facts about a strange individual named Roy Frankhauser who just happens to have been associated with both Oswald and Burros.

John George and Laird Wilcox, in *Nazis, Communists, Klansmen, and Others on the Fringe*, have provided us with a wealth of information about Frankhauser's operations inside domestic political organizations—the Minutemen in particular.

Here's what George and Wilcox wrote about the government's infiltration of the Minutemen and the role of the aforementioned Roy Frankhauser:

The Minutemen, in fact, were among the most thoroughly infiltrated of all domestic far right groups. According to Eric Norden, in his long essay on the paramilitary right appearing in the June 1969 issue of *Playboy* magazine, virtually all of the major Minutemen cases were cracked with the assistance of government infiltrators and informants.

One of these informants was a nightmare named Roy Frankhauser, a professional government infiltrator whose alliance with [Robert] DePugh [of the Minutemen] began in the early 1960s, shortly after the organization was formed. Frankhauser was well-known for having taken the Fifth Amendment thirty-three times when questioned about his Ku Klux Klan involvement by the House Un-American Activities Committee in 1965. Unaware of Frankhauser's role, Norden interviewed him extensively for his article. Frankhauser, whom DePugh had made a regional coordinator, portrayed the Minutemen to Norden as a neo-Nazi organization to be feared and reckoned with:

"Hitler had the Jews; we've got the niggers. We have to put our main stress on the nigger question, of course, because that's what preoccupies the masses—but we're not forgetting the Jew. If the Jews knew what was coming—and believe me, it's coming as surely as the dawn—they'd realize that what's going to happen in America will make Nazi Germany look like a Sunday-school picnic. We'll build better gas chambers, and more of them, and this time there won't be any refugees.

Norden notes that Frankhauser, having made this statement, "paused and seemed to brood for a few seconds," and then continued: "Of course, there are some good Jews, you know, Jews like Dan Burros, who was a friend of mine. Yeah, print that some of my best friends are Jews. Dan Burros was one of the most patriotic, dedicated Americans you'll ever meet in your life."

Norden commented: "Frankhauser fell silent. Burros was a fanatic American Nazi who served as [George Lincoln] Rockwell's [American Nazi party] lieutenant for years, then resigned in 1962 to edit a magazine called *Kill* and finally became a Klan leader. He had rushed into Frankhauser's house in October 1965 brandishing an issue of the *New York Times* that exposed his Jewish ancestry, snatched a loaded pistol from the wall and blew his brains out."

*What Norden did not say is that some conspiracy buffs believe that Frankhauser may have had more than a casual involvement in the killing, although no determination of that fact was ever made and the death was ruled a suicide. Another theory, also not confirmed, is that Frankhauser may have encouraged Burros's suicide inasmuch as his cover had been blown. Burros died from three bullet wounds, unusual in a bona fide suicide. DePugh, who examined the gun, said it was unlikely that Burros killed himself.*

*Other Frankhauser associates have ventured related opinions. What is also possible is that in 1965 Frankhauser was working as a government informant and that Dan Burros was too, perhaps reporting to Frankhauser. At the time of this writing Frankhauser still resides in the Reading, Pennsylvania, house where the death occurred; blood stains are still imbedded in the ceiling.* [emphasis supplied by the author of *Final Judgment*.]

But was Frankhauser a government informant and agent provocateur so early in his career? Frankhauser denies it, but his own U.S. Army records suggest otherwise. During an extensive interview under oath that took place during the period July 13 to 18, 1957, Army records reveal the following:

"(FRANKHAUSER) made a decision to infiltrate organizations such as the Neo-Nazi Party, the Communist Party, and the Ku Klux Klan, to determine their motives, identify the leaders, and report this information to the proper intelligence agency of the United States Government if their aims were ascertained to be inimical to the interest of the United States. FRANKHAUSER advised he had created a cover story which included causing people to think he was a true Communist or Nazi and the creation of an organization which was to be a large, well-organized unit, but which was composed of only one man—FRANKHAUSER. FRANKHAUSER'S aim at Fort Bragg was to get the Klans of the North together with the Klans of the South to give the United States government the opportunity to destroy these organizations."

During the 1960s, Minutemen were involved in three major terrorist acts in which Frankhauser was the possible informant, directly or indirectly, who tipped off the FBI."

In 1973, after DePugh was released from prison, Frankhauser became head of Minutemen intelligence . . . During October 1973 DePugh was a featured speaker at Liberty Lobby's annual Board of Policy meeting in Kansas City, Missouri. He had been released from prison six months earlier. Frankhauser, as security director, was his constant companion and lived with the DePugh family in Norborne [Missouri] for several weeks—all the time working for the ATF as an undercover informant.

Roy Frankhauser's background is much more convoluted. According to U.S. Army documents released under the Freedom of Information Act in 1988, Frankhauser was enmeshed in deep personal problems long before he entered the army. The victim of a broken home and an alcoholic mother, and regarded by school officials and various employers as emotionally unstable and unreliable, he enlisted in the U.S. Army on November 6, 1956. Long a collector of Nazi memorabilia and a Ku Klux Klan sympathizer even as a young man, he was engaged in a number of half-baked plots that immediately brought him to the attention of army authorities.

Military reports specified that Frankhauser joined the army and volunteered for airborne duty in order to be assigned to Germany. He developed a scheme to have himself declared officially dead so he could leave the army and join the neo-Nazi movement, hoping to rise to a position of prominence.

On July 2, 1957, Frankhauser stated that he planned to desert the U.S. Army and join the revolutionary forces in Cuba. In fact, he went AWOL and arrived in Miami, Florida, on July 5, 1957, to do precisely that. He was taken into custody shortly thereafter and returned to his military unit. Army records reflect that Frankhauser was discharged on November 18, 1957, under the provisions of AR-635209 (unfit for military service).

Frankhauser's rather incredible role as a government informant is well-documented. It first came to light in July 1975 when the *Washington Star* reported on his role in an undercover operation in Canada authorized by the top-secret National Security Council. Frankhauser was assigned to infiltrate the "Black September" terrorist organization. The CBS Evening News of July

28, 1975, did a feature on Frankhauser during which announcer Fred Graham noted that:

"Sworn testimony by federal agents [maintains] that Frankhauser has carried out a series of undercover missions for the government, including one approved by the National Security Council in the White House.

"One government source said Frankhauser had an uncanny ability to penetrate both right- and left-wing groups, that he could still help convict those who supplied the explosives that blew up school buses in Pontiac, Michigan, in 1971."

Frankhauser eventually ran afoul of his ATF superiors by going too far with his entrapment schemes and not clearing them with the ATF beforehand. This brought about his eventual indictment on February 28, 1974, on charges of stealing explosives, at which time he used his relationship with the agency as a defense. He was eventually convicted and sentenced to a period of probation, after which the ATF had a way of enforcing his cooperation and curbing his erratic behavior (or so it thought). An FBI teletype dated June 17, 1974, revealed:

"Frankhauser has proposed through his attorney that if allowed to plead guilty and receive probation on current bombing charges he will introduce federal agents to individuals who have approached him regarding his activities."

Frankhauser's ATF "handler," Edward N. Slamon, had written several internal memos describing Frankhauser as "an excellent infiltrator and confidential informant," according to the *Washington Star*.

Roy Frankhauser's involvement as a government undercover operative and agent provocateur began in the 1960s and continued sporadically until 1986, when he was indicted along with Lyndon LaRouche and several other defendants in the Boston LaRouche case involving credit card fraud and other charges. Frankhauser, who made his first contact with the LaRouche organization in 1975, had become their director of security! On December 10, 1987, Frankhauser was convicted of plotting to obstruct a federal investigation of the group.[743]

All of this intrigue and minutiae about the FBI, the CIA, the BATF and the ADL is interesting, of course. The fact that Dan Burros died under highly mysterious circumstances in the home of a long-time covert operative is likewise quite interesting.

It is probably relevant to note that one JFK assassination researcher, Peter Dale Scott, has long put forth the contention that Lee Harvey Oswald "working for a private investigator on federal government contract, was investigating the use of interstate mails for illegal arms sales [and has noted that] . . . the American Nazi Party, in 1963, was being investigated by the U.S. government . . . for its mail-order purchase of firearms."[744]

That Oswald was perhaps in contact with Burros (and there have been unsubstantiated rumors that Oswald himself may have been in the Washington, D.C. area—specifically Arlington, Virginia where Burros and the American Nazi Party were headquartered) and that Burros was in turn closely associated with a BATF undercover informant adds to the relevance of Scott's contention. However, as we noted in Chapter 15, it is more than likely that Oswald was, in fact, under deployment—through the office of

Guy Banister—by the ADL which, in turn, reportedly regularly to the FBI and other government agencies.

It is known, based upon official Justice Department documents that have been released under the Freedom of Information Act, that Frankhauser's government-sponsored undercover activities—on at least one occasion—were financed by a Jewish community organization. In that instance, the Jewish Community Center of Reading, Pennsylvania.[745] So the likelihood that the ADL also had a hand in Frankhauser's activities is very strong indeed. But the plot thickens. There is an even more explosive Frankhauser link to the JFK assassination.

## FRANKHAUSER AND OSWALD

What no JFK assassination researchers have ever yet pointed out, with one exception, is that the same Roy Frankhauser claimed to have met several times with not only Lee Harvey Oswald but also John and Ruth Paine, the Texas couple who played a key role in the final months of the life of Lee Harvey Oswald.

An article regarding Frankhauser's Oswald connection written by Scott M. Thompson and published in the November 20, 1975 issue of *New Solidarity* magazine is republished here in pertinent part.

Inclusion of this material is in no way intended by the author of *Final Judgment* to serve as an endorsement of the information related therein, but is simply provided so that there may be as complete a record as possible of all the little-known areas involving JFK assassination conspiracy research can be examined by independent-minded individuals who are truly interested in finding out the truth. The article states:

**In a series of exclusive interviews with IPS over the past month, former National Security Council operative Roy Frankhauser has provided information which conclusively demonstrates that the National Security Council planned and coordinated the Nov. 1963 assassination of President John F. Kennedy. Frankhauser provided details of numerous assassination teams organized for the Kennedy and other operations by known agents of the CIA and FBI within groups ranging from the left-wing Socialist Workers Party (SWP) and the Communist Party (USA) to right-wing groups such as the paramilitary Minutemen.**

**Also included in the preparations for the assassination were Cuban exile groups (Gusanos), the American Nazi Party, and such top CIA agents as G. Gordon Liddy, Frank Sturgis, and E. Howard Hunt, the convicted Watergate burglar and close associate of William F. Buckley. In early 1963, Frankhauser told IPS, "the word came down to get Kennedy and agent-led teams began to spring up all over the place."**

**Frankhauser confirms that two agents within the SWP periphery, who also had close ties to the Communist Party USA, were a direct part of the Kennedy operation. Frankhauser met the two, Ruth and John Paine, in 1960, when he was infiltrating the SWP in New York as an agent for the Mississippi White Citizens Council and for then Mississippi Governor Patterson. Both Paines have been closely linked to Lee Harvey Oswald (who described himself as the "patsy" in the Kennedy killing moments before he was shot in the Dallas jail)**

by both the Warren Commission and by independent investigators of the assassination.

In the months preceding the assassination, the Paines lived with Marina and Lee Harvey Oswald in Dallas. It was Ruth Paine who constructed Oswald's "radical" cover. She was the one who drove Oswald to Mexico City so that he could be photographed by the CIA in front of the Soviet Embassy. She also took Oswald to New Orleans where together they opened a franchise of the SWP front, Fair Play for Cuba, with the approval of SWP national leaders.

In New York, the Paines had recruited Frankhauser to a secret paramilitary "leftist" organization after a number of casual meetings at SWP functions. They told Frankhauser that the group had three goals: l) to break Martin Luther King out of jail should he be arrested; 2) to kill Alabama Sheriff "Bull" Connor, then a notorious opponent of integration; and 3) to assassinate President Eisenhower if revolution could not be fomented "legally." The Paines instructed Frankhauser to intensively study the SWP's paper, the Militant, in order "to learn the jargon of the left."

Actual military training for this group was conducted at Camp Midvale in the Ramapo Mountains of northern New Jersey. At this time Midvale was a Communist Party USA-controlled camp. Although all of Frankhauser's reports on this operation were turned over by Governor Patterson's office to the FBI in Mississippi, no arrests were made.

It was during this same period that Frankhauser first met Oswald at an International Scientific Socialist meeting in New York to which he was taken by the Paines.

Frankhauser's second meeting with Oswald was at a CIA training camp near Lake Ponchartrain in Louisiana.

Beginning in 1961, NSC agents launched an operation in the right-wing Minutemen—founded a year earlier to prepare for "guerilla warfare" against [what the Minutemen believed would be a] communist takeover of the U.S. [This] transformed the organization into a key NSC center for recruiting and coordinating the psychotic fringe of right-wing groups into a swarm of assassination teams, some of which were specifically selected and trained for the Kennedy assassination.

This takeover of the Minutemen was conducted under the auspices of FBI Operation COINTELPRO and CIA Operation Scorpio, and within a short time the entire Minutemen national executive committee was composed of agents — with the exception of the organization's founder Robert DePugh, who has remained a controlled dupe of the FBI ever since.

Frankhauser, at the time a CIA stringer, was himself deployed into the Minutemen, eventually becoming East Coast director of intelligence and national counterintelligence director.

Among the key figures in the Minutemen side of the Kennedy assassination operation, Frankhauser said, was Ken Duggan, who, was assistant director of Minutemen counterintelligence under Frankhauser. Also a CIA stringer, Duggan worked within the Buckley family network of Catholic fascist terrorists, recruiting Gusanos for the abortive Bay of Pigs invasion. Duggan also recruited and trained several teams in preparation for the Kennedy assassination.

Duggan, who later denounced the Buckleys, was murdered at New York's Rikers Island prison approximately a month ago. He was in prison as a result of a frame-up on attempted murder charges brought by one George Wilkie, a protege of leading members of the Buckleys' Conservative Party operation.

Also involved in profiling and selecting members of the Kennedy and other assassination teams were two agents active in the Connecticut Minutemen: Vincent De Palma and Eugene Tabbett. De Palma had been a leading CIA assassination expert in Latin America before being planted in the FBI. The FBI in turn deployed him into the Minutemen where he quickly became a national figure. Tabbett had worked for the FBI in the Klan Bureau of Intelligence before joining De Palma in Connecticut.

[Frankhauser's] 1964 subpeona to testify before the Warren Commission was quashed by the FBI on "national security" grounds. At that time Frankhauser was threatened by two Reading, Pennsylvania-based FBI agents, Kaufman and Davis, who told him that "if you release information on the Paines to the Commission, you'll be in deep trouble with the FBI." One day before their visit, Frankhauser was almost struck by two bullets fired through the window of his Reading home.[746]

How much of what Frankhauser claims is true is beyond the scope of this volume. However, JFK researchers who have tripped over themselves looking into the life and times of Lee Harvey Oswald have been notably delinquent in studiously ignoring the Frankhauser and Frankhauser-Burros connections to Lee Harvey Oswald. They would contribute much to their own research and to the search for the truth by pursuing these matters further—if indeed these researchers are seeking the truth.

## THE NOVO CONNECTION

It is interesting to note, and not just incidentally, the connections of the aforementioned Ken Duggan whom Frankhauser alleged had ties to some aspect of the JFK assassination conspiracy. Among those with whom Ken Duggan was associated were none other than two Cuban brothers, Guillermo and Ignacio Novo.

It was in Chapter 9 and in Chapter 16 where we learned of the Novo brothers trip to Dallas, Texas in the company of CIA contract agent Marita Lorenz. Upon their arrival in Dallas one day before the president's assassination, the Novos and their associates met with not only long-time CIA officer, E. Howard Hunt, but also Jack Ruby, who later killed Lee Harvey Oswald.

The Novo brothers were not only involved in some fashion in the circumstances surrounding the JFK conspiracy, but, in later years, were convicted in the murder of maverick Chilean diplomat Orlando Letelier. Their co-conspirator in the crime was, as we saw in Chapter 9, Michael Townley who had been an operative for Investors Overseas Service (IOS).

IOS, of course, was the operation run by financier Bernard Cornfeld, front man for veteran Mossad official Tibor Rosenbaum, one of the key figures behind Permindex, the shadowy corporate body linked to all the primary forces behind the JFK assassination.

What's more, as noted in Chapter 9, it was in the office of then New York Sen. James L. Buckley (brother of the aforementioned William F. Buckley, Jr.) that the Novos plotted the Letelier murder.

As we noted, particularly in Chapter 16, it appears likely that there were at least several assassination teams in place in or near Dealey Plaza before and during the JFK assassination, all part of a grand multi-levelled "false flag" operation. The allegations made by Frankhauser, indeed, jibe completely with the conclusions reached in *Final Judgment*.

The author is indebted to Van Loman, who brought the magnitude of the little-noticed Oswald-Burros connection to my attention after the second edition of this volume went to press.

Loman himself has his own unusual connection to the netherworld of intelligence. As a teenager Loman adopted as his father figure and mentor a cagey and colorful Cincinnati, Ohio-based roustabout named Jim Harris whose remarkably checkered career came to an end with his death in December of 1994.

Although Harris publicly postured as the Grand Dragon of the Ohio Ku Klux Klan, he was, in fact, a long-time informant for J. Edgar Hoover's FBI and a self-described contract agent for the CIA, actively collaborating in the CIA-Mafia plots against Castro—and perhaps more.

Among Harris' key associates was none other than Roy Frankhauser, his fellow intelligence operative. It was through Harris that Loman met Roy Frankhauser many years ago. Thanks indeed to Van Loman for pointing out the significance of the Oswald-Burros connection.

That Daniel Burros—whose name appeared in Lee Harvey Oswald's address book—should have died, under such mysterious circumstances, in the home of a known long-time federal government undercover operative inside both "leftwing" and "rightwing" political groups, it seems, should be of interest to JFK assassination researchers.

Yet, to dig too deeply into this little-explored area will, inevitably, begin turning up rocks under which the tentacles of the ADL and its collaborators in American intelligence lie hidden. This perhaps explains why some JFK assassination researchers have avoided this unpleasant mystery altogether.

This author believes that the Oswald-Burros connection is indeed another avenue that JFK assassination investigators should explore further and one which, in the end, adds further compelling evidence that solidifies the foundation upon which our final judgment is based.

## Afterword:

## The Continuing Cover-Up

The concurrent release of Oliver Stone's film, *JFK*—its many demerits notwithstanding—and Mark Lane's best-selling *Plausible Denial* sparked a renewed wave of interest in the assassination of John F. Kennedy. Now, today, millions of Americans—and people from around the globe—are convinced that there was indeed a conspiracy behind the assassination of the thirty-fifth president of the United States and that the United States government was a willing participant in the cover-up of the true facts about the murder of John F. Kennedy.

In the wake of the renewed public interest, growing demands for release of the secret JFK assassination files held by the government reached a fever pitch. Ultimately, there was indeed a bill introduced in Congress calling for the release of the documents.

### THE CIA LAUNDRY?

As far as the legislation to open the files was concerned, there were more than a few people who believed the legislation itself was suspect. Here's why:

First of all, the individual called in to lend his expertise as the primary architect of the legislation was the controversial G. Robert Blakey, the former director of the House Assassinations Committee.

In Chapter 10, of course, we reviewed Blakey's spurious findings which concluded that "The Mafia Killed JFK," and also examined Blakey's close relationship with the CIA which led his critics to suspect that perhaps the House investigation was being scuttled from within.

What's more, we also explored Blakey's enigmatic relationship with Morris Dalitz, one of Meyer Lansky's closest long-term associates and a major backer of the Israeli lobby in this country.

With all of this baggage—little known to the general public at least—Blakey was an unusual choice, unless, of course, Congress (as many suspect) doesn't really want to get to the truth.

However, the legislation that Blakey drafted is equally controversial. Under Blakey's proposal, the U.S. District Court of Appeals in Washington would appoint a five member citizen board to review and decide on the release of the assassination investigation documents. The legislation did specify that any persons previously involved in any investigation of the JFK assassination would not be eligible for appointment to the board.

However, it appears as though that proposed legislation itself was yet a continuing part of the cover-up—a sop to the public—an effort to make it appear as though "something is being done to solve the JFK assassination puzzle."

Why Congress and Blakey decided upon the federal appeals court in Washington, D.C. as the body which should select the "blue ribbon" document review panel is not so much of a mystery—that is, if one believes that the Establishment is still trying to keep the truth about the assassination hidden and buried forever.

It appears as though the proposed blue ribbon panel would have been nothing less than a government-sponsored CIA laundry which will make sure that any incriminating evidence in the files never sees the light of day.

## THE BUCKLEY FAMILY—AGAIN

In fact, one of the very judges on the appeals court which would select the panel—if it ever actually came into being—is former Sen. James L. Buckley—brother of ex-CIA man William F. Buckley, Jr., agency protege and longtime friend of E. Howard Hunt, himself implicated in the JFK murder.

(Buckley, in an even earlier incarnation, prior to his single term in the Senate, before being ousted by the voters of New York, had engaged in lucrative family oil dealings in Israel.)

As we saw in Chapter 9, it was in then-Senator Buckley's New York office that the anti-Castro Cuban brothers, Guillermo and Ignacio Novo, met with Mossad-linked mercenary Michael Townley to plot the assassination of Chilean diplomat Orlando Letelier.

The Novo brothers, of course, were named by ex-CIA operative Marita Lorenz as among those who traveled in a two-car caravan from Miami to Dallas, arriving on November 21, 1963. Upon arrival in Dallas the CIA hirelings were met by their CIA paymaster, E. Howard Hunt. They were also visited in their Dallas quarters by Dallas nightclub keeper Jack Ruby. The rest is history.

So it was that Judge James L. Buckley would have been one of those who would play a pivotal role in selecting the final arbiters of what the public will be allowed to see in the JFK assassination files—after, of course, those files had been carefully laundered by the CIA.

## A BILL IS PASSED

As it was, the Congress did act, after much debate, and approved a bill requiring government-wide disclosure of documents relating to the assassination. Former CIA Director George Bush, as president, even signed the bill into law. This bill is equally controversial as Blakey's first initiative.

The disclosure law sets up a five-member review board with the power to obtain assassination records from any government office, the CIA and FBI and committees of Congress. The board will also be permitted to hold hearings and subpoena witnesses or documents if necessary.

The five-member board is to be appointed by the president and confirmed by the Senate. Nominations to the panel must be made in 90 days, or by January 25, a few days after the presidential inauguration. No board member may be an employee of the federal government or a person who has been involved in any of the previous official investigations.

All of this, however, takes time and there are a few exceptions written into the bill that critics are suspicious about. For example, the review board has the authority to postpone the release of certain documents.

George Bush himself said, in signing the bill, that were it in his hands (which now it will not be in light of his re-election defeat) that he would exercise his Constitutional authority to keep secret executive branch deliberations, law enforcement information, and national security information.

Bush, however, may have had the last laugh. On May 31, 1993 the *Washington Post* reported that when President-elect Bill Clinton's staff took over the Bush White House they discovered that material critical to the formation of a document review board had already left the White House.

Recommendations for the review board issued by the American Historical Association, the Organization of American Historians, the Society of American Archivists and the American Bar Association were among the documents packed up by the Bush administration and shipped off, along with millions of other documents scheduled for inclusion in the future George Bush presidential library.

However, even though he proclaimed President John F. Kennedy to be his role model, and even though he himself said publicly that he suspected there had been a conspiracy behind the JFK assassination, it was after a considerably long delay before newly-elected President Bill Clinton appointed members to the document review board, even though the records disclosure legislation required the president to appoint the board within 90 days. What documents this review board will ultimately release, of course, remains to be seen. And whether the documents will be of any actual value whatsoever is another question altogether.

This is all the more ironic inasmuch as some 800,000 pages from the government's files were released to the public by the National Archives on August 23, 1993. However, many key documents were not among those released, much to the dismay of JFK assassination researchers.

## TRIVIALIZING THE ASSASSINATION

The dean of the Warren Commission critics, Mark Lane, whose own work proved conclusively that the CIA played a part in the president's assassination, does not believe that the record will be complete until a special prosecutor is appointed to review all of the files.

Lane has come down hard on former CIA director George Bush and others who have reacted so hysterically to the suggestion that segments of the American government (specifically the CIA) have been implicated—by the evidence—in the JFK assassination.

Lane scored former CIA director Bush for comparing those who believe that there was a conspiracy behind the assassination to those who believe that Elvis Presley is still alive. "To trivialize the death of our president is a major disservice to the American people. Those who believe that there was a conspiracy are derisively referred to as 'conspiracy buffs.' We are not 'conspiracy buffs.' We are the American people. We are farmers, lawyers, doctors, workers, teachers, housewives.

"Every single poll conducted for the last quarter of a century indicates that the vast majority of the American people believe that the Warren Commission was a lie. We want the truth. When President Bush makes a joke of this, he is making a joke of the deep beliefs of three-quarters of the American people on a very serious subject."

## WHERE IS THE MEDIA?

Lane is skeptical about the Establishment's decision to acknowledge the grass-roots demand that the secret files be released to the public.

"I've been asking to have those files released for the last 25 years. These are politicians reacting to the overwhelming sentiment of a large majority of the American people.

"At the time of the Warren Commission hearings here in Washington, the media was barred. I kept saying to the media, 'Where are you?' After all, in any other case, for example, the *New York Times*, the *Washington Post*, the American Civil Liberties Union and everybody else in the media are demanding to be let in.

"If Oswald had not been killed, there would have been an open trial. However, the Warren hearings were held in total secrecy. There was not one editorial, not one column, not one radio or TV editorial which said, 'Open up the hearings.'"

## THE MAFIA COVER STORY

"Now, however, that there is this growing demand for the truth, we see the next line of defense by the government. That is, 'The Mafia Killed JFK.' The government is now saying, 'OK, let's look at the files.' They want us to be satisfied with the opening of the files. This is not enough, however. Think of it this way: If there was a bank robbery and the police found out who did it, we would not be satisfied if they just opened the files so that everybody could look at the files and see what happened.

## A SPECIAL PROSECUTOR

"There should be a special prosecutor appointed to investigate and apply the rule of law. That special prosecutor should take all of the evidence and present it to a special grand jury. That's how they did it with the Iran-contra case and with Watergate. The only way to get the truth about the assassination is to appoint a special prosecutor who will bring those responsible to trial."

## WHERE IS THE TRUTH?

As this is written, however, it appears, unfortunately, that the release of the key files will be many months—even years—into the future. The government is determined that its dirtiest secrets be kept locked away forever. Indeed, it might take years before all of the incriminating evidence, pointing in whatever direction, can be erased from the public records forever.

However, it does seem unlikely that there will ever be uncovered any record which states flatly: "Israel, its allies in the CIA, and the Meyer Lansky Crime Syndicate orchestrated the assassination of John F. Kennedy."

And if such a document did somehow emerge, it is not likely that the Israeli lobby-influenced media would ever let the document reach the eyes of the public.

## PUBLISHING DISTORTIONS

This author had one interesting experience in seeking a publisher for this volume. Knowing that Shapolsky Publishers had released two books on the JFK assassination, my publicist sent an outline of *Final Judgment* to their offices in New York. Shortly thereafter my publicist received a handwritten postcard from Isaac Mozeson, Shapolsky's editorial director.

The ferocity and hysteria in Mozeson's response was unlike anything I had ever seen. He described the theory outlined in *Final Judgment* as being "infantile" and wrote of the "powerlessness" of Israel's Mossad. I was, frankly, amused by his response, but intrigued at the fury.

It was then I did some checking. The 1992 edition of *Writer's Market* reveals that 40% of Shapolsky's publications are of "Jewish interest." Shapolsky, it turns out, also just happens to be an affiliate of the Israeli-based Steimatsky Publishing House of North America. Interesting?

Shapolsky's two books on the assassination are worth noting. The first Shapolsky conconction was David Scheim's *Contract on America* which is notable for primarily being a rehash of Lansky Syndicate-linked and CIA defender Robert Blakey's book, *The Plot to Kill the President*, which fixes the blame on "The Mafia."

Scheim, as we noted in Chapter 10, would have us believe that Meyer Lansky was a little fish in a very big pond—hardly an influence at all. He also scoffs at Jim Garrison's prosecution of Clay Shaw—an innocent bystander who was guilty only of restoring lovely old buildings in the French Quarter of New Orleans.

The second Shapolsky book, *First Hand Knowledge*, by former CIA contract agent Robert Morrow, is subtitled "How I Participated in the CIA-Mafia Murder of President Kennedy."

This volume, an elaboration of Morrow's previous work, *Betrayal*, contains much useful information, beyond question, and obviously was written by someone who was privy to much of what was happening in the CIA at the time of the assassination.

However, what is notable about the volume is that Morrow specifically portrays the CIA's Mossad liaison, James J. Angleton, as somehow being out of the loop as far as the assassination and the cover-up was concerned. This, as we have seen, is just simply not true. He even suggested elsewhere that Angleton and Robert F. Kennedy were famous friends, without documenting this unlikely scenario.

And while Morrow does flatly accuse Clay Shaw of having been involved in the assassination conspiracy, even noting the Permindex link —which he portrays as strictly a CIA venture and not related directly to the assassination conspiracy—he would have the reader believe that the conspiracy against JFK by elements in the CIA went no higher than Shaw.

Morrow's contention is that Shaw headed a "rogue" element based in New Orleans operating outside the control of the CIA headquarters at Langley where Angleton's influence was then supreme.

Interestingly—for whatever it's worth—when Morrow was arrested for his participation in a CIA-orchestrated plan to counterfeit Cuban currency, the lawyer who handled his defense, Fred Weisgal, immigrated to Israel within a year after the JFK assassination and quickly became Israel's Deputy Minister of Justice, a high honor indeed. Perhaps Morrow hasn't told us everything he really knows and perhaps Weisgal's high post was a reward was for assisting in the JFK assassination cover-up.

## THE ISRAELI LOBBY RESPONDS

The response of the Israeli lobby to the release of the first edition of *Final Judgment* was quite interesting, to say the least. *Washington Jewish Week* (WJW), the leading newspaper of the pro-Israel lobby in the nation's capital, published a vituperative broadside blast at *Final Judgment* in a prominently placed full-page attack in its April 28, 1994 issue.

The weekly newspaper savaged the book as a "conspiracy theory" that presents the "latest JFK murder fantasy." According to WJW, "New kook-right book blames Israel."

The charge that *Final Judgment* is somehow "kook-right" in its orientation is, of course, specious at best, inasmuch as many of the primary sources for the documentation of JFK's bitter behind-the-scenes fight with Israel are far from being "right-wing," let alone "kook-right."

Never has anyone ever charged Pulitzer Prize winner Seymour Hersh, James and Leslie Cockburn, former Ambassador George Ball, historian Alfred Lilienthal or Stephen Green, among others, with being "kook-right." And, indeed, none of the JFK conspiracy theorists cited in *Final Judgment* have the reputation of being anything but good, old-fashioned liberals.

*Washington Jewish Week* claimed that "Piper spends most of his 302 pages quoting out-of-context secondary sources, making unlikely tenuous connections, and asserting untruths over and over as if their repetition will magically impart validity." In short, WJW was suggesting that this author simply "made up" his facts, pure and simple. WJW said that the thesis presented in *Final Judgment* is "speculative" and "bizarre."

According to WJW, the book is "anti-Jewish to its core" which, of course, is nonsense. In fact, among those who read the book prior to publication were Jewish authors, attorney Mark Lane, himself the nation's foremost authority on the JFK assassination, and Dr. Alfred Lilienthal, the pioneer American Jewish critic of Israel and its powerful lobby in this country. Neither found the book to be "anti-Jewish."

In seeking to discredit the Israeli connection to the JFK assassination conspiracy, WJW slipped up and, effectively, confirmed the explosive nature of the facts about the Israeli connection to the JFK murder.

WJW tried to discredit the 'Permindex connection' to the JFK assassination by pointing out that *Final Judgment* noted that Permindex is mentioned in Oliver Stone's film, *JFK*. Then WJW added that Stone's film "never claims to be factual," thus suggesting that Clay Shaw's Permindex connection was one of the instances of artistic license admittedly utilized by Stone in the making of the film. (And, ironically enough, as we have seen, Stone himself was gun-shy when it came to facing the so-called "French connection"—that is, the Israeli connection—head on.)

In short, WJW critiqued the film by a combination of name-calling, innuendo and playing fast and loose with the facts, an indirect admission that, clearly, *Final Judgment* hits perhaps too close to home.

## WHAT ABOUT THE JFK 'RESEARCHERS'?

In retrospect it may well be that Oliver Stone's stunning success with the film *JFK* may have done research into the JFK assassination controversy more harm than good. As we noted in Chapter 17, Stone's film focused new public interest on the controversy and gave millions of Americans and people worldwide a new perspective on the affair. The impact of the film was probably more significant, in the end, than a dozen best-selling books on the assassination combined.

However, because of Stone's apparent determination to avoid the so-called "French connection" (as documented in Chapter 17), and because of the multiple ties to the Israeli-Lansky combination on the part of Stone's corporate backers, we must indeed question the real motivation behind the decision to publicize an edited and factually-skewed representation of the facts surrounding the JFK assassination controversy.

Indeed—particularly in light of the fact that Stone's financial angel, Arnon Milchan just happened to be Israel's biggest arms dealer—one might conclude that Stone's film was nothing more than slickly-packaged and heavily-promoted black propaganda and propaganda-for-profit at that!

Because so many prominent and respected JFK assassination researchers took money from Stone and his backers—Jim Marrs, in particular, who received $300,000 for the rights to his book *Crossfire*—they may have been unwittingly compromised. They are in a unpleasant position in which they will look somewhat silly if they choose to criticize Stone.

Shortly after *Final Judgment* was published, I sent Jim Marrs a copy of the book, along with a letter noting Stone's strange reaction to the book and commenting on Stone's avoidance of the "French connection." I asked Marrs for any comments or criticisms. He never responded.

Can the researchers now honestly criticize Oliver Stone? Can they admit that Stone's version of the assassination conspiracy is off-base? Can they acknowledge that Stone's backers have intimate ties to the very powerful forces that stood to benefit by JFK's removal from the White House? These are questions that truth seekers must ask of the researchers.

**TRUTH BETRAYED . . .**

Even a devout JFK admirer such as James DiEugenio, author of *Destiny Betrayed*, must ask himself whether or not he has been fully forthcoming with his readers.

In his well-written volume, which was nothing less than a paean to Jim Garrison, DiEugenio compiled a compelling vindication of Garrison's case against Permindex board member Clay Shaw and his role in the JFK assassination conspiracy. Yet, DiEugenio was quite circumspect in his dissection of Shaw's Permindex connection. Never once did DiEugenio delve into the Israeli connection.

And although DiEugenio even went so far as to note Clay Shaw's relationship with the powerful Stern family of New Orleans, the owners of WDSU radio and television that played so central a part in portraying Lee Harvey Oswald as a "pro-Castro extremist," DiEugenio was circumspect, to say the least, in his treatment of the Stern-Shaw connection.

According to DiEugenio, the Stern family's motive for supporting Shaw was "obvious." According to DiEugenio: "They did not wish to see their city tarred with the conviction of one of its leading lights for conspiracy to murder President Kennedy." Was their motivation really that "obvious" or is DiEugenio skirting around the truth?

DiEugenio, despite his in-depth research into other aspects of the New Orleans connection to the assassination, never once referenced CIA operative Guy Banister's ties to ADL operative A. L. (Bee) Botnick, whose New Orleans office of the pro-Israel ADL received extensive funding from the Stern family (although, in all fairness, this may have been an oversight).

As we have seen, however, it is not an extraordinary leap of the imagination to conjecture that Lee Harvey Oswald's assignment working for Guy Banister—resulting in Oswald's public image as a "pro-Castro extremist"—may indeed have been part of an ADL-sponsored "fact-finding" operation carried out through Banister's detective agency.

DiEugenio actually had good reason to be so reticent in pulling his punches. After all, it was Sheridan Square Press that published his book. The prime movers behind Sheridan Square are Ellen Ray and William Schapp, founders of the so-called Institute for Media Analysis which includes among its financial backers the Stern Family Fund, the foundation established by Clay Shaw's friends, the Sterns of New Orleans.

All of this—at the very least—perhaps demonstrates how even the most dedicated JFK assassination researchers can be distracted or otherwise misdirected in their own efforts to seek the truth.

AN INTERESTING FOOTNOTE. For the record, it was Sheridan Square Press that also published Jim Garrison's own book, *On the Trail of the Assassins*. Would they have published that book if, per chance, Garrison had opted to pursue Clay Shaw's Permindex connection to its ultimate conclusion? This, of course, is a question that can never be answered. We do know, however, that when Garrison went after Shaw he was, in fact, looking in the right direction.

Garrison died, unfortunately, before *Final Judgment* was published and this, perhaps, is one of my great regrets. I believe that if Garrison had had the opportunity to study the facts presented in these pages that he, too, would have concluded that this book does indeed present a final judgment on the biggest case of his career.

## AVOIDING FINAL JUDGMENT . . .

Although I requested the opportunity to address the 1994 symposium of the JFK Assassination Information Center in Dallas, the ruling clique at the center  were careful not to include this author among the speakers, despite my repeated efforts to obtain a place on the official forum.

Likewise, neither the aforementioned James DiEugenio nor any of the other "big names" among JFK assassination researchers have even attempted to refute any of the substantive allegations appearing in the pages of *Final Judgment*. If the thesis of *Final Judgment* is foolish or misguided, one would think that it would be a simple process to discredit such a book.

## HINTS ABOUT ISRAEL . . .

One veteran JFK assassination researcher of some prominence, Peter Dale Scott, who has been cited extensively in the pages of *Final Judgment*, has come close to hinting at a possible Israeli role in the murky depths of the JFK assassination conspiracy.

In his excellent book *Deep Politics and the Death of JFK*, Scott has gone further than most JFK assassination researchers in exploring the recurring Meyer Lansky connection to Jack Ruby and the CIA, for example, and pointing out CIA man James Jesus Angleton's peculiar role in the JFK controversy which we have outlined in detail in these pages.

In these areas, among others, Scott has clearly done his research, but one cannot read his book without thinking that Scott has likewise tip-toed up to the Israeli connection, but refused to draw the obvious conclusions for his readers.

Scott says a lot about many things, but says nothing when it comes to the Israeli links to the JFK assassination that have been thoroughly documented in *Final Judgment*. And despite his in-depth research in a wide variety of subjects relating to the JFK controversy, Scott has absolutely nothing to say whatsoever about Clay Shaw's Permindex connection. It is something that he obviously would prefer not to discuss.

## SCOTT'S ISRAELI LOBBY SOURCES

It is interesting to note that in his acknowledgements, among those Scott thanks for assistance in the preparation of his book are two rather interesting sources: Wesley McCune of Group Research, Inc. and Michael Lerner. Group Research, Inc., while ostensibly an "independent" research entity, has generally been described by its critics as a "front" for the Anti-Defamation League (ADL) of B'nai B'rith, the influential self-styled "civil rights" organization that has been exposed as an intelligence and propaganda conduit for Israel's Mossad.

As noted in Chapter 17, the ADL's long-suspected Mossad link was brought to public light in a broad-ranging investigation by the San Francisco Police Department of the ADL's covert domestic spying operations aimed at a wide variety of both "right wing" and "left wing" political groups in the United States.

Scott's source Michael Lerner, a prominent liberal philosopher, also happens to be the publisher of *Tikkun* magazine, a Jewish-oriented journal which has emerged as a major voice in the American lobby for Israel.

That these two played a part in shaping Scott's final judgment (if it can be described as such) perhaps explains in part Scott's clear and repeated effort to avoid broaching the Israeli connection to the assassination of President Kennedy.

## DON'T RATTLE THE CAGE

This author can only conclude that these "researchers" who have spun their wheels, expended vast amounts of time, energy and money (not to mention having made money at that) in delving into the JFK affair would rather not cross the line, so to speak, and rattle the Israeli cage. I understand their reasoning, of course, but, at the same time, I am compelled to question their integrity.

To their credit, however, there have been a number of long-time JFK assassination researchers who have favorably acknowledged *Final Judgment* and the substance of its claims, whether they agree with its conclusions in the entirety or not.

I will not name them here and thereby burden them with the possibility of being tarred as "anti-Semites" or "extremists"—the favorite term reserved for those who dare to criticize the actions of Israel—but they know who they are and their support has been appreciated.

## SIMILAR CONCLUSIONS

Just before *Final Judgment* was first published, I was delighted to learn that one long-time JFK assassination researcher, Philip Ten Brink, working entirely independently of this author, not so surprisingly reached essentially the same conclusions reached in *Final Judgment*, even up to and including a number of fine points that some might find somewhat esoteric. I am compelled to repeat the old saw that "great minds think alike," but I would be overstating the case in so doing. It is simply that the facts are there for those who wish to recognize them for what they are.

Ten Brink discovered on his own that pointing the finger in the direction of Israel and the Mossad is not good public relations. When he spoke on his findings at the 1993 symposium of the JFK Assassination Information Center in Dallas, Ten Brink advised me, there were a lot of people who were uneasy, to say the least, that someone within their ranks was being "politically incorrect." Hats off to Ten Brink for having the guts to call the shots at he saw it. The same can't be said for those JFK assassination researchers who see the truth but are afraid to admit it.

## ANSWER THE QUESTION 'WHY?'

All of this further suggests that even those who purport to be seeking the truth about the JFK assassination are only willing to go so far. Will the "researchers" continue to dabble in esoteric questions as to "how many bullets were fired?" or "where did the bullets hit?" or will they once and for all attempt to answer that overwhelming question most important of all: Why was John F. Kennedy murdered and who, ultimately, was responsible?

To answer that question one cannot avoid the until-now secret fact of JFK's battle to prevent Israel from building the nuclear bomb, for Israel—like its allies in both organized crime and the CIA—did have a strong motive to move against JFK and indeed did.

## AN ISRAELI SUCCESS STORY ...

What about Israel and its aggressive campaign to build the nuclear bomb—the controversy that played so central a role in the events that led to the assassination of John F. Kennedy? In the end, it was Israel—not JFK—that had the last word on the matter.

The November 1994 issue of *Jane's Intelligence Review* reported that Israel had, by that time, developed seven nuclear installations and as many as 200 nuclear weapons—enough to make tiny Israel the world's sixth-largest nuclear power.

According to a summary of *Jane's* report that appeared in the Associated Press on November 19, 1994: "The Israeli government neither confirms nor denies having nuclear weapons, and has tried to keep the country's nuclear program secret. It has not signed the Nuclear Non-Proliferation Treaty, which would open its facilities to international inspection."

So much, then, for JFK's strenuous efforts to put a stop to nuclear expansion in the Middle East. Any hope of success came to a crashing halt on November 22, 1963.

## WHAT ABOUT THE KENNEDY FAMILY?

Many readers of *Final Judgment* have asked if the Kennedy family has responded to the allegations made in this volume. Not publicly, at least. But we can be confident that the Kennedy family—above all—does indeed know the truth about the JFK assassination

But don't expect the family to ever go public with any knowledge they might have of Mossad involvement in the affair. It will never happen. Too much is at stake.

If anything, the Kennedy family has been firmly coopted by the Mossad itself. The key to understanding this is Jacqueline Kennedy Onassis's ten year relationship—prior to her death—with the enigmatic Belgian-born Jewish diamond merchant Maurice Tempelsman.

After positioning himself as a permanent fixture in the center of Jacqueline's life—and then ensconcing himself as her live-in companion in the Kennedy widow's elegant Manhattan penthouse—Tempelsman reportedly doubled (perhaps even tripled, by some accounts) Jacqueline's already substantial fortune.

Although, upon her death, the major media dramatized the romance of Jacqueline and her companion, the media never once reported Tempelsman's long-time role as an international agent-in-place, operating in and out of Africa for the Israeli Mossad and its allies in the CIA. So it was that during Jacqueline's final days, Israel's Mossad was represented in the most intimate circles of the Kennedy family.

Ironically, in the end, perhaps, it doesn't really matter to the Kennedy family who was ultimately behind the assassination of the president and his brother. Two family members died violently and tragically, whoever was responsible. The family's loss was all too personal, far beyond any other international geopolitical ramifications that were very much of interest to the conspirators responsible for the two assassinations. Pursuing the truth about what really happened was never an option.

Sen. Edward M. Kennedy himself is probably lucky to still be alive, but he never achieved his dream of reclaiming the White House for the Kennedy dynasty. The likelihood that any other future family member will once again occupy the Oval Office is scant, at best

If truth be told, the Kennedy family has, in its own fashion, benefited immensely from the double tragedy, securing a place in history and legend that might otherwise have been lost had JFK lived out his term.

## THE MEDIA'S 'FINAL JUDGMENT'

It is somewhat ironic, indeed, that the Kennedy legacy, however, is being subjected to revision by the media.

Writing in the *Washington Post* on November 25, 1993, famed economist Robert Samuelson deviated from his area of expertise and delved into the subject of the Kennedy legacy.

His prominently placed column, appearing on the right-hand of the op-ed page was a full-tilt assault on the memory of John F. Kennedy, coming in the wake of the 30th anniversary of what may well have been the most stunning public event in our nation's history.

"We have come through another orgy of Kennedy remembrances," complained Samuelson, "and I confess that, finally, I am fed up. It is not just that his life and his assassination have been overdramatized, transforming him from a political figure into an entertainment phenomenon with a place in pop culture closer to Elvis than Harry Truman. The dissent goes deeper. Our Kennedy obsession obscures something crucial. he was, at best, a mediocre president or, less charitably, a lousy one."

## KENNEDY AND VIETNAM

Samuelson went on the blame Kennedy for the tragedy of the war in Vietnam. "It was Kennedy who made the critical commitment to Vietnam. All the subsequent speculation about whether he would or wouldn't have increased that commitment, as Johnson did, is really irrelevant. We can never know what Kennedy would have done, only what he did. And what he did was make a major military (and political) commitment to a country whose survival was not a vital national interest, and thereby, involves us in a conflict that politically we could not sustain. Once this happened, there was no easy exit. Bad judgment."

The opinionated columnist determined that JFK lacked "wisdom or good instincts" and that he did "not have the background or values to make good decisions by himself."

"The Kennedy who lives beyond the grave," concluded Samuelson, "commands neither my sympathy nor my interest. He is simplified, romanticized and exploited. He is not a person but a popular delusion."

So much for the memory of John F. Kennedy in the judgment of one of the nation's most respected opinion-makers. Perhaps, then, it should be no surprise that on November 22, 1994—the 31st anniversary of the JFK assassination—the *Washington Post*, America's political newspaper of record, said not a single word in commemoration of that tragic day.

## ASKING FOR A DEBATE

Just prior to the release of this edition of *Final Judgment*, I sent copies of the second edition to the a number of individuals inviting them to debate the thesis of *Final Judgment* with me—on radio or in any public forum or in writing. I gave them the opportunity refute the book in the manner they wished. Not an unfair offer, I should think.

Here are those who received copies of *Final Judgment* and the invitation to a debate:

**Jack Anderson** - The syndicated columnist and international wheeler-dealer who has promoted a number of conflicting theories about the JFK assassination, notably the myth that Cuba's communist dictator, Fidel Castro, was behind the president's murder.

**Robert Dornan** - The flamboyant California Republican congressman and presidential hopeful who has described himself as a "fan of Menachem Begin," the late former Israeli prime minister whose role in the JFK affair is outlined in *Final Judgment*.

**Jack Shafer** - Editor of Washington, D.C.'s popular *City Paper*, a freewheeling, liberal-oriented "alternative" newspaper.

**John Loftus** - Author of *The Secret War Against the Jews*, a new book which claims that anti-Israel partisans in the American intelligence community have sought to sabotage the state of Israel. (Loftus is a former attorney with the Nazi-hunting Office of Special Investigations.)

**Roland Pritikin** - Retired Brigadier General and internationally-known physician and founder of the Center for Global Security, an ad hoc pro-Israel lobby group which included among its advisors Luis Kutner, a former attorney for Jack Ruby, and General Julius Klein, the American military officer who played a major role in the establishment of the Mossad.

**Bob Grant** - The controversial broadcaster over WABC radio in New York who has often bragged of his friendly relations with the Anti-Defamation League (ADL) of B'nai B'rith and of his deep devotion to the state of Israel.

**Rush Limbaugh** - The biggest name in "conservative" talk radio known for being an outrageous and audacious critic of everything but Israel's misdeeds.

**Chuck Harder** - Host of the widely-heard "For the People" radio program, Harder refuses to mention the role of Israel in international misdeeds, although he is quick to find conspiracy and corruption of other sorts under almost every rock.

**G. Gordon Liddy** - The former CIA and FBI operative who was brave enough to stand up to a federal judge and go to prison for refusing to rat on his friends. Once frequently accused of being a Nazi sympathizer, Liddy is now a popular radio broadcaster—but never a critic of Israel.

**William F. Jasper** - Senior Editor of the John Birch Society's *New American* magazine which is a steadfast backer of the state of Israel and still enamored of Mossad-allied CIA man James Jesus Angleton's fantasy/cover story that "The Soviets Killed JFK."

**David Scheim** - Author of *Contract on America*, which claims that "The Mafia Killed JFK" and ignores the integral role of Israeli loyalist and CIA collaborator Meyer Lansky in the international crime syndicate. Scheim has been a major figure in the community of JFK assassination "reserchers" but, as we've noted in these pages, he refuses to acknowledge even the possibility of CIA involvement in the crime.

**Jack Newfield** - The liberal columnist for the *New York Post*, Newfield, an Israeli loyalist, has claimed that missing Teamster's Union boss Jimmy Hoffa was the prime mover behind the JFK assassination.

Issuing a call for a debate was not a search for publicity for *Final Judgment*—although any publicity would have been welcome and actually quite remarkable.

What I earnestly sought was for some individual to come forth and prove me wrong—to show me where the conclusions reached in *Final Judgment* were unsound.

## A SINGLE RESPONSE . . .

Of this vast array of individuals invited to debate, as of March 1, 1995 only General Pritikin had responded. His lengthy letter said that "Every statement in your book can be refuted, but I am not the one to do it." Pritikin told me that General Mark Clark said that "I wouldn't be surprised if thirty or forty years after the assassination of John F. Kennedy books will come out blaming the Jews."

"Your book" wrote Pritikin, "along with the writings of Grace Halsell and George Ball (who had a long record of treason) are considered [by the Arabs] the tryptych for the destruction of the USA and the extermination of the American people."

(Grace Halsell is a professional journalist of liberal inclinations who has written somewhat critically of Israel. Former Undersecretary of State George Ball is guilty of the same crime. Evidently Halsell, Ball and I are guilty of crimes of the same magnitude as far as General Pritikin is concerned.)

"You state in your letter," wrote Pritikin, "that no one has come forward to refute the allegations in your book. This is due to the fact that [the first edition] has no index. It is written in the style of Victor Hugo and Alexander Dumas. It reads like a beautiful, fictional novel because it has no index. That is why no one has come forward to refute anything."

"The discovery of oil in the Arabian Peninsula in the 1930s brought about the downfall of free western civilization, because the USA failed to have the foresight, the courage and the adamant will to combat the oil rich sheiks, and because we had traitors like Michael Collins Piper, Grace Halsell and George Ball."

## PRITIKIN'S 'PROOF'

In his letter General Pritikin cited the presence of a lovely memorial in Israel to John F. Kennedy as "proof" that the Israelis loved JFK more than any other American president.

This is scant "proof" indeed—of nothing. A cynic might be so crass as to suggest that the memorial was nothing more than a tribute by the Israelis to one of their own more outrageous public executions and the skill with which it was conducted.

Lest, however, that some pro-Israel zealot claim that this is my contention, for the record I will say that it is not. What I am saying is that such a memorial proves nothing: Only that the Mossad-dominated Israeli establishment wants to have it on the record—although the facts show otherwise—that "Israel loved JFK."

Perhaps the average man in the street in Tel Aviv did indeed admire John F. Kennedy. But Prime Minister David Ben-Gurion, Mossad assassinations chief Yitzhak Shamir and their allies in the CIA and in the Lansky Crime Syndicate did not.

Be all of this as it may, I can only conclude that the refusal by these "big names" to either debate me publicly or to attempt to repudiate my work in any way, shape or form is precisely because they cannot. *Final Judgment* is indeed, in my view, for all intents and purposes, the final judgment on what really happened in Dallas.

### A FINAL HOPE . . .

These, of course, are all things to ponder as we consider the way that the truth about the JFK assassination is treated by the media and about the way the facts and the so-called facts will be released to the public.

Those who are ostensibly seeking the truth about the murder of President Kennedy but who continue to ignore the very clear role played by Israel and its Mossad in the JFK assassination are perhaps, in the end, the greatest enemies of the truth. I seek no conflict or argument with these people—only their assistance in arriving at the truth. If I am wrong, I ask them to show me where I'm wrong.

If even President Kennedy's admirers are unable to face the truth and expose it to the light of day, then America and the world face a very grave crisis indeed. I hope that I am mistaken.

In the end I would have much preferred that someone else would have written a book such as *Final Judgment*, for, frankly, I do find it frustrating that others looking into the circumstances of the JFK assassination seem to have steered clear of that one controversial area of research that is so central to divining the truth about the murder of President Kennedy.

Despite all this, it is my hope that the release of *Final Judgment* will, in some way, contribute to a full understanding of not only the death of John F. Kennedy, but also of all of the world-shaking events that followed—events that changed the course of history.

# Postscript

A senior French diplomat, Bernard Ledun, died in Paris on February 1, 1994. His sudden death at age 50—ostensibly from a heart attack—may be another of the "convenient" deaths that have occurred in the wake of the JFK assassination and its cover-up and a direct consequence of the announcement, on November 22, 1993, of the impending release of the first edition of *Final Judgment*.

Ledun had been privy to "inside" information which confirmed the high-level intelligence status of the French source—quoted in Chapter 16 of *Final Judgment*—who provided this author information which establishes that the much-discussed "French connection" to the Kennedy assassination is, in fact, misnamed and is, instead, the Israeli connection.

Just prior to his sudden death, Ledun, a career officer in the French diplomatic corps, was scheduled to become Consul General for France in Johannesburg, South Africa. From October 1989 to December 1993 he served as Consul General for his native country in Vancouver, British Columbia, Canada.

While posted in Vancouver, Ledun committed a grievous—albeit honest—mistake that may have sealed his own fate. His unwitting action proved the high-level French intelligence status of the source, quoted in *Final Judgment*. The source—let's call him "Pierre"—asserted (based on his own inside knowledge) that Israel's secret service, the Mossad, utilized connections in French intelligence, in arranging the hiring of an assassin or assassins who were involved in the execution of President Kennedy.

In 1976, while serving in the French consulate in Vancouver, Canada, Ledun released copies of internal French intelligence documents to Pierre confirming that Pierre had indeed been a French intelligence officer privy to explosive state secrets.

Because of the incendiary nature of the information to which Pierre had been privy, French intelligence had denied for years that Pierre was engaged in intelligence work for his native country. The release of the documents by Ledun, however, provided hard evidence to the contrary.

Not only had Pierre learned specific details about how French intelligence had been manipulated by the Mossad in the JFK assassination conspiracy—information provided by his own allies in French intelligence—but Pierre himself had been brought into a previous assassination conspiracy conducted jointly by the Mossad and French intelligence.

The Mossad had contracted—through its key contact in French intelligence, Colonel Georges deLannurien—to arrange for Pierre to unwittingly play the role of "patsy" (*a la* Lee Harvey Oswald) in a Mossad plot to kill Egyptian President Gamal Abdel Nasser during the last week of October, 1956, just prior to the invasion at Port Said during the Suez Crisis.

(It was deLannurien, as we noted in Chapter 16, who was later the primary conduit between the Yitzhak Shamir of the Mossad and James J. Angleton of the CIA in the JFK assassination conspiracy.)

When Pierre realized that he, in fact, was the intended patsy in the Nasser assassination plot, he surrendered to Egyptian intellience at Cairo International Airport.

For refusing to give up his life in a Mossad-sponsored conspiracy, Pierre—the scion of a distinguished family and the son of a reknown French diplomat—became a man without a country. After fleeing to South America and then to Canada, Pierre was tried *in absentia* by a French military court and convicted of "treason" and "breach of external security of the state" and condemned to twenty years of forced labor.

When, in 1976, still in exile, Pierre sought clemency by approaching the French consul general's office in Vancouver, Canada, where he was then living, his request was rejected.

At that time, in a documented dated "5 OCT 1976" the French Ministry of Defense advised the French Consul General in Vancover that Pierre's request had been denied. It was Bernard Ledun at the French Consul General's office who released this letter of denial to Pierre, not realizing the explosive nature of the document.

As Pierre says, French intelligence was "furious with this gaffe of Mr. Ledun, an act very treasonable, that of giving to outsiders a letter of the minister of Defense giving credit to my allegations that I had been a diplomat and intelligence officer serving France in Libya and Italy.

"You may argue," Pierre acknowledges, "that this letter does not prove that I served the French Government. Well, where did you see a simple French citizen being accused of Treason and "*atteinte a la surete de l'Etat,*" condemned to the terrible sentence of 20 years of hard labor?

"Only if you believe in Santa," comments Pierre, "could you believe that anyone may be guilty of such horrendous 'crimes' without having knowledge of State secrets. And by the way, "*atteinte a la surete de l'Etat*" means, in good English 'trying to overthrow the State by a subversive act.'

"It supposes that I had the power to betray and harm the French State in the period referred to. That is, in the 1950's. That's credit indeed towards my allegations. And this is why Mr. Ledun had to pay the price of his mistake by death.

Pierre contends: "Mr. Ledun was murdered in Paris by French intelligence on February 1, 1994. He gave me the weapon by which I can sustain my allegations. If once I was convicted of 'treason,' why not a second time?

"Without this letter, French intelligence would answer to your allegations in *Final Judgment* that they never heard of me, that I am an imposter or some kind of nut, lunatic, crank or else. But this damned letter is in your hands. So if you decide to ask more questions now, they may tell you that I am a 'poor son of a bitch.' Yes!

"Please pray for the soul of Mr. Ledun who was a true gentleman—the first victim of *Final Judgment.*

"I thank you so for *Final Judgment*," Pierre told this author in a recent letter. "Your book is justice done. I may now die in peace. As Dag Hammarskjold, the late UN Secretary General commented, 'The truth is so simple that it is regarded as pretentious banality.' "

Pierre believes, beyond question, that Ledun was, in fact, murdered in retribution for his mistake in light of the forthcoming release of *Final Judgment*. Here's why . . .

You see, the first public announcment of the allegations appearing in *Final Judgment* came in a special full-page advertisement published on November 22, 1993 in Dallas, Texas in the program of the annual symposium conducted by the JFK Assassination Information Center.

The announcement revealed that *Final Judgment* had relied, in part, upon a French source for information detailing the Israeli Mossad connection to the JFK assassination and the French intelligence role therein.

Pierre believes that this announcement tipped off the Mossad and French intelligence that he was the source referenced in *Final Judgment*. As a consequence, Ledun's murder was an act of retribution against Ledun for his mistake of many years earlier—that is, confirming that Pierre had indeed been involved (however unwittingly) in a sensitive and high-level joint collaborative effort between the Mossad and French intelligence.

Had Pierre not courageously spoken out, filling in the missing link in the JFK assassination conspiracy, Bernard Ledun might indeed haved lived out the rest of his natural life in peace . . . but the truth about the Kennedy assassination might never have been told.

Pierre fears for his own life, but he does rest assured that he played a major role in helping resolve the greatest mystery of our modern era—the question of who really orchestrated the death of John F. Kennedy.

Perhaps someday Pierre's name can be revealed, but for the time being, he will have to remain an unsung hero in history.

MICHAEL COLLINS PIPER
Washington, D.C.
March 1, 1995

# Bibliography

Adelson, Alan. *The Ruby-Oswald Affair*. Seattle, Washington: Romar Books, Ltd., 1988.

Anson, Robert Sam. *They've Killed the President! The Search for the Murderers of John F. Kennedy*. New York: Bantam Books, 1975.

Ball, George and Douglas Ball. *The Passionate Attachment: America's Involvement With Israel, 1947 to the Present*. New York: W. W. Norton & Company, 1992.

Beit-Hallahmi, Benjamin. *The Israeli Connection—Who Israel Arms and Why*. New York: Pantheon Books, 1987.

Blakey, G. Robert & Richard N. Billings. *The Plot to Kill the President: Organized Crime Assassinated JFK—The Definitive Story*. New York: Times Books, 1981.

Blitzer, Wolf. *Between Washington and Jerusalem*. New York: Oxford University Press, 1985.

Blumenthal, Sid. Ed. *Government by Gunplay: Assassination Conspiracy Theories From Dallas to Today*. New York: Signet Books, 1976.

Bruck, Connie. *Master of the Game*. New York: Simon & Schuster, 1994.

Canfield, Michael & Alan J. Weberman. *Coup d'etat in America: The CIA and the Assassination of John F. Kennedy*. New York: The Third Press, 1975.

Cockburn, Andrew, and Leslie Cockburn. *Dangerous Liaison: The Inside Story of the U.S. Israeli Covert Relationship*. New York: Harper Collins Publishers, 1991.

Cohen, Mickey with John Peer Nugent. *Mickey Cohen: In My Own Words*. Englewood Cliffs, New Jersey: Prentice-Hall, Inc., 1975.

Curtiss, Richard. *A Changing Image: American Perceptions of the Arab-Israeli Dispute*. Washington, D.C.: American Educational Trust, 1986.

Davis, John H. *Mafia Kingfish: Carlos Marcello and the Assassination of John F. Kennedy*. New York: McGraw-Hill Publishing Company, 1989.

Deacon, Richard. *The Israeli Secret Service.* New York: Taplinger Publishing Co., Inc., 1978.

Demaris, Ovid. *The Last Mafioso: The Treacherous World of Jimmy Fratianno.* New York: Bantam Books, 1981.

Ehrenfeld, Rachel. *Evil Money: Encounters Along the Money Trail.* New York: Harper Collins Publishers, 1992.

Eveland, Wilbur Crane. *Ropes of Sand: America's Failure in the Middle East.* New York: W. W. Norton & Company, 1980.

Executive Intelligence Review. *Dope, Inc.* New York: New Benjamin Franklin House, First edition, 1978; second edition, 1986.

Executive Intelligence Review. *Moscow's Secret Weapon: Ariel Sharon and the Israeli Mafia.* Washington, D.C.: Executive Intelligence Review, 1986.

Executive Intelligence Review. *Project Democracy: The 'Parallel Government' Behind the Iran-Contra Affair.* Washington, D.C.: Executive Intelligence Review, April, 1987.

Executive Intelligence Review. *The Ugly Truth About the ADL.* Washington, D.C.: Executive Intelligence Review, 1992.

Fensterwald, Bernard, and the Committee to Investigation Assassinations. *Coincidence or Conspiracy?* New York: Zebra Books, 1977.

Findley, Paul. *They Dare to Speak Out: People and Institutions Confront Israel's Lobby.* Westport, Connecticut: Lawrence Hill & Company, 1985.

Flammonde, Paris. *The Kennedy Conspiracy: An Uncommissioned Report on the Jim Garrison Investigation.* New York: Meredith Press, 1969.

Forster, Arnold. *Square One.* New York: Donald I. Fine, Inc., 1988.

Forsyth, Frederick. *The Day of the Jackal.* New York: Bantam Books, 1972.

Fox, Stephen. *Blood and Power: Organized Crime in Twentieth Century America.* New York: William Morrow & Company, 1989.

Friedman, Robert I. *The False Phophet: Rabbi Meir Kahane: From FBI Informant to Knesset Member.* New York: Lawrence Hill Books, 1990.

Garrison, Jim. *On the Trail of the Assassins: My Investigation & Prosecution of the Murder of President Kennedy.* New York: Sheridan Square Press, 1988.

Gentry, Curt. *J. Edgar Hoover: The Man and the Secrets.* New York: W. W. Norton & Company, 1991.

Ghareed, Edmund (ed). *Split Vision: The Portrayal of Arabs in the American Media.* Washington, D.C.: American-Arab Affairs Council, 1983.

Giancana, Sam and Chuck Giancana. *Double Cross: The Explosive Inside Story of the Mobster Who Controlled America.* New York: Warner Books, 1992.

Gosch, Martin A. and Richard Hammer. *The Last Testament of Lucky Luciano.* Boston: Little Brown and Company, 1974.

Green, Stephen. *Taking Sides: America's Secret Relations With a Militant Israel.* New York: William Morrow & Company, 1984.

Harrison, Alexander. *Challenging DeGaulle: The OAS and the Counterrevolution in Algeria.* New York: Praeger Publishers, 1989.

Henissart, Paul. *Wolves in the City: The Death of French Algeria.* New York: Simon and Schuster, Inc., 1970.

Hepburn, James. *Farewell America.* Liechtenstein: Frontiers Company, 1968.

Hersh, Seymour M. *The Samson Option: Israel's Nuclear Arsenal and American Foreign Policy.* New York: Random House, 1991.

Hinckle, Warren and William W. Turner. *Deadly Secrets: The CIA-Mafia War Against Castro and the Assassination of JFK.* New York: Thunder's Mouth Press, 1992.

Horne, Alistair. *A Savage War of Peace.* Middlesex, England: Penguin Books, 1977.

Hougan, Jim. *Secret Agenda: Watergate, Deep Throat and the CIA.* New York: Random House, 1984.

Hougan, Jim. *Spooks: The Haunting of America—The Private Use of Secret Agents.* New York: William Morrow & Company, Inc., 1988.

House Select Committee on Assassinations, *The Final Assassinations Report.* New York: Bantam Books, 1979.

Hurt, Henry. *Reasonable Doubt: An Investigation into the Assassination of John F. Kennedy.* New York: Holt, Rinehart & Winston, 1985.

Hutchison, Robert. *Vesco.* New York: Praeger Publishers, 1974.

Kantor, Seth. *Who Was Jack Ruby?* New York: Everest House, 1978.

Katz, Leonard. *Uncle Frank: The Biography of Frank Costello.* New York: Drake Publishers, Inc., 1973.

Kenan, I. L. *Israel's Defense Line: Her Friends and Foes in Washington.* Buffalo: Prometheus Books, 1981.

Kirkwood, James. *American Grotesque: An Account of the Clay Shaw-Jim Garrison Affair in New Orleans.* New York: Simon & Schuster, 1970.

Krefetz, Gerald. *Jews and Money: The Myths and the Reality.* New York: Ticknor & Fields, 1982.

Kurzman, Dan. *Ben-Gurion: Prophet of Fire.* New York: Simon & Schuster, 1983.

Kwitny, Jonathan. *The Crimes of Patriots: A True Tale of Dope, Dirty Money, and the CIA.* New York: W. W. Norton & Company, 1987.

Kwitny, Jonathan. *Endless Enemies: The Making of an Unfriendly World.* New York: Penguin Books, 1986.

Lacey, Robert. *Little Man: Meyer Lansky and the Ganster Life.* Boston: Little, Brown & Company, 1991.

Lacouture, Jean. *DeGaulle: The Ruler.* New York: W.W. Norton & Company, 1993.

Lane, Mark. *A Citizen's Dissent.* New York: Dell, 1975.

Lane, Mark. *Plausible Denial.* New York: Thunders Mouth Press, 1991.

Lane, Mark. *Rush to Judgment.* New York: Thunder's Mouth Press, 1992.

Lane, Mark and Donald Freed. *Executive Action.* New York: Dell Books, 1973.

Lasky, Victor. *JFK: The Man & The Myth.* New York: Arlington House Publishers, 1966.

Leek, Sybil and Burt Sugar. *The Assassination Chain.* New York: Corwin Books, 1976.

Lewis, Ron. *Flashback.* Medford, Oregon: Lewcom Productions, 1933.

Lilienthal, Alfred M. *The Zionist Connection II.* New Brunswick, New Jersey: North American, 1982.

Loftus, John and Mark Aarons. *The Secret War Against the Jews,* New York: St. Martin's Press, 1994.

Mangold, Tom. *Cold Warrior—James Jesus Angleton: The CIA's Master Spy Hunter.* New York: Simon & Schuster, 1991.

Marrs, Jim. *Crossfire: The Plot That Killed Kennedy.* New York: Carroll & Graf Publishers, Inc., 1989.

Marshall, Jonathan and Peter Dale Scott and Jane Hunter. *The Iran-Contra Connection: Secret Teams and Covert Operations in the Reagan Era.* Boston: South End Press, 1987.

McCoy, Alfred W. *The Politics of Heroin: CIA Complicity in the Global Drug Trade.* Chicago: Lawrence Hill Books, 1991.

Messick, Hank. *Lansky.* New York: Berkley Medallion Books, 1971.

Messick, Hank and Burt Goldblatt. *The Mobs and The Mafia.* New York: Ballantine Books, 1972.

Messick, Hank. *Secret File.* New York: G. P. Putnam's Sons, 1969.

Milan, Michael. *The Squad: The U.S. Government's Secret Alliance With Organized Crime.* New York: Shapolsky Publishers, Inc., 1989.

Miller, Marvin. *The Breaking of a President: The Nixon Connection.* Covina, California: Classic Publications, 1975.

Moldea, Dan. *The Hoffa Wars: Teamsters, Rebels, Politicians and The Mob.* New York: Paddington Press, 1978.

Morrow, Robert D. *Betrayal: A Reconstruction of Certain Clandestine Events from the Bay of Pigs to the Assassination of John F. Kennedy.* Chicago: Henry Regnery Co, 1976.

Morrow, Robert D. *The Senator Must Die: The Murder of Robert F. Kennedy.* Santa Monica, California: Roundtable Publishing, Inc., 1988.

Mullins, Eustace. *The World Order.* Staunton, Virginia: The Ezra Pound Institute, 1992.

Nelson, Jack. *Terror in the Night: The Klan's Campaign Against the Jews.* New York: Simon & Schuster, 1993.

O'Brien, Lee. *American Jewish Organizations and Israel.* Washington, D.C.: Institute for Palestine Studies, 1986.

Oglesby, Carl. *The JFK Assassination: The Facts and The Theories.* New York: Signet Books, 1992.

Oglesby, Carl. *The Yankee and Cowboy War: Conspiracies From Dallas to Watergate.* Kansas City, Kansas: Sheed Andrews & McMeel, Inc., 1976.

Ostrovsky, Victor and Claire Hoy. *By Way of Deception: The Making and Unmaking of a Mossad Officer.* New York: St. Martin's Press, 1990.

Pilat, Oliver. *Drew Pearson: An Unauthorized Biography.* New York: Harper's Magazine Press, 1973.

Prouty, L. Fletcher. *The Secret Team: The CIA and Its Allies in Control of the United States and the World.* Costa Mesa, California: Institute for Historical Review, 1992.

Rafizadeh, Mansur. *Witness: From the Shah to the Secret Arms Deal— An Insider's Account of U.S. Involvement in Iran.* New York: William Morrow & Company, 1987.

Rappleye, Charles and Ed Becker. *All American Mafioso: The Johnny Rosselli Story.* New York: Doubleday, 1991.

Raviv, Dan and Yossi Melman. *Every Spy a Prince.* Boston: Houghton Mifflin Co., 1990.

Reid, Ed. *The Grim Reapers: The Anatomy of Organized Crime in America, City by City.* New York: Bantam Books, 1970.

Reid, Ed, and Ovid Demaris. *The Green Felt Jungle.* New York: Pocket Books edition, 1964.

Rockwell, George Lincoln. *This Time the World.* Liverpool, West Virginia: White Power Publications, 1963.

Roemer, William F. *War of the Godfathers.* New York: Donald I. Fine, Inc., 1990.

Rokach, Livia. *Israel's Sacred Terrorism.* Belmont, Massachusetts: AAUG Press, 1986.

Russell, Dick. *The Man Who Knew Too Much.* New York: Carroll & Graf Publishers, 1992.

Ryskind, Allan H. *Hubert.* New York: Arlington House, 1968.

Sale, Kirkpatrick. *Power Shift: The Rise of the Southern Rim and its Challenge to the Eastern Establishment.* New York: Random House, 1975.

Scheim, David E. *Contract on America: The Mafia Murder of President John F. Kennedy.* New York: Shapolsky Publishers, Inc., 1988.

Scott, Peter Dale. *Crime and Cover-Up: The CIA, the Mafia, and the Dallas-Watergate Connection.* Berkeley, California: Westworks Publishers, 1977.

Scott, Peter Dale. *Deep Politics and the Death of JFK.* Berkley, California: University of California Press, 1993.

Sheridan, Walter. *The Fall and Rise of Jimmy Hoffa.* New York: Saturday Review Press, 1972.

Smith, Richard Norton. *Thomas E. Dewey & His Times.* New York: Simon & Schuster, Inc., 1982.

Steven, Stewart. *The Spymasters of Israel.* New York: Ballantine Books, 1980.

Summers, Anthony. *Conspiracy.* New York: McGraw-Hill Book Company, 1980.

Summers, Anthony. *Official and Confidential: The Secret Life of J. Edgar Hoover,* New York: G. P. Putnam's Sons, 1993.

Tarpley, Webster Griffin and Anton Chaitkin. *George Bush: The Unauthorized Biography*. Washington, D.C.: Executive Intelligence Review, 1992.

Thompson, Scott. *The Buckley Family: Wall Street Fabians in the Conservative Movement*. New York: Campaigner Publications. (undated; circa 1980).

Tivnan, Edward. *The Lobby: Jewish Political Power and American Foreign Policy*. New York: Simon & Schuster, 1987.

Truman, Margaret. *Harry S. Truman*. New York: William Morrow & Company, Inc., 1973.

Wean, Gary L. *There's a Fish in the Courthouse*. Oak View, California: Casitas Books, 1987.

Whalen, Richard J. *The Founding Father: The Story of Joseph P. Kennedy*. New York: New American Library, 1964.

Winter-Berger, Robert N. *The Washington Pay-off: An Insider's View of Corruption in Government*. Secaucus, New Jersey: Lyle Stuart, Inc., 1972.

Wise, David. *The American Police State: The Government Against the People*. New York: Random House, 1976.

# Reference Notes

Note: Most of the volumes cited in the following reference notes are readily available in public libraries. However, for rare and/or out-of-print works, please contact the nation's leading source for JFK assassination literature:

**Last Hurrah Book Shop**
**937 Memorial Avenue**
**Williamsport, PA  17701**
**Tel: (717) 327-9338**

---

**Chapter One**
**The Tie That Binds**

1 *Entertainment Weekly*, January 17, 1992.
2 *Ibid.*
3 *Washington Report on Middle East Affairs*, March 1992.
4 *Ibid.*
5 *University Reporter*, January, 1992.
6 *Tikkun* , March/April 1992.
7 *Ibid.*

**Chapter Two**
**Off With His Head**

8 *Washington Report on Middle East Affairs*,  February  1992.
9 *Ibid.*
10 *Ibid.*
11 *Ibid.*
12 *Ibid.*
13 *Ibid.*
14 *Ibid.*
15 *Washington Times*, January 14, 1992.

16 *Ibid.*

17 Jim Marrs. *Crossfire: The Plot That Killed Kennedy.* (New York: Carroll & Graf Publishers, Inc., 1989), p. 582.

17 Margaret Truman. *Harry S. Truman.* (New York: William Morrow & Company, Inc. 1973), p. 489.

### Chapter Three
### A Bad Habit

19 *Tikkun*, March/April 1992.

20 *Ibid.*

21 Livia Rokach. *Israel's Sacred Terrorism.* (Belmont, Massachusetts: AAUG Press, 1986), p. 34.

22 *The Spotlight*, September 6, 1982.

23 *The Spotlight*, November 10, 1980

24 *Ibid.*

25 Jonathan Marshall, Peter Dale Scott and Jane Hunter. *The Iran-Contra Connection: Secret Teams and Covert Operations in the Reagan Era.* (Boston, Massachusetts: South End Press, 1987), p. 217.

26 *Ibid.*

27 *The Spotlight,* April 21, 1986.

28 *The Spotlight.*, November 10, 1986

29 *Ibid.*

30 *Ibid.*

31 *Ibid.*, September 27, 1982.

### Chapter Four
### No Love Lost

32 C. David Heymann, *A Woman Named Jackie.* (New York: New American Library, 1989), p. 151.

33 *Ibid.*

34 *Time*, October 19, 1992., p. 28.

35 Richard Whalen. *The Founding Father: The Story of Joseph P. Kennedy.* (New York: New American Library, 1964), pp. 366-367.

36 George Lincoln Rockwell. *This Time the World.* (Liverpool, West Virginia: White Power Publications, 1963), p. v.

37 *Ibid.*, p. 123.

38 Interview with DeWest Hooker, January 20, 1992.

39 *Ibid.*

40 Edward Tivnan. *The Lobby: Jewish Political Power and American Foreign Policy.* (New York: Simon & Schuster, 1987), p. 54.

41 Interview with De West Hooker.

42 Richard Curtiss. *A Changing Image*. [Washington, D.C.: American Educational Trust, 1986), p. 65.

43 *Ibid.*

44 *Ibid.*, p. 66.

45 *Ibid.*.

46 Jim Marrs. *Crossfire: The Plot That Killed Kennedy.* (New York: Carroll & Graf Publishers, Inc., 1989), p. 175.

47 Michael Milan. The Squad: The U.S. Government's Secret Alliance With Organized Crime. [New York: Shapolski Publishers, 1989], p. 166.

48 Stephen Fox. *Blood and Power: Organized Crime in Twentieth Century America.* (New York: William Morrow & Company, 1989), p. 307.

49 *Ibid.*

50 *Ibid.*, pp. 313-314.

51 *Ibid.*, p. 314.

52 *Ibid.*, p. 315.

53 Sam Giancana & Chuck Giancana. *Double Cross: The Explosive Inside Story of the Mobster Who Controlled America.* (New York: Warner Books, 1992), p. 75.

54 *Ibid.*, p. 227.

55 *Ibid.*, p. 229.

56 *Ibid.*, p. 230.

57 *Ibid.*, p. 280.

58 *Ibid.*, p. 284.

59 Heymann, p. 234.

60 Tivnan, p. 52.

61 Victor Lasky. *JFK: The Man & The Myth.* (New Rochelle, New York, 1966), p. 143.

62 Tivnan, *Ibid.*

63 Seymour M. Hersh. *The Samson Option: Israel's Nuclear Arsenal and American Foreign Policy.* (New York: Random House, 1991), p. 94.

64 *Ibid.*, p. 96.

65 *Ibid.*, p. 97.

66 Alfred M. Lilienthal. *The Zionist Connection II.* (New Brunswick, New Jersey: North American, 1982), p. 548.

67 *Ibid.*

68 Hersh, p. 103.

69 Giancana, p. 296.

70 Mickey Cohen with John Peer Nugent. *Mickey Cohen: In My Own Words.* (Englewood Cliffs, New Jersey: Prentice-Hall, Inc., 1975), p. 236.

71 Hersh, p. 97.

72 *Ibid.*
73 *Ibid.*

**Chapter Five**
**Genesis**

74 Seymour Hersh. *The Samson Option: Israel's Nuclear Arsenal and American Foreign Policy.* (New York: Random House, 1991), p. 98.
75 *Ibid.,* p. 99.
76 *Ibid.*
77 *Ibid.*
78 *Ibid.,* p. 100.
79 *Ibid.,* p. 113.
80 Richard Curtiss. *A Changing Image* (Washington, D.C.: American Educational Trust, 1986), p. 65.
81 *Ibid.,* p. 67.
82 *Ibid.*
83 *New Outlook Magazine,* January, 1964, p. 5.
84 Alfred Lilienthal. *The Zionist Connection II.* (New Brunswick, New jersey: North American, 1982), p. 545.
85 Curtiss, p. 66.
86 *Ibid.,* p. 66
87 *Washington Post,* November 20, 1962.
88 *Washington Post,* March 20, 1982.
89 Stephen Green. *Taking Sides: America's Secret Relations With a Militant Israel* (New York: William Morrow & Company, 1984), p. 182.
90 *Ibid.,* p. 181.
91 *Ibid.*
92 *Ibid.*
93 *Ibid.,* pp. 181-182.
94 *Ibid.,* p. 182.
95 *Ibid.,* pp. 182-183.
96 *Ibid.,* p. 154.
97 *Ibid.,* p. 159-160.
98 Dan Raviv and Yossi Melman. *Every Spy a Prince.* (Boston: Houghton Mifflin Co., 1990), pp. 71-72.
99 *Ibid.,* pp. 159-160.
100 Hersh, p. 100.
101 *Ibid.*
102 Green, p. 164.
103 *Ibid.*

104 *Ibid.*

105 *Ibid.*, pp. 164-165.

106 *Ibid.* , p. 164.

107 Hersh, p. 101.

108 *Ibid.*, p. 102.

109 *Ibid.*

110 *Ibid.*, p. 103.

111 *Ibid.*

112 *Ibid.*, p. 105.

113 *Ibid.*, p. 118.

114 George Ball and Douglas Ball. *The Passionate Attachment.* [New York: W. W. Norton & Company, 1992), p. 51.

115 Lilienthal, p. 547.

116 Hersh, p. 107.

117 *Ibid.*, p. 109.

118 *Ibid.*, p. 108.

119 *Ibid.*

120 *Ibid.*, p. 109.

121 *Ibid.*, p. 111.

122 Andrew Cockburn and Leslie Cockburn. *Dangerous Liaison: The Inside Story of the U.S.-Israeli Covert Relationship.* (New York: Harper Collins Publishers, 1991), p. 91.

123 I. L. Kenan. *Israel's Defense Line: Her Friends and Foes in Washington.* (Buffalo: Prometheus Books, 1981), p. 166.

124 *Ibid.*, pp. 166-167.

125 *Washington Post*, August 13, 1963.

126 *Ibid.*, p. 187.

127 *London Jewish Chronicle*, Nov. 22, 1963.

128 *Ibid.*

129 Hersh, pp. 125-126.

130 Dan Kurzman. *Ben-Gurion: Prophet of Fire.* (New York: Simon & Schuster, 1983), pp. 440-441.

131 Hersh, pp. 120-121.

132 *Ibid.*, p. 120.

133 *Ibid.*, p. 121.

134 *Ibid.*

135 *Ibid.*

136 *Ibid.*, pp. 121-122.

137 *Ibid.*, p. 124.

138 Quoted by Yossi Melman in the *Los Angeles Times*, Nov. 28, 1993.

139 Ball, pp. 51-52.

140 *Washington Times,* July 4, 1992.

141 *Ibid.*

142 *Ibid.*

**Chapter Six**
**The Coming of the Messiah**

143 John Davis. *Mafia Kingfish: Carlos Marcello and the Assassination of John F. Kennedy.* (New York: McGraw-Hill Publishing Company, 1989), p. 159.

144 Robert Lacey. *Little Man: Meyer Lansky and the Gangster Life.* (Boston: Little, Brown & Company, 1991), pp. 332-333.

145 Ed Reid and Ovid Demaris. *The Green Felt Jungle.* (New York: Pocket Books edition, 1964), pp. 217-219.

146 *Ibid.*

147 Robert Morrow. *The Senator Must Die* (Santa Monica, California: Roundtable Publishing, Inc., 1988), p. 126.

148 Robert N. Winter-Berger. *The Washington Pay-Off* (New York: Lyle Stuart, Inc., 1972), pp. 65-66.

149 *Ibid.,* p. 66.

150 Stephen Green. *Taking Sides: America's Secret Relations With a Militant Israel.* (New York: William Morrow & Company, 1984), p. 186.

151 *Ibid.*

152 I. L. Kenan. *Israel's Defense Line: Her Friends and Foes in Washington.* (Buffalo: Prometheus Books, 1981), p. 173.

153 Seymour Hersh. *The Samson Option: Israel's Nuclear Arsenal and American Foreign Policy.* (New York: Random House, 1991), p. 127.

154 *Ibid.,* p. 128.

155 Green, p. 185.

156 *Ibid.,* p. 186.

157 Richard Curtiss. *A Changing Image* (Washington, D.C.: American Educational Trust, 1986), p. 68.

158 *Ibid.*

159 Jean Lacouture. *DeGaulle: The Ruler.* (New York: W. W. Norton & Company, 1993), p. 446.

160 *Ibid.*

161 *Ibid,* p. 378.

162 *Ibid.*

163 Curtiss, *Ibid.*

164 *Ibid.*

165 *Ibid.*

166 *Ibid.*

167 Alfred Lilienthal. *The Zionist Connection II.* (New Brunswick, New Jersey: North American, 1982), p. 549.

168 Kenan, p. 173.

169 Curtiss, p. 75.

170 Green, p. 246.

171 *Ibid.*

172 Curtiss, p. 75.

173 Green, p. 186.

174 Richard Deacon. *The Israeli Secret Service.* (New York: Taplinger Publishing Co., Inc., 1978), p. 179.

175 *Ibid.*

176 Green, pp. 165-166.

177 *Washington Observer*, September 15, 1968.

178 Alan H. Ryskind. *Hubert.* (New York: Arlington House, 1968), pp. 79-84.

179 Ball, p. 52.

180 Green, pp. 186-187.

181 *Ibid.*

182 *Ibid.*, p. 251.

183 *Ibid.*, pp. 243-244.

184 *Ibid.*, p. 249.

185 *Ibid.*, p. 180.

186 *Washington Star,* June 4, 1967.

187 Ball, pp. 65-66.

188 Green, p. 250.

**Chapter Seven**
**Israel's Godfather**

189 Marvin Miller. *The Breaking of a President: The Nixon Connection.* (Covina, California: Classic Publications, 1975), p. 336.

190 *The Wall Street Journal,* November 19, 1969, p. 1.

191 Miller, p. 327.

192 Martin Gosch & Richard Hammer. T*he Last Testament of Lucky Luciano.* (Boston: Little Brown & Company, 1974), p. 229.

193 Robert D. Morrow. *The Senator Must Die: The Murder of Robert F. Kennedy.* (Santa Monica, California: Roundtable Publishing, Inc., 1988), p. 238.

194 *The Spotlight*, September 25, 1978.

195 Gosch & Hammer, p. 381.

196 *Ibid.*, p. 431.

197 Robert Lacey. *Little Man: Meyer Lansky and the Gangster Life.* (Boston: Little, Brown & Company, 1991), p. 386.

198 Hank Messick. *Lansky.* (New York: Berkley Medallion Books, 1971), pp. 8-10.

199 Gosch & Hammer, p. 146.

200 Peter Dale Scott. *Deep Politics and the Death of JFK.* (Berkeley, California: University of California Press, 1993), p. 192.

201 Peter Dale Scott. *Deep Politics and the Death of JFK.* (Berkeley, California: University of California Press, 1993), p. 187.

202 *Ibid.*

203 Mickey Cohen with John Peer Nugent. *Mickey Cohen: In My Own Words.* (Englewood Cliffs, New Jersey: Prentice-Hall, Inc., 1975), p. 35.

204 *Ibid.*

205 Messick, p. 215.

206 Executive Intelligence Review. *Dope, Inc.* (New York: New Benjamin Franklin House, 1986), p. 587.

207 Michael Milan. *The Squad: The U.S. Government's Secret Alliance With Organized Crime.* (New York: Shapolsky Publishers, 1989), p. 194.

208 Hank Messick. *Secret File.* (New York: G. P. Putnam's Sons, 1969), p. 185.

209 Interview with *Ma'ariv*, July 5, 1971.

210 Milan, p. 206.

211 *Washington Observer*, May 15, 1969.

212 *Twin Circle*, September 29, 1968.

213 Executive Intelligence Review. (*Dope, Inc.*), pp. 578-579.

214 Curt Gentry. J. *Edgar Hoover: The Man and the Secrets.* (New York: W. W. Norton & Company, 1991), p. 530.

215 *Ibid.*, p. 531.

216 Tom Mangold. *Cold Warrior.* (New York: Simon & Schuster, 1991), p. 235.

217 Peter Dale Scott. *Deep Politics and the Death of JFK.* (Berkeley, California: University of California Press, 1993), p. 64.

218 Morrow, p. 98.

219 Sam Giancana and Chuck Giancana. *Double Cross: The Explosive Inside Story of the Mobster Who Controlled America.* (New York: Warner Books, 1992), p. 255.

220 *Ibid.*, p. 256.

221 Gentry, p. 495.

222 *Ibid.*, p. 628.

223 Antony Summers. *Official and Confidential: The Secret Life of J. Edgar Hoover*, (New York: G. P. Putnam's Sons, 1993), pp. 244-245.

224 Messick, p. 276.

225 Lacey, p. 163.

226 *Ibid.*, p. 164.

227 Robert I. Friedman. *The False Prophet: Rabbi Meir Kahane: From FBI Informant to Knesset Member.* (New York: Lawrence Hill Books, 1990), p. 144.

228 Executive Intelligence Review. *Moscow's Secret Weapon: Ariel Sharon and the Israeli Mafia.* (Washington, D.C.: Executive Intelligence Review, March 1, 1986), p. 14.

229 *Ibid.*

230 *Ibid.*, pp. 14-15.

231 *Ibid.*

232 Andrew Cockburn and Leslie Cockburn. *Dangerous Liaison: The Inside Story of the U.S.-Israeli Covert Relationship.* (New York: Harper Collins Publishers, 1991), pp. 41-42.

233 Ed Reid. *The Grim Reapers: The Anatomy of Organized Crime in America, City by City.* (New York: Pocket Books edition, 1964), p. 293.

234 Messick, pp. 248-249.

235 Executive Intelligence Review (*Moscow*), p. 17

236 *Ibid*, p. 16.

237 *Ibid.*, p. 18.

238 *Life*, September 16, 1967.

239 Messick, Ibid.

240 Jim Hougan. *Spooks: The Haunting of America—The Private Use of Secret Agents.* (New York: William Morrow & Co., Inc., 1985), p. 172.

241 Executive Intelligence Review (*Moscow,*), p. 13.

242 *Ibid.*, p. 16.

243 Morrow, p. 152.

244 Executive Intelligence Review. *Project Democracy: The 'Parallel Government' Behind the Iran-Contra Affair.* (Washington, D.C.: Executive Intelligence Review, April 1987), pp. 271-272.

245 *Ibid.*, p. 272.

246 Hank Messick and Burt Goldblatt. *The Mobs and the Mafia.* (New York: Ballantine Books, 1972), p. 204.

247 *Newsweek*, November 29, 1971.

248 Lacey, p. 333.

249 *Wall Street Journal*, Ibid.

250 Lacey, pp. 383-384.

**Chapter Eight**
**Thick as Thieves**

251 Andrew Cockburn and Leslie Cockburn. *Dangerous Liaison: The Inside Story of the U.S.-Israeli Covert Relationship.* (New York: Harper Collins Publishers, 1991), p. 16.

252 *Ibid.*

253 Tom Mangold. *Cold Warrier—James Jesus Angleton: The CIA's Master Spy Hunter.* (New York: Simon & Schuster, 1991), p. 307.

254 *Ibid.,* p. 52.

255 Peter Dale Scott. *Deep Politics and the Death of JFK.* (Berkeley, California: University of California Press, 1993), p. 54.

256 Cockburn, p. 42.

257 *Ibid.,* pp. 42-43.

258 *Ibid.,* p. 43.

259 Mangold, p. 362.

260 *Ibid.*

261 Steven Stewart. *The Spymasters of Israel.* (New York: Ballantine Books, 1980, p. 119.

262 Wilbur Crane Eveland. *Ropes of Sand: America's Failure in the Middle East.* (New York: W. W. Norton & Company, 1980), p. 95.

263 Wolf Blitzer. *Between Washington and Jerusalem.* (New York: Oxford University Press, 1985), p. 96.

264 *Ibid.*

265 Cockburn, p. 69.

266 *Ibid.*

267 Richard Deacon. *The Israeli Secret Service.* (New York: Taplinger Publishing Co., Inc., 1978), pp. 170-171.

268 *Ibid.,* p. 171.

269 Cockburn, p. 80.

270 *Ibid.*

271 Seymour Hersh. *The Samson Option: Israel's Nuclear Arsenal and American Foreign Policy* (New York: Random House, 1991), p. 144.

272 Stephen Green. *Taking Sides: America's Secret Relations With a Militant Israel.* (New York: William Morrow & Company, 1984), p. 164.

273 Cockburn, p. 147.

274 Cockburn, pp. 42-43.

275 Deacon, p. 35.

276 Cockburn, p. 42.

277 Mangold, p. 314-315.

278 Robert I. Friedman. *The False Prophet: Rabbi Meir Kahane—From FBI Informant to Knesset Member.* (New York: Lawrence Hill Books, 1990), pp. 34-35.

279 Alfred W. McCoy. *The Politics of Heroin.* (Brooklyn, New York: Lawrence Hill Books, 1991), p. 25.

280 Alfred W. McCoy. *The Politics of Heroin.* (Brooklyn, New York: Lawrence Hill Books, 1991), p. 58.

281 Peter Dale Scott. *Deep Politics and the Death of JFK.* (Berkeley, California: University of California Press, 1993), p. 196.

282 Carl Oglesby. *The JFK Assassination: The Facts and the Theories.* (New York: Signet Books, 1992), p. 145.

283 *Ibid.*, 149.

284 Peter Dale Scott. *Deep Politics and the Death of JFK.* (Berkeley, California: University of California Press, 1993), p. 55.

285 *The New York Times,* December 24, 1974.

**Chapter Nine**
**A Little Unpleasantness**

286 *Washington Observer,* April 15, 1972.

287 Sam Giancana and Chuck Giancana. *Double Cross: The Explosive Inside Story of the Mobster Who Controlled America.* (New York: Warner Books, 1992), p. 301.

288 Mark Lane. *Plausible Denial.* (New York: Thunder's Mouth Press, 1992), p. 93.

289 *Ibid.*, pp. 99-100.

290 *Ibid.*, p. 100.

291 *The Spotlight,* February 17, 1992.

292 *Ibid.*

293 *Ibid.*

294 L. Fletcher Prouty. *The Secret Team: The CIA and its Allies in Control of the United States and the World.* (Costa Mesa, Calif.: Institute for Historical Review, 1990), p. 416.

295 Lane, pp. 107-108.

296 *Ibid.*

297 Anthony Summers. *Conspiracy.* (New York: McGraw-Hill Book Company, 1980), p. 193.

298 *The Spotlight,* October 28, 1991.

299 *The Spotlight,* February 17, 1992.

300 *Ibid.*

301 *Ibid.*

302 Victor Ostrovsky and Claire Hoy. *By Way of Deception: The Making and Unmaking of a Mossad Officer.* (New York: St. Martin's press, 1990), pp. 217-218.

303 John Dinges and Saul Landau. *Assassination on Embassy Row.* (New York: Pantheon Books, 1980), pp. 98-99.

304 *Ibid.*, p. 396.

305 *Ibid.*, pp. 96-97.

306 *Washington Observer*, November 1, 1971.

307 Jim Marrs. *Crossfire: The Plot That Killed Kennedy.* (New York: Carroll & Graf Publishers, Inc., 1989), p. 200.

308 Michael Canfield and Alan J. Weberman. *Coup d'etat in America: The CIA and the Assassination of John F. Kennedy.* (New York: The Third Press, 1975), p. 29.

309 John Loftus and Mark Aarons. *The Secret War Against the Jews.* (New York: St. Martin's Press, 1994), p.

310 *Ibid.*, pp. 29-30.

311 Alistair Horne. *A Savage War of Peace.* (Middlesex, England: Penguin Books, 1977), p. 498.

312 *Ibid.*, p. 445.

313 *Ibid.*, pp. 445-446.

314 *Ibid.*, p. 447.

315 Alexander Harrison. *Challenging DeGaulle: The OAS and the Counterrevolution in Algeria.* (New York: Praeger Publishers, 1989), p. 70.

316 Alistair Horne. *A Savage War of Peace.* (Middlesex, England: Penguin Books, 1977), p. 498.

**Chapter Ten**
**Little Man's Little Man**

317 David E. Scheim. *Contract on America: The Mafia Murder of President John F. Kennedy.* (New York: Shapolsky Publishers, Inc., 1988), p. 120.

318 *Ibid.*

319 *Ibid.*, p. 48.

320 Jim Garrison. *On the Trail of the Assassins* (New York: Sheridan Square Press, 1988), p. 163-164.

321 Peter Dale Scott. *Deep Politics and the Death of JFK.* (Berkeley, California: University of California Press, 1993), p. 55.

322 Mark Lane. *Plausible Denial.* (New York: Thunder's Mouth Press, 1991), p. 34.

323 William Roemer. *War of the Godfathers*. (New York: Donald I. Fine, Inc., 1990), p. 53.

324 *Ibid.*, p. 55.

325 *Ibid.*, pp. 166-178.

326 G. Robert Blakey & Richard N. Billings. *The Plot to Kill the President: Organized Crime Assassinated JFK—The Definitive Story*. (New York: Times Books, 1981), p. 401.

327 Hank Messick, Lansky. (New York: Berkley Medallion Books, 1971), pp. 82-83.

328 Martin A. Gosch & Richard Hammer. *The Last Testament of Lucky Luciano*. (Boston: Little Brown & Company, 1974), pp. 156-157.

329 Messick, *Ibid.*

330 *Ibid.*, pp. 86-87.

331 *Ibid.*, p. 87.

332 *Ibid.*

333 *Ibid.*, p. 129.

334 Robert D. Morrow. *The Senator Must Die: The Murder of Robert F. Kennedy*. (Santa Monica: CA: Roundtable Publishing, Inc., 1988), p. 16.

335 Sam Giancana and Chuck Giancana. *Double Cross: The Explosive Inside Story of the Mobster Who Controlled America*. (New York: Warner Books, 1992), p. 298.

336 Morrow, p. 30.

337 Giancana, p. 255.

338 Anthony Summers. *Conspiracy*. (New York: McGraw-Hill Book Company, 1980), p. 316.

339 Giancana, p. 63.

340 Messick, p. 84.

341 Seth Kantor. *Who Was Jack Ruby?* (New York: Everest House, 1978), p. 28.

342 *Ibid.*

343 House Select Committee on Assassinations. *The Final Assassinations Report*. (New York: Bantam Books, 1979), p. 204.

**Chapter Eleven**
**Cuban Love Song**

344 Curt Gentry. *J. Edgar Hoover: The Man and the Secrets*. (New York: W. W. Norton & Company, 1991), p. 496.

345 Anthony Summers. *Conspiracy*. (New York: McGraw-Hill Book Company, 1980), pp. 266-267.

346 Jim Hougan. *Spooks: The Haunting of America—The Private use of Secret Agents.* (New York: William Morrow & Company, Inc., 1988), pp. 335-226.

347 *Free Cuba News,* December 15, 1965.

348 Summers, p. 193.

349 Charles Rappleye and Ed Becker. *All American Mafioso: The Johnny Rosselli Story.* (New York: Doubleday, 1991), p. 189.

350 Robert Morrow. *The Senator Must Die: The Murder of Robert F. Kennedy.* (Santa Monica, CA: Roundtable Publishing, Inc., 1988), p. 59.

351 Rappleye and Becker, *Ibid.*

352 *Yipster Times* (no date available)

353 Peter Dale Scott. *Deep Politics and the Death of JFK.* (Berkeley, California: University of California Press, 1993), p. 180.

354 Rappleye and Becker, p. 245.

355 *Ibid.,* p. 256.

356 *Ibid.,* p. 334.

357 *Ibid.,* p. 354.

358 Rappleye and Becker, p. 327.

359 Giancana, p. 355.

360 *Ibid.,* pp. 354-355.

361 Scott, p. 71.

## Chapter Twelve
## An Opiate for the Masses

362 Alfred McCoy. *The Politics of Heroin: CIA Complicity in the Global Drug Trade.* (Chicago: Lawrence Hill Books, 1991), pp. 40-41.

363 Hank Messick. *Lansky.* (New York: Berkley Medallion Books, 1971), pp. 210-211.

364 *Ibid.*

365 Dan Moldea. *The Hoffa Wars: Teamsters, Rebels, Politicians and the Mob,* (New York: Paddington Press Ltd., 1978), p. 123.

366 Messick, p. 215.

367 *Ibid.*

368 McCoy, p. 40.

369 *Ibid.,* pp. 44-45.

370 Messick, p. 199.

371 McCoy, *Ibid.*

372 *Ibid.,* pp. 64-65.

373 *Ibid.*, pp. 60-61.

374 *Ibid.*

375 *Ibid.* p. 19.

376 Sam Giancana and Chuck Giancana. *Double Cross: The Explosive Inside Story of the Mobster Who Controlled America.* (New York: Warner Books, 1992), p. 259.

377 *Ibid.*, p. 258.

378 McCoy, p. 462.

379 Bernard Fensterwald and the Committee to Investigate Assassinations. *Coincidence or Conspiracy?* (New York: Zebra Books, 1977), p. 187.

380 McCoy, p. 477.

381 Executive Intelligence Review. *Project Democracy: The 'Parallel Government' Behind the Iran-Contra Affair.* (Washington, D.C.: EIR News Service, 1987), p. 287.

382 Jonathan Kwitny. *Endless Enemies: The Making of an Unfriendly World.* (New York: Penguin Books, 1986), p. 331.

383 *The Wall Street Journal,* December 19, 1991.

384 Rachel Ehrenfeld. *Evil Money: Encounters Along the Money Trail.* (New York: Harper Collins Publishers, 1992), p. 259.

385 *Ibid.*

386 Henry Hurt. *Reasonable Doubt: An Investigation into the Assassination of John F. Kennedy.* (New York: Holt, Rinehart & Winston, 1985), pp. 417-419.

387 Dick Russell. *The Man Who Knew Too Much.* (New York: Carroll & Graf Publishers, Inc., 1992), p. 563.

388 McCoy, p. 14.

389 Giancana, p. 215.

**Chapter Thirteen**
**A Missing Link**

390 A. J. Weberman writing in *The Yipster Times* (no date available)

391 Hank Messick. *Lansky.* (New York: Berkley Medallion Books, 1971), p. 153.

392 Michael Milan. *The Squad: The U.S. Government's Secret Alliance With Organized Crime.* (New York: Shapolsky Publishers, Inc., 1989), p. 195.

393 Mickey Cohen with John Peer Nugent. *Mickey Cohen: In My Own Words.* (Englewood Cliffs, New Jersey: Prentice-Hall, Inc., 1975), p. 82.

394 *Ibid.*, p. 90.

395 *Ibid.*

396 *Ibid.*, p. 91.

397 Ovid Demaris. *The Last Mafioso.* (New York: Bantam Books, 1981), p. 32.

398 Cohen, *Ibid.*

399 *Ibid.*, pp. 91-92.

400 Gary L. Wean. *There's a Fish in the Courthouse.* (Oak View, California: Casitas Books, 1987), p. 681.

401 *Ibid.*

402 Robert Morrow. *The Senator Must Die: The Murder of Robert F. Kennedy.* (Santa Monica, California: Roundtable Publishing, Inc., 1988), p. 16.

403 John Davis. *Mafia Kingfish: Carlos Marcello and the Assassination of John F. Kennedy* (New York: McGraw-Hill Publishing Co., 1989), p. 239.

404 Wean, pp. 678-679.

405 *Ibid.*, p. 679.

406 *Ibid.*, p. 677.

407 *Ibid.*,

408 *Ibid.*

409 Curt Gentry, *J. Edgar Hoover: The Man and the Secrets.* (New York: W. W. Norton & Company, 1991), p. 493.

410 Wean, pp. 687-688.

411 Ibid., p. 688.

412 *Ibid.*, p. 689.

413 *Ibid.*

414 *Ibid.*

415 *Ibid.*, p. 739.

416 Peter Dale Scott. *Deep Politics and the Death of JFK.* (Berkeley, California: University of California Press, 1993), p. 143.

417 *Ramparts* (No date available).

**Chapter Fourteen**
**The Errand Boy**

418 Stephen Fox, *Blood and Power.* (New York: William Morrow & Company, 1989), p. 307.

419 Bernard Fensterwald and the Committee to Investigate Assassinations. *Coincidence or Conspiracy?* (New York: Zebra Books, 1977) pp. 371-372.

420 Seth Kantor. *Who Was Jack Ruby?* (New York: Everest House, 1978) pp. 13-14.

421 Peter Dale Scott. *Deep Politics and the Death of JFK.* (Berkeley, California: University of California Press, 1993), p. 180.

[422] *Ibid.*, p. 184.

[423] *Ibid.*, p. 183.

[424] *Ibid.*, p. 182.

[425] Jim Marrs, *Crossfire: The Plot That Killed Kennedy* (New York: Carroll & Graf Publishers, Inc., 1989), p. 392.

[426] Scott, p. 141.

[427] *Ibid.*, p. 144.

[428] *Ibid.*, p. 141.

[429] *Ibid.*, p. 71.

[430] *Ibid.*, p. 71.

[431] *Ibid.*, p. 70.

[432] *Ibid.*, p. 151.

[433] *Ibid.*, p. 193.

[434] *Ibid.*, p. 19.

[435] *Ibid.*, p. 21.

[436] *Ibid.*, p. 181.

[437] *Ibid.*, p. 151.

[438] *Ibid.*, p. 201.

[439] *Ibid.*

[440] *Ibid.*, p. 349.

[441] Sam Giancana and Chuck Giancana. *Double Cross: The Explosive Inside Story of the Mobster Who Controlled America.* (New York: Warner Books, 1992), p. 329.

[442] Robert Morrow. *The Senator Must Die: The Murder of Robert F. Kennedy.* ( Santa Monica: CA: Roundtable Publishing, Inc., 1988), p. 19.

[443] *I bid.*, p. 49.

[444] John Henshaw,*The National Enquirer*, May 17, 1964.

[445] *Ibid.*

[446] John Henshaw, *The Washington Observer* , July 1, 1969.

[447] Private correspondence in author's files.

[448] Kantor, p. 127.

[449] *Ibid.*, p. 209.

[450] Mike Milan. *The Squad: The U.S. Government's Secret Alliance With Organized Crime.* (New York: Shapolsky Publishers, 1989), pp. 232-234.

[451] *Ibid.*

[452] David Scheim. *Contract on America: The Mafia Murder of President John F. Kennedy.* (New York: Shapolsky Publishers, Inc., 1988), pp. 45-47.

[453] G. Robert Blakey and Richard N. Billings. *The Plot to Kill the President: Organized Crime Assassinated JFK.* (New York: Times Books, 1981), p. 396.

454 Fensterwald, p. 288.
455 Mickey Cohen with John Peer Nugent. *Mickey Cohen: In My Own Words.* (Englewood Cliffs, New Jersey: Prentice-Hall, Inc., 1975), p. 129.
456 Milan, p. 10.
457 Peter Dale Scott. *Deep Politics and the Death of JFK.* (Berkeley, California: University of California Press, 1993), p. 143.
458 Cohen, p. 200.
459 Ibid.
460 Blakey & Billings, p. 325.
461 *Ibid.*, p. 327.
462 *Ibid.*
463 *Ibid.*
464 Mark Lane. *A Citizens Dissent* (New York: Holt, Rinehart & Winston, 1968), pp. 30-31.
465 *Ibid.*
466 *Ibid.*
467 *Ibid.*
468 *Ibid.*, p. 34.
469 *Ibid.*
470 *Ibid.*, p. 36.
471 *Ibid.*
472 Private memorandum supplied to author and interview with source who supplied the memorandum.
473 *Washington Daily News*, Oct. 6, 1966.
474 *Philadelphia News*, February 22, 1964.
475 Alan Adelson. *The Ruby-Oswald Affair.* (Seattle, Washington: Romar Books, Ltd., 1988), p. 6.

**Chapter Fifteen**
**The Twain Shall Meet**

476 Paris Flammonde. *The Kennedy Conspiracy: An Uncommissioned Report on the Jim Garrison Investigation.* (New York: Meredith Press, 1969), p. 219.
477 Peter Dale Scott. *Deep Politics and the Death of JFK.* (Berkeley, California: University of California Press, 1993), pp. 300-301.
478 *Ibid.*, p. 106.
479 *Ibid.*, p. 214 (paraphrasing *Paesa Sera*, March 4, 1967).
480 *Ibid.*, p. 215.

481 *Ibid.*

482 *Ibid.*, p. 216.

483 *Ibid.*, p. 95.

484 *Ibid.*, p. 97.

485 *Ibid.*, p. 333.

486 *Ibid.*, p. 97.

487 *Ibid.*, pp 102-106.

488 *Ibid.*, p. 333.

489 *Ibid.*, p. 218.

490 Jim Garrison. *On the Trail of the Assassins: My Investigation and Prosecution of the Murder of President Kennedy.* (New York: Sheridan Square Press, 1988), p. 87.

491 Flammonde, p. 218.

492 Executive Intelligence Review, p. 429.

493 Dick Russell, *The Man Who Knew Too Much* [New York: Carroll & Graf Publishers, 1992), p. 792.

494 *Ibid.*, p. 430.

495 Flammonde, p. 31.

496 Garrison, p. 118.

497 Flammonde, p. 224.

498 E. Mullins, *The World Order* (Ezra Pound Institute, 1992), p. 157.

499 Tom Mangold. *Cold Warrior—James Jesus Angleton: The CIA's Master Spy Hunter* (New York: Simon & Schuster, 1991), p. 43.

500 Executive Intelligence Review, *Dope, Inc.*, p. 433.

501 *Ibid.*, p. 435.

502 Executive Intelligence Review. *Dope, Inc.* (1978 edition), p. 354.

503 *Ibid.*

504 Flammonde, p. 221.

505 Executive Intelligence Review, p. 438.

506 *Ibid.*, p. 439.

507 *Ibid.*, pp. 440-441.

508 Richard Deacon. *The Israeli Secret Service.* (New York: Taplinger Publishing Co., Inc., 1978), p. 22.

509 Robert Morrow. *The Senator Must Die: The Murder of Robert F. Kennedy.* (Santa Monica, CA: Roundtable Publishing, Inc., 1988), p. 123.

510 *Ibid.*, p. 133.

511 *Ibid.*, p. 148.

512 *Ibid.*, p. 219.

513 Michael Canfield and Alan J. Weberman. *Coup d' etat in America: The CIA and the Assassination of John F. Kennedy* (New York: The Third Press, 1975), p. 40.

514 Flammonde, *Ibid.*

515 *Ibid.* , p. 28.

516 Executive Intelligence Review. *Dope, Inc.* (New York: New Benjamin Franklin House, 1986), p. 434.

517 Jean Lacouture. *DeGaulle: The Ruler.* (New York: W. W. Norton & Company, 1993), p. 278.

518 *Ibid.*, p. 296.

519 Alistair Horne. *A Savage War of Peace.* (Middlesex, England: Penguin Books, 1977), p. 499.

520 Paris Flammonde. *The Kennedy Conspiracy.* (New York: Meredith Press, 1969), p. 223.

521 Gerald Krefetz. *Jews and Money.* (New York: Ticknor and Fields, 1982), p. 104.

522 Lacouture, p. 324.

523 Alexander Harrison. *Challenging DeGaulle: The OAS and the Counterrevolution in Algeria.* (New York: Praeger Publishers, 1989), p. 67.

524 *Ibid.*, p. 87.

525 *Ibid.*, p. 87.

526 Paul Henissart. *Wolves in the City: The Death of French Algeria.* (New York: Simon & Schuster, 1970), p. 346.

527 *Ibid.*, p. 347.

528 Benjamin Beit-Hallahmi. *The Israeli Connection—Who Israel Arms and Why.* (New York: Pantheon Books, 1987), pp. 44-45.

529 *Ibid.*

530 Executive Intelligence Review, *Dope, Inc.*, p. 442-443.

531 Dick Russell. *The Man Who Knew Too Much.* [New York: Carroll & Graf Publishers, 1993), p. 396.

532 Peter Dale Scott. *Deep Politics and the Death of JFK.* (Berkeley, California: University of California Press, 1993), p. 109.

533 *Ibid.*, p. 562.

534 Robert Morrow. *Betrayal: A Reconstruction of Certain Clandestine Events from the Bay of Pigs to the Assassination of John F. Kennedy.* (New York: Warner Books, 1976), p. 84.

535 Anthony Summers. *Conspiracy.* (New York: McGraw-Hill Book Company, 1980), p. 324-325.

536 Executive Intelligence Review. *The Ugly Truth About the ADL* [Washington, D.C.: Executive Intelligence Review, 1992], p. 73.

537 Jack Nelson. *Terror in the Night.* [New York: Simon & Schuster, 1993], p.214.

538 *San Francisco Weekly*, April 28, 1993.
539 A. Forster. *Square One* [New York: Donald Fine, Inc., 1988], p. 56.
540 *Ibid.*
541 *Ibid.*
542 Peter Dale Scott. *Deep Politics and the Death of JFK.*
(Berkeley, California: University of California Press,
1993), p. 243.
543 *Washington Observer*, June 15, 1970.
544 Hutchison, Robert,*Vesco.* (New York: Praeger Publishers, 1974), p. 97.
545 John Loftus and Mark Aarons. *The Secret War
Against the Jews.* (New York: St. Martin's Press, 1994),
p. 134.

**Chapter Sixteen
Double Cross in Dallas?**

546 Dick Russell. *The Man Who Knew Too Much.* [New York: Carroll &
Graf, 1993), p. 588.

547 See Mark Lane. *Plausible Denial.* (New York: Thunder's Mouth
Press, 1991).
548 *The Spotlight,* October 28, 1992
549 *The Spotlight*, August 14, 1978.
550 Wilmington, Delaware *Sunday News Journal,* August 20, 1978.
551 Dick Russell, *The Man Who Knew Too Much* [New York: Carroll & Graf
Publishers, Inc., 1992), p. 475.
552 *Ibid.*
553 Lane, pp. 45-46.
554 *Ibid.*, p. 64.
555 *Ibid.*, p. 82.
556 *Ibid.*, p. 64.
557 *Ibid.*, p. 78.
558 *Ibid.*, p. 83
559 Bernard Fensterwald and the Committee to Investigate Assassinations .
*Coincidence or Conspiracy?* (New York: Zebra Books, 1977), p. 184.
560 Peter Dale Scott. *Deep Politics and the Death of JFK.*
(Berkeley, California: University of California Press,
1993), p. 44.
561 *Ibid.*
562 *Ibid.*
563 *Ibid.*, pp. 184-185.
564 Jim Hougan. *Secret Agenda: Watergate, Deep Throat and the CIA.*
(New York: Random House, 1984), p. 220.

565 *New American View*, February 1, 1992.

566 James Hepburn. *Farewell America*. [Liechtenstein: Frontiers Company, 1968], p. 349.

567 Gary Wean. *There's a Fish in the Courthouse*. (Oak View, California: Casitas Books, 1987), p. 695.

568 *Ibid.*, p. 697.

569 *Ibid.*

570 *Ibid.*, p. 698.

571 *Ibid.*, p. 699.

572 *Ibid.*, p. 698.

573 *Ibid.* p. 699.

574 *Ibid.*, pp. 699-700.

575 *Ibid.*, p. 701.

576 *Ibid.*, pp. 702-703.

577 Anthony Summers. *Conspiracy*. (New York: McGraw-Hill Book Co., 1980), p. 451.

578 *Ibid.*

579 Dan Moldea. *The Hoffa Wars: Teamsters, Rebels, Politicians and the Mob*. (New York: Paddington Press Ltd, 1978), p. 279.

580 Dick Russell. *The Man Who Knew Too Much*. (New York: Carroll & Graf Publishers, 1992), p. 693.

581 *Ibid.*, p. 477.

582 *Ibid.*, pp. 703-704.

583 *Ibid.* p. 539.

584 *San Diego Tribune*, February 9, 1992.

585 *Newsweek*, December 23, 1991.

586 Michael Milan. *The Squad: The U.S. Government's Secret Alliance With Organized Crime*. (New York: Shapolsky Publishers, Inc., 1989) pp. 232-234.

587 *Ibid.*

588 Victor Ostrovsky and Claire Hoy. *By Way of Deception: The Making and Unmaking of a Mossad Officer*. (New York: St. Martin's Press, 1990), p. 141-143.

589 Executive Intelligence Review. *The Buckley Family: Wall Street Fabians in the Conservative Movement*. (New York: Campaigner Publications), p. 11.

590 Russell, p. 506.

591 Hepburn, pp. 337-338.

592 Warren Hinckle and William Turner. *Deadly Secrets*. [New York: Thunder's Mouth Press, 1992), p. 434.

593 Private communication to author, dated August 15, 1993.

594 *Ibid.*

595 Russell, p. 785.

596 Tom Mangold. *Cold Warrior.* (New York: Simon & Schuster, 1991), p. 133.

597 *Ibid.* p. 558.

598 *Ibid.*, pp. 559-560

599 Dan Kurzman. *Ben-Gurion: Prophet of Fire.* (New York: Simon & Schuster, 1985), p. 417.

600 Dan Raviv and Yossi Melman. *Every Spy a Prince.* (Boston: Houghton, Mifflin & Company, 1990), p. 73.

601 *Ibid.*, p. 563.

602 Henry Hurt. *Reasonable Doubt.* (New York: Holt, Rinehart & Winston, 1985), p. 418.

603 Robert Morrow. *First Hand Knowledge.* [New York: Shapolski Publications, 1992), p.191.

604 Dick Russell. *The Man Who Knew Too Much* (New York: Carroll & Graf Publishers, 1992), p. 785.

605 Jean Lacouture. *DeGaulle: The Ruler.* (New York: W. W. Norton & Company, 1993), p. 297.

606 *Ibid.*, p. 325.

607 Alexander Harrison. *Challenging DeGaulle: The OAS and the Counterrevolution in Algeria.* (New York: Praeger Publishers, 1989), p. 123.

608 Paul Henissart. *Wolves in the City: The Death of French Algeria.* (New York: Simon & Schuster, 1970), p. 174

609 Richard Deacon. *The Israeli Secret Service.* (New York: Taplinger Publishing Co., Inc., 1977), p. 177.

610 Stewart Steven. *The Spymasters of Israel.* (New York: Ballantine Books, 1980), p. 242.

611 *Ibid.*, p. 561.

612 Frederick Forsyth. *The Day of the Jackal.* (New York: Bantam Books, 1972), p. 17.

613 Alfred W. McCoy. *The Politics of Heroin.* (Brooklyn, New York: Lawrence Hill Books, 1991), p. 69.

614 *Ibid.*

615 Benjamin Beit-Hallahmi. *The Israeli Connection—Who Israel Arms and Why.* (New York: Pantheon Books, 1987), p. 46.

616 Stewart Steven. *The Spymasters of Israel.* (New York: Ballantine Books, 1980), p. 242.

617 Dan Raviv and Yossi Melman. *Every Spy a Prince.* (Boston: Houghton Mifflin Co., 1990), p. 158.

618 Dan Raviv and Yossi Melman. *Every Spy a Prince.* (Boston: Houghton Mifflin Co., 1990), pp. 158-159.

619 Steven, p. 252.

620 *Ibid.*

621 Dick Russell. *The Man Who Knew Too Much* (New York: Carroll & Graf Publishers, 1992), p. 785.

622 Jim Marrs. *Crossfire: The Plot That Killed Kennedy.* (New York: Carroll & Graf Publishers, Inc., 1989), pp. 202-209.

623 *Ibid.*, pp. 401-405.

624 Tom Mangold. *Cold Warrior.* (New York: Simon & Schuster, 1991), p. 134.

## Chapter Seventeen
## They Dare Not Speak Out

625 Sid Blumenthal (editor). *Government by Gunplay: Assassination Conspiracy Theories From Dallas to Today.* (New York: Signet Books, 1976), p. 231.

626 Jim Garrison, *On the Trail of the Assassins.* (New York: Sheridan Square Press, 1988), p. 251.

627 *Ibid.*

628 Anthony Summers, *Official and Confidential: The Secret Life of J. Edgar Hoover.* {New York: G. P. Putnam's Sons, 1992), pp. 244-245.

629 James Kirkwood. *American Grotesque: An Account of the Clay Shaw-Jim Garrison Affair in New Orleans.* (New York: Simon & Schuster, 1970), p. 47.

630 *Washington Observer*, August 1, 1970.

631 Walter Sheridan. *The Fall and Rise of Jimmy Hoffa.* New York: Saturday Review Press, 1972), p. 418.

632 *Los Angeles Times,* February 13, 1970.

633 Jim Garrison. *On the Trail of the Assassins: My Investigation & Prosecution of the Murder of President Kennedy.* (New York: Sheridan Square Press, 1988), p. 168.

634 Dick Russell. *The Man Who Knew Too Much.* [New York: Carroll & Graf Publishers, 1992), p. 400.

635 *Ibid.*, pp. 401-402.

636 *Ibid.*, p. 430.

637 Warren Hinckle and William Turner. *Deadly Secrets.* [New York: Thunder's Mouth Press, 1992), p. 252.

638 Executive Intelligence Review. *Moscow's Secret Weapon.* [Washington, D.C.: Executive Intelligence Review, March 1, 1986), p. 119.

639 Peter Dale Scott. *Deep Politics and the Death of JFK.* (Berkeley, California: University of California Press, 1993), p. 187.

640 *Ibid.,* p. 173.

641 Kirkwood, p. 162.

642 Garrison, p. 270.

643 David Wise. *The American Police State: The Government Against the People*. (New York: Random House, 1976), pp. 200-201.

644 Wise, *Ibid.*

645 Richard Deacon. *The Israeli Secret Service*. (New York: Taplinger Publishing Co, Inc., 1978), p. 171.

646 *Twin Circle*. September 29, 1968.

647 Lee O'Brien. *American Jewish Organizations and Israel*. (Washington, D.C.: Institute for Palestine Studies, 1986), p. 99.

648 *Ibid.*

649 *Ibid.*, p. 100.

650 *Washington Post*, March 3, 1967.

651 Charles Rappleye and Ed Becker. *All American Mafioso: The Johnny Rosselli Story*. (New York: Doubleday, 1991), p. 471.

652 Ovid Demaris. *The Last Mafioso: The Treacherous World of Jimmy Fratianno*. (New York: Bantam Books, 1981), p. 389.

653 Rappleye and Becker, p. 475.

654 *Ibid.*

655 *Ibid.*

656 Peter Dale Scott. *Crime and Cover-up: The CIA, the Mafia, and the Dallas-Watergate Connection*. (Berkeley, California: Westworks Publishers, 1977), p. 26.

657 *Ibid.*, p. 25.

658 *Ibid.*

659 *Washington Observer*, April 1, 1967

660 *Washington Observer*, June 15, 1968.

661 Oliver Pilat. *Drew Pearson: An Unauthorized Biography*. (New York: Harper's Magazine Press, 1973), p. 241.

662 *Ibid.*, p. 183.

663 *Ibid.*, p. 17.

664 *Ibid.*, p. 169.

665 Interview with Alec deMontmorency, January 25, 1992.

666 Pilat, p. 183.

667 *Ibid.*

668 *Washington Observer*, February 15, 1967.

669 *Washington Observer*, November 1, 1968.

670 Mickey Cohen with John Peer Nugent. *Mickey Cohen: In My Own Words*. (Englewood Cliffs, NJ: Prentice-Hall, Inc., 1975), pp. 232-233.

671 *Uncle Frank: The Biography of Frank Costello* (New York: Drake Publishers, Inc., 1973), p. 230.

672 *Washington Observer*, July 1, 1969.

673 Pilat, p. 233.

674 J. Hougan. *Secret Agenda*. (New York: Random House, 1984), p. 89.

675 *Washington Observer*, February 1, 1971.

676 Robert Lacey. *Little Man: Meyer Lansky and the Gangster Life*. (Boston: Little, Brown & Company, 1991), p. 417.

677 *Washington Observer*, Ibid.

678 *Ibid.*

679 Alexander Harrison. *Challenging DeGaulle: The OAS and the Counterrevolution in Algeria*. (New York: Praeger Publishers, 1989), p. 15.

680 *New York Post*, January 14, 1992.

681 *The Spotlight*, February 17, 1992.

682 Dan Moldea. *The Hoffa Wars: Teamsters, Rebels, Politicians and the Mob*. (New York: Paddington Press, 1978), p. 421.

683 *The Washington Times*, January 19, 1992.

684 *Human Events*, January 4, 1982.

685 *Covert Action Information Bulletin*, Summer 1989.

686 *Moscow's Secret Weapon*. [Washington, D.C.: Executive Intelligence Review, March 1, 1986], pp. 82-84.

687 *Covert Action Information Bulletin, Ibid.*

688 Mark Lane. *Rush to Judgment*. (New York: Thunder's Mouth Press, 1992), p. xxvii.

689 *The Spotlight*, July 17, 1978.

690 *Ibid.*

691 Connie Bruck. *Master of the Game*. (New York: Simon & Schuster, 1994), p. 52.

692 *The Spotlight*, October 5, 1981.

693 *Ibid.*

694 *Ibid.*, August 10, 1981.

695 *Ibid.*

696 Ron Lewis. *Flashback*. (Medford, Oregon: Lewcom Productions, 1993), p. 119.

697 Alexander Cockburn, *The Nation*, May 18, 1992.

**Chapter Eighteen**
**The Heir to the Throne**

698 Private interview with former RFK campaign volunteer who was present at the scene when Robert Kennedy was assassinated.

699 G. Robert Blakey and Richard Billings. *The Plot to Kill the President.* (New York: Times Books, 1981), p. 395.

700 Seymour Hersh. *The Samson Option: Israel's Nuclear Arsenal and American Foreign Policy.* (New York: Random House, 1992), p. 100.

701 Robert Morrow. *The Senator Must Die: The Murder of Robert F. Kennedy.* (Santa Monica, California: Roundtable Publishing, Inc., 1988). NOTE: The reconstruction of the RFK assassination by Morrow as described in this chapter appears, essentially, within pages 119-227 of Morrow's book.

702 *Ibid.,* p. 49.

703 Andrew Cockburn and Leslie Cockburn. *Dangerous Liaison: The Inside Story of the U.S.-Israeli Covert Relationship.* (New York: Harper Collins Publishers, 1991), p. 99.

704 *Ibid.,* p. 101.

705 *Ibid.,* p. 102.

706 *Ibid.,* p. 103.

707 *Ibid.*

708 Mansur Rafizadeh. *Witness: From the Shah to the Secret Arms Deal— An Insider's Account of U.S. Involvement in Iran.* (New York: William Morrow & Company, 1987), p. 393.

709 Cockburn., p. 104.

710 Morrow, p. 10.

711 *Ibid.,* p. 33.

712 Rafizadeh, p. 124.

713 *Ibid.,* p. 126.

714 Morrow, p. 178.

715 *Ibid.,* p. 11.

716 *Ibid.,* p. 117.

717 *Ibid.*

**Appendix One**
**Where Was George ?**

718 Mark Lane. *Rush to Judgment.* (New York: Thunder's Mouth Press, 1992), pp. xxv-xxvi.

719 Mark Lane. *Plausible Denial.* (New York: Thunder's Mouth Press, 1991), p. 331.

720 *Covert Action Information Bulletin,* Summer 1992.

721 *Ibid.*

722 *Ibid.*

723 *Ibid.*

724 *Ibid.*
725 *Ibid.*
726 Lane. *Plausible Denial.* pp. 32-33.
727 *Covert Action Information Bulletin.*
728 *The Spotlight,* March 22, 1982.
729 *Covert Action Information Bulletin.*
730 *Ibid.*
731 *Covert Action Information Bulletin.* Winter 1990.
732 *Ibid.*
733 *The Spotlight,* June 21, 1982.
734 *Covert Action Information Bulletin,* Summer 1992.
735 *Ibid.*
736 *Spy,* August 1992.
737 *Ibid.*
738 *Ibid.*
739 *Ibid.*
740 Webster Griffin Tarpley and Anton Chaitkin. *George Bush: The Unauthorized Biography* [Washington, D.C.: Executive Intelligence Review, 1992], pp. 247-248.
741 *Ibid.*
742 Executive Intelligence Review. *Dope, Inc.* (1992 edition), p. 608.

**Appendix Two**
**The Man From The Klan**

743 John George and Laird Wilcox. *Nazis, Communists, Klansmen and Others on the Fringe.* (New York: Prometheus Books, 1992), pp. 285-290.
744 Peter Dale Scott. *Deep Politics and the Death of JFK.* (Berkley, California: University of California Press, 1993), pp. 248-250.
745 Letter to Roy Frankhauser from Robert Curran, U.S. Attorney for the Eastern District of Pennsylvania, November 21, 1973.
746 *New Solidarity* newspaper, November 20, 1975.

# INDEX

# *About the author . . .*

**Michael Collins Piper** has been a Washington-based journalist for some 15 years. A political correspondent for *The Spotlight*, a national weekly newspaper published by Liberty Lobby on Capitol Hill in Washington, Piper is a prolific writer with thousands of published works that have appeared in *The Spotlight* and elsewhere.

Piper's explosive 1987 investigative report on the truth behind the bizarre public suicide of Pennsylvania State Treasurer R. Budd Dwyer was nominated for a Pulitzer Prize. Dwyer's widow later credited Piper's work with having forced an in-house Justice Department investigation of its own prosecution of Dwyer on trumped-up corruption charges.

A frequent guest on two nationally-broadcast radio talk shows, *The Editors' Roundtable* and *Radio Free America*, Piper has also been a contributor to the new monthly historical journal, *The Barnes Review*.

He is also the author of the book *Best Witness* which is an account of the widely-publicized Mel Mermelstein affair involving Liberty Lobby that was the subject of the made-for-television film *Never Forget*. Mark Lane, the attorney best known as the author of *Rush to Judgment*, the groundbreaking critique of the Warren Commission Report on the JFK assassination, represented Liberty Lobby in the Mermelstein case and wrote the introduction to *Best Witness*.

Piper was the first journalist ever to expose the identity of San Francisco-based Roy Edward Bullock as a long-time deep cover intelligence operative for the Anti-Defamation League (ADL) of B'nai B'rith. In 1993—nearly seven years after Piper first unmasked Bullock in *The Spotlight*—the ADL informant's real identity was finally acknowledged in the Establishment media. Piper later compiled and edited a volume entitled *The Garbage Man* which examined the ADL spy scandal in detail.

A student of the JFK assassination for some 25 years, Piper combined this interest with a keen knowledge of U.S. Middle East policy and a broad-ranging expertise in the history of organized crime in the researching and writing of *Final Judgment*. According to Piper:

"I don't pretend to have all the answers about what ultimately happened in Dallas on November 22, 1963—nobody ever will—but I do believe that I have come as close as anyone ever will in outlining the framework of the conspiracy that ended the life of President Kennedy.

"I have simply sorted out all of the evidence that I could find and I have laid it on the table for people to consider. I encourage debate on this issue as on all issues and hope that people are willing to examine the facts that I have put forth. Unfortunately, in the past, people have approached the JFK assassination with certain blinders on—and that's wrong."

"My thesis is controversial, to be sure," says Piper, "but I think that all who profess to be interested in finding out the truth at last will be forced to look at the fruits of my research and conclude, indeed, that the final judgment reached in this volume is very much a scenario that does indeed make ultimate sense."

Tear out this page and mail